Interdisciplinary Studies in Human Rights

Volume 13

Human rights are one of the normative cornerstones of contemporary international law and global governance. Due to the complexities of actual or potential violations of human rights and in light of current crises, new and interdisciplinary research is urgently needed. The series Interdisciplinary Studies in Human Rights recognizes the growing importance and necessity of interdisciplinary research in human rights. The series consists of monographs and collected volumes addressing human rights research from different disciplinary and interdisciplinary perspectives, including but not limited to philosophy, law, political science, education, and medical ethics. Its goal is to explore new and contested questions such as the extraterritorial application of human rights and their relevance for non-state actors, as well as the philosophical and theoretical foundations of human rights. The series also addresses policy questions of current interest including the human rights of migrants and refugees, LGBTI rights, and bioethics, as well as business and human rights.

The series editors are Members of the Centre for Human Rights Erlangen-Nürnberg (CHREN), an interdisciplinary research center at Friedrich-Alexander-University Erlangen-Nürnberg. The Advisory Board brings together human rights scholars from a wide range of academic disciplines and regional backgrounds. The series welcomes suggestions for publications of academic research falling into the series subject matter.

Danielle Anne Pamplona
Carolina Olarte-Bácares • Olena Uvarova
Editors

Business and Human Rights from the Lens of Women

Voices from the Global South

Springer

Editors
Danielle Anne Pamplona
Pontifical Catholic University of Paraná PUCPR
Curitiba, Brazil

Carolina Olarte-Bácares
Pontificia Universidad Javeriana
Bogota, Colombia

Olena Uvarova
UNDP Business and Human Rights ProgrammeYaroslav Mudryi National Law University
Kharkiv, Ukraine

ISSN 2509-2960 ISSN 2509-2979 (electronic)
Interdisciplinary Studies in Human Rights
ISBN 978-3-032-04035-0 ISBN 978-3-032-04036-7 (eBook)
https://doi.org/10.1007/978-3-032-04036-7

This Springer imprint is published by the registered company Springer Nature Switzerland AG
The registered company address is: Gewerbestrasse 11, 6330 Cham, Switzerland

Foreword

The business and human rights agenda has been evolving rapidly in recent years. The uptake of the UN Guiding Principles on Business and Human Rights by different stakeholders globally has grown significantly and human rights occupy an increasingly central space in contemporary discussions on sustainable and responsible business operations. However, the dominant narrative has often overlooked the specific experiences and perspectives of women. Though there are numerous efforts to incorporate a gender lens into the business and human rights work, more concrete, strong steps need to be taken to bring more voices from women in the Global South to the table. And this is precisely the aim of this book, which comes at a very timely moment, offering critical visions on a broad range of issues.

This publication delves into the unique challenges faced by women vis-a-vis business activities, exploring specific regional realities, from Latin America to Africa, Asia, and Eastern Europe. From women scholars working on business and human rights to female workers in global supply chains, the authors unpack the specific impacts businesses can have on the lives of women, what it means to incorporate a gender perspective into business and human rights frameworks, and how to ensure gender equality advances within companies, among others.

Key salient issues are tackled along the chapters, including the impact of COVID-19, the use of new technologies, or the urgency of the just transition. The book does not shy away from addressing other complex issues such as business operating in contexts of conflict, particularly in the war on Ukraine, or grave human rights abuses such as modern slavery.

This collection of texts will be an important source for business and human rights scholars, practitioners, and policymakers. By centering the voices of women from the Global South, it adds more layers of complexity to the discussions on the impacts of business activities and what responsible business conduct would look like for women in the margins. It also calls for policies, practices, and regulations that are truly inclusive, equitable, just, and sustainable.

As a woman from the Global South myself, I welcome this publication and hope that as we navigate the current global context, the invaluable contributions of women to the field of business and human rights are recognized and celebrated worldwide.

UN Working Group on Business and Human Rights Fernanda Hopenhaym,
Geneva, Switzerland

Contents

Introductory Chapter: Intellectual Production by Women from Peripheral Countries in Business and Human Rights: Conditions and Barriers

Danielle Anne Pamplona, Diana Carolina Olarte-Bácares, Olena Uvarova, and Angela Schembri Peña

Abstract This chapter aims to introduce the book which arises from the realization that the area of study recognized as 'Business and Human Rights' suffers from an affliction identified in the sciences in general: the lack of visibility of women from peripheral countries. The purpose of this preliminary chapter is to discover the role of gender approach in business and human rights scholarship, to map gender related theoretical studies and practical tools to implement the UN Guiding principles on business and human rights with indication of women voices engagement in these developments. Introductory chapter also presents the methodology of the survey and the analysis of the data on the conditions and possible barriers and limits for the publication and dissemination of intellectual production on business and human rights issued by women from peripheral countries. The principal barriers which are analysed are the following: household care, language barrier, restricted time schedule, lack of economic benefit, gender-based discrimination, pandemic impact, lack of information for publishing, administrative burdens, maternity leave.

This book arises from a critical realization: the field of study known as 'Business and Human Rights' (BHR) mirrors a broader issue within the sciences—the significant lack of visibility accorded to women scholars from peripheral countries. While

D. A. Pamplona
Pontifícia Univ. Católica do Paraná, Curitiba, Brazil
e-mail: danielle.pamplona@pucpr.br

D. C. Olarte-Bácares
Pontificia Universidad Javeriana, Bogota, Colombia
e-mail: c.olarte@javeriana.edu.co

O. Uvarova (✉)
UNDP Business and Human Rights ProgrammeYaroslav Mudryi National Law University, Kharkiv, Ukraine
e-mail: o.o.uvarova@nlu.edu.ua

A. S. Peña
Department of Public Law of the Pontificia Universidad Javeriana, Vitry Sur Seine, France
e-mail: angela.schembri@javeriana.edu.co

D. A. Pamplona et al. (eds.), *Business and Human Rights from the Lens of Women*, Interdisciplinary Studies in Human Rights 13,
https://doi.org/10.1007/978-3-032-04036-7_1

academic production in BHR is well-established and organized in the Global North, particularly in nations like the United States, Canada, England, France, the Netherlands, and Germany, bolstered by platforms such as the Cambridge University Press *Business and Human Rights Journal*, the contributions of women from outside this traditional core often remain obscured. This introductory chapter serves as a gateway to the volume, which seeks to discover the role of a gender approach within BHR scholarship, map relevant theoretical studies and practical tools for implementing the UN Guiding Principles on Business and Human Rights (UNGPs), and highlight the engagement of women's voices in these developments.

The chapter specifically presents the methodology and findings of a survey conducted to explore the conditions, barriers, and limitations affecting the publication and dissemination of BHR intellectual production by women scholars originating from or working in peripheral countries. Our point of departure is the conviction that this invisibility is a matter of public concern. Understanding the precarious situation many women face in academia, hearing their perspectives, and learning from their experiences are crucial steps. Overcoming the barriers to publication requires collective effort. Thus, this work aims to raise consciousness about the problem and amplify the voices of women from peripheral countries who possess valuable insights for the BHR field's development, ultimately seeking to enhance their opportunities and academic impact.

1 Contextualizing the Barriers

The challenges faced by authors from peripheral countries are well-documented, often including significant language and cultural constraints, particularly when their mother tongue is not English.[1] For women scholars, these hurdles are frequently compounded by gender-specific barriers prevalent within academia,[2] leading to further invisibility. This situation has been exacerbated, especially during the pandemic, which saw a considerable decrease in female academic production. This complex panorama stems partly from women's historical difficulties in attaining senior academic positions and securing institutional resources comparable to their male colleagues.[3] The persistent 'glass ceiling',[4] fueled by factors like the struggle to balance personal and professional responsibilities within patriarchal cultural contexts, further restricts the time and resources available for women to conduct and disseminate research, directly impacting publication output.

The COVID-19 pandemic starkly exposed and intensified existing gender inequalities. Many women, including academics, found themselves shouldering

[1] Amano et al. (2016), pp. 533–542; Beveridge (1998); Piszcz and Sierocka (2020), pp. 533–542.

[2] Generoso Meneguetti and Vier Machado (2018), pp. 141–159; Agrello and Garg (2009), pp. 1305.1–1305.6.

[3] Fuchs Epstein et al. (1995), pp. 295–449.

[4] Jackson and O'Callaghan (2009), pp. 460–482.

increased domestic and childcare responsibilities while attempting to maintain their professional activities.[5] This did not translate into more time for research but rather significantly less.[6] Studies confirm this trend, indicating a drop in women's academic productivity compared to men's during the pandemic, with fewer women participating in new projects.[7] For instance, one prestigious social science journal reported a decline in manuscripts submitted by female authors from 38% to 13% between the first and second quarters of the first pandemic year.[8] Even research focused on the pandemic itself was predominantly led by male voices; preliminary data analyzing expert sources in major US newspapers during the early pandemic showed that men accounted for nearly 65% of cited experts.[9] This early evidence suggested that women's intellectual contributions were not prioritized during the crisis realignment of tasks.[10]

Furthermore, research highlights the disproportionate burden borne by women in emerging economies during the pandemic. Data collected by McKinsey & Company reveals that significantly higher percentages of women in countries like Brazil, Mexico, China, and India, compared to those in developed economies (Canada, US, France, Germany, Ireland, UK), reported challenges related to physical and mental health, and particularly, household responsibilities imposing stress burdens.[11] As Windsor and Crawford note, many women, especially those from traditionally underrepresented backgrounds, entered the pandemic already facing strategic disadvantages due to factors like implicit bias and the 'hidden curriculum' of academia.[12] The essential requirements for academic production—quiet and concentration—become elusive amidst demanding family care responsibilities. This disparity is often rooted in traditional gender roles where male professional work, being monetized, is prioritized.[13] Despite awareness of these issues and proposals for remedies, institutional responses have often been lacking, leaving university structures seemingly neutral yet effectively blind to the specific needs of women scholars.[14]

[5] Power (2020), pp. 67–73.

[6] Power (2020), pp. 67–73.

[7] Goldsmith Weil and Bauer (2021), pp. 1–9.

[8] Goldsmith Weil and Bauer (2021), pp. 1–9.

[9] Fletcher et al. (2021), pp. 1011–1016.

[10] Goldsmith Weil and Bauer (2021), pp. 1–9.

[11] Fletcher et al. (2021), pp. 1011–1016.

[12] Windsor and Crawford (2021), pp. 1–11.

[13] Power (2020), pp. 67–73.

[14] Rosario Undurraga et al. (2021), pp. 1–28.

2 Survey Methodology and Findings

To empirically investigate these conditions, we conducted a survey between June and October 2022.[15] The survey targeted women members of the Teaching Business and Human Rights Forum[16] and the Global Business and Human Rights Scholars Association.[17] Participation was voluntary, and the purpose was clearly communicated. Thirty women responded, providing a valuable sample for analysis.

- **Respondent Profile:** The respondents predominantly identified as scholars in law (83.3%), with smaller representations from social sciences (6.7%), business ethics (3.3%), and other disciplines (6.7%). A significant portion (41.4%) are members of the Global Business and Human Rights Scholars Association, and 31% belong to the Teaching Forum, with 44.8% involved in other associations. In terms of age, the largest group was between 55–60 years old, with notable cohorts also in the 40–45 and 25–30 age brackets. This distribution is relevant as barriers can shift with age and career stage, impacting younger women seeking visibility and those potentially managing childcare responsibilities. Professionally, respondents are primarily engaged in academia as faculty members (full-time or adjunct) or PhD/Master's students (totaling over 76%), while others work as researchers in various organizations or hold other roles. In BHR practice outside direct academic roles, the most common positions were consultant/advisor (40%) and independent researcher (30%).
- **Geographic and Educational Background:** The survey respondents originated from a diverse range of countries, with Brazil (33.4%) and Colombia (23.4%) being the most represented, alongside individuals from Chile, Croatia, Denmark, Greece, Guatemala, Lebanon, Pakistan, Ukraine, and the United States. Correspondingly, the primary mother tongues reported were Portuguese (33.3%) and Spanish (26.7%), languages in which high-impact Q1 and Q2 journals are scarce. Despite this, the respondents demonstrate high levels of educational attainment. All hold bachelor's degrees, overwhelmingly obtained in their country of origin (86.8%). Postgraduate studies show a strong trend towards institutions in the Global North (including France, UK, Switzerland, Denmark, Germany, Spain), with nearly half (46.7%) holding a Doctoral degree and 43.3% an LLM or Master's degree. More than half completed their highest degree within the last 1–5 years, indicating recent engagement with advanced scholar-

[15] Link to the survey: https://docs.google.com/forms/d/e/1FAIpQLScKCuweSC7WFpEzti828vqJ02MpdDZnCHupYTnuN6bnk7XlLg/viewform.

[16] The **Teaching Business and Human Rights Forum** is a unique platform for collaboration among individuals teaching business and human rights worldwide. The Forum seeks to promote and strengthen business and human rights education by fostering collaboration among teachers. Teaching Business and Human Rights Forum | Promoting Business and Human Rights Education.

[17] The **Business and Human Rights Scholars Association** is an association of business leaders, academics and policymakers united to promote research and teaching of human rights worldwide.

ship. This contrasts sharply with their current work locations: a majority (66.6%) reported mainly working on BHR issues *in* peripheral countries (Brazil and Colombia being most frequent, but also including Congo, Gabon, Greece, Guatemala, Indonesia, Italy, Lebanon, Ukraine, and the UK/Denmark for some respondents). This divergence between postgraduate training location and primary work location may reflect factors like the availability of specialized BHR programs or a strategic move to gain visibility through Global North institutions before returning to focus on issues relevant to their home regions.

- **Publication and Impact:** While 80% of respondents have published books or book chapters on BHR (with publications reported across 40 instances in peripheral countries[18] and 37 instances in Global North countries[19]), the picture for journal articles is different. Forty percent have *not* published or had articles approved in the BHR field. Furthermore, only 26.7% reported publishing in high-impact Q1 or Q2 ranked journals, compared to 16.6% in Q3 or Q4 journals. A striking 83.3% of respondents believe that women, in general, face barriers to publishing in indexed Q1 and Q2 journals. This suggests that while book publishing might offer more accessible routes, penetrating top-tier journals remains a significant challenge, potentially limiting visibility within mainstream global academia. In contrast, participation in conferences and workshops is high (96.7%), with respondents taking on multiple roles including panelists, listeners, organizers, moderators, and occasionally, keynote speakers. These activities spanned numerous countries across the Global North and South.

Regarding academic impact (defined through citations, H-index, publication count, publisher prestige, and public policy influence), respondents were divided: 56.7% felt they have an academic impact, while 43.3% felt they do not. Notably, public policy impact was cited by 53.3% as a source of their impact, and citations by 50%. Fewer pointed to the prestige of the publisher (30%) or their H-index (10%). This may suggest that while traditional citation-based metrics might not fully capture their influence, their work often has tangible relevance in shaping public policy, locally or globally—a crucial contribution to society, even if it does not always translate into high visibility within Global North academic circuits. This aspect warrants deeper investigation.

- **Identified Barriers:** A large majority (83.3%) confirmed facing barriers to publication. The most frequently cited were: responsibility for care of people at home (cited by 20 women), restricted time schedules (20 women), language barriers (15 women), lack of sufficient economic benefit from publishing (15 women), and gender-based discrimination (14 women). Other significant barriers included the impact of the pandemic (13 women), lack of information on how

[18] 11 in Brazil, 10 in Colombia, 5 in Mexico, 2 in Chile, 2 in Costa Rica, 1 in Guatemala, 1 in Indonesia, 1 in Lithuania, 1 in Estonia, 1 in Argentina, 1 in Cameroon, 1 in Pakistan, 1 in Peru and 1 in Ukraine.

[19] 10 in United Kingdom, 7 in the United States of America, 5 in France, 4 in Spain, 3 in Germany, 2 in Norway, 1 in Denmark, 1 in Italy, 1 in Belgium, 1 in Portugal, 1 in Sweden, 1 in Switzerland.

and where to publish (12 women), administrative burdens (11 women), and maternity leave (11 women). Furthermore, 86.7% agreed that women from and working in countries outside Western Europe, the USA, and Canada face *additional* barriers when trying to publish in indexed journals.

When invited to elaborate freely, respondents highlighted resistance from mainstream outlets to decolonial critiques and frameworks developed outside the Global North. They noted a preference for theoretical work grounded in Western literature and a perceived lack of interest in topics specific to the Global South. Experiences of discrimination, xenophobia, and challenges establishing credibility were reported. The language barrier was emphasized again, particularly concerning technical academic language. Critically, respondents pointed to difficulties accessing Global North networks, which hinders opportunities for collaboration and, importantly, access to funding.

3 Strategies for Overcoming Barriers

Respondents offered insightful strategies to address these publication barriers. Suggestions included fostering a change in attitude among publishers towards women and authors from peripheral countries, developing more regional workshops to strengthen connections and mitigate language barriers, and promoting the creation of more ranked journals based in peripheral countries or allowing submissions in languages other than English. For existing journals in Western Europe, the USA, and Canada, there was a call to actively address representation, improve the inclusion of diverse agendas, and ensure greater diversity among author profiles, while consciously combating stereotypes and discrimination.

Crucially, there was an emphasis on recognizing and valuing the unique knowledge, experiences, and contexts that women from the Global South bring to BHR issues. Respondents stressed the need for empowerment, suggesting the creation of regional focus groups, women-led research projects, gender-sensitive publishing policies, mentoring schemes, and broader academic networks built on equal partnerships. Clear academic guidelines on publishing processes and financial support to overcome funding access difficulties were also identified as vital needs. A key suggestion was to enhance the perceived 'value of the field' by being more open to findings that may lack extensive precedent in established Western literature but reflect the realities and shortcomings of BHR application in diverse contexts, particularly where field research is more prevalent. The innovative nature of research emerging from peripheral countries was underscored, alongside an appeal for Western European, US, and Canadian academia to become more receptive to these new approaches.

4 The Contribution of This Volume

The chapters within this book exemplify the relevant and often critical research being produced by women scholars examining BHR from perspectives outside the US-Western European axis. These perspectives offer different readings and potential solutions to the complex challenge of regulating business activities concerning human rights. They draw attention to worldviews and lived realities that may not align with the assumptions underpinning dominant frameworks, thereby enriching the global BHR discourse.

Contributors demonstrate, for instance, how soft law mechanisms like the Sustainable Development Goals or corporate social responsibility initiatives, as well as sustainability reporting guidelines, may prove insufficient or overlook critical information when viewed from the vantage point of countries experiencing exploitation of labor and natural resources. They question the adequacy of concepts like 'social sustainability' when evaluation criteria fail to engage with local needs. Similarly, they analyze how frameworks like the UNGPs can falter in addressing economic, social, cultural, or environmental rights violations, potentially failing to protect women facing intersectional vulnerabilities.

This book is relevant not only because it presents these vital research results but also because it represents a conscious effort—the first known initiative of its kind—to bring together women researchers focusing on BHR from peripheral countries. By shedding light on their work and outlining the significance of their role, we hope this volume contributes to a more inclusive and comprehensive understanding of business and human rights. We anticipate that more initiatives of this nature will follow, and that the participation of these researchers in mainstream journals and workshops will soon become as commonplace as it always should have been.

References

Agrello DA, Garg E (2009) R.Mulheres na física: poder e preconceito nos países em desenvolvimento. Revista Brasileira de Ensino de Física [online] 31(1):1305.1–1305.6. ISSN 1806-9126. https://doi.org/10.1590/S1806-11172009000100005

Amano T, Gonzalez-Varo JP, Sutherland WJ (2016) Languages are still a major barrier to global science. PLoS Biol 14(12):e2000933. https://doi.org/10.1371/journal.pbio.2000933

Beveridge BJ (1998) How culture, law, and language are all barriers to effective cross-cultural legal communication, specifically international commercial contracts (T). University of British Columbia. https://open.library.ubc.ca/collections/ubctheses/831/items/1.0077531

FletcherS,JoeMB,HernandezS,TomanI,HarrisonT,RuzyckiS(2021)ThegenderofCOVID-19experts in newspaper articles: a descriptive cross- sectional study. J Gen Intern Med 36(4):1011–1016. https://pesquisa.bvsalud.org/global-literature-on-novel-coronavirus-2019-ncov/resource/pt/covidwho-1037994

Fuchs Epstein C Sauté R, Bonnie Oglensky B, Gever M (1995) Glass ceilings and open doors: women's advancement in the legal profession. Fordham Law Rev 64. https://ir.lawnet.fordham.edu/flr/vol64/iss2/2

García-Bullé S (2020) Pandemia académica: la cuarentena acentúa la desigualdad de género en la academia. Insituto para el Futuro de la Educación. https://observatorio.tec.mx/edu-news/academicas-pandemia-covid19

Goldsmith Weil J, Bauer K (2021) «Editorial: Re-imaginando diversidad en la academia, en tiempos de activismo feminista y pandemia», Polis [En línea], 59 | 2021. http://journals.openedition.org/polis/20230

Hayashi MCPI et al (2014) Indicadores da participação feminina em Ciência e Tecnologia. Transinformação 19(2):169–187. ISSN 2318-0889

Jackson JFL, O'Callaghan EM (2009) What do we know about glass ceiling effects? A taxonomy and critical review to inform higher education research. Res High Educ 50(5):460–482. http://www.jstor.org/stable/29782936

Meneguetti G, Vier Machado V (2018) A Invisibilidade das Mulheres nas Ciências Criminais. Gênero & Direito, [S. l.], 7(2). https://doi.org/10.22478/ufpb.2179-7137.2018v7n2.39283. https://periodicos.ufpb.br/ojs/index.php/ged/article/view/39283

Piszcz A, Sierocka H (2020) The role of culture in legal languages, legal interpretation and legal translation. Int J Semiot Law 33:533–542. https://doi.org/10.1007/s11196-020-09760-3

Power K (2020) The COVID-19 pandemic has increased the care burden of women and families. Sustain: Sci Pract Policy 16(1):67–73. https://doi.org/10.1080/15487733.2020.1776561

Undurraga R, Simbürger E, Mora C (2021) «Desborde y desazón versus flexibilidad y concentración: Teletrabajo académico y género en tiempos de pandemia», Polis [En línea], 59 | 2021. http://journals.openedition.org/polis/20244

Windsor L, Crawford K (2021) Differential effects of pandemic parenting. ADVANCE J, Oregon State University, 2. https://doi.org/10.5399/osu/advjrnl.2.3.4

Positive Duties on Private Mining Companies to Fulfil Socio-Economic Rights in Africa: Developments Towards Strengthening the Legal and Conceptual Foundations

Elsabé Boshoff

> *"The intervention of multinational corporations may be a potentially positive force for development if the State and the people concerned are ever mindful of the common good and the sacred rights of individuals and communities." ACHPR in the SERAC case, para 69.*

Abstract This chapter argues that important theoretical work done by key thinkers in Africa in relation to socio-economic responsibilities of non-state actors, as well as recent legal developments at the regional, sub-regional and national levels in Africa, has pushed the frontiers of thinking about corporate responsibility and socio-economic rights adjudication. These developments also strengthened the legal and conceptual foundations for positive duties on private mining companies in fulfilling socio-economic rights in Africa. The chapter highlights way in which the duties on corporate actors have been extended in Africa, including as a consequence of the kinds of functions that they have come to fulfil in African societies. These duties go beyond both the UNGPs and corporate social responsibility, to set a new frontier in corporate human rights accountability. It draws on recent developments in particular from the African regional human rights system, and considers the case study of South Africa as an example of a progressive jurisdiction in relation to holding corporations accountable. This chapter concludes that corporations in Africa are recognised as corporate citizens, which not only have rights but also have duties to contribute to the realisation of sustainable development and equality in the countries and areas where they operate, not merely on a voluntary basis or in terms of commitments that they deem important, but as part of wider development and human rights frameworks. The next step would be to develop frameworks at the regional

E. Boshoff (✉)
Norwegian Centre for Human Rights, University of Oslo, Oslo, Norway

D. A. Pamplona et al. (eds.), *Business and Human Rights from the Lens of Women*, Interdisciplinary Studies in Human Rights 13,
https://doi.org/10.1007/978-3-032-04036-7_2

level through which these obligations can be enforced, where states are unable or unwilling to do so.

1 Introduction

The United Nations Guiding Principles on Business and Human Rights (UNGPs or the Principles) represent the current global consensus on the human rights obligations of corporations and the duties of states to hold them accountable.[1] The UNGPs provide an international framework for addressing the accountability gap which exists in many countries in the world where national legal, structural and institutional arrangements are insufficient to effectively hold corporations accountable for human rights violations.[2] Yet, while the UNGPs set important standards in relation both to the duty of corporations to refrain from impacting adversely on human rights, and additionally imposes a duty on corporations to pay compensation and make reparations for instances where violations do take place, the Principles stop short of imposing the full range of human rights responsibilities—to protect and fulfil human rights, in addition to respecting them—on non-state actors. While the UNGPs do not preclude companies from taking up positive realisation of rights, it does not consider this a duty. Therefore, while the UNGPs are an important starting point for human rights accountability by corporations, there are circumstances which may require the extension of corporate obligations. In the context of mining, moral arguments can be made for such an extension of corporate obligations, for example where mines are required to generate electricity for their own use because host states are unable to provide electricity, in which case they might then have a moral obligation to share this with mining adjacent communities.

Against this background, this chapter argues that important theoretical work done in Africa in relation to socio-economic responsibilities of non-state actors and recent legal developments at the regional, sub-regional and national levels in Africa, contribute to strengthening the legal and conceptual foundations for positive duties on private mining companies in fulfilling socio-economic rights in Africa. It highlights ways in which the duties on corporate actors have been extended in Africa, including as a result of the kinds of functions that they have come to fulfil in African

[1] Efforts are underway at the UN level since 2014 to develop a "draft legally binding instrument to regulate, in international human rights law, the activities of transnational corporations and other business enterprises" (UN draft legally binding instrument), but it is unclear when and whether it will be adopted or receive enough ratifications to enter into force.

[2] Recent developments have seen the elaboration of national laws on corporate accountability, for example the Norwegian Transparency Act, 2022 and the German Act on Corporate Due Diligence to Prevent Human Rights Violations in Supply Chains which entered into force in 2023, as well as the recently adopted European Union Corporate Sustainability Due Diligence Directive, 2024. These laws provide important new pathways for corporate accountability in the home states, but a full discussion of this falls beyond the scope of this chapter.

societies. These duties go beyond both the UNGPs and corporate social responsibility, to set a new frontier in corporate human rights accountability.

This chapter is organised as follows: following this introductory section, Sect. 2 provides a grounding for the kinds of circumstances in which it would make sense to extend corporate accountability beyond that provided for in the UNGPs. Section 3 discusses the ways in which the boundaries of thinking about corporate responsibility and socio-economic rights adjudication have been pushed by key thinkers in the field. Section 4 sets out the international and regional legal frameworks applicable to Africa on the extent to which there is an emerging recognition of positive duties on companies. Section 5 considers the case study of South Africa from both a legislative and jurisprudential perspective, as an example of a progressive jurisdiction in relation to holding corporations accountable. Section 6 draws on the preceding sections to conclude on the extent to which the African regional and local developments move beyond corporate social responsibility and corporate responsibility to respect, and towards binding socio-economic obligations on companies.

2 Circumstances and Considerations for the Extension of Corporate Accountability for Socio-economic Obligations

A first consideration about circumstances where is makes sense to extend corporate obligations to fulfilling socio-economic rights relates to the role of corporations in African societies in which they operate. Access to basic necessities for a dignified life remains low in many African countries. In 2016, "6 out of 10 people did not have access to electricity" in sub-Saharan Africa,[3] while in 2020 "only 57% of the population report having an improved water supply that is fully functional, available when needed, easily accessible and provides good quality and safe water".[4] Mining companies equally require consistent and extensive sources of electricity and water to run their operations, including in extraction and refinement processes.[5] Often mining companies are granted exclusive rights to use certain aquafers, thereby excluding the local communities from access this life-giving resource.[6] On the face of it, this brings the needs of the corporations and the local communities affected by the mining activities into conflict with each other. However, where communities did not have access to electricity or safe drinking water before the arrival of the mine, the infrastructure developed by corporations may also benefit local communities. In

[3] Arlet et al. (2019) https://blogs.worldbank.org/developmenttalk/barriers-urban-electrification-sub-saharan-africa-perspective-end-users.

[4] Thomas et al. (2020), p. 2.

[5] Banerjee et al. (2015), p. 33.

[6] See for example, Van Wyngaardt (2018) https://www.miningweekly.com/article/orca-gold-gets-water-use-permit-for-sudan-project-2018-02-08/rep_id:3650.

Ghana, for example, the gold mining industry brought benefits to the community by providing the local community with "infrastructural developments like schools, clinics, roads, boreholes and pipe borne water supplies".[7] In South Africa, the African Rainbow Minerals' Khumani mine provided toilets and hygiene facilities to two communities in which they operate.[8] However, in most countries there is no obligation on corporations to provide mining affected communities with access to such infrastructure. So where they do so, it is usually on the basis of voluntarily accepted corporate social responsibility (CSR) considerations.[9] This means that these contributions to society are not considered to be a requirement, but are rather private self-regulation, charitable practices or "an expression of good will to the broader society in which they operate".[10] Strong moral arguments could however be made for the extension of the services they already provide to themselves, to the mining affected communities, as will be discussed further below.

Secondly, through a wave of constitution-making on the African continent since the 1990s the majority of African countries now have progressive constitutions which provide for not only civil and political rights, but also economic and social rights protection, either as justiciable rights or as "directive principles". Furthermore, all but three African states[11] have ratified the International Covenant on Economic, Social and Cultural Rights (ICESCR)[12] and all but one African state[13] are Parties to the African Charter on Human and Peoples' Rights (African Charter). The rights of all people to workers' rights, right to education, housing, food and health care, among others, are thus not contested on the continent. While states are the main duty bearers under international human rights law, under the African human rights system non-state actors also have obligations, both positive and negative, in relation to the realisation of human rights.[14]

Thirdly, the COVID-19 pandemic has exposed some of the deep structural inequalities in societies around the world and the need to rethink the ways in which health, education, housing and other services are delivered to people, including the most vulnerable. For example, during the first months of the COVID-19 pandemic, major mining companies across the African continent made substantive financial

[7] Appiah and Buaben (2012), p. 1044.

[8] International Council on Mining and Minerals https://miningwithprinciples.com/growing-access-to-sanitation-and-hygiene-in-mining-communities/.

[9] South Africa is one notable exception in this regard on the African continent, where legislation requires mines to adopt a social and labour plan prior to commencing mining operations and in consultation with communities, which is then binding on the corporation. This will be discussed in more detail in Sect. 3 below.

[10] Bilchitz (2010), p. 1.

[11] Botswana, South Sudan and Mozambique have not yet ratified the ICESCR.

[12] UN General Assembly, International Covenant on Economic, Social and Cultural Rights, 16 December 1966, United Nations, Treaty Series, vol. 993, p. 3, available at: https://www.refworld.org/docid/3ae6b36c0.html.

[13] Morocco is not a State Party to the African Charter.

[14] This is further unpacked in Sect. 4 below.

contributions to the communities within which they operate, including Richards Bay Minerals in South Africa, which "committed R1.5-million [approximately $80 000] towards meeting mine community food, water and health needs", Glencore corporation, which provided "support to the #Khomani San community who suffer from a loss of tourism income and lockdown restrictions" and Barrick Gold corporation, which "contributed $1.7-million in the form of critical equipment and expertise to help prevent the spread of the virus in Tanzania and $1.5-million in the DRC".[15] The International Council on Mining and Metals (ICMM) proudly summarises the contribution of their members to COVID-19 efforts as follows:[16]

> As of June 2020, ICMM company members had donated more than US$315 million to global response efforts through COVID-19 funds and individual company donations to national relief efforts. Member companies have also been donating company facilities for use as field hospitals and testing centres, providing access to clean water and sanitation facilities, engaging in awareness-raising campaigns on hygiene and other preventative measures, providing food and care packages, investing in online education programmes, supplying medical transport vehicles, building mechanical ventilators, 3D printing PPE equipment, taking steps to avoid discrimination against those who test positive for COVID-19, and building labs and creating testing capacity to support government responses, especially where public capacity is limited.

While these contributions were not obligatory, it provides a platform from which to consider the role of corporations in delivering these services, and the need for stronger positive obligations, including in times of crisis but also in addressing more long-term structural challenges, particularly in developing countries where state capacity is limited. With these considerations in mind, the next section looks at the reasoning developed by key African thinkers about the moral grounding for positive corporate obligations to realise socio-economic rights.

3 Theoretical Grounding for Holding Mining Companies Accountable for Positive Obligations in Realising Socio-economic Rights

This section considers three angles on the duty of non-state actors to fulfil socio-economic rights and the moral and theoretical justifications developed by (mainly) African scholars for why these duties should be imposed on corporations. The first relates to broadly whether corporations as non-state actors can be held accountable for human rights violations, and socio-economic rights more specifically, the second concerns the recognition of positive duties in relation to socio-economic rights, and the third whether corporations have a positive duty to fulfil socio-economic rights.

---

[15] African Commission on Human and Peoples' Rights (2020), p. 28.

[16] Prescott et al. (2020), p. 6.

3.1 *Non-state Actors' Accountability for (Socio-economic) Human Rights Violations*

Bilchitz argues that the point of departure for thinking about human rights obligations should not be the duty bearer but rather the rights holder.[17] In his view, the very nature of human rights (if considered from the perspective of the natural scholars)[18] means that the duties in relation to respecting, protecting and fulfilling these rights cannot be limited to one type of duty bearer, namely the state, but that all actors who may have an impact on human rights have duties in this regard.[19] Chirwa supports the view that the state cannot be the only duty bearer in relation to socio-economic rights, even if it remains the main duty bearer. Specifically in relation to socio-economic rights, he argues that there is a need for a "combination of efforts of various duty holders in the realisation of socio-economic rights".[20] According to Chirwa, the duties on other actors should primarily be determined in relation to state obligations. Therefore, where a private person carries out the functions of the state or exercises "power akin to or greater than that of the state", they should be held to the same standard as the state, including in fulfilling human rights obligations.[21] Bilchitz is more cautious in assigning the same obligations on corporations as on states. In his view corporations should be characterised as "'partially public, partially private' entities". Because of their partially public nature, they should be able to bear direct responsibilities under international human rights law.[22] Nevertheless, because they maintain a partially private nature, they cannot be burdened with all the same obligations as the state, even in cases where they do perform state functions. This is because a core element of the nature of corporations, unlike the state, is to further the self-interest of the persons who created it.[23] On the other hand, its dual nature means that corporations are "not entitled in all circumstances to privilege its own self-interest over others and must seek to consider its effect on the rights of others as placing important constraints on what it may do".[24]

---

[17] See generally Bilchitz (2013), Bilchitz and Deva (2013), Bilchitz (2016).

[18] See generally Dembour (2010).

[19] Bilchitz (2016), p. 144.

[20] Chirwa (2002), p. 4.

[21] Chirwa (2002), p. 6.

[22] Bilchitz (2016), p. 143.

[23] Bilchitz (2016), pp. 164–165.

[24] Bilchitz (2016), p. 168.

3.2 *Positive Duties in Relation to Socio-economic Rights*

Positive duties enjoin "the duty bearer to take some action to make possible the enjoyment of the right by the right bearer".[25] One of the reasons why duties in fulfilling rights are not traditionally imposed on non-state actors, is because these duties are considered to be more onerous than negative duties.[26] Liebenberg sums up this position as follows:[27]

> A prevailing dichotomy of liberal rights theory is the distinction between the negative and positive duties imposed by human rights norms. A strong duty of accountability is imposed when the State is perceived to interfere with people's enjoyment of human rights, whether through the conduct of officials or legislative, executive or administrative action. Non-existent or much weaker accountability is imposed when State responsibility is attributed to omissions.

Liebenberg argues that in contrast to this view, all human rights, including civil and political as well as economic, social and cultural rights, should be understood to entail both positive and negative obligations, and therefore that the dichotomy between economic and social rights on the one hand, and civil and political rights on the other, cannot be maintained.[28] Nolan holds that "efforts to argue that the horizontal application of ESR would constitute an even greater encroachment of liberty/freedom (and particularly economic freedom) than the horizontal application of civil and political rights [...] are doomed to failure".[29] This is because the notion that civil and political rights are "cost-free and give rise to exclusively negative duties" has been proven to be false.[30] De Schutter concurs on this point, because of what he sees as the impossibility of "tracing a line between the 'negative' duty to respect human rights and the 'positive' duties to protect and to fulfil them" due to an "intrinsic continuity between these various dimensions".[31]

If corporations thus can have positive human rights obligations, De Schutter asks whether it is possible to directly apply the obligations under international instruments to corporations, or whether such rights are "too vague and indeterminate, or simply unsuitable for application to corporate actors."[32] In particular he notes that "States discharge their positive duties to protect and to fulfil human rights by using their regulatory powers or by providing public services to the population, relying on the tool of taxation and following a ranking of the priorities [...] settled through

[25] Madlanga (2018) https://www.groundup.org.za/article/human-rights-we-should-not-only-target-state/.

[26] Chirwa (2002), p. 4.

[27] Liebenberg (2011), p. 37.

[28] Liebenberg (2011), p. 38.

[29] Nolan (2014), p. 80.

[30] Nolan (2014), p. 80.

[31] De Schutter (2014), p. 201.

[32] De Schutter (2014), p. 198.

democratic debate", powers which corporations do not have.[33] De Schutter argues that one way in which to delineate the responsibilities of corporations is by limiting their required obligations to their "sphere of influence".[34] De Schutter argues that in determining the duty bearer, the focus "should not be the private or the public nature of the actor" but rather on the "degree of dependency" between the right holder and duty bearer or level of control over the good.[35] Similarly, Nolan argues that in practically determining the *kinds* of obligations that should be imposed on non-state actors (NSA), these should be interpreted broadly and should include "consideration of the level of dependence of the former on the latter, any responsibility that the NSA may owe the rights-holder as the result of a special relationship", the importance of the right for the survival and dignity of the rights holder, and the likelihood of the right being met by someone other than the NSA.[36]

3.3 Corporations Having a Positive Duty to Fulfil Socio-economic Rights

Bilchitz is critical of the UNGPs, stating that the limitations of the scope of responsibility for corporations to the negative duty to respect "rest on a mistaken conception of the social role of business as well as a limited understanding of democratic legitimacy", and that as a result there is a "serious lacuna at the international level which has significant implications given the potential role of business in helping to address important challenges such as global poverty and environmental sustainability".[37] Bilchitz addresses three arguments advanced by the UN Special Rapporteur, John Ruggie, the main person behind the UNGPs, for why corporate responsibility should be limited to the duty to respect. These are: (1) corporations have a specialised (economic) function in society, which may be undermined by "wider social obligations", (2) there is a need for a "clear principled differentiation" between the kinds of obligations that states and corporations have, otherwise corporations may fulfil governance functions for which they "lack democratic legitimacy" and (3) states may shirk their responsibilities by transferring it to corporations.[38]

In response to the first argument, Bilchitz argues that not wanting to impact negatively on the economic viability of a corporation might be a factor to *limit* the extent of corporate social obligations, but would not as such constitute a bar on having such obligations *at all*.[39] In response to the second point, what he calls the legitimacy

[33] De Schutter (2014), p. 200.

[34] De Schutter (2014), p. 204.

[35] De Schutter (2014), p. 207.

[36] Nolan (2014), p. 90.

[37] Bilchitz (2013), p. 108.

[38] Bilchitz (2013), pp. 128–135.

[39] Bilchitz (2013), p. 128.

argument, Bilchitz argues that while corporations should engage to understand the needs of the affected community in order to have participatory legitimacy and should ensure that their actions have normative legitimacy, such actions would not necessarily lack legitimacy just because corporations are not democratically elected.[40] He argues that underlying the legitimacy arguments is a notion that state and corporate obligations would be in competition, and that this is an incorrect assumption, as they can also function collaboratively.[41] In relation to the third argument, Bilchitz argues that placing some responsibilities on corporations should not be equated with transferring all government functions, and government would always retain important functions, even if mainly in coordinating or planning services delivered by a network of actors.[42] Ultimately he thus concludes that there are no legitimate reasons to exclude positive obligations for corporations, and that given the extent of human rights failures, the collaboration of all actors is necessary to alleviate it.

This section provided an overview of the current theoretical discourse in support of the recognition of positive human rights obligations for corporations, in particular in relation to the fulfilment of socio-economic rights. It is clear from the above that contrary to a legal positivist approach characterising many national and international legal discourses around corporate human rights obligations, the moral and theoretical basis is in place for imposing more onerous obligations on corporations that merely not infringing human rights. The extent to which this thinking has found its way into the human rights framework applicable to African states is discussed in the next section.

4 Positive Corporate Obligations Under the International Human Rights Framework Applicable to Africa

Chirwa notes that already in the preamble to the Universal Declaration of Human Rights, 1948, human rights obligations are not limited to states.[43] He argues that in providing that "'every individual and every organ of state...shall strive...to secure' the universal and effective recognition and observance of all human rights", human rights obligations, including positive obligations, on non-state actors is already implied in this early human rights framework.[44] Furthermore, international bodies such as the Committee on Economic, Social and Cultural Rights and the International Labour Organisation have also explicitly stated that non-state actors, including

[40] Bilchitz (2013), pp. 132–134.

[41] Bilchitz (2013), p. 135.

[42] Bilchitz (2013), pp. 135–136.

[43] Chirwa (2002), p. 3.

[44] Chirwa (2002), p. 3.

business actors, have duties in ensuring access to food and health care, and in creating employment opportunities and safe working environments.[45]

However, under the UNGPs adopted in a UN resolution in 2011, and representing the current consensus on the duties of corporations, corporations are primarily required to respect the law, including as it relates to human rights and to act with "due diligence". Where there is a breach of this duty to respect or where there are human rights impacts which they "cause or contribute to through its own activities, or which may be directly linked to its operations, products or services by its business relationships",[46] they are expected to provide a remedy, usually through compensation. While the UNGPs do not preclude companies from taking up positive realisation of rights, it does not consider this a duty. Importantly, the UNGPs provide that:[47]

> Business enterprises may undertake other commitments or activities to support and promote human rights, which may contribute to the enjoyment of rights. But this does not offset a failure to respect human rights throughout their operations.

This means in practice that corporate social responsibility undertakings cannot "make up" for human rights violations in other areas. For example, the use of corporate funds for the building of a school cannot be used as an excuse for violation of labour rights. Another important element of the UNGPs is that they require that specific attention be paid to particular vulnerable group, enumerated as including "indigenous peoples; women; national or ethnic, religious and linguistic minorities; children; persons with disabilities; and migrant workers and their families".[48] This is an important element of a human rights based approach to business operations and is cross-cutting, in that it should be taken into account in all actions undertaken by corporations. Furthermore, according to the UNGPs, "a business enterprise's 'activities' are understood to include both actions and omissions" which result in a failure to respect human rights.[49]

In relation to the obligations of states, the UNGPs require of states to protect people from human rights violations by corporations, including by putting in place and enforcing laws that require corporations to respect human rights.[50] Thus states have a duty to take judicial, administrative, legislative or other appropriate steps to ensure access to effective remedies where human rights abuses occur.[51] The UNGPs do not provide for states to place any obligations on companies beyond respecting

---

[45] Chirwa (2002), p. 3.

[46] Special Representative of the Secretary-General on the issue of human rights and transnational corporations and other business enterprises, *Guiding Principles on Business and Human Rights: Implementing the United Nations "Protect, Respect and Remedy" Framework*, 2011) (UNGPs), p. 17.

[47] UNGPs, p. 13.

[48] UNGPs, p. 14.

[49] UNGPs, p. 15.

[50] UNGPs, p. 4.

[51] UNGPs, p. 27.

human rights, however, as noted above, this does not preclude them to do so, as the UNGPs aim only to establish minimum standards application at the international level.

At the global level there are thus not specific standards which require corporations to contribute positively to the realisation of the rights of the communities in which they operate, they only have negative obligations not to infringe on rights and the positive duties to mitigate the consequences of activities which infringe on human rights and "where appropriate" remediate the consequences.[52] One exception is that corporations are required to "comply with all applicable laws" at the national level.[53] This means that in cases where there are more stringent obligations on corporations at national level, they would be required to comply with it.[54]

An additional source of corporate obligations at the international level is the voluntary frameworks within which corporations have taken up positive functions within the communities in which they operate, including for the medical and health support provided during the COVID-19 pandemic, referenced above. One example is the ICMM Mining Principles, which "define good practice environmental, social and governance requirements for the mining and metals industry through a comprehensive set of performance expectations".[55] Some of the biggest mining companies operating in Africa are members of the ICMM, including African Rainbow Minerals, Anglo American, Anglo Gold Ashanti, Barrick Gold, Glencore, Rio Tinto and Sibanye Stillwater, among others. Liebenberg and Moyo argue convincingly that such voluntary corporate standards are in fact developing "into a system of transnational governance for business" in that "as these voluntary initiatives begin to incorporate stronger accountability mechanisms, the lines between strictly voluntary and mandatory spheres for participants become blurred".[56] This view is also held by Kotze and Fuo, who argue that such regimes are "conducive to facilitating more adaptive, responsive, productive, multi-actor and decentralised forms of regulation that do not exclusively depend on the state for their legitimacy and effectiveness".[57] They refer to this as a shift in focus from government to multi-actor governance. As soft law developments, these voluntary obligations may also lay down principles which over time could be adopted into more formal law.

At the African regional level, the African Charter makes no distinction between economic, social and cultural rights on the one hand and civil and political rights on the other. This means that socio-economic rights are equally enforceable against duty bearers in the same way as civil and political rights, including in relation to the duty to fulfil these rights. Furthermore, the African Charter also makes provision for

---

52 UNGPs, p. 13.

53 UNGPs, p. 1.

54 See the example of South Africa discussed below.

55 International Council on Mining and Metals "Mining Principles" https://www.icmm.com/en-gb/members/member-requirements/mining-principles.

56 Khulekani and Liebenberg (2015), pp. 714–715.

57 Kotzé and Fuo (2016), p. 293.

horizontal application of rights through a provision on duties of individuals. These duties include duties towards "family and society, the State and other legally recognized communities and the international community", to exercise rights with due regard to others, to contribute to the national community and to pay tax in the interest of society.[58]

The approach of the African Commission in its jurisprudence has been similar to that followed at the global level, in that states are considered to be the main duty bearers of human rights, with the duty to protect their people against the negative consequences of corporations. In the case of *Social and Economic Rights Action Center (SERAC) and Center for Economic and Social Rights (CESR) v. Nigeria* (SERAC case), the Commission stated that this duty to protect "requires the State to take measures to protect beneficiaries of the protected rights against political, economic and social interferences" by corporations.[59] Oloka-Onyango criticised the approach followed by the Commission in not holding the corporation in this case directly accountable, in that he argues that "every individual" referred to in the section on individual duties "covers both natural and artificial persons, and should therefore impose obligations on corporations as well.[60]

In the case of *Zimbabwe Human Rights NGO Forum v Zimbabwe*[61] and again in *Centre on Housing Rights and Evictions vs The Sudan*,[62] the Commission confirmed the state's duty to act with due diligence in holding non-state actors accountable, failure of which would result in a violation of the state's duty to protect. The case of the *Institute for Human Rights and Development in Africa and Others v. Democratic Republic of the Congo* (*Kilwa* case) dealt *inter alia* with the involvement of an Australian mining company in supporting human rights violations in the DRC. In this case the Commission found that the state had "failed not only to investigate and punish the involvement of the Anvil Mining Company but also to provide redress for the victims against the Company for the role it played in the perpetration of the violations". The Commission further stressed "the need and the legal imperative that entities engaged in the extractive industries undertake their activities with due regard to the rights of the host communities".[63] While this case did not relate to socio-economic or positive obligations on corporations, it did signal a willingness

[58] African Charter on Human and Peoples' Rights, Articles 27 & 29.

[59] *Communication 155/96: Social and Economic Rights Action Center (SERAC) and Center for Economic and Social Rights (CESR) / Nigeria* (African Commission on Human and Peoples' Rights), para 46.

[60] Oloka-Onyango (2003), pp. 903 & 910.

[61] *Communication 245/02: Zimbabwe Human Rights NGO Forum v. Zimbabwe* (African Commission on Human and Peoples' Rights), para 115.

[62] *Communication 279/03: Sudan Human Rights Organisation & The Sudan; 296/05 – Centre on Housing Rights and Evictions/The Sudan* (African Commission on Human and Peoples' Rights), para 148.

[63] *Communication 393/10 - Institute for Human Rights and Development in Africa and Others v. Democratic Republic of the Congo* (African Commission on Human and Peoples' Rights) [English quote from the 2018 Newsletter of the Working Group on Extractive Industries, Environment and Human Rights of the ACHPR, p. 12].

of the Commission to acknowledge that corporations may have obligations under the regional human rights law. While not directly finding a violation by a corporation, the Commission's recommendations to the state did include the prosecution of Kilwa employees for the perpetration of human rights violations.

Recently, the African Court on Human and Peoples' Rights (the Court) in *LIDHO v Cote d'Ivoire*[64] for the first-time commented on the accountability of non-state actors, in particular corporations, for the violation of human rights. It held that "even though the responsibility [...] to respect the obligations of international law is incumbent primarily on States, it is also true that this responsibility is incumbent on companies, notably, multinational companies". The Court held that "[s]uch a responsibility requires enterprises to commit themselves to public policies in prevention and reparation, due diligence in continuous identification of the consequences of their activities and lastly, setting up procedures aimed at solving problems caused by their action". A minority dissenting opinion proposes that "[t]he Court should horizontally extend the positive obligations contained in the African Charter to the powerful multinational companies that mastermind massive human rights violations on the continent". While, again, this does not extend to fulfilment of socio-economic rights, it does signal a directional change and an opening for further developments in this regard in future.

The jurisprudence at the sub-regional level, for example in the Court of Justice of the Economic Community of West African States (ECOWAS Court) in the *SERAP v. Federal Republic of Nigeria*[65] case, based on the same facts as the *SERAC* case, is similar to that of the Commission. The ECOWAS Court found that Nigeria had "defaulted in its duties in terms of vigilance and diligence".[66] Unfortunately, in a recent judgement which "diverges in several significant respects from international jurisprudence on corporate misconduct and the duty owed by states to protect their citizens from the abuses of non-state actors", the Court in *Molmou v Guinea*[67] held that non-state actors cannot be the subject of human rights claims in international law, as only states are subjects under international law.[68] There thus seems to be a retrogression at the level of the ECOWAS Court in relation to corporate accountability.

However, in a recent soft law development, the Commission went significantly further in its interpretation of the duties on corporations, particularly those engaged in the extractive industries, in its 2018 State Reporting Guidelines on Articles 21 and 24 of the African Charter. These Guidelines explicitly state that corporations do have duties under the African human rights system. The reasoning of the Commission

[64] African Court on Human and Peoples' Rights, *LIDHO and Others v Republic of Cote d'Ivoire* (Application 041/2016) [2023] AfCHPR 21 (5 September 2023).

[65] *SERAP (Socio-Economic Rights and Accountability Project) v Nigeria, Merits, General list no ECW/CCJ/APP/08/09, Judgment no ECW/CCJ/JUD/18/12, IHRL 1963 (ECOWAS 2012)* (ECOWAS Court).

[66] SERAP case, para 112.

[67] *Marie Molmou & 114 Ors. v Guinea, Judgment*, ECW/CCJ/JUD/16/16, May 17, 2016.

[68] Loua and Kaufman (2017), p. 151.

in this regard is that whereas the African Charter provides for duties not only on states but also on individuals, and given the significant impact of corporations on human rights which would result in a "human rights vacuum" if they were not subject to accountability, corporations do have human rights obligations under the African human rights system.[69] In the words of the Commission, "[c]learly, if this obligation can be imposed on individuals, there is an even stronger moral and legal basis for attributing these obligations to corporations and companies".[70] According to the Commission, in addition to the negative duty to respect, or to do no harm, and to ensure that those that act on their behalf or to their benefit respect human rights, "in certain circumstance companies also bear certain positive obligations".[71] These obligations include "fiscal responsibilities and transparency obligations", consultation and participation of communities and the undertaking of environmental, social and human rights impact assessments.[72]

Most important for purposes of the current analysis, the Guidelines provide for duties on corporations to "contribute to the development needs of the host communities". This duty is justified on the basis of "the social and economic impacts of the operations of companies and the nature of the power that they exercise". Importantly, the Commission stresses that these are not CSR based voluntary principles but are *legal obligations*, which include "supporting community-based employment and economic diversification to reduce reliance on the extractive industries as the sole source of income, educational, health, agricultural or pastoral development projects, as well as providing access to mine facilities and infrastructure".[73] The Guidelines place a corresponding duty on states to "adopt the required institutional measures for monitoring and enforcing the fiscal, environmental, labour, health and human rights observance standards by third parties" and to "lay down the administrative, civil and criminal liabilities that result from the failure of non-state actors including businesses such as those in extractive industries to comply with these standards and any harm or violations arising from such non-compliance".[74]

This however, raises further questions. In the first place, it raises questions about the allocation of responsibility between the various levels of the state (national and local) and mining companies for the provision of employment opportunities, development projects, health care or education. Secondly, while there are established international standards and best practices regarding some of these obligations, such as participation of community members in decisions affecting them, and how impact assessments should be conducted, there is no clear guidance in this document or elsewhere on the obligations that corporations have to fulfil in relation to

[69] African Commission on Human and Peoples' Rights (2018) State Reporting Guidelines and Principles on Articles 21 and 24 of the African Charter Relating to Extractive Industries, Human Rights and the Environment, p. 37.

[70] African Commission on Human and Peoples' Rights (2018), p. 37.

[71] African Commission on Human and Peoples' Rights (2018), p. 39.

[72] African Commission on Human and Peoples' Rights (2018), pp. 39–40.

[73] African Commission on Human and Peoples' Rights (2018), p. 40.

[74] African Commission on Human and Peoples' Rights (2018), p. 34.

development and socio-economic needs of the community. It is consequently hard to determine when they would be considered to be in breach of these obligations. While corporations clearly have more power and socio-economic impacts than individuals, in most cases corporations have less power and less socio-economic impacts than states. According to Ratner, corporate responsibility is "'down from state responsibility and up from individual responsibility".[75] Given that, according to the UNGPs, corporations are "specialized organs of society performing specialized functions",[76] to what extent may they be held accountable for these more general functions? It is also not clear from the Guidelines if the Commission through recognising human rights obligations on corporations intends to extend its jurisdiction beyond the State Parties to the Charter. One indication that it may be extending its powers in this regard, was the action taken by the Chairperson of the Working Group on Extractive Industries, Environment and Human Rights in Africa after the adoption of the *Kilwa* decision, of writing to the company concerned, requesting it to "acknowledge responsibility for breaching its duty of care through a public statement and contribute to the reparations".[77]

From the international human rights framework applicable in Africa, it seems to be clear that the most commonly followed approach is for states to be held accountable for their failure to protect their citizens against the human rights impacts of corporations. The UNGPs, while maintaining the primary responsibility on states to protect, also recognise the obligation of corporations to respect human rights and recognises some positive duties, such as to engage the affected people, undertake impact assessments and put in place grievance mechanisms. The dissenting opinion in the African Court decision in *LIHDO v Cote d'Ivoire,* and the State Reporting Guidelines of the African Commission push at the boundaries of corporate obligations, based on the unique characteristic of the African human rights system of recognising individual duties. In the case of the State Reporting Guidelines, it goes so far as to propose that corporations may have positive legal obligations to contribute to the wellbeing and development of the communities in which they operate. In considering how this obligation may be concretised, the next section considers the case study of South Africa, a country where there is explicit recognition of the positive socio-economic obligations of corporations, to see how the allocation of responsibility to corporate actors may work in practice.

---

[75] This view is also held by S Ratner (2001) Corporations and Human Rights: A Theory of Legal Responsibility. Yale Law Journal 111, p. 488, quoted in Bilchitz (2013), p. 129.

[76] UNGPs, p. 1.

[77] African Commission on Human and Peoples' Rights (2017) https://www.achpr.org/pressrelease/detail?id=65.

5 Legal Framework in South Africa Providing for Positive Duties of Companies in Relation to Socio-economic Rights

The South African Constitution, 1996, is the highest law of the land and provides a clearly established basis for constitutional duties on non-state actors. The Constitution in section 8 (2) provides that "natural and juristic" persons have human rights duties, where this is required by the *nature of the right* and the *nature of the obligation* arising from the right. The Constitution also provides for a range of socio-economic rights which should be protected for everyone, including "access to adequate housing, health care services, sufficient food and water, social security, and further education" as well as fair labour practices.[78]

If the argument of Bilchitz above is followed in that the rightsholders should be central to human rights realisation, this would mean that all who impact on these rights should also have duties in relation to their fulfilment. This was confirmed by the South African Constitutional Court in the *Government of the Republic of South Africa and Others v. Grootboom and Others* in which the Court held that a "right of access to adequate housing also suggests that it is not only the state who is responsible for the provision of houses", but that private actors also have a role.[79] The Court further held that "other agents within our society [...] must be enabled by legislative and other measures to provide housing".[80] Kotze and Fuo argue that this means that in practice "the positive obligation on non-state actors to fulfil socio-economic rights is limited to the extent that these actors must only comply with and contribute to policies, programmes and laws that the state enacts".[81] The approach in *Grootboom* was reconfirmed in the *Modderklip Boerdery (Pty) Ltd. v. Modder East Squatters & Anor.* case, in which the Supreme Court of Appeal held that "circumstances can indeed be envisaged where the right [to housing] would be enforceable horizontally", however, it did not find it necessary to apply it in this case.[82]

While in the aforementioned cases the Courts did not find a violation of a horizontal application, in *Governing Body of the Juma Musjid Primary School & Others v Essay N.O. and Others*[83] the Constitutional Court found a violation of a negative horizontal obligation in relation to the right to education. The Court further "underlined how the alleged watertight distinction between public and private power would serve to disguise private power's public dimension,"[84] thereby following the same

[78] Nolan (2014), p. 74.

[79] *Government of the Republic of South Africa and Others v Grootboom and Others (CCT11/00) [2000] ZACC 19* SAFLII (South African Constitutional Court), para 35.

[80] Grootboom case, para 35.

[81] Kotzé and Fuo (2016), p. 309.

[82] *Modderklip Boerdery (Pty) Ltd. v. Modder East Squatters & Anor.* 2001 (4) SA 385 (W) at 394J–395A–B, para 31.

[83] *Governing Body of the Juma Musjid Primary School & Others v Essay N.O. and Others* (CCT 29/10) [2011] ZACC 13.

[84] Nolan (2014), p. 84.

logic as Bilchitz above that corporations are entities with both private and public functions. In two further cases the Constitutional Court found a violation of a positive socio-economic duty of a non-state actor. Firstly, in the *City of Johannesburg Metropolitan Municipality v Blue Moonlight Properties 39 (Pty) Ltd and Another*[85] the Constitutional Court found that private building owners had a duty to provide unlawful occupants with accommodation for a period of time, since they would have been rendered homeless had they been evicted.[86] Secondly, in *Daniels v Scribante and Another*[87] the Constitutional Court set out the criteria for when positive duties can be imposed on non-state actors, as including: "the nature of the right; what is the history behind the right; what does the right seek to achieve; how best can that be achieved; what is the "potential of invasion of that right by persons other than the State or organs of state"; and, would letting private persons off the net not negate the essential content of the right?". Many of these considerations are echoed by Nolan above, and in relation to whether the right would be negated if not fulfilled by the non-state actor, the Court is applying the same logic as Bilchitz above that rights holders and not specific duty bearers are at the core of human rights realisation. The Court however confirmed what has been stated by theorists that "[i]t would be unreasonable [...] to require private persons to bear the exact same obligations under the Bill of Rights as does the state".[88]

In relation to socio-economic rights, the South African courts have generally followed an approach of "strong negative and weak positive obligations".[89] Whereas all societal actors are considered to have negative duties not to interfere with rights, in the *Grootboom* case and later jurisprudence, the Constitutional Court has limited the positive realisation of socio-economic rights based on "reasonableness, progressive realisation and the State's available resources".[90] This is in contrast to the approach followed by the African Commission, which requires states, even in situations of emergency, to comply with "at least the core obligations with respect to economic, social and cultural rights".[91] Beyond the core obligations, states must "take 'concrete and targeted steps', while taking full advantage of the 'available resources' within *the state and other sources*" [emphasis added].[92]

---

[85] *City of Johannesburg Metropolitan Municipality v Blue Moonlight Properties 39 (Pty) Ltd and Another* (CC) [2011] ZACC 33; 2012 (2) BCLR 150 (CC); 2012 (2) SA 104 (CC) (1 December 2011).

[86] Madlanga (2018) https://www.groundup.org.za/article/human-rights-we-should-not-only-target-state/.

[87] *Daniels v Scribante and Another* (CCT50/16) [2017] ZACC 13; 2017 (4) SA 341 (CC); 2017 (8) BCLR 949 (CC) (11 May 2017), para 39.

[88] Daniels case, para 40.

[89] Liebenberg (2011), p. 40.

[90] Liebenberg (2011), p. 40.

[91] Ssenyonjo (2016), p. 94.

[92] Ssenyonjo (2016), p. 107, quoting *Communication No. 241/2001 - Purohit and Moore v. The Gambia (2003) 16th Annual Activity Report; (2003) AHRLR 96 (ACHPR 2003).*

Under South African law, the Companies Act 71 of 2008 in section 7 (a) explicitly provides for the promotion of compliance with the Bill of Rights of the Constitution in the application of company law. The Mineral and Petroleum Resources Development Act 28 of 2002 (MPRDA) further requires of all mining companies to adopt social and labour plans (SLPs) as a prerequisite to the granting of mining licences, and progress under it must be reported on.[93] One of the fundamental principles underlying the MPRDA is to "ensure that holders of mining and production rights contribute towards the socio-economic development of the areas in which they are operating".[94] The SLPs must be developed in consultation with the affected mining communities and in consultation with "other economic development frameworks", and "should address infrastructure related needs and contribute towards income generation", by providing for example housing, roads, access to water and electricity to mine workers and those affected by the mining operations.[95] In response to "loadshedding" from the national energy generator ESKOM,[96] and other government failures, some mines have also started "embedded generation" of electricity for their own consumption.[97] Civil society has been placing pressure on mines to ensure that the electricity generated in this way is owned by the community and is renewable, primarily solar or wind energy.[98] This is arguably one way in which corporations can fulfil socio-economic rights of those who they directly impact through their operations. However, the regulatory framework has been criticised for not providing sufficient criteria on fulfilment, lack of transparency in that documents are not publicly available and for its lack of formal grievance mechanism for affected communities in cases of non-compliance.[99] The South African legal framework on corporate accountability for fulfilling socio-economic rights, already arguably embedded in the Constitution, has thus been developed and given content through laws as well as constitutional jurisprudence. Important principles have been laid down for such obligations, as well as mechanisms for ensuring that corporations, particularly mining companies, comply with at least some, prior agreed on, obligations to fulfil socio-economic rights.

[93] MPRDA, section 23.

[94] MPRDA, section 2 (i).

[95] South African Department of Mineral Resources, *Guideline for the submission of a Social and Labour Plan* (2010), p. 17; Kotzé and Fuo (2016), p. 311.

[96] Eskom Holdings, https://loadshedding.eskom.co.za/LoadShedding/Description.

[97] Interview conducted with South African human rights activist in 2023.

[98] Interview conducted with South African human rights activist in 2023.

[99] Ronald Ozzy Lamola (2017) A Critical Analysis of the Enforceability of Social And Labour Plans In The South African Mining Industry. Master's Thesis at Pretoria University (unpublished), p. 2.

6 Lessons for the Application of Positive Corporate Duties on Mines in Relation to Socio-economic Rights at the African Regional Level

Through the normative work that has been done, it is clear that the distinction drawn between positive and negative duties on companies—a distinction between merely respecting rights and actually promoting and fulfilling them—is an artificial delineation, which cannot be supported on legal, practical or normative grounds. The theory as well as the approach demonstrated by the South African courts, support the approach taken by the African Commission in relation to more expansive corporate obligations rather than the more limited approach of the UNGPs.

Both the South African Constitution and the African Charter recognise that individuals may be duty bearers, and extrapolate this to also provide for duties of corporations. However, while the Constitution creates a strong horizontal application for all human rights, the duties in the African Charter are on paper more limited. Under the Charter, persons are not considered duty bearers in relation to all the rights (including socio-economic rights) under the Charter, but have specific delineated duties, set out in Articles 27 to 29. These duties include duties to exercise rights with due regard to the rights of others, respect fellow beings without discrimination, to serve the national community, preserve national solidarity and independence and work to the best of his abilities and competence. While these do not directly include socio-economic duties, the Commission's interpretation reads in duties which basically require compliance with Charter obligations, such as providing access to information and to contribute to the realisation of socio-economic needs of communities where they operate. Nevertheless, because the horizontal application of the Charter is not explicitly stated, the application of positive socio-economic duties on corporations remains less "grounded" than in the South African case.

However, as argued by Liebenberg, in practice the positive fulfilment of socio-economic rights in South Africa so far received only weak application, with various criteria being applied to determining whether the state has complied with its obligations, and considerations such as available resources given primary consideration. On the other hand, the African Charter does not draw a distinction between the obligations in relation to the realisation of civil and political rights on the one hand and socio-economic rights on the other. This is because while in the South African context socio-economic rights are explicitly subject to progressive realisation, no such limitation is found in the Charter, and the African Commission has followed the approach of other international bodies of recognising that there is a minimum core of socio-economic rights which have to be fulfilled. From this discussion it appears that while the South African context does recognise stronger obligations on corporations than many other national jurisdictions, it does not yet go far enough in establishing a framework within which the corporate obligations under the African Charter can be fully realised.

Having nevertheless established through the African regional and national frameworks that corporations can be duty bearers in relation to positive obligations, the next question is how far these obligations should go? While the arguments of Bilchitz about the public/private nature of corporations, the language of dependency or control used by De Schutter, and the criteria set out by the South African Constitutional Court in the *Daniels* case differ in some respects, their all agree on the notion that corporations have more power than individual persons, but less power than the state, and that their duty to fulfil human rights would be adjusted accordingly. If the view of Kotze and Fuo above is followed, which also accords with the approach of the UNGPs, then the only positive duties on corporations in relation to socio-economic rights would be those that are explicitly required of them in government legislation and policies that are enacted. However, given that these positive duties flow not only from national obligations but also from international obligations on corporations, which exist independently of the obligations of the state, this conception of positive obligations on corporations seems too narrow.[100] This also raises a challenge in terms of enforcement, as it again places the full responsibility on the state to ensure compliance by corporations.

In terms of enforcement, despite the limited measures taken by the African Commission to get the Anvil Mining Company to take direct responsibility for human rights violations which they aided and abetted in the DRC, on the whole "international law does not contain mechanisms to enforce its prescriptions vis-à-vis corporations".[101] Consequently, it would remain largely up to national level enforcement to ensure compliance with positive socio-economic responsibilities. However, such an approach would greatly limit the efficacy of the direct obligations on corporations under international law, as the challenges faced by governments in developing countries to hold corporations accountable has been well documented. Therefore, it may be time for the African Commission or African Court to take the next logical step, and to find a violation of Charter rights by a corporation, thereby remedying the oversight in the *SERAC* case and starting a new epoch of corporate accountability in Africa, which goes beyond the inadequate CSR and corporate-responsibility-to-respect paradigms.

Most of the discussion above related to the obligations of corporations in general. However, since the State Reporting Guidelines are limited to the context of extractive industries, it is important to consider the kinds of obligations that would be imposed on mining companies specifically. Kotze and Fuo undertook a case study regarding the possibility of mining companies in the South African context having a duty to contribute to realising the right to water, because of "the ecological impact of mines on water resources and resultant socio-economic externalities that

---

[100] This is part of the reasoning that had spurred the development of the UN draft legally binding instrument. However, in its current version (updated draft of July 2023) the obligations remain with individual future state parties to the instrument to enforce the responsibilities on corporations.

[101] De Schutter (2014), p. 197. The current UN draft legally binding instrument may be a first, if limited, step in this direction.

are passed on to society".[102] I believe these authors correctly argue that while the responsibility for fulfilling socio-economic rights should not be shifted away from the state, that "the mining sector […] [should] take on a more proactive role in supporting the state in fulfilling its obligations", given their power, resources and their impact on and special relationship with the communities in which they operate.[103] Kotze and Fuo advance another argument for why mining companies could be held accountable for provision of socio-economic rights such as water, in that "unlike the function to arrest and detain people, water provision is not an exclusive state prerogative, as the increasingly popular trend to privatise water services suggests".[104] However, when it comes to the specific functions, they argue mining companies should include in their SLPs "social and labour related aspects *it deems important*"[emphasis added]. Such an approach is not satisfactory in that it allows corporations freedom in setting their own agenda, similar to the CSR framework. While it may be argued that SLPs are made binding through reporting and are therefore superior to CSR, and should be subject to public participation, it does not help to clarify which positive duties corporations should have under a human rights regime.

7 Conclusion

Clearly, no consensus has yet been established among academics or in practice on the extent of the positive socio-economic duties of corporations. However, a number of guidelines have crystalised from the above which can be applied on a case-by-case basis to determine the extent of such positive obligations: (1) while corporate positive obligations do not extend as far as state obligations, they are more rigorous that obligations on individuals; (2) the degree of dependency/special relationship/sphere of influence of the corporation, and related to that, the power or level of control of the corporation over the means to realise the right; (3) what the right seeks to achieve, including its importance for survival and a life of dignity of right holders; (4) whether the non-realisation by the corporation would negate the essential content of the right, or whether there is another duty holder able and better placed to fulfil the right; (5) delimiting the obligations so as not to undermine the economic viability of the corporation; (6) engagement and consultation with the affected community to identify the needs that they consider a priority; (7) taking account of the specific needs and rights of vulnerable groups. Core to almost all of these considerations, is the idea of placing the rights holder, rather than any potential duty bearer, at the centre of a human rights approach to fulfilling socio-economic rights.

If these considerations are applied to the context of mining companies fulfilling socio-economic rights in developing countries in Africa, the following can briefly

[102] Kotzé and Fuo (2016), p. 285.

[103] Kotzé and Fuo (2016), pp. 291–307.

[104] Kotzé and Fuo (2016), p. 304.

be said in relation to these considerations. Firstly, in most, if not all cases, there is a special relationship or relationship of dependency between communities affected by mining and the mining companies. This is because mining operations usually disrupt the normal livelihoods and social structures which were in place before their presence, often resulting also in the relocation of entire communities. Secondly, while it is not possible to create a hierarchy of rights, the fulfilment of some socio-economic rights is at the very core of life and dignity, including the rights to food and shelter, health and education. Additionally, even if the maximum availability of state resources were applied to the realisation of socio-economic rights, in most African countries large sections of the society still are not able to share in these benefits, and the non-fulfilment of the rights by mining companies for the people that they directly impact on, would leave them without access to their rights. Crucially, not all communities affected by mining have the same needs, and effective consultation and participation in decision-making is therefore necessary in determining which rights fulfilment should enjoy priority, within the available resources of the corporation, while not infringing on its viability. In the COVID-19 situation, based on these considerations, there was a duty on mining companies to assist the communities they impact on with the necessary health care and PPE, as well as access for children to electronic means of education. This is because African states in these cases were not able to provide these functions effectively to the whole of society, corporations in many cases already had the infrastructure available for these purposes, the very lives of people were in the balance, and the needs of vulnerable groups, such as children should be a core consideration. Therefore, to the extent that governments were not able to provide these necessities, corporations had a duty, at least from a moral and regional law perspective, to ensure the realisation of these rights. Whether these duties also extend to the wider community is not one that is addressed in the State Reporting Guidelines, where duties to fulfil are limited to the affected communities, and thus remains an open question.

It is clear that at least in the African context, corporate obligations today go beyond the CSR and corporate duty to respect frameworks. While this view was previously applied cautiously at national level in countries such as South Africa, and has been much theorised upon, the African Commission as one of the bodies mandated to interpret the African Charter has now authoritatively confirmed these obligations. Corporations in Africa are recognised as corporate citizens, which not only have rights but also have duties to contribute to the realisation of sustainable development and equality in the countries and areas where they operate, not merely on a voluntary basis or in terms of commitments that they deem important, but as part of wider development and human rights frameworks. The next step would be to develop frameworks at the regional level through which these obligations can be enforced, where states are unable or unwilling to do so.

References

African Commission on Human and Peoples' Rights (2017) Press release: 'Letter to Anvil Mining Company on its role in human rights violations in the DRC', 19 December 2017. https://www.achpr.org/pressrelease/detail?id=65

African Commission on Human and Peoples' Rights (2018) State Reporting Guidelines and Principles on Articles 21 and 24 of the African Charter Relating to Extractive Industries, Human Rights and the Environment

African Commission on Human and Peoples' Rights (2020) 67th Ordinary Session of the African Commission on Human and Peoples' Rights, Inter-session Activity Report of Commissioner Dersso

Appiah DO, Buaben JN (2012) Is gold mining a bane or a blessing in Sub-Saharan Africa: the case of Ghana. Int J Dev Sustain 1:1033–1048

Arlet J, Ereshchenko V, Lopez Rocha S (2019) Barriers to urban electrification in Sub-Saharan Africa from the perspective of end-users. World Bank Blogs 2 May 2019. https://blogs.worldbank.org/developmenttalk/barriers-urban-electrification-sub-saharan-africa-perspective-end-users

Banerjee ZRSG, McMahon G, Toledano P, Robinson P, Arroyo IP (2015) World Bank Report on the power of the mine: a transformative opportunity for Sub-Saharan Africa

Bilchitz D (2010) Do corporations have positive fundamental rights obligations? Theoria 57:1–35

Bilchitz D (2013) A chasm between 'is' and 'ought'? A critique of the normative foundations of the SRSG's Framework and the Guiding Principles. In: Bilchitz D, Deva S (eds) Human rights obligations of business beyond the corporate responsibility to respect? Cambridge University Press, UK, pp 107–137

Bilchitz D (2016) Corporations and the limits of state-based models for protecting fundamental rights in international law. Indiana J Global Leg Stud 23:143–170

Bilchitz D, Deva S (2013) The human rights obligations of business: a critical framework for the future. Cambridge University Press, UK

Chirwa DM (2002) Non-state actors' responsibility for socio-economic rights: the nature of their obligations under the South African Constitution. ESR Rev 3:2–6

De Schutter O (2014) Corporations and economic, social, and cultural rights. In: Riedel E, Giacca G, Golay C (eds) Economic, social, and cultural rights in international law: contemporary issues and challenges. Oxford University Press, UK, pp 193–224

Dembour M (2010) What are human rights? Four schools of thought. Hum Rts Q 32:1–20

Eskom Holdings SOC. What is load shedding? https://loadshedding.eskom.co.za/LoadShedding/Description

International Council on Mining and Metals. Mining Principles. https://www.icmm.com/en-gb/members/member-requirements/mining-principles

International Council on Mining and Minerals. Growing access to sanitation and hygiene in mining communities. https://miningwithprinciples.com/growing-access-to-sanitation-and-hygiene-in-mining-communities/

Khulekani M, Liebenberg S (2015) The privatization of water services: the quest for enhanced human rights accountability. Hum Rights Q 37:691–727

Kotzé LJ, Fuo O (2016) Bridging the public-private regulatory divide: South African mines and the right of access to water. J Energy Nat Resour Law 34:285–312

Liebenberg S (2011) Grootboom and the seduction of the negative/positive rights dichotomy. South Afr Public Law 26:37–59

Loua FF, Kaufman J (2017) Molmou v Guinea: The ECOWAS Court of Justice at the Service of its Member States. Bus Hum Rights J 2:149–155

Madlanga M (2018) Human rights: we should not only target the state, says Constitutional Court judge. Groundup, 5 September 2018. https://www.groundup.org.za/article/human-rights-we-should-not-only-target-state/

Nolan A (2014) Holding non-state actors to account for constitutional economic and social rights violations: experiences and lessons from South Africa and Ireland. ICON 12:61–93. https://doi.org/10.1093/icon/mot066

Oloka-Onyango J (2003) Reinforcing marginalized rights in an age of globalization: international mechanisms, non-state actors, and the struggle for peoples' rights in Africa. Am Univ Int Law Rev 18:851–914

Prescott DMD, Torres-Rahman Z, Nelson J (2020) Report by International Council on Mining and Metals (ICMM), Business Fights Poverty (BFP) and The Partnering Initiative (TPI), Building forward better COVID-19 framework: mining as a partner in supporting more inclusive and resilient societies

South African Department of Mineral Resources (2010) Guideline for the submission of a Social and Labour Plan

Ssenyonjo M (2016) The protection of economic, social and cultural rights under the African Charter. In: Chirwa D, Chenwi L (eds) The protection of economic, social and cultural rights in Africa. Cambridge University Press, UK, pp 91–120

Thomas MLH, Channon AA, Bain RES, Nyamai M, Wright JA (2020) Household-reported availability of drinking water in Africa: a systematic review. Water 12:1–28

Van Wyngaardt M (2018) Orca Gold gets water use permit for Sudan project. Mining Weekly, 8 February 2018. https://www.miningweekly.com/article/orca-gold-gets-water-use-permit-for-sudan-project-2018-02-08/rep_id:3650

Business and Women's Human Rights Framework in Brazil: An Analysis from *Fábrica de Fogos* Case

Melina Girardi Fachin

Abstract The research analyses the Brazilian normative framework regarding the relation between businesses and human rights under a gender-based perspective. The key problem of the article is that this framework still has not embraced such a perspective and, for this reason, seems to be inefficient in protecting women's human rights within the business's activities. The research has a descriptive character and the method applied is inductive. The article reviews and compares the national and international normative diplomas in relation to the international jurisprudence and concrete episodes of human rights violations that occurred in Brazil. It concludes that the mentioned framework is not sufficient to prevent impunity and human rights violations by businesses and, also, that there is no sufficient legal protection to women's rights, since the international references concerning the issue were not incorporated into the Brazilian legislation. Therefore, in spite of the progress made in Brazil with respect to the regulation of business activities for the specific purpose of protecting human rights, significant protective gaps still exist in relation to gender issues and women's rights within the largest portion of the Brazilian business sector.

1 Introduction

The Covid-19 pandemic showed that inequality between men and women is still very present, which can be seen in access to health, care economy, domestic violence, and the greater precariousness of work. The promotion of gender equality, as it depends on public policies to face inequalities, requires investments. Thus, the insufficiency of States' resources disproportionately impacts women since they depend on them more than men, first, because of structural inequalities and, secondly, because the lack of investment will delay the achievement of substantial

M. G. Fachin (✉)
Federal University of Paraná, Curitiba, PR, Brazil

D. A. Pamplona et al. (eds.), *Business and Human Rights from the Lens of Women*, Interdisciplinary Studies in Human Rights 13,
https://doi.org/10.1007/978-3-032-04036-7_3

gender equality, far from being achieved. In other words, the loss of corporate taxes, whether due to tax abuses committed by companies or the granting of tax benefits by States without compensation, means the deprivation of resources for investment in public policies in favor of gender equality and combating discrimination.

The proposal, therefore, is the analysis of this correlation from the human rights approach and specifically the Human Rights and Companies, considering that there are currently no binding international instruments that hold companies responsible for failing to pay taxes, nor that expressly deal with state obligations regarding the granting of tax benefits to companies. An interpretation of the Guiding Principles for Business and Human Rights is an essential tool for the analysis, presenting perspectives for the responsibility of companies and States in relation to tax collection and its relationship with gender equality.

The object of this research are the normative conditions, including the constitutional framework, about the relation between businesses and human rights in Brazil and, more precisely, gender issues and the human rights of women. The premise adopted as the key problem of the article is that, despite mirroring international standards established by the UN, in Brazil such regulatory conditions on the issue are still incipient and don't incorporate a gender perspective.

Those conditions are provided for by Decree No. 9571 of 2018, which adopts the UN Guiding Principles for Business and Human Rights into the Brazilian legal apparatus. However, as shall be argued, the passive adoption of these normative standards meant the maintenance of their original defects, such as, among others, their non-mandatory character, and the lack of a specific protection, at the national level, of women's rights, especially with regard to the majority of the business sector (of micro and small companies).

In addition to the scarcity of scientific sources related to the issue that integrates the object of the article, the research justifies itself also by recent concrete cases that occurred in Brazil, such as the rupture of the Fundão dam in 2015 in the city of Mariana and the dam rupture disaster in Brumadinho in 2019. Among many other violation episodes, the one central to the article is the "Fábrica de Fogos" disaster, which occurred in 1998 in Santo Antônio de Jesus and, in 2020, was judged by the Inter-American Court of Human Rights (Employees of the Santo Antônio de Jesus Fireworks Factory v. Brazil) in disfavour to the Brazilian State. The centrality of the case lies in its paradigmatic potential regarding the economic, racial and gender inequality that it demonstrates as persistent in Brazil.

For this reason, the research has a descriptive character, for its objective is to present the national legal basis applicable to the issue here presented, its flaws and the empirical bases that indicate them. The method applied in the article is inductive, for the general premise that shall integrate the conclusion is drawn from the articulated analysis of the legislation and the concrete cases narrated. Finally, as its research technique, the article reviews and compares the national and international normative diplomas in relation to the international jurisprudence, the protection of companies and human rights under a gender perspective.

2 Framework Regarding Business and Human Rights in Brazil

The Working Group's visit to Brazil in 2015 concluded that "Brazil has a well-developed legal framework and regulations and mechanisms to protect human rights against business-related harm",[1] having signed the main international human rights instruments.[2]

The framework regarding Business and Human Rights in Brazil strongly reflects the main international benchmark on the subject: the UN Guiding Principles for Business and Human Rights.[3] However, the importation of the legal reference does so mirroring both the positive innovations of the principles as well as the gaps that were left behind. Among other gaps that will be indicated, are the mechanisms for reparation and remediation posited in chapter IV of the Decree.

For example, article 13 of the Decree states that the State must only "encourage" ("*incentivar*" in Portuguese) the adoption, by businesses, of such mechanisms, among which are mere pecuniary compensations and public apologies. That is to say, the mechanisms are not severe at all and to the State is attributed a passive or weak role. Similar arguments could be presented with respect to article 14, which states that public administration have, once again, the simple task of encouraging business to establish and participate in the mechanisms of complaint and reparation in relation to possible violations to human rights within the business environment.

The implementation of the Guiding Principles into the national framework occurred with the Decree 9571 in 2018,[4] establishing the National Guidelines on Business and Human Rights.

---

[1] Human Rights Council (2016) Report of the Working Group on the issue of human rights and transnational corporations and other business enterprises on its mission to Brazil. par. 40. Available in: https://documents-dds-ny.un.org/doc/UNDOC/GEN/G16/096/43/PDF/G1609643.pdf?OpenElement. Accessed 09 July 2021.

[2] "Brazil has signed and ratified, or acceded to, eight of the nine core international human rights treaties. It has signed and, in some cases, ratified all the Optional Protocols, except for two. Brazil has also ratified seven of the eight International Labour Organization (ILO) fundamental conventions that cover four categories of principles and rights, namely, the right to organize and bargain collectively; abolition of forced labour; abolition of child labour; and elimination of discrimination in employment and occupation. It has ratified three of the four ILO governance conventions and 86 of the 177 ILO technical conventions.". Human Rights Council (2016) Report of the Working Group on the issue of human rights and transnational corporations and other business enterprises on its mission to Brazil. para 40, para 9. Available in: https://documents-dds-ny.un.org/doc/UNDOC/GEN/G16/096/43/PDF/G1609643.pdf?OpenElement. Accessed 09 July 2021.

[3] Office of the High Commissioner for Human Rights (2011) Guiding Principles on Business and Human Rights. Available in: https://www.ohchr.org/Documents/Publications/GuidingPrinciplesBusinessHR_EN.pdf. Accessed 09 July 2021.

[4] Brazil (2018) Decree No. 9.571. Establishes the National Guidelines on Business and Human Rights. Available in: http://www.planalto.gov.br/ccivil_03/_ato2015-2018/2018/decreto/D9571.html. Accessed 09 July 2021.

One of the main differences between the Guiding Principles and the Brazilian decree is that, while the international principles are applied to "all business enterprises, both transnational and others, regardless of their size, sector, location, ownership of structure",[5] the national framework limits the principles' applicability to big, medium, and multinational enterprises that operate in Brazil. With regard to micro and small companies, the normative wording refers to the *extent of their capabilities* in terms of the first paragraph of article 1 here translated: "(…) *micro and small businesses may, to the extent of their capabilities, comply with the Guidelines referred to in this Decree, subject to the provisions of art. 179 of the Constitution*".[6]

The National Guidelines determine that the Decree "may" be complied with by microenterprises and small enterprises, observing their capacities and in respect to article 179 of the Brazilian Constitution. The mentioned article states that micro and small enterprises shall have differentiated legal treatment, aiming to stimulate them by simplifying, reducing and/or eliminating administrative, taxation, pension expenses and credit obligations. To illuminate this, the Brazilian Federal Supreme Court has reaffirmed on different occasions this comprehension, restating the normative scope of article 179. Also, in the judgement of Direct Action of Unconstitutionality (*Ação Direta de Inconstitucionalidade*) No. 1.643, Justice Maurício Corrêa ruled that "*there is no offense to the principle of tax equality if the law, for extra-fiscal reasons, gives unequal treatment to micro and small businesses with different taxpayer capacity*".[7] Also, in the judgement of Extraordinary Appeal (*Recurso Extraordinário*) No. 627.543, Justice Dias Toffoli ruled that "*[article] 179 of the Federal Constitution, aims to simplify and reduce the obligations of these companies, granting them a different legal treatment, which is in perfect consonance with the principles of contributory capacity and isonomy*"[8]

However, small businesses are a major part of Brazil's economy. In 2016, of the 6.4 million existing establishments in the country, 99% were micro or small

[5]Office of the High Commissioner for Human Rights (2011) Guiding Principles on Business and Human Rights. Available in: https://www.ohchr.org/Documents/Publications/GuidingPrinciplesBusinessHR_EN.pdf. Accessed 09 July 2021.

[6]Article 1 of Decree n°. 9.571/2018, which (in free translation) states the following: "This Decree establishes the National Guidelines on Companies and Human Rights, for medium and large companies, including multinational companies with activities in the country". Brazil (2018) Decree No. 9.571. Establishes the National Guidelines on Business and Human Rights. Available in: http://www.planalto.gov.br/ccivil_03/_ato2015-2018/2018/decreto/D9571.html. The citations above were freely translated. Accessed 09 July 2021.

[7]Brazil's Supreme Federal Court (2003) Direct Action of Unconstitutionality No. 1.643. Available in: https://redir.stf.jus.br/paginadorpub/paginador.jsp?docTP=AC&docID=266708. Accessed 09 July 2021.

[8]Brazil's Supreme Federal Court (2013) Extraordinary Appeal No. 627.543. 2013. Available in: https://redir.stf.jus.br/paginadorpub/paginador.jsp?docTP=TP&docID=7066469. Accessed 09 July 2021.

enterprises, employing 52% of the registered private sector workers.[9] Such an expressive part of the Brazilian economy cannot be left out of compliance with National Guidelines. It is important to emphasize that the case proposed here for analysis of the Fireworks Factory is a case of a small business, hence the importance of this specific reflection, as shown below.[10]

Human Rights must not be seen as a burden, but as part of businesses, regardless of size.[11] Although this is not a unanimous position. Some authors—here, for all, Zanitelli (2011)—indicate that the debate about the obligation of businesses to be subject to human rights guidelines (and to sanctions for violating them) can be divided into two groups. On the one hand, according to the author, there are the so-called "voluntarists" ("*voluntaristas*", such as Georg Kell and John Ruggie), who defend that companies should freely adhere, without state coercion, to business practices aligned with human rights. On the other hand, the "obligationists" ("*obrigacionistas*", such as Peter Utting and Surya Deva), who carry a certain disbelief in relation to soft law instruments and understand that it is necessary for companies to be compelled, under risk of penalty (both nationally and internationally), to comply with guidelines arising from international law of human rights.

Furthermore, the national framework suffers from two additional problems which are also objects of criticism regarding the Guiding Principles. The first is the fact that the guidelines are not mandatory, but voluntary mechanisms subject to compensation. Paragraph 3 of article 1 states that the Ministry of State will institute the "Business and Human Rights" label for enterprises that voluntarily adopt the guidelines. The fact that the national framework is not compulsory, and the possibility of consensual dispute resolution established in the Decree can create a scenario of impunity for the violation of human rights by companies, as it is made clear by events that took place in Brazil.

An emblematic example is the consecutive disasters involving the mining industry in the state of Minas Gerais. On 5 November 2015, the rupture of the Fundão tailings dam, operated by the mining company Samarco Mineração SA, owned by BHP and Vale, in the district of Mariana, was considered one of the worst environmental disasters in Brazil. In March 2016, the company agreed to settle a civil

[9] SEBRAE (2016) Pequenos negócios em números. Available in: https://www.sebrae.com.br/sites/PortalSebrae/ufs/sp/sebraeaz/pequenos-negocios-em-numeros,12e8794363447510VgnVCM1000004c00210aRCRD. Accessed 09 July 2021.

[10] As stated in the Inter-American Court of Human Rights's decision on the Employees of the Santo Antônio de Jesus Fireworks Factory v. Brazil case, "[...] the fireworks factory was a small private business, which operated in an informal economy scheme." (Freely translated from footnote no. 248). Inter-American Court of Human Rights (2020) Employees of the Santo Antônio de Jesus Fireworks Factory v. Brazil. p. 48. Available in: https://www.corteidh.or.cr/docs/casos/articulos/seriec_407_por.pdf. Accessed 09 July 2021.

[11] Zanitelli (2011).

public claim.[12] Five years after the tragedy, the civil public suit was reopened because the terms of the agreement were not complied with by the companies involved.[13]

In January 2019, three years after the disaster in Mariana, a new rupture of the tailings dam in Brumadinho involving Vale, the same mining company responsible for the previous rupture, is considered the biggest labor accident in Brazil and the second greatest industrial disaster of the century.[14] Although the violation of women's rights in the cases of mining company Vale is not direct, the impact of mining projects has devastating impacts on communities, as in the cases above, and has disproportionate effects on women. This example shows that voluntary mechanisms for business and human rights are not enough, granting impunity for the companies and lacking reparation to the victims.

The visit of the Working Group on Business and Human Rights "found that, while some companies have specific policies and guidance on human rights in line with the Guiding Principles, it was clear that this was not the case for a majority of business enterprises in Brazil".[15] "The Working Group noted that human rights risks were mainly seen as risks to a company's operations, rather than risks faced by vulnerable rights holders".[16] Additionally, "(…) many interlocutors mentioned efforts to reduce child slavery or forced labor. While important, these do not comprise all the issues covered by the Guiding Principles".[17]

Included in the issues that are not covered by the Decree, because of the lack of treatment by the Guiding Principles on the matter, is the gender issue regarding women's rights. The words "gender" and "woman" appear only twice in the

[12] Human Rights Council (2016) Report of the Working Group on the issue of human rights and transnational corporations and other business enterprises on its mission to Brazil. para 28–33. Available in: https://documents-dds-ny.un.org/doc/UNDOC/GEN/G16/096/43/PDF/G1609643.pdf?OpenElement. Accessed 09 July 2021.

[13] Mauricio (2020) Ministérios Públicos e Defensorias pedem retomada de ação de R$155 bilhões contra a Vale, Samarco e BHP. https://observatoriodamineracao.com.br/ministerios-publicos-e-defensorias-pedem-retomada-de-acao-de-r-155-bilhoes-contra-a-vale-samarco-e-bhp/. Accessed 09 July 2021.

[14] Gortázar (2019) A maldição das minas no Brasil: entre o medo do desemprego e o fantasma da impunidade. https://brasil.elpais.com/brasil/2019/05/04/politica/1556925352_146651.html. Accessed 09 July 2021.

[15] Human Rights Council (2016) Report of the Working Group on the issue of human rights and transnational corporations and other business enterprises on its mission to Brazil. para 12. Available in: https://documents-dds-ny.un.org/doc/UNDOC/GEN/G16/096/43/PDF/G1609643.pdf?OpenElement. Accessed 09 July 2021.

[16] Human Rights Council (2016) Report of the Working Group on the issue of human rights and transnational corporations and other business enterprises on its mission to Brazil. para 13. Available in: https://documents-dds-ny.un.org/doc/UNDOC/GEN/G16/096/43/PDF/G1609643.pdf?OpenElement. Accessed 09 July 2021.

[17] Human Rights Council (2016) Report of the Working Group on the issue of human rights and transnational corporations and other business enterprises on its mission to Brazil. para 12. Available in: https://documents-dds-ny.un.org/doc/UNDOC/GEN/G16/096/43/PDF/G1609643.pdf?OpenElement. Accessed 09 July 2021.

Brazilian law,[18] and are not enough to promote the necessary gender perspective to business and human rights.

3 Special Dimension of Women's Rights in the BHR Framework

The need for a special dimension of women's rights was perceived by the Working Group on the issue of human rights and transnational corporations and other business enterprises, since women experience the impacts of business activities disproportionately. Considering that it is urgent "that measures taken by States and business enterprises to implement the UNGPs are gender responsive",[19] the UN Working Group and the United Nations Development Program created a booklet for a gender guidance for the Guiding Principles.[20]

The Gender Dimensions of the Guiding Principles on Business and Human Rights,[21] however, were not incorporated into the Brazilian Decree together with the applicable framework on Business and Human Rights. Therefore, the Decree lacks the necessary gender perspective to fight inequalities related to discrimination against women within business activities.

Women play an important role in the economy as a whole and specifically in the performance of companies, yet they bear the burden disproportionately, without the benefits of economic development being reversed. Therefore, the need for a gender approach to corporate issues does not arise in 2019 but derives from the inequalities of the process of neoliberal globalization and economic development itself.

Globalization, as a new global order, has reduced borders and allowed the emergence of new international actors, including transnational companies, which has generated a redefinition of the sovereignty of States. States, primarily responsible for guaranteeing human rights, as a result of globalization, have seen their sovereignty shifted to market dominance. Aiming to attract foreign investment to drive

---

[18] Articles 8, I, VII, IX and 10, IV. In: Brazil (2018) Decree No. 9.571. Establishes the National Guidelines on Business and Human Rights. Available in: http://www.planalto.gov.br/ccivil_03/_ato2015-2018/2018/decreto/D9571.html. Accessed 09 July 2021.

[19] United Nations Development Programme (2019) Gender Dimensions of the Guiding Principles on Business and Human Rights. Available in: https://www.undp.org/content/undp/en/home/librarypage/democratic-governance/gender-dimensions-guiding-principles-on-business-n-human-rights.html. Accessed 09 July 2021.

[20] United Nations Development Programme (2019) Gender Dimensions of the Guiding Principles on Business and Human Rights. Available in: https://www.undp.org/content/undp/en/home/librarypage/democratic-governance/gender-dimensions-guiding-principles-on-business-n-human-rights.html. Accessed 09 July 2021.

[21] Office of the High Commissioner for Human Rights (2019) Gender dimensions of the Guiding Principles on Business and Human Rights - Report of the Working Group on the issue of human rights and transnational corporations and other business enterprises. 2019b. Available in: https://ap.ohchr.org/documents/dpage_e.aspx?si=A/HRC/41/43. Accessed 09 July 2021.

economic growth, States have adapted their economic and financial barriers to the will of transnational companies, granting favorable regulation, involving tax incentives and flexibilization of labor laws. This new scenario between the need for investment in developing countries and the expansion of corporate power has created precariousness in the protection of human rights, especially regarding the most vulnerable groups such as women.

With privatization, the provision of services that used to belong to the States is also transferred on a large scale to transnational companies. With a view to profit and not the holistic development of human rights, the impact on social rights is disproportionately suffered by women, suffering the negative consequences of globalization. The lack of redistribution of privatization profits, instead of increasing the quality of life of all and reducing inequalities, has women as victims, increasing the distance in achieving gender equality.

Policies for the implementation of substantial gender equality from an intersectional approach have been rejected in favor of profit, and when the issue is addressed, it must be critically analyzed in order not to fall into the trap of the empty discourse of corporate marketing. In opposition to the movement of the last centuries, inaugurated with the Universal Declaration of Human Rights, the present neoliberal model promotes the emptying of individual and collective human rights, instead of promoting them. In this sense, the recognition of human rights in general and the human rights of women in particular has been threatened.

The context weakens the already precarious position of women's rights. Therefore, women's rights that have never been properly considered face new violations with the insertion of the role of transnational corporations amid globalization, with the further weakening of the role of States.

In the area of human rights and transnational corporations, there is no focus on the necessary treatment of vulnerable groups, as demonstrated in the case of the Guiding Principles for Human Rights and Business. It also imposes an additional challenge in guaranteeing the rights of women in relation to abuses committed by companies, which is the impunity of these actors, considering that they are not considered subjects of international law. The case of the "Fábrica de Fogos" that is presented below is an example of what is affirmed.

4 The "Fábrica de Fogos" Case

Business will find itself on a dangerous path if it pursues policies that just benefit its own interests at the expense of communal interests, that is, of society.[22] Although a series of improvements in women's access to the labor market, educational attainment, health outcomes and labor force participation across countries, they still are at disadvantage.

---

[22] Véras (2015), pp. 109–123.

There are many differences between the genders' ability to make effective choices around the world. Discrimination against women and the non-recognition of the value of their contribution to society are common in many countries. In addition, women's impressive gains in rights can be held back by lack of improvement in rights. When laws reinforce traditional prejudices, women have less access to resources, credit, education, employment, decision-making positions and lower income.[23]

One extreme and paradigmatic case that represents women's inequality in the labor area is the Employees of the Santo Antônio de Jesus Fireworks Factory v. Brazil, judged by the Inter-American Court of Human Rights. Brazil's condemnation for the deaths and violations of human rights of the workers at the Fireworks Factory,[24] at Santo Antônio de Jesus, in the Recôncavo Baiano region, represents an iconic case involving structural discriminations based on race, gender and social conditions.

The tragedy took place on December 11, 1998, and left dozens of dead. Of the 64 workers killed in the explosion, 63 were women and most of them were black. Among the victims, 22 were children and adolescents.

Although there is no instrument with binding force to hold companies accountable for human rights violations, the dialogue between the different levels will enable the expansion of the scope of protection and the promotion of women's rights. The sentence of Fábrica de Fogos v. Brazil addressed the issue of business and human rights—citing the Guiding Principles—and gender discrimination—citing the understanding of the CEDAW Committee—to complement the right to equality provided for in the American Convention on Human Rights—to condemn the Brazilian State to present "*a report on the implementation and application of the National Guidelines on Business and Human Rights, especially with regard to promoting and supporting measures of inclusion and non-discrimination, through the creation of incentive programs for the hiring of vulnerable groups*".

Although the Inter-American Court did not establish a direct relationship between the area of human rights and business and gender discrimination, as intended in this paper, the conclusion of the judgment demonstrates that the gap in the area of human rights and business—that also comes up against the lack of accountability of companies for human rights violations—as far as women's rights are concerned, may be narrowed by multilevel constitutionalism: the Inter-American Court (regional system), citing the Guiding Principles and CEDAW (global scope), ordered Brazil to apply of the National Guidelines on Business and Human Rights (local scope).

Considering that companies are not subjects of international law, they cannot be held directly responsible for violations of human rights treaties, which is why the Brazilian State was condemned in the above-mentioned case and why most of the

[23] Walters and Mason (1994).

[24] Inter-American Court of Human Rights (2020) Employees of the Santo Antônio de Jesus Fireworks Factory v. Brazil Case. Available in: https://www.corteidh.or.cr/docs/casos/articulos/seriec_407_por.pdf. Accessed 09 July 2021.

instruments address the obligation of the States, which is also portrayed in the Guiding Principles, still strongly linked to state obligations. However, with the growing power of business, it is necessary to look not only at the role of business as human rights violators, but also at the potential to translate economic growth into sustainable development, which includes achieving substantive gender equality.

This case also represents the relation between gender and racial discrimination with situations of poverty. According to the Court, the victims "were in a situation of structural poverty, most of them were Afro-descendant women and girls, four of whom were pregnant, and they had no other economic option but to accept dangerous work under exploitative conditions". Therefore, the condemnation decision is the international recognition of the State's responsibility to adopt protecting measures for those people affected by structural and intersectional discrimination.

The Court recognized that the Brazilian State was aware that hazardous industrial activities were carried out at the factory and did not properly inspect the place. Because of that, it exposed the workers to a high risk and imminent danger of life, personal integrity and health. The factory employed the Santos Antônio de Jesus's inhabitants, who had no choice but to accept the high-risk, low-paid work in the manufacture of fireworks.

The ruling convicts Brazil to adopt a series of structural measures, such as the creation of economic alternatives for the economic and labor insertion of the explosion victims and their family members. The ruling also establishes the creation and execution of a socioeconomic development program for the town's population and determines that Brazil must hold the perpetrators liable for the damages caused by the explosion.

The fact that all 64 fatal victims of the explosion were either women or children is directly related to Brazil's failure to address gender inequality. In Santo Antônio de Jesus, women constitute most of the city's low-income workers, representing 74% of those who earn up to 1/4 of the minimum wage and 62% of those who are paid between 1/4 and 1/2 of it. They also make for 65% of the unemployed economically active persons.[25]

Assigned gender roles concerning unpaid care work are also a main reason why these women turn to fireworks. The fireworks manufacturing allows them to either take their children to factories or bring production into their homes.

It appears from this case that only when women achieve equality of access and opportunity, will they realize their full potential to contribute to economic and social well-being. This can be done with women's empowerment, which can be defined as women's ability to make strategic life choices where that ability had been previously denied.

Enterprise development can make a significant contribution to women's empowerment and gender equality. To reach that goal it is necessary to generate more and better economic opportunities for women to reap the maximum benefit from WBEs

[25] Brigagao (2019).

(Women's Business Enterprises).[26] By doing this, clarifies Véras, it is possible to improve societies and enable women to play a more central role in the global economy.[27]

Companies are more aware that long-term success can be achieved through the creation of the same value for shareholders and the community in which they operate. Women are special because they can shape new models of leadership, experiencing unique processes, values of work and family, and the personal dynamics of change with the processes of developing and leading their businesses.[28]

5 The InterAmerican Standards

In the Fábrica de Fogos Case, the Inter-American Court devoted significant space in the judgment to examine the conjunctural conditions of the facts, such as the characteristics of the population and the municipality. The situation denounced a case of human labor exploitation and economic inequality in a context marked by the damages resulted from slavery. Therefore, issues such as informality, poverty, and unskilled labor subjugated a large part of the population of Santo Antônio de Jesus to economic and social vulnerability.

In the judgment, Judge Mac-Gregor (2020, p. 02) outlined some crucial elements of the case, which are protected and discussed in the Inter-American System, of which the following stand out: 1) poverty as part of economic discrimination; 2) the guarantee of substantive equality and 3) the state's obligation to guarantee rights against the actions of private individuals. Given that the impaired efficacy of social, economic, and cultural rights provides an opportune scenario for the violation of other rights, the Inter-American perspective fell on the safeguarding of these guarantees and is in a phase of recognition and consolidation in the Inter-American System, being perceived through a logic of indivisibility and interdependence among human rights. This means that they must be fully understood as human rights, without hierarchy among them, and enforceable in all cases by the competent authorities, so that the violation of one of these rights affects the others.

The Court identified multiple social factors that demean the individual due to discriminatory beliefs and understood that, when combined in the same situation and person, they aggravate the victim's vulnerability in a case of rights violation. In this debate, the concepts of intersectionality and intersectional discrimination are discussed as intensifiers of the structural discrimination process of gender, which must be understood when adopting a gender perspective in the analysis of cases of violence and/or subordination of historically marginalized groups.

---

[26] Véras (2015), p. 112.

[27] Véras (2015), p. 112.

[28] Véras (2015), p. 114.

In the decision of the case Employees of the Fireworks Factory of Santo Antônio de Jesus Vs. Brazil, the Inter-American Court takes a careful look to investigate the situation of vulnerability of the victims in a context of structural and intersectional discrimination, marked by various vulnerable factors. The case dealt with the factual consequences of state failures on labor irregularities and clandestine fireworks manufacturing activities. The outcomes affected the lives of 60 workers, including children and pregnant women. The constructions on the incidence of a structural dimension in the case of discrimination were like those developed in the case Workers of the Hacienda Brasil Verde Vs. Brazil (2016), directed at the economic position that placed the victims in a situation of structural vulnerability. However, in this case in question, the Inter-American Court added a new focus: the intersectional. Therefore, in addition to the social marker of poverty, the frailties of gender and race were also considered to assess the situation of vulnerability.

Therefore, understanding that the establishment of a dangerous and clandestine economic activity, such as the manufacturing of fireworks, took place in a space marked by poverty and marginalization of the social environment, offering the members of that population a unique and necessary alternative to ensure their subsistence due to low levels of education, the Inter-American Court concluded that economic and social disadvantages, when related to those referring to interiorized population groups, can impose greater disadvantages and risks.

Once again, the Court highlighted the essentiality of constructing affirmative measures with a differential outlook, assimilating the specificities that such violations accommodate (Inter-American Court 2020, p. 35). In this sense, the Inter-American Court reinforces the understanding that, in situations of discrimination that affect groups in a particularly vulnerable situation, state duties are accentuated (Inter-American Court 2020, p. 55). Thus, the Court's stance established that in a case of structural discrimination, it must be considered to what extent the victimization of the specific case evidences the vulnerability of people who belong to a group.

Considering this, the convergence of discriminatory elements in the present context has resulted in an exacerbated amplification of the inequalities faced by the alleged victims, since they shared specific discriminatory characteristics that affect social groups already vulnerable, such as individuals in economic need, women, and Afro-descendants. However, it is crucial to note that beyond this, they are subjected to a unique form of discrimination, arising from the intersection of these factors, and, in certain cases, due to pregnancy, the condition of being minors, or the conjunction of these two circumstances. In this context, it is relevant to underline that the Inter-American Court established that the condition of pregnancy can be interpreted as a state of fragility, and that, in some instances of victimization, a differentiated impact due to this condition.

In view of this, the following measures were determined as guarantees of non-repetition: adoption of measures to implement a systematic policy of periodic inspections at fireworks production sites; development and execution of a social and economic development program specially aimed at the population of Santo Antônio de Jesus, in coordination with the victims and their representatives; presentation of a report on the progress of the legislative process of the legislative project (which proposes to establish a new regulation for the manufacture, trade, and use of fireworks, repealing the existing legislation); and presentation of a report on the implementation and application of the National Guidelines on Businesses and Human Rights, especially with regard to the promotion and support of inclusion and non-discrimination measures.

When a group, such as women, is placed in a situation of continuous subordination and interiorization, cases of deprivation or restriction of rights must adhere to a set of factors related to the environment, no longer focusing solely on the specific case as an isolated violation. In the realm of professions and professional institutions, the presence of hierarchical structures that establish predominant standards responsible for determining the inclusion or exclusion of individuals from the category of members is notable. The notion of "dominance" and "excellence" can simultaneously express evaluations of competence and, implicitly, justify discriminatory tendencies. Indeed, it is important to observe that evaluations of competence often intertwine with considerations related to the social identity of the individual, aspects that are sometimes irrelevant to the evaluation of their professional competence.

When confronting such understandings with the female labor context, the existence and reproduction of patterns (of subordination) and ideals (about the worker figure) place the female gender in a place distant from expectations about workers. Although both men and women may experience subordination in the economic context, women systematically experience this subordination in both dimensions.

The dimensions to consider for understanding this subordination system include the social imaginary, the business imaginary, and the imaginary of public agents and policymakers. Regarding the first, it translates as a set of common-sense representations, maintained by individuals in general, about the distributions conferred to men and women, about their positions and assignments, in the family, at work, and in public and private social life. Regarding the business imaginary, this related to business perspectives on these same topics, is linked to the decisions of such economic agents on hiring, investment in training, assignment of tasks and responsibilities, definition of remuneration levels, and promotion of men and women based on a set of ideals about family, work, and society. The third sphere pertains to the complex of conceptions, perspectives, and concepts that make up the idea of political actors and policymakers. These representations constitute the core of the decisions made in this area and, consequently, have a direct influence on the opportunities, as well as the living and working conditions of men and women.

From these constructions, an interpretive parameter developed in the decisions of the cases Los Buzos Miskitos (Lemoth Morris et al.) Vs. Honduras (2021) and Olivera Fuentes Vs. Peru (2023) deserves highlight: the responsibility of companies regarding human rights. Multinational corporations cannot exempt themselves from the jurisdiction of international human rights law. Even in the absence of an international treaty that explicitly and specifically obliges them, it is feasible to infer the existence of a general obligation attributable to these companies, in the sense of respecting human rights. This obligation does not depend on their classification as legal entities of International Law since it is subject to execution and supervision within the framework of national states.

The accountability of transnational companies is a matter of persistent controversy, but some possible approaches to address this challenge are already outlined. In the context of Latin American states, the issue of corporate accountability in relation to human rights is exacerbated by the absence of effective regulation that ensures supervision and application of sanctions against those who commit violations, due to the economic power of these entities. An alternative under consideration is extraterritorial jurisdiction, which implies the accountability of corporations before their country of origin. However, this approach proves to be flawed in certain scenarios due to the decentralized nature of transnational companies, which makes both the identification of the state of origin and the geographical distance between the court and the site of the violations challenging.

The focus of regulations and treatment on human rights, notably those conferred to cases of structural discrimination, needs to be able to encompass multiple factors (social, economic, and contextual) to ensure a safe assessment of the vulnerability of victims and create adequate policies, and thus, developing strategies that can effectively combat the interconnected manifestations of oppression in the labor context. This involves a meticulous analysis of analytical categories that contribute to a deeper understanding of the complex interactions and interdependencies in social relations, as well as efforts to combat the various interconnected manifestations of oppression (Hirata 2014, p. 69). In the labor context, this manifests in the different levels of subordination of women, black women, and poor black women.

The economic position of those belonging to a historically subordinated group, such as women, is also a basis for exacerbating a situation of structural discrimination and was used as a parameter to identify the case of discrimination by the Inter-American Court in the decision of the case Workers of the Hacienda Brasil Verde Vs. Brazil (2016). By analyzing "poverty" as a prohibited criterion of discrimination, the Inter-American Court adopted a comprehensive interpretation, incorporating this criterion within the scope of the prohibition of discrimination based on "economic position." In this perspective, the Court recognized that the "poverty" criterion is one of the suspect categories not explicitly outlined in Article 1.1 of the American Convention on Human Rights, however, due to the flexibility of the formulation of this provision, deserves special treatment due to its condition of vulnerability.

These elements are intrinsically linked to the fundamental social right to work, which is based on the capacity for individual emancipation and the stimulation of economic growth. However, it is imperative that both conceptions are integrated, as the coexistence of human freedom and dignified work is incompatible with forms of economic development that exploit in a predatory manner. On the contrary, economic growth should not be used to undermine work and the human condition. Thus, the low financial condition of the individual, besides problematizing their insertion into the labor market, making them susceptible to accepting degrading work situations, can also limit their employment opportunities and exacerbate situations of structural and historical discrimination, propagating a cycle of subordination. These consequences of the economic position obstruct the movement of personal (when linked to historically marginalized groups) and financial emancipation (with the limitation of labor opportunities).

With the application of the interpretive parameters constructed by the Inter-American Court of Human Rights in the decisions of the analyzed and systematized cases, it is possible to understand that, in cases of structural discrimination, notably when involving a specific social group, the situations share common elements of vulnerability, which radiate effects to areas beyond those related to life, society, and family. The labor context is presented as one of these areas, since it is a fertile space for the proliferation and reproduction of systematized treatments of exclusion, which includes conditioning stereotypes and discriminatory, the intersection of elements of vulnerability, and standardized violence.

The Brazilian conviction in the case Employees of the Fireworks Factory of Santo Antônio de Jesus Vs. Brazil (2020) added to the structural lenses of equality the intersectional focus, providing a comprehensive reading under these biases. The Inter-American Court positioned itself to: 1) identify an aggravation of the situation of structural discrimination when there is the intersection of specific factors of discrimination; 2) highlight the essentiality of constructing affirmative measures with a differential outlook, assimilating the specificities that such violations accommodate, and 3) recognize the economic and social disadvantages, understanding that when related to those referring to population groups, can impose greater disadvantages.

6 Some Conclusions

As shown, by placing themselves as non-mandatory and by allowing disputes to be resolved within consensual means, the Brazilian Decree's guidelines seem to weaken their protective potential. The cases of Brumadinho and Mariana exemplify such legal shortcomings. That is, the national legal basis is not sufficient to prevent impunity and human rights violations arising from business activities and, besides that, there is no legal protection from a gender perspective, since the international references concerning the issue were not incorporated into the Brazilian legislation.

Likewise, the recent judgment within the Employees of the Santo Antonio de Jesus Fireworks Factory v. Brazil case by the Inter-American Court of Human Rights supports the conclusion presented above. Given the longstanding and persistent gender (and racial) inequality in the country, the legal arrangements aimed at protecting vulnerable groups in the business environment prove themselves to be laconic and inefficient. And more than that, the case acts as an example that gender equality and socioeconomic benefits are correlated variables, given that to guarantee equitable access to economic opportunities can also be favorable for the economic purposes of the business sector.

Thus, in spite of the advances made in Brazil with regard to the regulation of business activities for the specific purpose of protecting human rights, significant protective gaps still exist. By restricting its applicability to large, medium-sized and multinational companies, the protective condition of the national normative arrangements cannot reach a large portion of the Brazilian business sector, which is mostly made up of small companies and employs more than half of the private sector workers.

Also, in adopting the UN Guiding Principles for Business and Human Rights via Decree No. 9571 of 2018, Brazil missed the opportunity to enlarge the legal scope in order to encompass a gender perspective, leaving behind the long-needed women's rights protection as it was made clear, among others, in the emblematic Employees of the Santo Antonio de Jesus Fireworks Factory v. Brazil case.

The impact on women's rights and the absence of a gender-specific lens to address the harm caused by business are clear. In the decision by the Inter-American Court of Human Rights, whose facts were narrated above, the Brazilian State was condemned and it was made clear the intersectional discrimination suffered by female workers, as well as the relationship with the issue of human rights and companies. There is, however, no specific relationship between gender and business theme in the sentence. It should also be noted that the case's name is male, despite the recognition of the gender issue by the Inter-American Court and the fact that 59 of the 60 victims were women.

The judgment of the Inter-American Court, despite deepening the theme of human rights and companies, portrays the consolidated jurisprudence of the Inter-American Human Rights System, which mirrors the other human rights courts regarding the exclusive responsibility of States for violations committed by private actors. The context is one of impunity for powerful multinational corporations that not only violate human rights, but also undermine the duty of States to achieve substantive gender equality.

The absence, at the national, regional or global levels, of an answer to the problem of gender inequality in the performance of transnational companies demonstrates that the dialogue between the three levels, taking advantage of the best that each system has to offer, from an approach to the constitutionalization of international law, is an important technique that should be applied. To combine the efforts of the Latin American countries with the common objective of reinforcing the constitutional guarantees for gender equality in the face of corporate threats is an urgently needed measure.

References

Brazil (2018) Decree No. 9.571. Establishes the National Guidelines on Business and Human Rights. Available in: http://www.planalto.gov.br/ccivil_03/_ato2015-2018/2018/decreto/D9571.html. Accessed 09 July 2021

Brazil's Supreme Federal Court (2003) Direct Action of Unconstitutionality No. 1.643. Available in: https://redir.stf.jus.br/paginadorpub/paginador.jsp?docTP=AC&docID=266708. Accessed 09 July 2021
Brazil's Supreme Federal Court (2013) Extraordinary Appeal No. 627.543. Available in: https://redir.stf.jus.br/paginadorpub/paginador.jsp?docTP=TP&docID=7066469. Accessed 09 July 2021
Brigagao N (2019) Workers of the Fireworks Factory of Santo Antônio de Jesus and their family members vs. Brazil and why we need to talk about socioeconomic gender inequality. Oxford Human Rights Club. Available in: https://ohrh.law.ox.ac.uk/workers-of-the-fireworks-factory-of-santo-antonio-de-jesus-and-their-family-members-vs-brazil-and-why-we-need-to-talk-about-socioeconomic-gender-inequality/. Accessed 09 July 2021
Gortázar NG (2019) A maldição das minas no Brasil: entre o medo do desemprego e o fantasma da impunidade. https://brasil.elpais.com/brasil/2019/05/04/politica/1556925352_146651.html. Accessed 09 July 2021
Human Rights Council (2016) Report of the Working Group on the issue of human rights and transnational corporations and other business enterprises on its mission to Brazil. Available in: https://documents-dds-ny.un.org/doc/UNDOC/GEN/G16/096/43/PDF/G1609643.pdf?OpenElement. Accessed 09 July 2021
Inter-American Court of Human Rights (2020) Employees of the Santo Antônio de Jesus Fireworks Factory v. Brazil Case. Available in: https://www.corteidh.or.cr/docs/casos/articulos/seriec_407_por.pdf. Accessed 09 July 2021
Mauricio A (2020) Ministérios Públicos e Defensorias pedem retomada de ação de R$155 bilhões contra a Vale, Samarco e BHP. https://observatoriodamineracao.com.br/ministerios-publicos-e-defensorias-pedem-retomada-de-acao-de-r-155-bilhoes-contra-a-vale-samarco-e-bhp/. Accessed 09 July 2021
Office of the High Commissioner for Human Rights (2011) Guiding Principles on Business and Human Rights. Available in: https://www.ohchr.org/Documents/Publications/GuidingPrinciplesBusinessHR_EN.pdf. Accessed 09 July 2021
Office of the High Commissioner for Human Rights (2019) Gender dimensions of the Guiding Principles on Business and Human Rights - Report of the Working Group on the issue of human rights and transnational corporations and other business enterprises. Available in: https://ap.ohchr.org/documents/dpage_e.aspx?si=A/HRC/41/43. Accessed 09 July 2021
SEBRAE (2016) Pequenos negócios em números. Available in: https://www.sebrae.com.br/sites/PortalSebrae/ufs/sp/sebraeaz/pequenos-negocios-em-numeros,12e8794363447510VgnVCM1000004c00210aRCRD. Accessed 09 July 2021
United Nations Development Programme (2019) Gender Dimensions of the Guiding Principles on Business and Human Rights. Available in: https://www.undp.org/content/undp/en/home/librarypage/democratic-governance/gender-dimensions-guiding-principles-on-business-n-human-rights.html. Accessed 09 July 2021
Véras EZ (2015) Female entrepreneurship: from women's empowerment to shared value creation. RISUS, São Paulo 6(2):109–123. ISSN 2179-3565
Walters VEL, Mason G (1994) Women in Top Management in Africa: The Sierra Leone Case. AAPAM - Public Administration and Management. Available in: https://citeseerx.ist.psu.edu/viewdoc/download?doi=10.1.1.529.3345&rep=rep1&type=pdf. Accessed 09 July 2021
Zanitelli L (2011) Corporações e Direitos Humanos: o debate entre voluntaristas e obrigacionistas e o efeito solapador das sanções, Sur - Revista Internacional de Direitos Humanos 8(15) 2011. Available in: https://core.ac.uk/download/pdf/16033942.pdf. Accessed 09 July 2021

Women in the Ukrainian Private Sector: Ensuring Gender Equality and Responsible Business Conduct in the Context of the War

Daria Nagaivska

Abstract This paper examines how Gender Equality and Women's Empowerment (GEWE) in the workplace, supply chains and local communities need to be ensured by private sector through responsible business conduct in a situation of global emergencies and recovery. The coronavirus disease (Covid-19) pandemic and the full-scale Russia aggression against Ukraine created momentum when public and private companies operating in Ukraine were forced to balance conflicting needs and expectations of different social groups by rebuilding business processes in a highly challenging and fast changing context.

Limited capacities and funds are among the most popular arguments used to postpone implementation of the Human Rights Due Diligence (HRDD) and to shrink corporate support of employees, suppliers and community members, which puts the most vulnerable groups at risk. Armed conflicts, pandemics and disasters affect women with children the most, and businesses need to identify, assess and mitigate their specific human rights risks in any specific operating context to ensure social justice and decent work.

GEWE plays a significant role in preventing crises, enabling a gender-responsive recovery and building resilience for sustainable growth. This paper considers the ways in which GEWE is compatible with the Business and Human rights (BHR) framework and, based on the example of Ukraine, identifies how the GEWE instruments should be incorporated into corporate policies, practices and procedures aimed to ensure that the company is not involved in human rights abuses and is contributing to gender-responsive recovery to build the sustainable and inclusive future.

Funding Information: Research Council of Finland, grant 359718.

D. Nagaivska (✉)
Aalto University School of Business, Espoo, Finland
e-mail: daria.nagaivska@aalto.fi

D. A. Pamplona et al. (eds.), *Business and Human Rights from the Lens of Women*, Interdisciplinary Studies in Human Rights 13,
https://doi.org/10.1007/978-3-032-04036-7_4

1 Introduction

Global challenges and emergencies, including the Covid-19 pandemic and the full-scale invasion of the Russian Federation in Ukraine, disproportionately affect women and girls,[1] and push them into extreme poverty, financial dependence and economic exclusion, which increase the risks of violence against them. The women's empowerment programs and initiatives, designed and implemented by the international development partners, governments, private actors and non-governmental organizations to '*break the cycle of intergenerational poverty and vulnerability*',[2] remain not efficient in closing the gender-poverty gap and protecting women and girls from violence and discrimination, especially in conflict-affected context. In the last decades, in support of the Commission on the Status of Women and the Beijing Platform for Action, UN agencies launched a series of multistakeholders initiatives to engage private sector to make commitments and contribute to the inclusive and sustainable economic growth, among them – the Ten Principles of the United Nations Global Compact,[3] Women's Empowerment Principles,[4] Gender Equality Accelerators[5] and many others.

One of the reasons, why women remain underrepresented in the decision-making process, have limited access to finance, bear a disproportionate burden of the care work, experience digital gender gap and struggle with launching and developing their businesses, is that the United Nations Guiding Principles on Business and Human Rights (UNGPs),[6] the OECD Guidelines for Multinational Enterprises[7] and other business and human rights instruments are not properly addressing the gender equality issues[8] by stating that people experience human rights harms in the same way,[9] including in the situation of the global emergency.

By declaring '*individuals from groups or populations that may be at heightened risk of becoming vulnerable or marginalized, and with due regard to the different*

[1] See UN Economic and Social Council Agreed Conclusions on the Sixty-eighth session of the Commission on the Status of Women E/CN.6/2024/L.3 (2024).

[2] Ibid, para 13.

[3] See UNGC, The Ten Principles of the UN Global Compact, https://unglobalcompact.org/what-is-gc/mission/principles.

[4] UN Women, Women's Empowerment Principles, https://www.weps.org/.

[5] UN Women, Gender Equality Accelerators, https://www.unwomen.org/en/what-we-do/gender-equality-accelerators.

[6] See UN Human Rights Council, Report of the Special Representative of the Secretary-General on the Issue of Human Rights and Transnational Corporations and Other Business Enterprises John Ruggie. A/HRC/17/31 (2011).

[7] See OECD Guidelines for Multinational Enterprises (2011).

[8] See Meyersfeld (2013), pp. 193–217.

[9] For more details see Martignoni and Umlas (2018); Götzmann and Brainton (2021), pp. 171–182; Simons and Handl (2019), pp. 113–150; Goldblatt and Rai (2020).

risks that may be faced by women and men',[10] UNGPs *'do not address the differentiated impacts of business activity on women in any crosscutting way'*,[11] nor provide some guidance to the public or private sector actors on how to address these challenges and ensure that the polices and decisions are gender sensitive, and the business conduct in the workplace, supply chains and local communities is responsible. The business managers are expected to act in the best interests of investors and shareholders, and this duty does not require them to protect or empower women.[12] Guidelines, further developed to address gender blindness of the UNGPs, state that companies *'should contribute to achieving substantive gender equality and avoid exacerbating or reproducing existing discrimination against women throughout their operations'*.[13] However, the proposed approach is rather added to UNDPs tha integrated into them, and is not reviewing the concept of gender equality, existing power relationships and established structures.

OECD Guidelines are not referring to gender or gender equality by mentioning that *'enterprises should respect the human rights of individuals belonging to specific groups or populations that require particular attention'*,[14] and naming women among other vulnerable groups. The OECD Due Diligence Guidance for Responsible Business Conduct is encouraging enterprises to think *'through how real or potential adverse impacts may differ for or may be specific to women'*,[15] and to implement some approaches to identify and manage adverse impacts on women (by analyzing sex-disaggregated data, implementing gender responsive policies, engaging women to decision-making process, etc.), but is leaving any detailed instructions aside.

The private sector is possessing the corporate power over human rights, which emerges as *'the production, by business enterprises, in and through social relations, of effects that shape the capacities of individuals to enjoy their human rights'*,[16] and which growths extremely when *'corporations control large parts of marketized socio-economic rights'*,[17] for example, as providers of essential goods and services. Business is playing a crucial role in defining and mitigating human rights related risks, especially regarding influence of the emergency situations on women, including in the labour market and in entrepreneurship. But do the companies have the clear guidelines and understanding on how to ensure responsible business conduct by addressing the gender equality issues and the disproportionate influence of global challenges and emergencies on women and girls?

---

[10] UN Human Rights Council, Report of the Special Representative of the Secretary-General on the Issue of Human Rights and Transnational Corporations and Other Business Enterprises John Ruggie. A/HRC/17/31 (2011), p. 6.

[11] Simons and Handl (2019), p. 137.

[12] Simons and Handl (2019).

[13] See UN General Assembly, Report of the Working Group on the Issue of Human Rights and Transnational Corporations and other Business Enterprises, A/HRC/41/43 (2019), para 21.

[14] See OECD Guidelines for Multinational Enterprises (2011), para 40.

[15] See OECD Due Diligence Guidance for Responsible Business Conduct (2018), Annex Q2.

[16] See Birchall (2021), p. 43.

[17] Ibid, p. 51.

Existing international and national mechanisms aimed to ensure gender equality in the private sector often apply the top-down approach by trying to mitigate the harm caused to women and avoiding '*the transformation of deep-seated patriarchal structures across the entire range of themes, actors and contexts within which the effects of multiple layers of inequality are experienced and perpetuated*'.[18] The participatory, inclusive and transformative political solutions[19] have to be developed and implemented to ensure that women are seen as agents of the influence and participants of the decision-making process, especially in the conflict-affected contexts and during recovery processes. The 'building back better' and 'leaving no one behind' principles, articulated by the international development organizations, governmental institutions and private sector, are meant to navigate the efforts of different actors in balancing power relations and influencing local population, especially vulnerable groups.

In the last years many Business and Human Rights (BHR) scholars and experts are focused on the gender dimension of the economic growth and responsible business conduct by providing some concrete recommendations and examples on how to address business-related human rights abuses by reconstructing BHR principles and other guidelines issued by intergovernmental organizations.[20] Still, it remains unclear how exactly the unequal power structures and relations should be managed in the conflict-affected context to ensure that women haven't been locked into the future harms, and which gender responsive approaches should be used to ensure that private sector in not contributing to the human rights abuses. Another challenge is presented by the common women's empowerment practices that don't identify how companies themselves '*can simultaneously be the sites and causes of poverty and gender discrimination*'.[21] In this case, empowerment strategies are seeing women as caregivers, mothers, members of the local communities and advocates for the sustainable growth, by providing some solutions to support them in carrying these responsibilities.[22]

This article aims to illustrate, based on the example of Ukraine, the gender equality challenges that emerge during a situation of global emergencies which companies are facing, and to identify how GEWE instruments should be incorporated into corporate policies, practices and procedures aimed to ensure that company is not involved in the human rights abuses and is contributing to gender-responsive recovery to build the sustainable and inclusive future.

---

18 Götzmann et al. (2022), p. 3.

19 For more details see Federici (2019).

20 For more details see Kristiansson and Götzmann (2020), pp. 1–17 and Leite and Kohonen (2021).

21 Götzmann et al. (2022), p. 4.

22 See Bellows et al. (2016) and Arora-Jonsson (2011), pp. 744–751.

2 The Impact of Emergency Situations on the Ukrainian Business

The Ukrainian business has been severely impacted by the geopolitical tensions and emergencies at least three times during the last 10 years: during the annexation of the Crimean Peninsula by the Russian Federation and partially occupation of the territories of the Donetsk and Luhansk regions in 2014, the coronavirus disease (Covid-19) pandemic since 2020, and the full-scale invasion of the Russian Federation to Ukraine which started in February 2022.

The invasion of the Russian Federation to Ukraine in 2014 disrupted industrial production, supply chains and exports by causing the reduced investors' confidence, increased inflation rate, drop in GDP and the deepening economic recession.[23] This led to the reduced enterprises' capacity to ensure employees decent work and pay, which negatively affected socio-economic rights of vulnerable groups, notably those living in rural areas. Destruction of plants and infrastructure complicated access to opportunities for work in neighboring areas mostly for people with disabilities, older people and people with family responsibilities. The continuing hostilities, landmine threats, loss of suppliers and reduced access to internal and external sales markets, forced numerous enterprises, notably those in the proximity to the 'contact line', to switch into a survival mode.[24] Because of the air alerts and missile attacks, companies faced difficulties to ensure safety and security of the workplace and the continuity of production processes, which increased risks of causing or contributing to human rights abuses or being linked to such abuses through business relationships.[25]

In 2020, the Covid-19 pandemic significantly impacted the companies by introducing the quarantine restrictions which caused reduced revenue and demand. Consequently, Ukraine experienced a net outflow of investment, increased inflation of 10 percent and increased unemployment rate of 9.6 percent.[26] In response, many companies have taken cost-cutting measures by starting to use online sales channels, develop flexibility in management and decision-making (e.g., by arranging

[23] For more details see the World Bank, Ukraine Economic Update (2015). https://www.worldbank.org/content/dam/Worldbank/document/eca/ukraine/ua-macro-april-2015-en.pdf. Assessed 10 March 2024; The Page Ukraine (2024). https://en.thepage.ua/economy/economic-decline-caused-by-russias-war-in-2014-and-2022. Accessed 10 March 2024.

[24] See UNDP Report 'Business and Human rights in Ukraine: Accelerating sustainable and equitable development through implementation of the UN Guiding Principles on Business and Human rights' (2022).

[25] See Business and Human Rights Resource Center, Briefing 'Russian invasion of Ukraine: Analysis of companies' human rights due diligence' (24 May 2022). https://www.business-humanrights.org/en/from-us/briefings/business-response-to-the-russian-invasion-of-ukraine/. Accessed 10 February 2024.

[26] OECD, Report 'Covid-19 Crisis in Ukraine' (2022). https://www.oecd.org/eurasia/competitiveness-programme/eastern-partners/COVID-19-CRISIS-IN-UKRAINE.pdf. Accessed 10 February 2024.

remote work conditions, implementing online planning tools, etc.), reduce employees' working hours and salaries, as well as develop customized solutions for women employees and employees with parental responsibilities.[27]

Since 2022, massive damage to infrastructure, blackouts, and supply and value chains disruptions led to the closure of many businesses.[28] Up to 50 percent of companies have suspended their activities, and 30 percent of pre-war employment has been lost.[29] In late 2022, a new wave of rocket and drone attacks damaged or destroyed almost 50 percent of Ukraine's electricity system, causing power outages in 10 out of 24 regions that in some cases will take years to fix.[30] In the end of 2022, 83 percent of companies had seen revenues decrease, the majority by over 20 percent.[31] The top 5 challenges Ukrainian companies reported were safety and security of employees, logistics and transport, absence of clients or orders, decline in partners' businesses, and export-import operations.[32]

Small and medium enterprises (SMEs) are the major contributor to the Ukrainian economy. In 2020, SMEs accounted for 73 percent of the country's employment and generated 63 percent of gross sales. Almost two-thirds of Ukrainian SMEs were located in the regions which have been exposed to active land warfare[33] and were therefore more susceptible to the shocks caused by the war than large companies. By the end of 2022, SMEs have seen their income decrease by 43 percent and employment by 22 percent.[34] The war has led to higher costs throughout value chains while the volume of bank loans has decreased, and SMEs were often unable to secure alternative financial resources.[35] SMEs remain more vulnerable in times of

---

[27] See Ukrainian Corporate Equality Index report 2020. https://www.womanactual.org/ua/projects/equalityindex/. Accessed 10 February 2024.

[28] Results of the Eighth monthly survey of companies managers 'Ukrainian business in conditions of war' (December 2022). Companies reported the following obstacles to conducting business: interruptions in electricity, water and heat supply (80%), rising prices for raw materials and materials (70%), safety and security at work (46%), and disruption of supply chains (37%).

[29] See 'Report on the application of the resolution concerning the Russian Federation's aggression against Ukraine from the perspective of the mandate of the International Labour Organization' (2022) and Lyvch et al. (2022).

[30] https://www.theguardian.com/world/2022/oct/27/kyiv-facing-sharp-deterioration-electric-supply-russian-strikes.

[31] According to the report published by the European Business Association, only 6% of respondents reported no changes to revenue, and another 11% reported revenue growth (30 January 2023). https://eba.com.ua/en/u-83-kompanij-eva-vidbulosya-padinnya-biznesu-u-2022-rotsi/. Accessed 15 February 2024.

[32] See report published by the American Chamber of Commerce in Ukraine (23 August 2022). https://chamber.ua/news/doing-business-after-six-months-of-war-in-ukraine-amcham-ukraine-latest-survey-results-72-of-members-fully-operational/. Accessed 15 February 2024.

[33] See UNDP Analytical Report 'Rapid Assessment of the War's Impact on Micro, Small and Medium Enterprises in Ukraine (2022), p. 10.

[34] See EBRD publication (1 March 2023). https://www.ebrd.com/news/2023/ebrd-usa-and-sweden-assess-impact-of-war-on-smes-in-ukraine.html. Accessed 15 February 2024.

[35] See publication of the Atlantic Council (1 February 2023). https://www.atlanticcouncil.org/blogs/ukrainealert/ukrainian-smes-hold-the-key-to-the-countrys-economic-revival/. Accessed 15 February 2024.

crisis compared to large companies because of the absence of a financial safety cushion and leverage that large business normally has.

Most companies in Ukraine, especially SMEs, were not prepared for the full-scale invasion and had neither business contingency plan nor human rights due diligence in action. The lack of knowledge and capacities to implement the human rights assessment led to the situation when most companies were doing 'right things' by relying on the intuition of their managers, common sense and moral values. The BHR framework mostly was not applied to the business operations and the decision-making process, and this put the different groups of the society, especially vulnerable groups living close to the frontline or on the occupied or deliberated territories of Ukraine, in jeopardy because of the increased risks of human rights violations.

3 Dynamics of the Emergency Situations and Their Impact on Women and Girls

The outbreak of the Covid-19 pandemic, declared by the World Health Organization on March 11, 2020 as an international concern,[36] caused more than 7 million deaths worldwide by putting different countries in the situation of the global emergency. In Ukraine, since 2020 more than 4 million cases of the disease were laboratory confirmed, and 105 505 deaths of people infected with coronavirus were registered.[37] The crises disproportionately impacted women because of their high exposure to the virus as they accounted for 82 percent of the health and social workers who faced significantly increased workload and emotional burnout.[38] Also, women suffered from the domestic violence which increased by 30 percent as well as the unfair distribution of unpaid domestic and care work. The crises exposed deep divides in income and job security between officially employed and self-employed workers, especially for those working remotely, in the informal sectors of economy or in the rural areas, most of whom are women who became more vulnerable to the economic downtown due to the lack of social protection and low savings.[39]

The one crisis followed the next, and in two years the Russian military troops attacked the biggest cities and rural areas of Ukraine. The start of the full-scale war was particularly dramatic in the first two months, as Ukrainian cities drastically transformed from peace to massive shelling, with more than 20% of the territory of

[36] See WHO publication on Covid-19 outbreak (2020). https://www.who.int/emergencies/diseases/novel-coronavirus-2019. Accessed 15 February 2024.

[37] See the website of the Ministry of Health of Ukraine on Covid-19 pandemic in Ukraine. https://covid19.gov.ua/en. Accessed 15 February 2024.

[38] See UNDP, UN Women and UN Food and Agriculture Organization Report 'COVID-19 in Ukraine: Impact on Households and Businesses' (2020).

[39] Ibid.

the whole country being occupied in the first week only. The full-scale invasion in February 2022 led to violations of international humanitarian and international human rights law,[40] namely forced transfers and deportations of children, attacks which caused civilian harm in populated areas, attacks targeting Ukraine's energy infrastructure, patterns of willful killings, unlawful confinement, torture, rape, and unlawful transfers of detainees, sexual and gender-based violence, and cyber-attacks. This marked a start of the large displacement and refugee crisis.

Two years after the beginning of the full-scale invasion, in February 2024, the UN Human Rights Monitoring Mission verified 30.457 civilian casualties in Ukraine, the conflict-related violence has killed at least 10.582 civilians and injured 19.875.[41] More than 3.69 million people have been internally displaced while 39 percent among them have been displaced more than once.[42] In 2024, over 14.6 million people of Ukraine needed humanitarian assistance, primarily in ensuring and providing protection, wash, shelters, health, food security and livelihoods.[43] The internally displaced people needed financial support, power banks and generators, health services and clothes.[44] The number of returnees was constantly growing and in 2024 reached 2 million people,[45] 76 percent of people who moved abroad because of the full-scale war, were hoping or planning to return to Ukraine.[46] This means, that the need of the population in humanitarian assistance was growing, and the government, international development partners, private sector and NGOs needed to develop and implement innovative decisions in addressing humanitarian crisis, delivering services and ensuring sustainable economic growth.

The situations of global emergencies disproportionately negatively influence women and girls by worsening inequalities and discrimination, especially among internally displaced people and other vulnerable groups.[47] Since the beginning of the full-scale war, women and children presented the majority of Ukrainian refugees (68 percent).[48] Women-headed households reported extreme livelihood needs and increased unpaid care burdens for older parents, children and relatives with

---

[40] See UN Human Rights Council Report of the Independent International Commission of Inquiry on Ukraine, A/HRC/52/62 (2023).

[41] See UNHCR Report 'Two-Year Update - Protection of civilians: impact of hostilities on civilians since 24 February 2022' (2024).

[42] See IOM, 'Ukraine Internal Displacement Report – General Population Survey Round 15' (2023).

[43] See UNHCR 'Humanitarian Needs and Response Plan Ukraine' (2023).

[44] See IOM, 'Ukraine Internal Displacement Report – General Population Survey Round 15' (2023).

[45] See UNHCR report on Ukraine Refugee Situation (2023). https://data.unhcr.org/en/situations/ukraine. Accessed 22 April 2024.

[46] See UNHCR report on Intentions and Perspectives of Refugees from Ukraine (2023). https://data.unhcr.org/en/dataviz/304?sv=54&geo=0. Accessed 22 April 2024.

[47] See Report 'Rapid Damage and Needs Assessment: February 2022 - February 2023' (2023). https://ukraine.un.org/en/224376-ukraine-rapid-damage-and-needs-assessment. Accessed 22 April 2024.

[48] See UNHCR, 'Ukraine Situation Regional Refugee Response Plan (March-December 2022)' (2022).

disabilities, which restricted their abilities to participate in income-generating activities.[49] During the war, women spent over 16 hours per week more than men on unpaid domestic work and represented 72 percent of people registered as unemployed.[50] Women were underrepresented in higher-ranked positions in peacebuilding, politics and economics, on average earn 18.6 percent less than men and were more frequently employed in the informal sectors of the economy, especially in rural areas.

The World Economic Forum Global Gender Gap Reports for 2020, 2021 and 2022 showed that despite legislative advancement and international commitments, gender inequality persisted in Ukraine.[51] While the 2020 report ranked Ukraine in 59th place, Ukraine was ranked 81st out of 146 countries in 2022. The 2021 Gender Inequality Index ranked Ukraine 103rd out of 156 countries on women's political participation, with a slight improvement in 2022 (to position 100),[52] and a significant improvement in 2023 (to position 66).[53] Since the beginning of the full-scale invasion, Ukraine ratified the Istanbul Convention, developed GEWE policy framework presented by the State Strategy on Ensuring Equal Rights and Opportunities for Women and Men till 2030 and the National Strategy for Bridging the Gender Pay Gap for the period up to 2030, and adopted legislative and policy instruments to comply with the international GEWE commitments, including in the frame of the EU accession process, which started in 2023.

Still, more efforts should be made to overcome existing barriers for women in the labour market and entrepreneurship regarding the underrepresentation of women on the top positions, in decision-making process and in several profitable sectors of the Ukrainian economy. In the context of the full-scale invasion and recovery, the private sector may implement the heightened human rights due diligence to ensure that the companies are not causing, contributing to, or linked to adverse impacts on human rights in their business operations, or to which it may be linked through their operations, products, or services in supply and value chains. Despite the negative effects of the global emergency situations, Ukrainian companies continued to implement flagship initiatives to support the groups of society which are suffering the most. The main tendencies in providing support to women by the private sector are described in the next chapter.

---

[49] See European Parliament publication 'Russia's war on Ukraine: A gender-sensitive humanitarian response' (2022). https://www.europarl.europa.eu/RegData/etudes/ATAG/2022/729328/EPRS_ATA(2022)729328_EN.pdf. Accessed 10 March 2024.

[50] See Report 'Rapid Damage and Needs Assessment: February 2022 – December 2023' (2024). https://ukraine.un.org/sites/default/files/2024-02/UA%20RDNA3%20report%20EN.pdf. Accessed 10 March 2024.

[51] For more details see World Economic Forum Global Gender Gap reports in 2020–2022. https://www3.weforum.org/docs/WEF_GGGR_2020.pdf; https://www3.weforum.org/docs/WEF_GGGR_2021.pdf; https://www3.weforum.org/docs/WEF_GGGR_2022.pdf. Accessed 10 March 2024.

[52] World Economic Forum Global Gender Gap report (2022).

[53] World Economic Forum Global Gender Gap report (2023).

4 Women's Empowerment Initiatives Implemented by Companies in 2020–2024

The studies conducted in the last years showed that businesses adhering to the principle of diversity are for 50 percent more efficient and have a 70 percent higher chance of entering new markets than male-only companies, and companies with women in the board earn 20 percent more.[54] However, women are still underrepresented in the top positions in the companies, earn lower salaries and face horizontal segregation by being pushed to the low-income sectors of economy, such as health care, provision of social assistance and education.[55] Additionally, many companies '*are finding in women new forms of profit enhancement*'[56] by seeing them as '*a form of gender capital*'[57] which can be used for corporate goals.

According to the Ukrainian Corporate Index,[58] employees are considering company's compliance with the gender equality principles as important by choosing a job. During the Covid-19 pandemic, many international companies operating in Ukraine have implemented gender equality or non-discrimination policies, used standardized interviews when hiring, and collected data to provide diversity in the staff and develop a promotion plan for vulnerable employees.[59] Around 80 percent of companies reported they are interested to track gender equality issues in their supply and value chains. SMEs mostly systematically emphasized respect for gender equality and published gender-neutral job vacancies, but did not prepare non-financial reports and avoided to assess impact of their business operations on human rights.[60] Both large companies and SMEs were facing challenges in implementing a special mechanism for reporting cases of discrimination, harassment and misconduct, available for employees and people from outside the company.

Despite the efforts of gender equality champions among public and private Ukrainian companies, many issues had to be addressed to overcome existing barriers for career and professional growth which women and other vulnerable groups were facing and which became stronger in the labour market and in entrepreneurship because of the Covid-19 pandemic. The study conducted by the author at that

---

[54] See EY publication 'Diversity and inclusiveness means growth'. https://www.ey.com/en_gl/diversity-inclusiveness/diversity-and-inclusiveness-means-growth. Accessed 14 March 2024.

[55] For more details see website of the State Statistics Service of Ukraine, https://ukrstat.gov.ua.

[56] See Russell (2022), p. 91.

[57] See Russell (2019), pp. 627–640.

[58] The Ukrainian Corporate Equality Index is a national survey of corporate policies, rules and practices of private and public companies to support diversity and inclusion and prevent discrimination in the workplace. The last report was published in 2021 at: https://www.womanactual.org/en/projects/equalityindex/. In the Ukrainian Corporate Equality Index are mostly participating the leaders of the profitable sectors of economy, therefore, this analysis is not representing the state of affairs in the corporate sector on gender equality, but can be used as a benchmark for further developments.

[59] Ibid.

[60] Ibid.

time showed that women were experiencing the lack of available funds for their capacity building, heavy workload and work-life imbalance, discrimination in the workplace, including restrictions in promotion because of the gender segregation and existing gender pay gap. During the interviews, women employees shared numerous examples of discrimination. Short descriptions of some of them are listed below:

> I recently saw an ad: "We will employ a woman with a nice appearance up to 28 years without children with 10 years of experience, the position – a flower seller".

> Once I had my first interview with an assistant economist-logistician, then the CEO came and pushed me out the door. I stand behind that thin door and heard him shout at an HR manager: "I said, don't employ the beautiful ones, only the ugly ones, because wife will kill me".

> Once at the interview in the state company, they said to me: "As you will understand, the attractive young woman will distract employees. Eventually, you will want to be married and start your maternity leave, but we need a regular worker".

> I'm 58. It's simply unrealistic to get a job in my specialty. It is offered to work in laundry, as a janitor, etc. Did I need to get two higher education degrees for that?

> In Ukraine, the owner of the company twice arranged a meeting for me and twice tried to force me to sign an agreement that I would not get married and would not have children for at least 5 years. Because he thought I wouldn't be able to work then. I didn't show up for the third meeting because I realized there was no point in arguing with him.

The Covid-19 pandemic significantly increased inequalities between different social groups by putting women in the most vulnerable position. In response to the crises, Ukrainian companies started to implement some initiatives aimed to support women employees by providing remote work opportunities and flexible working schedule, but in general the workplace remained unfriendly to women due to the gender stereotypes stating that women need to take care about family members first, and because of that are not motivated and efficient at work. This was the time when companies started to revise their procedures on work life balance to support employees with parental responsibilities and arrange rooms for children in their offices.

The companies which made their policies and procedures more employee-friendly during the Covid-19 pandemic, turned out to be more prepared to overcome the challenges of the full-scale war invasion in February 2022. The programs of staff relocation, delivering psychological and financial support to employees and their family members, arrangement of shelters and rooms for children equipped with power generators, drinking water and food supplies, flexible and remote work arrangements became the basis of personnel management strategies of many Ukrainian companies from the first weeks of the full-scale invasion.[61] As many

[61] See UN Women, Report on analysis results of the private sector' best practices in women economic empowerment during the full-fledged Russian war against Ukraine (2023). https://ukraine.unwomen.org/uk/digital-library/publications/2023/08/zvit-za-rezultatamy-analizu-naykrash-

members of the staff moved abroad or to the other regions of Ukraine due to the safety reasons and men joined the Ukrainian Armed Forces, companies launched reskilling, upskilling, leadership and mentorship programs to engage and promote women employees, including in the sectors of the economy in which women were traditionally underrepresented (for example, freight and municipal transportation, extractive industries, energy sector, etc.).

In 2022–2024, twenty five Ukrainian companies signed the Women's Empowerment Principles (WEPs) and made their public commitments on supporting women and ensuring gender equality in the workplace, supply chains and local communities. The analysis of their policies and practices is a basis to conclude that most of them were at the beginning stage of WEPs implementation by showing good progress in achieving gender equality in the workplace, including by (a) ensuring professional development and promotion of women, (b) preventing violence, harassment and sexual exploitation, (c) implementing non-discrimination and equal opportunity policy, (d) using standardized recruitment procedures, (e) providing maternity leave and supporting work life balance. Despite this, companies were facing big challenges in ensuring gender equality in the marketplace as they did not have sufficient knowledge and capacity to engage women-owned businesses into their supply chains, track supplier performance on gender equality, implement gender responsible marketing practices by using gender sensitive language and restrict sexist advertising, as well as ensure product and service development with a gender lens.

Regardless the fact that many companies were very familiar with corporate social responsibility, philanthropy, advocacy and partnerships frameworks to support gender equality, they were not effectively applying a gender lens to community relations. This means that private sector representatives had awareness and attitudes towards gender equality and anti-discrimination in the workplace, but were struggling with transforming the theoretical knowledge and best practices of other companies to their context of operations. Additionally to the need to review their gender equality commitments in the broader perspective, companies had to improve their capacities to avoid and address adverse impacts on human rights that a business may cause or contribute to through its own activities, or to which it may be directly linked through its operations, products, or services via its business relationships, which is a part of the (heightened) human rights due diligence.

chykh-praktyk-biznesu-z-ekonomichnoho-upovnovazhennya-zhinok-pid-chas-povnomasshtabnoyi-rosiyskoyi-viyny-proty-ukrayiny. Accessed 5 March 2024.

5 Heightened Human Rights Due Diligence in the Conflict-Affected Context

Gender equality an integral part of the business and human rights agenda and, respectively, of the heightened human rights due diligence[62] (hHRDD) which allows companies to assess the potential and actual human rights impacts that may arise in the conflict-affected context and determine mitigating or preventative actions to '*avoid infringing on the human rights*'.[63] The means through which businesses meet the responsibility to respect human rights can vary by size, sector, operating context, and risk profile. Nevertheless, this responsibility extends to both large companies and SMEs, which may rely on less formal and less extensive due diligence processes as they may lack the capacity and leverage of larger businesses.[64] Companies should incorporate a vulnerability lens and conduct gender equality assessment to address the differentiated impacts of conflict on certain groups of people and ensure meaningful, safe stakeholder engagement undertaken in a sensitive way to avoid exacerbating conflict dynamics.[65]

For companies operating in Ukraine, the hHRDD should include (a) conflict analysis by identifying root causes of tensions and potential triggers, (b) mapping the main actors in the conflict and their motives, capacities and opportunities to inflict violence, and (c) identification and anticipation of the ways in which the companies' operations, products and services impact the conflict and the workers operating in a conflict area.[66] International Humanitarian Law obliges businesses to ensure that they and their employees are not contributing to war crimes,[67] and this obligation is fully aligned with implementation of the hHRDD procedure which provides instruments to ensure companies are equipped to prevent or mitigate their negative impacts.[68]

The responsible business conduct framework is developing in Ukraine since 2017, when the Pilot study on business and human rights in Ukraine was conducted.

[62] Principle 7 of the UNGP provides that 'the risk of gross human rights abuses is heightened in conflict-affected areas.' It means that companies also bear a responsibility to identify their impact within a conflict to be sure that their actions do not contribute to the conflict, do not participate in it and do not profit from it. For more details see UN General Assembly Report on the issue of human rights and transnational corporations and other business enterprises, A/75/212 (2020).

[63] See UN Human Rights Council, Report of the Special Representative of the Secretary-General on the Issue of Human Rights and Transnational Corporations and Other Business Enterprises John Ruggie. A/HRC/17/31 (2011), p. 13.

[64] See OECD Due Diligence Guidance for Responsible Business Conduct (2018).

[65] See UNDP Guide on Heightened Human Rights Due Diligence for business in conflict-affected contexts (2022).

[66] See UN General Assembly Report on the issue of human rights and transnational corporations and other business enterprises, A/75/212 (2020), para 46–49.

[67] Geneva Convention Relative to the Protection of Civilian Persons in Time of War (Fourth Geneva Convention, 1949).

[68] See Konopka and Patz (2022).

Since that time, Ukraine joined the OECD Declaration on International Investment and Multinational Enterprises and launched a National Contact Point to ensure its effective implementation, defined UNGPs implementation among strategic activity areas for the Parliamentary Commissioner for Human Rights, adopted the Action plan on socially responsible business[69] and adopted the National Human Rights Strategy with a Chapter on ensuring human rights in business activities.[70]

Despite the efforts of the expert community in collaboration with the government on implementing a framework for the responsible business conduct in Ukraine, the study[71] conducted by UNDP in 2021 identified the following main challenges: (a) the lack of business and human rights awareness and capacities both in public and private sector, (b) the policy incoherence at national, local, and corporate levels in ensuring its substantive compliance with human rights standards and the principle of respect for human dignity, (c) the lack of effective state and non-state remedies to prevent and protect against business-related human rights abuse. At that time, Ukrainian companies were mostly engaged in the implementation of the corporate social responsibility initiatives aimed to improve their image and reputation to gain new customers and attract investments. Businesses have mostly reported about what good they have done by avoiding to conduct the human rights risk assessment and developing a comprehensive action plan to address actual and potential negative influence of business operations on human rights.

Since the beginning of the full-scale war, owners and managers of Ukrainian companies driven by the motivation "to do good things", launched various initiatives to support their employees, local communities and the Ukrainian Armed Forces, incl. by providing humanitarian and financial support. In general, companies did not conduct a human rights risk assessment and analyze their impact on the conflict dynamics and different social groups. The study on responsible business conduct published by UNDP in 2023[72] provided evidence on (a) the low awareness of Ukrainian companies on responsible business conduct and the hHRDD, (b) the absence of governmental recommendations for companies on how to operate in a wartime or make a responsible exit from the areas beyond the control of the Government of Ukraine and war-affected territories, (c) the negative impact of the deregulation on the guarantees for employees' rights and strengthening of the freedom of employer's discretion, (d) safety and labour discrimination as the most salient issues, especially for the most vulnerable groups of people (people with

[69] Approved by the Decree of the Cabinet of Ministers of Ukraine № 853-r dated July 1, 2020 'On approval of the Action plan for the implementation of the Concept of realization of the state policy on promoting development of socially responsible business in Ukraine for the period until 2030'.

[70] Approved by the Decree of the President of Ukraine dated March 24, 2021 'On the National strategy on Human Rights'.

[71] UNDP Report 'Business and Human rights in Ukraine: Accelerating sustainable and equitable development through implementation of the UN Guiding Principles on Business and Human rights' (2022).

[72] See UNDP Context assessment Study 'Responsible Business Conduct during war in Ukraine' (2023).

disabilities, people with family and caregiving responsibilities, older people, and people with incurable diseases), (e) the implementation of the Business Contingency Plan, creation of an Internal Crisis Management Team, conducting an employee needs assessment among the best hHRDD tools developed by Ukrainian companies to overcome the negative consequences of the full-scale war. This means, that the flagship initiatives launched by businesses in response to the full-scale war should be supplemented by the nuanced and ongoing hHRDD which addresses the gender equality and vulnerability issues.

Applying a gender lens throughout the hHRDD procedure implies a public commitment of the company on gender equality (for example, by signing WEPs), conducting a human rights assessment and development of the Gender Action Plan to mitigate the actual or potential negative impact of the business operations or products on human rights and address existing inequalities in the workplace, supply chains and local communities. Also, companies need to map business activities and relationships across their value chains to identify and assess any human rights harms they may be causing, contributing to, or linked to, and check the performance of their suppliers and contractors in the regard of actual or potential human rights violations, incl. connected to the gender inequality and discrimination issues. The business contingency and emergency plans may apply the vulnerability lens by addressing the needs and interests of the different groups of employees, community members and other stakeholders by ensuring that they have access to remedy through internal or external grievance mechanisms and can submit their reports or claims about the human rights abuses.

Application of the vulnerability lens means that business entities may pay particular attention to the social groups which face discrimination, especially in the double or multiple form on the grounds of gender, age, displacement, cultural background, ability/disability, and other factors. It is crucial to introduce measures to ensure inclusion and safety across vulnerable groups and raise awareness of employees on how to interact with diverse groups in a rights-respecting manner, apply a test on the proportionality of means implied to achieve a legitimate aim, and react on the cases of misconduct and discrimination in the workplaceand beyond a company. The implementation of the mechanisms aimed to prevent and respond to the cases of the sexual harassment and domestic violence by submitting anonymous complaints, providing compensation for damage, and protection of complainants, is an important part of ensuring safe working conditions.

According to the results of the study, the rebuilding and recovery programs developed in Ukraine '*still do not focus on the business and human rights issues of responsible exit/return and responsible business conduct*',[73] and do not identify the role of companies in transitional justice processes and the mechanisms for bringing them to justice in the case of direct or indirect involvement in human rights harms. At the same time, the Government of Ukraine expresses increasing interest in ensuring responsible business conduct, which reflects the demands, policies and

[73] Ibid, p. 6.

procedures of the international development partners, donors and investors who are contributing to the realization of the strategic and operational frameworks on humanitarian response, rebuilding and recovery processes in a post-war Ukraine.

6 Business Contribution to the Gender Responsive Recovery

The 'productive power' of corporations,[74] or the power over knowledge, is realized in their abilities '*to define their own human rights responsibilities, priorities, exclusions, and to influence the field of BHR'*.[75] The business entities may use different instruments (cutting salary, not paying bonuses, restricting career growth, not confirming vacations, etc.), to defend themselves by putting employees who witnessed human rights abuses under pressure and influencing their ability to ensure their human rights. Nowadays we are observing the shift from business and human rights, to the business of human rights.[76] This can be illustrated by the numerous cases of collaboration between the private companies from the most risky sectors of economy and the international development partners, including UN, when businesses use human rights commitments to improve their reputation along 'social purpose' lines.[77] The risks of covering the business misconduct by spreading messages about corporate responsible initiatives are extremely high in the conflict-affected areas, where companies may collaborate with the government to contribute to the realization of the defense strategy, including by attracting the investments for producing military goods, rebuilding roads and housing infrastructure as well as building extractive or energy facilities without consulting with local citizens, including avoiding to engage women to participate in the decision-making process.

In February 2024, the third Rapid Damage and Needs Assessment (RDNA3) estimated that recovery and reconstruction would cost $486 billion,[78] with costs significantly increasing since then due to the massive attacks of the Russian Federation on the energy infrastructure located in different regions of Ukraine in March 2024. According to the RDNA3, the most affected sectors have been housing, transport, commerce and industry, energy, and agriculture. With the support of its international partners, the Government of Ukraine has begun to carry out reconstruction and recovery efforts. Ukrainian line ministries have identified US$15 billion in priorities for 2024, with particular focus on the industry and services sector,

[74] See Barnett and Duvall (2005), pp. 39–42.

[75] Birchall (2021), p. 52.

[76] Deva (2020), p. 5.

[77] Green (2018), pp. 573–580.

[78] See The World Bank, Ukraine – Third Rapid Damage and Needs Assessment in February 2022 – December 2023 (2024).

housing and utilities, energy, social infrastructure and services, transport, and cross-sectoral issues.[79]

Also, in the beginning of 2024, the Cabinet of Ministers approved the Government Action Plan for 2024,[80] which contained almost 450 objectives across 15 strategic fields of work, including development of the *Resilient Economy*. In March 2024, the Cabinet of Ministers of Ukraine approved the Ukraine Facility Plan, which became a basis for the implementation of the EU's financial support programme for Ukraine in 2024–2027.[81] The Ukraine Facility Plan includes more than 150 indicators in 69 reform areas to be implemented by 2027, also by covering *Investment and Business environment*. The Ukraine's Reform Matrix 2024[82] presented by the Government of Ukraine in February 2024, includes 6 clusters, 33 chapters and about 230 conditionalities and recommendations for Ukraine set in cooperation with international partners.

Ukraine's recovery and reconstruction framework provides significant opportunities to build back better, more equal, and in an inclusive manner that strengthens good governance, the rule of law, gender equality, sustainable socio-economic development, environmental sustainability and human rights for the benefit of all people in the country, including those most vulnerable and marginalized.[83] The Outcome document of the Ukraine Recovery Conference 2022 in Lugano underlines a guiding principle on gender equality which stated that '*the recovery process has to be inclusive and ensure gender equality and respect for human rights, including economic, social and cultural rights. Recovery needs to benefit all, and no part of society should be left behind. Disparities need to be reduced*'.[84] The declarative norm on gender equality needs to be implemented in the policy and program documents developed by the government to ensure that private sector is incorporating these principles into the day-to-day business activities.

There are several fields that need a special attention of the government, international development partners, financial institutions, private sector, research institutions, civil society and other stakeholders to ensure the strong engagement of the private sector for gender-responsive recovery by improving the investment and business environment. This model of cooperation may include the following fields of work:

---

[79] Ibid.

[80] The Order of the Cabinet of Ministers of Ukraine № 137 dated February 16, 2024 'On approval of the plan of priority actions of the Government for 2024'.

[81] The Ministry of Economy of Ukraine (2024) Government approves plan to implement Ukraine Facility programme. https://www.kmu.gov.ua/en/news/uriad-zatverdyv-plan-dlia-realizatsii-prohramy-ukraine-facility. Accessed 24 March 2024.

[82] The Cabinet of Ministers of Ukraine (2024) Ukraine's Reforms Matrix: reforms and Conditionalities. https://www.kmu.gov.ua/storage/app/sites/1/reform_images/presentation-on-ukraines-reforms-matrix.pdf. Accessed 24 March 2024.

[83] See UN Women Policy Brief 'A Gender Responsive Recovery for Ukraine: Introduction' (2023).

[84] See Outcome Document of the Ukraine Recovery Conference URC2022 'Lugano Declaration' (2022), p. 3.

I. Integration of the gender equality and women's empowerment principles into the framework supporting the business environment as well as implementation of the distinct programs and supportive measures for women's businesses, integrating domestic women's enterprises into global markets, and engaging them into the supply chains of companies operating in other countries.
II. Implementation of the gender-responsive procurement in the public sector by developing gender-responsive standards for suppliers, facilitating data collection on women's enterprises and gender-responsive enterprises, creating business development services for women, advocating legal frameworks that promote women's entrepreneurship and decent work enterprises, and supporting institutional capacity building in relevant purchasing organizations, namely through enhancing legislative framework and the competencies and professional qualifications of staff in procuring entities, refining procurement procedures and practices to implement public investment projects aimed at recovery, reconstruction and modernization.
III. Integration of the gender-sensitive quantitative and qualitative performance indicators, collection and analysis of the quality data on target groups, incl. women's enterprises and gender-responsive enterprises, with distribution by gender and other characteristics at the stages of design and implementation of recovery and reconstruction initiatives. In Ukraine, this may be ensured through (a) improving the mechanism for attracting private investments using the public-private partnership mechanism to accelerate the restoration of war-destroyed objects and the construction of new objects associated with post-war reconstruction of the economy of Ukraine; (b) integrating digital solutions, accelerating sustainable development, spreading of circular economy practices and stimulating economic growth; (c) taking measures for improving the business environment and investment climate, establishing the strategic framework for SMEs and improving SME's innovation capacity; (d) developing and implementing the amended grant programs to support SMEs; (e) developing and implementing normative and program documents aimed to revitalize agri-food sector.
IV. Support of capacity building in gender responsive planning and budgeting of government institutions at all levels, public and private companies and non-governmental organizations to take part in recovery's design, implementation, monitoring and evaluation phases, and ensure that civil society and legislators can provide oversight.
V. Development of the long-term projects on social infrastructure development, aimed to create favorable conditions for balancing work and family responsibilities, to provide support to working women with children and other groups of employees who have family responsibilities (e. g. those who give care to elderly family members or persons with disabilities), namely in the process of developing and implementing of normative and program documents aimed to provide employees with working conditions, payment of remuneration and dismissal terms as well as the opportunities for mobility of workforce.

VI. Implementation by the public and private companies of the existing codes of conducts for advancing gender equality and women's empowerment in the workplace, marketplace and communities such as the Women Empowerment Principles (WEPs), which will ensure that recovery and reconstruction initiatives are aligned with needs and interests of women and girls.

In 2024, UN Women published the Women's Empowerment Strategy by defining the economic empowerment as a process, '*through which all women enjoy their economic and social rights, exercise agency and power in ways that challenge inequalities and level the playing field and gain equal rights and access to ownership of and control over resources, assets, income, time and their own lives*'.[85] In the context of the full-scale war and recovery, it means that the governmental institutions and local authorities, international development organizations, business associations, public and private companies as well as non-governmental organizations and academia need to develop a framework aimed to ensure that women are equally participating in the economy by gaining equal rights and access to ownership of and control over resources, assets, income, time and their own lives, have access to remedy and are using grievance mechanisms to submit reports or claims about the human rights abuses or negative impact caused by the private sector.

The above listed interventions aimed to ensure a gender responsible recovery, present the model which can be implemented by private sector in global emergency situations. The businesses need to pay special attention to identify, assess and mitigate their specific human rights risks in any specific operating context to ensure social justice and decent work and contribute to the sustainable and inclusive economic growth.

7 Conclusion

This paper argues that private sector plays a crucial role in ensuring gender equality and women's empowerment (GEWE) in the workplace, supply chains and local communities in a situation of global emergencies and recovery. Women and girls were disproportionately affected by the coronavirus disease (Covid-19) pandemic and the full-scale Russia aggression against Ukraine, which significantly worsened existing inequalities and discrimination. The situations of global emergencies are forcing companies to balance conflicting needs and expectations of different social groups by rebuilding business processes in a highly challenging and fast changing context. The heightened human rights due diligence (hHRDD) procedure is an effective tool to ensure responsible business conduct through avoiding and addressing potential or actual adverse impacts on human rights that a business may cause

[85] See UN Women Women's Empowerment Strategy (2024). https://www.unwomen.org/sites/default/files/2024-03/un-women-womens-economic-empowerment-strategy-en.pdf. Accessed 10 March 2024.

or contribute to through its own activities, or to which it may be directly linked through its operations, products, or services via its business relationships.

Application of the vulnerability lens means that business entities may pay particular attention to the social groups which face discrimination, especially in the double or multiple form on the grounds of gender, age, displacement, cultural background, ability/disability, and other factors. It is crucial to introduce measures to ensure inclusion and safety across vulnerable groups and raise awareness of employees on how to interact with diverse groups in a rights-respecting manner, apply a test on the proportionality of means implied to achieve a legitimate aim, and react on the cases of misconduct and discrimination in the workplace, supply chains and local communities. The business contingency and emergency plans may apply the vulnerability lens by addressing the needs and interests of the different groups of employees, community members and other stakeholders by ensuring that they have access to remedy through internal or external grievance mechanisms and can submit their reports or claims about the human rights violations.

The framework aimed to ensure that women are equally participating in the economy by gaining equal rights and access to ownership of and control over resources, assets, income, time and their own lives, may include the following fields of work: (a) integration of gender equality and women's empowerment principles into the framework supporting the business environment, (b) implementation of the gender-responsive procurement in the public sector, (c) integration of the gender-sensitive quantitative and qualitative performance indicators, collection and analysis of the quality data on target groups, (d) support of capacity building in gender responsive planning and budgeting of government institutions, companies and non-governmental organizations to take part in recovery's design, implementation, monitoring and evaluation phases, (e) development of the long-term projects on social infrastructure development, aimed to create favorable conditions for balancing work and family responsibilities, (f) implementation by the public and private companies of the existing codes of conduct for advancing gender equality and women's empowerment in the workplace, marketplace and communities.

The governmental institutions, international development organizations, business associations, public and private companies, local authorities as well as non-governmental organizations and academia may join their efforts to overcome the negative consequences of the global emergency situations on women and girls and ensure that the recovery processes are gender responsible and address the needs and interest of the vulnerable groups. The businesses need to pay special attention to identify, assess and mitigate their specific human rights risks in any specific operating context to ensure social justice and decent work and contribute to the sustainable and inclusive economic growth.

References

Arora-Jonsson S (2011) Virtue and vulnerability: discourses on women, gender and climate change. Global Environ Change 21(2):744–751

Barnett M, Duvall R (2005) Power in international politics. Int Organ 59(1):39–75

Bellows AC et al (2016) Gender, nutrition, and the human right to adequate food: toward an inclusive framework. Routledge, Abingdon

Birchall D (2021) Corporate power over human rights: an analytical framework. Bus Hum Rights J 6:42–66. https://doi.org/10.1017/bhj.2020.23

Deva S (2020) From 'business or human rights' to 'business and human rights': what next? In: Deva S, Birchall D (eds) Research handbook on human rights and business. Edward Elgar, Cheltenham, pp 1–21

Federici S (2019) Re-enchanting the world: feminism and the politics of the commons. PM Press, Oakland

Goldblatt B, Rai S (2020) Remedying depletion through social reproduction: a critical engagement with the United Nations' Business and Human Rights Framework. Eur J Polit Gender. SSRN: https://ssrn.com/abstract=3551809

Götzmann N, Brainton N (2021) Embedding gender-responsive approaches in impact assessment and management. Impact Assess Proj Apprais 39(3):171–182

Götzmann N et al (2022) From formalism to feminism: gender, business and human rights. Bus Hum Rights J 7(1):1–11

Green SJ (2018) Going beyond ethics and compliance: the growing corporate movement to embrace social value creation. Loyola Law J 49(3):573–580

Konopka I, Patz C (2022) Corporate due diligence in times of armed conflict. European Coalition for Corporate Justice and Frank Bold, Brussels

Kristiansson L, Götzmann N (2020) National implementation processes for the UNGPs: towards gender-responsive approaches. Aust J Hum Rights 26(2):1–17

Leite M, Kohonen M (2021) Engendering business and human rights: applying a gender lens to the UN Guiding Principles on Business and Human Rights and binding treaty negotiations. Christian Aid, London

Lyvch D et al (2022) Impact of war assessment: rapid assessment of the impact of war in Ukraine on micro- and small enterprises in the worst-affected areas of Ukraine as well as in regions where the security situation is relatively stable – opportunities and challenges for strengthening employment and income generation. Ukraine, IOM Ukraine

Martignoni JB, Umlas E (2018) Gender-responsive due diligence for business actors: human rights-based approaches. The Geneva Academy of International Humanitarian Law and Human Rights, Geneva

Meyersfeld B (2013) Business, human rights and gender: a legal approach to external and internal considerations. In: Deva S, Bilchitz D (eds) Human rights obligations of business: beyond the corporate responsibility to respect. Cambridge University Press, Cambridge, pp 193–217

Russell R (2019) Gender as a catalyst for corporate reform. In: Sjåfjell B, Bruner C (eds) The Cambridge handbook of corporate law, corporate governance and sustainability. Cambridge Law Handbooks. Cambridge University Press, pp 627–640

Russell R (2022) Women and the 'business' of human rights: the problem with women's empowerment projects and the need for corporate reform. Bus Hum Rights J 7(1):84–99

Simons P, Handl M (2019) Relations of ruling: a feminist critique of the United Nations Guiding Principles on Business and Human Rights and violence against women in the context of resource extraction. Can J Women Law 31(1):113–150

Exploring the Business and Human Rights Environment for Ugandan Women Working Within Supply Chains

Destiny Mugasha Kebirungi

Abstract Women are vital to global supply chains and play varied roles in both formal and informal economies. Gender equality is a principle of all the leading human rights instruments, including the International Covenant on Economic, Social, and Cultural Rights (ICESCR), the International Covenant on Civil and Political Rights (ICCPR), and the Convention on the Elimination of Discrimination Against Women (CEDAW).

Gender inequality, however, remains a significant barrier for women. As a result, both state (Uganda) and non-state actors (multinational corporations (MNCs)) must pay more attention to the various human rights violations and barriers that disproportionally affect women. Although there are existing initiatives to promote gender equality both by state and non-state actors, structural changes are needed to ensure both actors recognise that substantive equality is key to social and economic justice.

Abbreviations

ACHPR	African Charter on Human and People's Rights
BHR	Business and Human Rights
CEDAW	Convention on the Elimination of Discrimination Against Women
CRC	China Railways Corporation
EOC	Equal Opportunities Commission
GBV	Gender Based Violence
HRDD	Human rights due diligence
ICCPR	International Covenant on Civil and Political Rights
ICESCR	International Covenant on Economic, Social and Cultural Rights
ILO	International Labour Organisation
MNCs	Multinational corporations
NAPE	National Association of Professional Environmentalists

D. M. Kebirungi (✉)
Cheshire, UK

D. A. Pamplona et al. (eds.), *Business and Human Rights from the Lens of Women*, Interdisciplinary Studies in Human Rights 13,
https://doi.org/10.1007/978-3-032-04036-7_5

UDHR	Universal Declaration of Human Rights
UNGPs	UN Guiding Principles
UWEA	Uganda Workers Education Association
UWEAL	Uganda Women Entrepreneurs Association Limited
WGBHR	The UN Working Group on Business and Human Rights
WoMin	Women against Mining

1 Introduction

The emerging area of Business and Human Rights (BHR) in international law seeks, in part, to address the power disparity between developed countries, multinational corporations (MNCs) and developing world societies. MNC is any corporation which owns, controls and manages production or service facilities outside its home state in more than one host state.[1] I will use the terms enterprises, corporations and business in some contexts. Attempts to deal with this power disparity have, ironically, side-lined another well-documented imbalance of power, which is gender inequality.[2] Gender inequality is one of the oldest manifestations of discrimination, and it remains a significant barrier for women in the BHR environment.[3] The UN Charter[4] and the Universal Declaration of Human Rights (UDHR),[5] all recognise that all human beings have human rights for the simple reason of being human.[6] In fact, the notion that men and women should be able to enjoy their human rights equally[7] is part of all the leading international human rights instruments, which include the International Covenant on Civil and Political Rights (ICCPR)[8] and the International Covenant on Economic, Social and Cultural Rights (ICESCR).[9] Another significant international instrument whose goal is to promote gender equality is The Convention on the Elimination of Discrimination Against Women (CEDAW), since its entry in 1981.[10] More recently, the #MeToo movement has empowered more women to speak about the gender inequality and sexual violence

[1] Muchlinski (2007), p. 6.

[2] Meyersfeld (2013), p. 198.

[3] Marston (2014), p. 5.

[4] See United Nations, *Charter of the United Nations,* (adopted 24 October 1945, 1 UNTS XVI).

[5] See Universal Declaration of Human Rights (adopted 10 December 1948 UNGA Res 217 A (III) (UDHR).

[6] Leeuwen (2013), p. 245.

[7] Ibid.

[8] International Covenant on Civil and Political Rights (adopted 16 December 1966, entered into force 23 March 1976) 999 UNTS 171 (ICCPR).

[9] International Covenant on Economic, Social and Cultural Rights (adopted 16 December 1966, entered into force 3 January 1976) 993 UNTS (ICESCR).

[10] Pauw (2013), pp. 51–52.

that they face in a workplace environment.[11] UN Human Rights experts have hailed this movement as a tipping point for gender equality and have supported the UN human rights mechanisms.[12]

Human rights violations are not gender neutral, and it is widely recognised that in their pursuit of economic prosperity, businesses are responsible for various human rights violations and abuses that affect women disproportionally.[13] Women are vital to global supply chains and play varied roles in both formal and informal economies. They work as raw material producers, small business owners, and executives, to mention but a few, which helps businesses to succeed and grow.[14] However, different women may experience multiple and intersectional forms of discrimination based on various variables such as age, occupation, language, ability, and family status, to mention but a few.[15] For instance, women working in the informal economy experience discrimination and the violation of rights in unique ways.[16] Meyersfield notes that both States and MNCs have a role to play in eliminating gender-based obstacles in both the formal and the informal sectors.[17] I agree with her emphasis that special attention should be given to the informal employment sector.[18] This is because where supply chains rely on workers in the informal sector, this will have implications on their 'responsibility to respect'.[19]

This article will begin by critically analysing the application of gender equality to both state (Uganda) and non-state actors (MNCs) in international law. Following the guidance of the *UN Guiding Principles on Business and Human Rights* (UNGPs),[20] it will discuss what appropriate steps Uganda has taken to ensure that

---

[11] Gieseler (2019), p. 2.

[12] See United Nations Human Rights: Office of the High Commissioner (2018) "#MeToo: 'A transformative movement, liberating and empowering,' https://www.ohchr.org/EN/NewsEvents/Pages/DisplayNews.aspx?NewsID=22767&LangID=E Accessed 12 March 2021.

[13] Söderberg (2019).

[14] For a more detailed analysis see, Research Report, Women's Empowerment in Global Value Chains: A Framework for Business Action to Advance Women's Health, Rights and Wellbeing, https://www.bsr.org/reports/BSR-Report-Womens-Empowerment-Supply-Chains.pdf Accessed 12 February 2021.

[15] United Nations Human Rights Office of the High Commissioner, 'The Gender Dimensions of the UN Guiding Principles on Business and Human Rights 'UN Working Group 2019) https://www.ohchr.org/Documents/Issues/Business/BookletGenderDimensionsGuidingPrinciples.pdf Accessed 13 March 2021, p. 6.

[16] Marston (2014), p. 5.

[17] Meyersfeld (2013), p. 204.

[18] Ibid.

[19] Ibid.

[20] United Nations Human Rights Office of the High Commissioner, 'Guiding Principles on Business and Human Rights: Implementing the United Nations "Protect, Respect and Remedy" Framework' (2011) United Nations https://www.ohchr.org/sites/default/files/documents/publications/guidingprinciplesbusinesshr_en.pdf Accessed 13 March 2021.

all businesses operating within its territory respect women's rights[21] and what role MNCs and/or their subsidiaries have played in promoting gender equality.[22] It will further discuss the main issues faced by Ugandan women in attaining equality and explore what structural changes are needed both at state and business level, to promote and ensure gender equality.

2 A Preliminary Structure of Safe Guards and Gender Equality

The international law discussion regarding MNCs and human rights now oscillates around the Protect, Respect and Remedy framework.[23] The UNGPs were issued by Special Rapporteur John Ruggie and are based on a three-pillared structure revolving around the State duty to protect from corporate human rights abuses, the corporate responsibility to respect human rights, and the need for more effective access to remedy by victims.[24] Rivera notes that the three pillars are interconnected and attempt to focus on the actual processes and mechanisms established both at the state and business level, to address, at an early stage, any possible impact on human rights, and where this is not possible, to mitigate or redress their negative effects.[25] In 2019, The UN Working Group on Business and Human Rights (WGBHR), developed a Gender Framework[26] for the UNGPs and provided Gender Guidance[27] for all 31 principles.

This section will focus on Pillars I and II, which are, the state's duty to protect and the corporate responsibility to respect, in respect of gender. It will also discuss what initiatives are currently in place to promote gender equality, both at the state and company level.

[21] United Nations Human Rights Office of the High Commissioner, 'The Gender Lens to the UN Guiding Principles on Business and Human Rights: Report of the Working Group on the issue of human rights and transnational corporations and other business enterprises.' (2019), United Nations https://documents-dds-ny.un.org/doc/UNDOC/GEN/G19/146/08/PDF/G1914608.pdf?OpenElement Accessed 13th March 2021, Principle 1.

[22] Ibid, Principle 11.

[23] See the "Protect, Respect and Remedy Framework" (2011) for a more detailed analysis.

[24] Rivera (2017), p. 1201.

[25] Ibid.

[26] See the guidance under The Gender Lens to the UN Guiding Principles on Business and Human Rights (2019), pp. 14–26 for a more detailed analysis.

[27] Ibid.

2.1 *State Duty to Protect*

Under Pillar I (state duty to protect), the first principle stipulates that states must protect against human rights abuses from MNCs within their territory.[28] Bernaz notes that the scope of the state's duty to protect is broad.[29] Principle 1 clarifies that the state's duty to protect, concerns the full range of human rights obligations. This means that states should 'prevent, investigate, punish sexual harassment and redress corporate human rights abuses through 'effective policies, legislation, regulations and adjudication'.[30] As Ruggie puts it, the State's duty to protect is 'the bedrock of protection against corporate human rights abuse'.[31]

Principle 2 notes that home states should set clear expectations that all MNCs respect human rights throughout their operations.[32] Therefore, the notion of state responsibility for the protection of harm by MNCs is particularly relevant to the protection against discrimination or harm against women.[33] Bonnitcha and McCorquodale note that the positive obligation of states to protect individuals from infringements of human rights within their territory by MNCs is moored in the concept of due diligence.[34] This was first articulated in Velásquez-Rodríguez v. Honduras,[35] where the due diligence standard requires states to take active measures to protect against, prosecute and punish private actors who commit human rights violations.[36] Therefore, this standard is at the core of states' responsibilities in respect of preventing MNCs,[37] from causing or exacerbating gender inequality[38]

A close analysis of the Ugandan Constitution (the Constitution)[39] reveals that especially onerous obligations arising from positive rights are clearly and expressly imposed on the state. For example, the duty to take affirmative action to protect the rights of women is specifically assigned to the state.[40] This duty involves the provision of facilities and opportunities necessary to enhance the welfare of women.[41]

---

[28] See Principle 2 under the Guiding Principles on Business and Human Rights: Implementing the United Nations "Protect, Respect and Remedy" Framework' (2011).

[29] Bernaz (2017), p. 194.

[30] Ibid, pp. 193–194.

[31] Ruggie (2013), p. 90.

[32] See Principle 2 under the Guiding Principles on Business and Human Rights: Implementing the United Nations "Protect, Respect and Remedy" Framework' (2011).

[33] Meyersfeld (2013), p. 206.

[34] Bonnitcha and McCorquodale (2017), pp. 899–904.

[35] *Velásquez Rodríguez v. Honduras [1988] Inter-Am.Ct.H.R. (Ser. C) No. 4.*

[36] Meyersfeld (2010), p. 151.

[37] Meyersfeld (2013), p. 207.

[38] *Opuz v. Turkey [2009] App. No. 33401/02.*

[39] See Uganda: Constitution of the Republic of Uganda, 22 September 1995, https://www.wipo.int/edocs/lexdocs/laws/en/ug/ug002en.pdf Accessed 16th March 2021.

[40] Ibid Article 32.

[41] Ibid Article 33.

2.1.1 Uganda and Gender Equality

Uganda is party to several international instruments which have clearly defined and encouraged state parties to address gender inequality, including ICESCR,[42] ICCPR,[43] CEDAW,[44] the African Charter on Human and People's Rights (ACHPR),[45] among others. CEDAW remains the most overarching international tool for tackling all forms of discrimination against women, including the numerous legal and social norms that create barriers for women at work.[46] CEDAW directs State parties to take appropriate measures to eliminate discrimination against women in all fields, including the workplace.[47] Uganda ratified this convention on 22 July 1985, and domesticated the provisions of CEDAW in its Constitution in 1995.

Article 20 of the Ugandan Constitution confers a responsibility for all non-state actors, including corporations, to respect human rights. However, this basis of the state responsibility for non-state actors has not yet been tested in Ugandan courts.[48] Unlike the duty to respect and promote, which are expressly recognised under Article 20 (2) of the Ugandan Constitution, the duty to protect human rights is not.[49] Nevertheless, Article 45 of the Constitution states that the duties relating to the fundamental rights and other human rights mentioned in chapter four do not exclude others not explicitly mentioned.[50] As the duty to protect is now well established in international law, it must be regarded as forming part of the duties that Uganda has within its constitutional framework. As noted in the *Honduras* case, the duty to protect requires the state to exercise due diligence to prevent human rights violations and to react to them.[51] So far, the duty to protect remains to be litigated in Ugandan courts, although violations of human rights by non-state actors that could be redressed via this duty are common in Uganda.[52] For instance, in *Baleke Kayira Peter & Others v Attorney General and Others,*[53] there was clear evidence that the

---

[42] Ratified in 1987.

[43] Ratified in 1995.

[44] Ratified in 1985.

[45] See the African Charter on Human and People's Rights (adopted 27 June 1981, entered into force 21 October 1986) CAB/LEG/67/3 rev. 5, 21 I.L.M. 58 (1982). Uganda ratified this Convention in 1986.

[46] Marston (2014), p. 7.

[47] See Article 11, CEDAW Convention.

[48] Uganda Consortium on Corporate Accountability (2016) 'The State of Corporate Accountability in Uganda: A Baseline Study Report for the Uganda Consortium on Corporate Accountability,' https://www.iser-uganda.org/images/downloads/16_09_21_UCCA_The_State_of_Corporate_Accountability_in_Uganda.pdf Accessed 12 March 2021, p. 38.

[49] Ibid.

[50] Ibid.

[51] See *Velásquez Rodríguez v Honduras*.

[52] See Uganda Consortium on Corporate Accountability (2016), p. 36, for a more detailed analysis.

[53] *Baleke Kayira Peter & Others v Attorney General and Others,* [2002] Civil Suite No 179.

state's defence forces were used in the violent eviction that resulted in the deprivation of access to homes, land, food and other possessions.[54]

Article 40(1) of the Ugandan Constitution requires the Parliament to enact laws to provide for the right of persons to work under satisfactory, safe and healthy conditions, the right to ensure equal work for equal pay, and the right to rest and reasonable working hours.[55] Several Acts address these rights, and these include the Employment Act 2006, the Occupational Safety and Health Act 2006, the Workers Compensation Act 2000, the National Social Security Fund Act, the Labour Unions Act 2006, and the Labour Disputes (Arbitration and Settlement) Act 2006.[56] Given that labour rights are directly applicable to non-state actors such as corporations, these acts regulate public and private employment.[57] However, it is important to note that the Employment Act, the Occupational Safety and Health Act, the Workers Compensation Act and the National Social Security Fund deal principally with formal employment and not informal employment.[58] Within the Ugandan context, as I will discuss later, this is a major oversight and has left informal workers without legislative protection.[59]

In the effort to attain gender equality, so far, Uganda has adopted the Gender Equality Seal for Public and Private Enterprises which is a corporate certification process that recognises good performance of UNDP Country Offices in delivering transformational gender equality results.[60] It rests on the insight that increasing collaborations between different domains of gender mainstreaming can catalyse both organisational transformation and development results.[61] It is important to note that Uganda was the first country in Africa to endorse the gender equality seal for private enterprises, and by 2018, forty-one enterprises had adopted the Gender Seal Certification Programme for Private Enterprises in Uganda.[62] Recently, Stanbic Bank joined the UNDP Gender Equality Seal programme in 2019.[63]

The Ugandan Parliament has also set up the Equal Opportunities Commission 'EOC' under Article 32(3) and Article 32 (4) of the Ugandan Constitution, and the Equal Opportunities Commission Act 2007, which is mandated to eliminate

---

[54] See Uganda Consortium on Corporate Accountability (2016), p. 36, for a more detailed analysis.

[55] Ibid, 51.

[56] Ibid.

[57] Ibid.

[58] Ibid.

[59] Ibid.

[60] UNDP (2023) UNDP Gender Equality Seal: Paving the Way for Gender Inclusivity in Uganda's Private Sector https://www.undp.org/uganda/blog/undp-gender-equality-seal-paving-way-gender-inclusivity-ugandas-private-sector Accessed 14 March 2021.

[61] Ibid.

[62] For a more detailed analysis see, Admin-Alg (2018).

[63] Uganda Business News (2019) Stanbic Bank joins UNDP Gender Equality Seal Programme', https://ugbusiness.com/2019/08/company-releases/stanbic-bank-joins-undp-gender-equality-seal-programme#gref Accessed 14 March 2021.

discrimination and inequalities against any individual or group of persons.[64] Its mandate is broad and extends to private businesses and enterprises.[65] In addition, Uganda adopted the National Policy on Gender-Based Violence,[66] which seeks to address Gender Based Violence (GBV) in all its forms as an integral part of achieving gender equality.[67]

2.2 Corporate Responsibility to Respect

Pillar II stipulates that it is the corporate responsibility to respect human rights.[68] This means that MNCs need to act with Human Rights Due Diligence (HRDD) to avoid infringing on the rights of others and address their potential adverse impacts, both direct and indirect.[69] HRDD implies an obligation by MNCs to take steps 'to become aware of, prevent and address adverse human rights impacts.'[70] Deva argues that this is the central tool proposed to enable MNCs to meet their responsibility to respect human rights.[71] Ruggie makes an excellent point when he points out that MNCs indeed have a corporate responsibility to respect human rights and that carrying out 'philanthropic good deeds' does not compensate for violating human rights in the territories in which they operate.[72] In addition, while the corporate responsibility to respect is limited in terms of the measures that is expected from MNCs, it concerns all human rights, which is emphasised in Guiding Principle 12.[73] Bernaz notes that this constitutes one of the greatest achievements of the UNGPs.[74] Furthermore, UNGP 14 points out that all business enterprises, including micro-,

---

64 See the Equal Opportunities Commission, 'Overview,' https://www.eoc.go.ug/about-us/ Accessed 20 February 2021.

65 See the Equal Opportunities Commission, 'EOC launches NBFP and SBFP on Gender and Quity requirements FY 2019/2020 (2019), https://www.eoc.go.ug/eoc-launches-nbfp-and-sbfp-gender-and-quity-requirements-fy-20192020/ Accessed 17 February 2021.

66 For a more detailed analysis see, Ministry of Gender, Labour and Social Development, 'The National Policy on Elimination of Gender Based Violence in Uganda,' (2016).

67 See Akinana Mama Wa Africa and Hivos, 'Tusikize; Listen to us, Experiences of Sexual Harassment Against Women in the World of Work in Uganda,' <https://www.akinamamawaafrika.org/wp-content/uploads/2020/07/Sexual-Harassment-Study.pdf> accessed 10 March 2021, p. 11.

68 See Pillar II. under the Guiding Principles on Business and Human Rights: Implementing the United Nations "Protect, Respect and Remedy" Framework' (2011).

69 See Principle 15, under the Guiding Principles on Business and Human Rights: Implementing the United Nations "Protect, Respect and Remedy" Framework' (2011).

70 See Principle 17, under the Guiding Principles on Business and Human Rights: Implementing the United Nations "Protect, Respect and Remedy" Framework' (2011).

71 Deva (2012), p. 106.

72 Ruggie (2013), p. 95.

73 See Principle 12, under the Guiding Principles on Business and Human Rights: Implementing the United Nations "Protect, Respect and Remedy" Framework' (2011).

74 Bernaz (2017), p. 194.

small and medium-sized enterprises, should take appropriate steps in line with the Guiding Principles to respect women's human rights, including those working in the informal economy.[75]

2.2.1 What Rights Are MNCs Bound by Under the Ugandan Constitution?

As I mentioned earlier, MNCs are required to respect human rights under Article 20(2) of the Ugandan Constitution. This raises the question of, where gender inequality prevails,can MNCs and/or their subsidiaries use their leverage to change harmful social norms in the areas where they operate?

The answer is yes. Corporations have a role to play by using their leverage to promote gender equality inside and outside the fence, but not alone.[76] UNGP 11 notes that business enterprises have a responsibility to avoid infringing on women's human rights.[77] UNGP 13 notes that business enterprises should not cause or contribute to adverse impacts on women's human rights and should address such impacts when they occur.[78] In addition, they should also take adequate measures to prevent or mitigate adverse impacts on women's human rights that are directly linked to their operations, products or services by their business relationships.[79] For instance, in 2015, following serious allegations of sexual misconduct and abuse by contractors, the World Bank cancelled the Uganda Transport Sector Development Project (TSDP),[80] until it was satisfied that the Ugandan government had fully addressed these issues in Kamwenge.[81]

Big corporations like MTN Uganda, a South African company, have played a big role in promoting gender equality in Uganda. For example, MTN Group signed the United Nations Women Empowerment Principles, pledging its commitment to the advancement of Gender Equality and the Empowerment of Women.[82] There have also been public awareness campaigns addressing issues faced by women in some enterprises, for instance, Nile Breweries Uganda launched a behavioural change campaign called 'No- Excuse,' to address the predicament of sexual harassment

---

[75] See Principle 14 under The Gender Lens to the UN Guiding Principles on Business and Human Rights.

[76] Paz (2020).

[77] See Principle 11 under The Gender Lens to the UN Guiding Principles on Business and Human Rights.

[78] Ibid, Principle 13(a).

[79] Ibid, Principle 13(b).

[80] The World Bank (2015) World Bank Statement on Cancellation of the Uganda Transport Sector Development Project (TSDP) https://www.worldbank.org/en/news/press-release/2015/12/21/wb-statement-cancellation-uganda-transport-sector-development-project Accessed 17 March 2021.

[81] Mwesigwa (2016).

[82] MTN (2020) MTN Group commits to bridging the gender divide https://www.mtn.com/mtn-group-commits-to-bridging-the-gender-divide/ Accessed 19 March 2021.

faced by women in Uganda[83] and to bring about a change in long-established societal behaviours and attitudes, towards sexual harassment, by encouraging stakeholders to support the victims to access appropriate support services.[84]

Within the flower farm sector, a Gender Scan undertaken by the Uganda Workers Education Association (UWEA) in 2019 indicated that the major flower companies have developed and/or are developing policies and procedures on some issues faced by women, such as sexual harassment.[85] This is largely as a result of interventions by NGOs (through partners of the women@work campaign), as well as Fair Trade requirements. These companies have also done some awareness raising about these policies, though it is not always consistent nor does it reach all the workers.[86] In addition, whilst structures have been put in place to address incidents of sexual harassment, these structures are not always effective.[87] Furthermore, a study that analysed the experiences of the China Railways Corporation (CRC) road construction project in Uganda found that a consistent and persistent emphasis on awareness raising was critical to addressing issues women face, such as sexual harassment.[88] The company was able to incorporate discussions about sexual harassment at various points during its training activities for staff, by having monthly staff meetings, as well as having sessions in which people from outside the company were invited to take part in the discussions, including officials from the Ministry of Gender Labour and Social Development (MGLSD).[89]

2.3 *Advocacy Coalition Groups*

In the effort to address the gender inequality problem, where the state and businesses have failed, advocacy coalition groups have been formed such as WoMin in collaboration with the National Association of Professional Environmentalists (NAPE), whose role is to amplify the voices of female minors and advocate for authorities to take appropriate action in addressing the inequalities that women face.[90]

[83] Nile Breweries (2019) Nile Special 'No Excuse' Campaign to highlight Sexual Harassment, https://www.nilebreweries.com/pledge-to-stand-against-sexual-harassment/#:~:text=The%20 16%20days%2C%20designated%20by,sexual%20harassment%20in%20the%20country. Accessed 20 March 2021.

[84] See Akinana Mama Wa Africa and Hivos, p. 24.

[85] Ibid, 14.

[86] Ibid.

[87] Ibid.

[88] Ibid.

[89] Ibid 23.

[90] National Association of Professional Environmentalists (NAPE): Challenges of Salt Mining: An account of Katwe women salt miners, https://womin.africa/wp-content/uploads/2020/09/uganda-report.pdf Accessed 20 March 2021.

Other groups that have been formed to advocate for 'equal pay for equal work' are organizations such as Akina Mama Wa Afrika, SIHANETWORK, which run an advocacy campaign #makehervisible, with the aim of formalising street trade in Uganda.[91] Uganda Women Entrepreneurs Association Limited (UWEAL) which was established in 1987 to promote women in business and provide necessary support and guidance to women in business,[92] and ZimbaWomen,[93] to mention but a few.

3 Obstacles Faced by Women Working in Supply Chains

The human rights violations that women face in the context of business activities combine existing gender discrimination with vast power imbalances between business actors and individual women.[94] There is no doubt that the issue of corporate accountability is pertinent in Uganda and requires investigation.[95] With the government aggressively promoting foreign direct investment and business as a means of improving the national economy and addressing poverty, corporations have in turn, gained unprecedented support from the government.[96]

With the state's failure to provide effective statutory and other protection against such exploitation, it has failed in its duty to protect against the violation of Article 11 of CEDAW.[97] This now leaves the question, what is the cost of promoting of business with MNCs in Uganda?[98]

It is important to note that the case law on the application of the Bill of Rights to MNCs in Uganda remains scanty. It is therefore not possible to draw general conclusions on a handful of cases that address this question either directly or indirectly.[99]

3.1 Maternity and Childcare Discrimination

Article 33(3) and Article 33(6) of the 1995 Ugandan Constitution recognize the need to protect the maternal functions of women. Section 56 of the Employment Act 2006 provides for maternity leave. However, within the informal sector, the

[91] SIHA Network (2019) A move to formalise street trade in Kampala: #MakeHerVisible https://sihanet.org/a-move-to-formalise-street-trade-in-kampala/ Accessed 17 March 2021.

[92] See, UWEAL Trade Information Point, 'Who we are,' https://uweal.co.ug/#about-us Accessed 1 April 2021.

[93] See, Zimba Women, 'About us' https://www.zimbawomen.org/about-us accessed 12 March 2021.

[94] Marston (2014), p. 29.

[95] See Uganda Consortium on Corporate Accountability (2016), p. 6, for a more detailed analysis.

[96] Ibid.

[97] Meyersfeld (2013), pp. 208–209.

[98] Ibid.

[99] See Uganda Consortium on Corporate Accountability (2016), p. 31, for a more detailed analysis.

constitution makes no provision for maternity leave beyond the provisions within the formal employment sector. Most of these employees don't have the security of tenure and often work throughout their pregnancies with little or no protection. Fears of loss of jobs force them not to take leave. Case studies within the flower farm industries share a dark light on this.[100] Women cannot even attempt to apply for maternity leave as it can lead to termination of employment and in some cases where they take a few days during their pregnancy, it will be deducted from annual leave or it will be looked at as days taken off without pay.[101]

Internationally, the ILO Convention confers maternity leave as one form of contingency that must be undertaken within the broader social protection measures in place for all workers. The ILO Maternity Protection Convention, 2000 (No. 183), greatly broadens the scope around social protection of women in the workforce and is designed to promote equality of all women in the workforce and the health and safety of the mother and child. The Convention spells out specific provisions for extending maternity protection to all women workers, including those within the informal economy and those engaged in atypical forms of dependent work.[102] However, Uganda has not ratified the convention and is yet to strengthen provisions advancing maternity leave protections beyond the formal sector.

All in all, although Uganda has a policy framework on maternal and child health rights, the national legal framework does not explicitly address the issue of maternity leave within the informal sector. It is therefore very difficult to enforce maternity leave for women who work in informal sectors where formal work agreements hardly exist.

3.2 *Sexual Harassment*

As I mentioned earlier, discourse on sexual harassment has captured the public imagination both globally, regionally and nationally following the #MeToo movement. The Uganda Employment law defines sexual harassment as intimidation, bullying, or coercion of a sexual nature, or the unwelcome or inappropriate promise of rewards in exchange for sexual favours.[103] General Recommendation No. 12 (1989) made by the CEDAW Committee recommends that states should include in their periodic reports to the Committee information about legislation in force to protect women against the incidence of all kinds of violence including Sexual harassment at the workplace.[104] The Beijing Platform for Action para. 178, recognises sexual harassment as a form of violence against women and calls for the enactment of laws

[100] Chimbi (2019).

[101] Ibid.

[102] ILO, C183 - Maternity Protection Convention, 2000 (No. 183).

[103] See the Uganda Employment Act, section 7.

[104] See Akina Mama Wa Africa and Hivos p. 11.

on sexual harassment.[105] The ILO Convention No. 111 of 1958, the Discrimination (Employment and Occupation) Convention, and No. 169, the Indigenous and Tribal Peoples Convention also specifically prohibit sexual harassment in the workplace.[106] Furthermore, the Protocol to the African Charter on Human and People's Rights on the Rights of Women in Africa (Maputo Protocol) obligates State parties to take appropriate measures to protect women from all forms of abuse, including gender inequality.[107]

Sexual harassment constitutes a crime in Uganda[108] and the Uganda Penal Code Act, notes that sexual harassment is liable for imprisonment for one year.[109] Furthermore, the Uganda Gender Policy 2007, recognised sexual harassment as a form of gender-based violence.[110] Following a study done by Akina Mama Wa Afrika in implementing the Women@Work Campaign, sexual harassment was found to be one of the key issues faced by women working within global supply chains.[111] It was found that women working in both formal and informal sectors faced similar experiences of sexual harassment.[112] Many problematic dynamics allow for sexual harassment to continue unmitigated and these include shame surrounding reporting harassment and abuse, practical difficulties in reporting, and misconceptions of what constitutes harassment.[113]

However, although sexual harassment is recognised as a violation and is encoded in the law in Uganda,[114] public views about sexual harassment are still largely dismissive of women's experiences and concerns.[115] For instance, the Employment Act requires employers employing more than twenty-five employees to put in place measures to prevent sexual harassment from occurring at their workplace.[116] The challenge with the law only recognising institutions with over twenty-five employees to put a sexual harassment prevention measure in place is problematic because the majority of workplaces/businesses in Uganda are in the informal sector and are small and medium-sized businesses, most of which do not have more than 25 employees.[117] In addition, the Employment Act defines a perpetrator of sexual harassment as an employee who has authority over the person alleging sexual

[105] Ibid.

[106] Ibid.

[107] Ibid.

[108] The Employment (Sexual Harassment) Regulations, 2012 (S.I. 2012 No. 15).

[109] Uganda Penal Code Act, Section 128(3).

[110] See Akina Mama Wa Africa and Hivos, p. 11.

[111] Ibid, 7.

[112] Ibid, 5.

[113] Mlynska et al. (2015), p. 10.

[114] Akinana Mama Wa Africa and Hivos, p. 5.

[115] Ibid.

[116] Employment Act, Section 7(4).

[117] Akinana Mama Wa Africa and Hivos, p. 12.

harassment or has authority in the work place.[118] This definition suggests that someone of the same rank cannot perpetrate sexual harassment against a co-worker because they do not have power over them and assumes that power can only be acquired through positional leadership. Imbalance of power relations between genders means that men in the same rank as women, and sometimes even a lower rank will have the power and by extension the entitlement to sexually harass women.[119] Furthermore, the sexual offences bill, which seeks to protect women and girls, has never been passed in the parliament.[120]

Addressing sexual harassment is central to ensuring the security of working people, particularly the most marginalised for example, the structure of work relations in the World Bank halted funding for the $265 million transport scheme after serious allegations of sexual misconduct and abuse by contractors.[121] The exact magnitude of sexual harassment occurring in the workplace in Uganda remains unclear due to the lack of statistics or the absence of a designated database by responsible oversight institutions.[122] Whilst anecdotal evidence suggests that sexual harassment at the workplace is very common—the prevalence rate remains unclear as many incidents are not reported.[123] Furthermore, many companies in Uganda either do not have specific policies in place to address sexual harassment in their work environment or do not have the scope within other employment policies and procedures to deal with the problem should it arise.[124]

3.3 Discriminatory Laws/or Social Norms

Marston notes that sex discrimination remains the most prevalent form of inequality in the work arena.[125] This is because women continue to face a number of legal and social barriers that keep them from contributing to their full potential.[126] One of the most significant barriers is unequal laws.[127] Despite CEDAW and other provisions such as the UNGPs, there is still prevalent discrimination among women in the workplace, especially within the norms.

[118] Employment Act, Section 7.

[119] Akinana Mama Wa Africa and Hivos, p. 12.

[120] Ibid.

[121] For a more detailed analysis, see, The World Bank, World Bank Statement on Cancellation of the Uganda Transport Sector Development Project (TSDP) (2015).

[122] Akinana Mama Wa Africa and Hivos, p. 13.

[123] Ibid.

[124] Ibid.

[125] Marston (2014), p. 6.

[126] Ibid 13.

[127] Ibid.

The governance gaps between developed and developing countries often result in inconsistencies between gender equality in the workplace of a corporation's home state and that in the workplace of its host State.[128] These gaps allow for the exploitation of women in host state countries in a manner that would be unlawful in the home state of the corporation. Women therefore continue to be significantly underrepresented in leadership in the business sphere.[129] I agree with Awori et al, who argue that the power inequalities, patriarchal systems and entrenched discrimination have a disproportionate impact on women.[130]

This is because Uganda is a patriarchal society where the culture and systems generally see to it that men are treated as superior beings.[131] Men are the heads of homes, clans, and communities.[132] As long as women are not given equal opportunities and are perceived as second-class citizens whose job is to ensure that men are given what they want at whatever cost, the unfair treatment and harassment will continue.[133] This context not only breeds sexual harassment, but all other forms of gender-based violence.[134] In addition, patriarchal culture is permissive of sexual harassment, and a key factor that may reduce the likelihood of reporting sexual harassment is a highly male-dominated organization and patriarchal culture. In very patriarchal work cultures, some men use sexual harassment as way to subjugate women and women for fear of retaliation play along with sexual harassment.[135]

3.4 *Low-Level Positions*

While the discussion about women's leadership is gaining traction globally, there remains a significant gap with respect to top leadership in business.[136] Women continue to be significantly underrepresented in leadership in the business sphere.[137] The absence of women's voice and/or leadership in institutions can also play a part in lack of action towards issues faced by women such as sexual harassment for example. In the institutions where women occupy positions of leadership and have voice to influence policy, there are policies and even mechanisms to address sexual harassment, whereas in institutions where women's voice was not particularly

[128] Ibid.

[129] Ibid 11.

[130] Awori et al. (2018), pp. 285–285.

[131] Ibid.

[132] Akinana Mama Wa Africa and Hivos, p. 13.

[133] Ibid 14.

[134] Uganda National Action Plan on Elimination of Gender Based Violence 2016–2021.

[135] Akinana Mama Wa Africa and Hivos, p. 15.

[136] Marston (2014), p. 10.

[137] Ibid 11.

encouraged, there was an absence of sexual harassment policies.[138] Marston argues that women still continue to face discrimination with respect to access of decision and leadership positions.[139] Furthermore, women still continue to be underrepresented on board of directors and decision making bodies.[140]

For instance, recently in 2019, Stanbic Bank appointed its first female CEO, Anne Juuko.[141] Although this is progressive, Ugandan women still have fewer leadership roles, compared to their male counterparts.[142] As of 2019, only ten women sit on boards of Uganda's listed companies.[143] I agree with Marston, who notes that the inclusion of women in governance and leadership positions in business is critical.[144]

3.5 *Poor Working Conditions*

Another challenge faced by women is poor working conditions. Within the extractive industry, for instance, salt miners are exposed to a number of economic, social and health challenges, of which women are affected the most.[145] These impacts, however, are not well documented or well publicised, leaving the miners to suffer in silence.[146] Within the salt mining extractive industry, it was found that women in Katwe were working without protective gear despite the dangers of exposure to brine and other corrosive chemicals that are part and parcel of the mining process.[147] Some of the workers were also found to work in extreme temperatures, under direct sun, with limited access to drinking water.[148]Another example was when women working for a Dutch MNC, Royal Van Zanten flower farm, were poisoned by pesticides because they were not given protective gear.[149] The state failed to protect these

[138] Akinana Mama Wa Africa and Hivos, p. 20.

[139] Marston (2014), p. 6.

[140] Ibid, 11.

[141] CNBC Africa (2020) Stanbic Bank names Anne Jukko as its first Ugandan female CEO, https://www.cnbcafrica.com/2020/stanbic-bank-names-anne-jukko-as-its-first-ugandan-female-ceo/ Accessed 20 March 2021.

[142] Daily Monitor (2019) Women in boardrooms: Why they are still few https://www.monitor.co.ug/uganda/business/prosper/women-in-boardrooms-why-they-are-still-few-1810880 Accessed 19 March 2021.

[143] Ibid.

[144] Marston (2014), p. 5.

[145] See National Association of Professional Environmentalists (NAPE): Challenges of Salt Mining: An account of Katwe women salt miners.

[146] Ibid.

[147] Ibid.

[148] Ibid.

[149] Khisa (2016).

women, since the Minister for Trade, Industry and Cooperatives at the time, dismissed the workers claims to protect the flower industry.[150]

Furthermore, one of the most frequently cited concerns of flower farmer workers regarding health and safety is the impact of pesticides on both their own and their communities' health.[151] Constant, unprotected exposure to certain chemicals can result in grave long-term health problems, including respiratory problems and eye damage, whilst for pregnant women, certain chemicals can induce miscarriage.[152] Other health problems stem from the arduous nature of the work such as body and back pain from bending, crouching or standing for several hours a day or repetitive strain injuries.[153] Furthermore, failing to provide certain necessary provisions, such as clean water, toilet facilities, can also harm workers.

3.6 Poor and Discriminatory Pay

Women workers are over-represented in the informal economy in environments characterized by an absence of social, labour and legal protections. This is exacerbated by gender stereotypes about women's work that results in job segregation and gendered disparities in wages and benefits.[154] One major issue that continues to inform public concern is one of equal pay for equal work, especially the gender pay gaps. The 1997 Gender policy takes cognisance of the fact that "Uganda is a patriarchal society where men are the dominant players in decision making, although women shoulder most reproductive, productive and community management responsibilities, many of which are not remunerated or reflected in national statistics."[155]

Following a study exploring the impacts of salt mining for female salt miners at Katwe, done by NAPE with the support of Women against Mining (WoMin), it was found that women earned between UGX 4000 and 10,000 (USD 1–3) per day for 10 hours of labour.[156] This money is not enough to buy domestic needs and medication

[150] Ibid.

[151] Mlynska et al. (2015), p. 15.

[152] Ibid.

[153] Ibid.

[154] Awori et al. (2018), p. 285.

[155] The National Gender Policy (Ministry of Gender, Labour and Social Development-Uganda, 1997), http://www.nzdl.org/cgi-bin/library.cgi?e=d-00000-00%2D%2D-off-0unescoen%2D%2D00-0%2D%2D%2D%2D0-10-0%2D%2D-0%2D%2D-0direct-10%2D%2D-4%2D%2D%2D%2D%2D%2D-0-11%2D%2D11-en-50%2D%2D-20-about%2D%2D-00-0-1-00-0-0-11-1-0utfZz-8-10&cl=CL1.7&d=HASH01880894b537b738a103f022.3&x=1 Accessed 13 March 2021.

[156] See National Association of Professional Environmentalists (NAPE): Challenges of Salt Mining: An account of Katwe women salt miners.

but most female minors have no choice as salt mining is their only means of survival and they have to feed their families.[157]

A study undertaken by the UWEA on 12 farms (11 flower farms and one fruit and vegetable farm) found a huge disparity between male and female pay. Shortly before leaving her job, one female manager reported, "I cannot make any decision here unless I seek permission from either the General Manager or Managing Director." This manager, who had earned a salary of Ugx 300,000, was succeeded by a male Human Resources Manager who was paid a salary of close to Ugx 1,500,000.[158] UWEA commented, "Whatever the reason, this practice demonstrated an unfair social practice that discriminated against women and which should be discouraged."[159]

4 Recommendations to Promote Gender Equality

States and businesses should address gender equality comprehensively and should also nurture organisational cultures that promote gender equality and women's rights.

4.1 National Policy and Legislation

Firstly, there needs to be a review of the Employment (Sexual Harassment Regulations) to respond to several gaps, including updating definitions of Sexual harassment to respond to contemporary experiences and ensuring the policy applies to all institutions regardless of the number of employees.[160]

Secondly, the Sexual Offences Bill 2019 needs to be fast-tracked to provide complementary support to the Sexual Harassment Regulations, 2012, particularly in terms of remedies and penalties for more egregious sexual offences committed in the workplace.[161] Advocacy on policies and laws like the sexual offences bill will help protect women from being sexually exploited, advocacy around the employment policy has also reduced discrimination against women based on their sex and gender.

Thirdly, Uganda should ratify the ILO Convention 190 on violence and harassment at work, which has more robust and comprehensive provisions to deal with

[157] Ibid.

[158] UWEA in Collaboration with WWW (2011) Developing Strategies for Change for Workers in African horticulture -The case of Uganda, available at: https://www.women-ww.org/_files/ugd/4111d6_48e2970f6c1d4ca2a1a5a9d8cf5c87c2.pdf p. 45. Accessed 17 March 2021.

[159] Ibid.

[160] Akinana Mama Wa Africa and Hivos, p. 28.

[161] Ibid, 29.

sexual harassment, for instance, in the workplace. Ratification should be followed by domestication, which can include reviewing and updating existing regulatory frameworks to incorporate stipulations such as extending protections for people in the informal sector or exploring stand-alone instruments.[162] It should be noted that in June 2019, recognizing that sexual harassment is incompatible with decent work, the ILO adopted Convention 190 on eliminating violence and harassment in the world of work to provide a global standard for violence-free workplaces. The Convention expands the scope of the world of work and, by the same stroke, the protections that workers enjoy in work, taking into consideration violations occurring in the course of, linked with or arising out of work.[163] This offers protection to women in the informal sector against sexual harassment in contrast to Uganda's current employment law whose scope can be interpreted to be limited to the formal sector. The ratification and domestication of this convention is critical to inform the review of the current legal framework for the expansion of the definition of workplaces and to specifically provide for the protection of women in the informal sector.[164]

Fourthly, the State should acknowledge its duty to protect working women from discriminatory actions committed by corporations and, when they occur, to investigate them and hold the corporation accountable.[165] The Ministry of Gender, Labour, and Social Development (MGLSD) should put in place a system to regularly monitor whether companies have internal policies to address sexual harassment and the extent to which these are being adhered to. In addition to sanctions, the MGLSD should also provide recognition and rewards to companies that have the right policies and practices.[166]

Fifthly, The Uganda National Action Plan on Business and Human Rights should also pay special attention to the unique circumstances and experiences of vulnerable or marginalized sections of society, such as women and address issues of inequality.[167]

[162] Ibid, 28.

[163] Art 3, C190- Violence and Harassment Convention, 2019.

[164] Akinana Mama Wa Africa and Hivos, p. 12.

[165] See Principle 3 under The Gender Lens to the UN Guiding Principles on Business and Human Rights.

[166] Akinana Mama Wa Africa and Hivos, p. 29.

[167] Initiative for Social and Economic Rights (2019) Background paper for Uganda's National Action Plan on Business and Human Rights, https://iser-uganda.org/wp-content/uploads/2022/07/Background_paper_for_Ugandas_NAP_on_business_and_human_rights.pdf Accessed 2 April 2021.

4.2 Gender Equality in Business

Corporate engagement with the goal of gender equality is indispensable to the realisation of human rights. Business enterprises should internalize gender as an equality issue, rather than treating it as a "tick-box exercise" or as an add-on to human rights due diligence. The first step is making visible the bias and unequal laws and practices we have come to accept as part of the business and cultural landscape around us. This requires dedicated efforts to further establish sexual harassment a baseline of where we are, identify targets for where we need to be and track the progress along the path between the two.[168] For gender equality to be achieved, companies must adopt a strategic and long-term view to mainstream gender in the business.

Firstly, companies should provide space and promote women's voice and participation in the leadership and governance structures of women working in both the formal and informal economy.[169] Companies can draw on Kampala Capital City Authority's (KCCA's) good practices on safeguards for their work in road construction in this respect.[170]

Secondly, companies should build transparent and trustworthy reporting mechanisms that ensure protection for survivors of sexual harassment and enable accountability regardless of rank.[171] This can involve developing appropriate sector-relevant sexual harassment committees to respond to cases of harassment. The group of staff that compose the committee should be clearly defined in the sexual harassment with complementary Terms of Reference.[172] Oxfam International also provides a great example of safeguarding policies that organizations and businesses facing sexual harassment allegations can adopt to ensure that the culture of violence is dealt with and prevented from reoccurring.[173]

Thirdly, companies should provide clear pathways for wage negotiations and promotions to ensure that female employees are not abused as they undertake this.[174] Fourthly, companies should ensure that they have well-constructed and managed sanitation facilities, separated by gender, especially for women working within the informal economy, to protect the women from being sexually harassed by their male

[168] Marston (2014), p. 46.

[169] Martin and Gammelgard (2020).

[170] Kampala City Council, 'GIC 2016 Thematic Areas,' <https://www.kcca.go.ug/ptf-gic-evaluation-criteria> Accessed 2 April 2021.

[171] Akinana Mama Wa Africa and Hivos, p. 29.

[172] Ibid.

[173] Oxfam International, 'Improving safeguarding and culture at Oxfam,' https://oi-files-d8-prod.s3.eu-west-2.amazonaws.com/s3fs-public/2020-12/Improving%20Safeguarding%20and%20Culture%20at%20Oxfam%20Report%20April%20-%20September%202020.pdf Accessed 19 March 2021.

[174] Ibid.

counterparts.[175] Fifthly, companies should ensure physical security within and the surroundings of places of work, particularly large establishments like factories, markets and flower farms, for example, by installing streetlights and security cameras where possible to ensure the security of their employees.[176]

Sixthly, to ensure decent work, companies should protect expectant mothers from exposure to hazardous chemicals or heavy lifting at work and provide paid parental leave.[177] Companies need to identify and address gender-related risks that negatively impact women's right to health and wellbeing and their equal participation at work.[178] For example, companies should develop and implement gender-sensitive policies and practices to create an enabling work environment for women and a simple case in point is to ensure that women workers in particular can access maternity leave without fear of losing their jobs.[179] Martin and Gammelgard, make an excellent point when they note that companies should also implement recruitment and hiring practices that reduce gender stereotypes, bias, and barriers to women's labour force participation.[180] They should also collect sex-disaggregated data on pay and promotions to close the gender pay gap and support women's access to the talent pipeline.[181]

Lastly, to combat the financial, emotional, and logistical burdens presented by COVID-19, businesses can take the following steps, inspired by UNICEF's 7 Ways Employees Can Support Working Parents During the Outbreak,[182] to respect the human rights of single working mothers.[183]

5 Conclusion

In conclusion, although international law has already put in place applicable mechanisms to address gender inequality, as discussed above, these mechanisms have not fully addressed gender inequality. I agree with Marston who points out that equality for women is, first and foremost, a matter of human rights.[184] A state-business collaboration is therefore needed since most states and business enterprises still pay little or inadequate attention to the diverse experiences of women in implementing

[175] Ibid.

[176] Ibid.

[177] Martin and Gammelgard (2020).

[178] Ibid.

[179] Ibid.

[180] Ibid.

[181] Ibid.

[182] UNICEF, '7 ways employers can support working parents during the coronavirus disease (COVID-19) outbreak' https://www.unicef.org/azerbaijan/7-ways-employers-can-support-working-parents-during-coronavirus-disease-covid-19-outbreak Accessed 17 March 2021.

[183] Green (2020).

[184] Marston (2014), p. 5.

their respective duties and responsibilities under the UNGPs. To eliminate all forms of discrimination against women and achieve substantive gender equality, Uganda as a state and businesses should work together with women's organisations and all other relevant actors to ensure systematic changes to discriminatory power structures that are barriers to women's equal enjoyment of human rights in all spheres.

The quick spread of COVID-19 has highlighted the aggravated gender discrepancies of women working within supply chains.[185] Furthermore, the Eastern African Sub-Regional Support Initiative for the Advancement of Women (EASSI) executive director appealed to stakeholders and the government to find ways in which they can encourage cross-border women traders to form cooperatives that will enable them to conduct well-structured trade, following the closure of at least 64.2 per cent of women-owned businesses as a result of the COVID-19 Pandemic.[186]

This is therefore, an opportunity to reflect on the way businesses operate within supply chains. It is time for a new system. We need supply chains in which everyone is acknowledged for their contribution, wealth is more equally distributed and women are treated equally. Everybody within the supply chain should earn at least a living wage. This will make people more resilient and supply chains more sustainable and fairer.

To sum up, it is time to change the paradigm and to understand that the profound transformation of the system will only be possible if we recognise that substantive equality is key to social and economic justice. There is no democracy without women.

Cases

Baleke Kayira Peter & Others v Attorney General and Others, [2002] Civil Suite No 179
Opuz v. Turkey [2009] App. No. 33401/02
Velásquez Rodríguez v. Honduras [1988] Inter-Am.Ct.H.R. (Ser. C) No. 4

Legislation

1995 Constitution of the Republic of Uganda
African Charter on Human and People's Rights (adopted 27 June 1981, entered into force 21 October 1986) CAB/LEG/67/3 rev. 5, 21 I.L.M. 58 (1982)
Employment Act 2006
Equal Opportunities Commission Act, 2007

[185] Nabukeera (2020), pp. 116–133.
[186] Lyatuu (2021).

ICCPR - International Covenant on Civil and Political Rights (adopted 16 December 1966, entered into force 23 March 1976) 999 UNTS 171 (ICCPR)
ICESCR - International Covenant on Economic, Social and Cultural Rights (adopted 16 December 1966, entered into force 3 January 1976) 993 UNTS (ICESCR)
ILO, C183 - Maternity Protection Convention, 2000 (No. 183)
Labour Disputes (Arbitration and Settlement) Act 2006
National Social Security Fund Act, the Labour Unions Act 2006
Occupational Safety and Health Act 2006
The Employment (Sexual Harassment) Regulations, 2012
The National Policy on Gender Based Violence, 2010
The Uganda Penal Code Act
The Uganda Penal Code Act
UDHR - Universal Declaration of Human Rights (adopted 10 December 1948 UNGA Res 217 A (III) (UDHR)
Uganda Gender Policy, 2007
United Nations, *Charter of the United Nations,* (adopted 24 October 1945, 1 UNTS XVI)
Universal Declaration of Human Rights (adopted 10 December 1948 UNGA Res 217 A (III) (UDHR
Workers Compensation Act 2000

UN Documents

The National Gender Policy, Ministry of Gender, Labour and Social Development-Uganda, 1997
United Nations Human Rights Office of the High Commissioner, 'The Gender Dimensions of the UN Guiding Principles on Business and Human Rights 'UN Working Group 2019) https://www.ohchr.org/Documents/Issues/Business/BookletGenderDimensionsGuidingPrinciples.pdf. Accessed 13 March 2021
United Nations Human Rights Office of the High Commissioner, 'The Gender Lens to the UN Guiding Principles on Business and Human Rights: Report of the Working Group on the issue of human rights and transnational corporations and other business enterprises.' (United Nations 2019) https://documents-dds-ny.un.org/doc/UNDOC/GEN/G19/146/08/PDF/G1914608.pdf?OpenElement. Accessed 13th March 2021
United Nations Human Rights Office of the High Commissioner, 'Guiding Principles on Business and Human Rights: Implementing the United Nations "Protect, Respect and Remedy" Framework' (United Nations 2011) https://www.ohchr.org/documents/publications/GuidingprinciplesBusinesshr_eN.pdf. Accessed 13 March 2021

References

Secondary Sources

Admin-Alg (2018) 28 new enterprises sign-up for the UNDP Gender Equality Seal Certification Programme for Private Enterprises. In: América Latina Genera. https://americalatinagenera.org/informate-noticias/28-new-enterprises-sign-up-for-the-undp-gender-equality-seal-certification-programme-for-private-enterprises/. Accessed 15 Mar 2021

Akinana Mama Wa Africa and Hivos, Tusikize; Listen to us, Experiences of Sexual Harassment Against Women in the World of Work in Uganda. <https://www.akinamamawaafrika.org/wp-content/uploads/2020/07/Sexual-Harassment-Study.pdf>. Accessed 10 Mar 2021

Awori S et al (2018) A feminist approach to the binding instrument on transnational corporations and other business enterprises. Bus Hum Rights J 3:285–285. https://doi.org/10.1017/bhj.2018.3

Bernaz N (2017) Business and human rights: history, law and policy: bridging the accountability gap. Routledge, Milton Park, Abingdon, Oxon

Bonnitcha J, McCorquodale R (2017) The concept of 'due diligence' in the UN guiding principles on business and human rights. Eur J Int Law 28:899–904. https://doi.org/10.1093/ejil/chx042

Chimbi J (2019) Women working in flower farms often denied maternity leave. https://hivos.org/women-working-in-flower-farms-often-denied-maternity-leave/. Accessed 20 Mar 2021

CNBC Africa (2020) Stanbic Bank names Anne Jukko as its first Ugandan female CEO. https://www.cnbcafrica.com/2020/stanbic-bank-names-anne-jukko-as-its-first-ugandan-female-ceo/. Accessed 20 Mar 2021

Daily Monitor (2019) Women in boardrooms: why they are still few https://www.monitor.co.ug/uganda/business/prosper/women-in-boardrooms-why-they-are-still-few-1810880. Accessed 19 Mar 2021

Deva S (2012) Regulating corporate human rights violations: humanizing business. Routledge

Equal Opportunities Commission, EOC launches NBFP and SBFP on Gender and Quity requirements FY 2019/2020 (2019a). https://www.eoc.go.ug/eoc-launches-nbfp-and-sbfp-gender-and-quity-requirements-fy-20192020/. Accessed 17 Feb 2021

Equal Opportunities Commission, Overview. <https://www.eoc.go.ug/about-eoc>. Accessed 20 Feb 2019b

Gieseler C (2019) The voices of #Me Too: from grassroots activism to a viral roar. Rowman & Littlefield

Green K (2020) Twice the work and half the support: COVID-19 and single working mothers: how can businesses help to reduce the pandemic's unequal burden on single mothers? https://www.openglobalrights.org/covid-19-and-single-working-mothers. Accessed 17 Mar 2021

Initiative for Social and Economic Rights (2019) Background paper for Uganda's National Action Plan on Business and Human Rights. https://iser-uganda.org/wp-content/uploads/2022/07/Background_paper_for_Ugandas_NAP_on_business_and_human_rights.pdf. Accessed 2 Apr 2021

Kampala City Council, GIC 2016 Thematic Areas. <https://www.kcca.go.ug/ptf-gic-evaluation-criteria>. Accessed 2 Apr 2021

Khisa I (2016) Poison at Dutch flower farm. https://www.independent.co.ug/poison-dutch-flower-farm/. Accessed 1 Apr 2021

Leeuwen F (2013) Women's Rights Are Human Rights!: The Practice of the United Nations Human Rights Committee and the Committee on Economic, Social and Cultural Rights. In: Hellum A, Aasen H (eds) Women's human rights: CEDAW in international, regional and national law. Cambridge University Press

Lyatuu J (2021) Women businesses need help to mitigate COVID-19 challenges. https://www.monitor.co.ug/uganda/business/finance/women-businesses-need-help-to-mitigate-covid-19-challenges%2D%2D3331120. Accessed 23 Mar 2021

Marston A (2014) Women, business and human rights: a background paper for the UN Working Group on Discrimination Against Women in Law and Practice. Marston Consulting
Martin L, Gammelgard N (2020) Why women's right to health and gender equality should be your business. https://www.openglobalrights.org/why-womens-right-to-health-and-gender-equality-should-be-your-business/. Accessed 12 Mar 2021
Meyersfeld B (2010) Domestic violence and international law. Hart Publishing
Meyersfeld B (2013) Business, human rights and gender: a legal approach to external and internal considerations. In: Deva S, Bilchitz D (eds) Human rights obligations of business: beyond the corporate responsibility to respect? Cambridge University Press
Ministry of Gender, Labour and Social Development. The National Policy on Elimination of Gender Based Violence in Uganda (August, 2016). <http://ngbvd.mglsd.go.ug/docs/2838GBV%20POLICY%2031st%2007%202019%20Final..pdf>. Accessed 15 Mar 2021
Mlynska A et al (2015) Thorns Amongst the Roses A Cross-country analysis of Human Rights Issues in Flower Farms in East Africa
MTN (2020) MTN Group commits to bridging the gender divide. https://www.mtn.com/mtn-group-commits-to-bridging-the-gender-divide/. Accessed 19 Mar 2021
Muchlinski P (2007) Multinational enterprises and the law, 2nd edn. Oxford University Press, Oxford
Mwesigwa A (2016) World Bank cancels funding for Uganda road amid sexual assault claims. https://www.theguardian.com/global-development/2016/jan/12/world-bank-cancels-uganda-road-sexual-assault-claims#:~:text=In%20an%20unusual%20step%2C%20the,staff%20working%20on%20the%20project. Accessed 17 Mar 2021
Nabukeera M (2020) Prevention and response to gender-based violence (GBV) during novel covid-19 lock-down in Uganda. J Adult Protect 23:116–133. https://doi.org/10.1108/jap-08-2020-0032
National Association of Professional Environmentalists (NAPE): Challenges of Salt Mining: An account of Katwe women salt miners, https://womin.africa/wp-content/uploads/2020/09/uganda-report.pdf. Accessed 20 Mar 2021
Nile Breweries (2019) Nile Special 'No Excuse' Campaign to highlight Sexual Harassment. https://www.nilebreweries.com/pledge-to-stand-against-sexual-harassment/#:~:text=The%2016%20days%2C%20designated%20by,sexual%20harassment%20in%20the%20country. Accessed 20 Mar 2021
Oxfam International, Improving safeguarding and culture at Oxfam. https://oi-files-d8-prod.s3.eu-west-2.amazonaws.com/s3fs-public/2020-12/Improving%20Safeguarding%20and%20Culture%20at%20Oxfam%20Report%20April%20-%20September%202020.pdf. Accessed 19 Mar 2021
Pauw M (2013) Women's rights: from bad to worse? Assessing the evolution of incompatible reservations to the CEDAW convention. Utrecht J Int Eur Law 29:51–65. https://doi.org/10.5334/ujiel.bw
Paz C (2020) Can corporations play a role in changing harmful social norms? https://www.openglobalrights.org/can-corporations-play-a-role-in-changing-harmful-social-norms/. Accessed 17 Mar 2021
Research Report, Women's Empowerment in Global Value Chains: A Framework for Business Action to Advance Women's Health, Rights and Wellbeing. https://www.bsr.org/reports/BSR-Report-Womens-Empowerment-Supply-Chains.pdf. Accessed 12 Feb 2021
Rivera H (2017) Negotiating a treaty on business and human rights: the early stages. Univ New South Wales Law J 40:1200. https://doi.org/10.53637/kqps5871
Ruggie J (2013) Just business: multinational corporations and human rights. W. W. Norton & Company
SIHA Network (2019) A move to formalise street trade in Kampala: #MakeHerVisible. https://sihanet.org/a-move-to-formalise-street-trade-in-kampala/. Accessed 17 Mar 2021

Söderberg P, Human rights violations at the work place aren't gender blind. So why are regulators? (2 April 2019). https://www.thegovernancepost.org/2019/04/un-human-rights-fails-gender-issues/. Accessed 10 Mar 2021

The National Gender Policy (Ministry of Gender, Labour and Social Development-Uganda, 1997). http://www.nzdl.org/cgi-bin/library.cgi?e=d-00000-00%2D%2D-off-0unescoen%2D%2D00-0%2D%2D%2D%2D0-10-0%2D%2D-0%2D%2D-0direct-10%2D%2D-4%2D%2D%2D%2D%2D%2D-0-11%2D%2D11-en-50%2D%2D-20-about%2D%2D-00-0-1-00-0-0-11-1-0utfZz-8-10&cl=CL1.7&d=HASH01880894b537b738a103f022.3&x=1. Accessed 13 Mar 2021

The World Bank (2015) World Bank Statement on Cancellation of the Uganda Transport Sector Development Project (TSDP). https://www.worldbank.org/en/news/press-release/2015/12/21/wb-statement-cancellation-uganda-transport-sector-development-project. Accessed 17 Mar 2021

Uganda Business News (2019) Stanbic Bank joins UNDP Gender Equality Seal Programme. https://ugbusiness.com/2019/08/company-releases/stanbic-bank-joins-undp-gender-equality-seal-programme#gref. Accessed 14 Mar 2021

Uganda Consortium on Corporate Accountability (2016) The State of Corporate Accountability in Uganda: A Baseline Study Report for the Uganda Consortium on Corporate Accountability. https://www.iser-uganda.org/images/downloads/16_09_21_UCCA_The_State_of_Corporate_Accountability_in_Uganda.pdf. Accessed 12 Mar 2021

UNDP (2023) UNDP Gender Equality Seal: Paving the Way for Gender Inclusivity in Uganda's Private Sector. https://www.undp.org/uganda/blog/undp-gender-equality-seal-paving-way-gender-inclusivity-ugandas-private-sector#:~:text=On%20August%2019%2C%202016%2C%20the,Seal%20(GES)%20Certification%20Programme. Accessed 12 Mar 2021

UNICEF, 7 ways employers can support working parents during the coronavirus disease (COVID-19) outbreak. https://www.unicef.org/azerbaijan/7-ways-employers-can-support-working-parents-during-coronavirus-disease-covid-19-outbreak. Accessed 17 Mar 2021

United Nations Human Rights: Office of the High Commissioner (2018) "#MeToo: 'A transformative movement, liberating and empowering'. https://www.ohchr.org/EN/NewsEvents/Pages/DisplayNews.aspx?NewsID=22767&LangID=E. Accessed 12 Mar 2021

UWEA in Collaboration with WWW (2011) Developing Strategies for Change for Workers in African horticulture -The case of Uganda. Available at: https://www.women-ww.org/_files/ugd/4111d6_48e2970f6c1d4ca2a1a5a9d8cf5c87c2.pdf, p 45. Accessed 17 Mar 2021

UWEAL Trade Information Point, Who we are. https://uweal.co.ug/#about-us Accessed 1 Apr 2021

Zimba Women, About us. https://www.zimbawomen.org/about-us. Accessed 12 Mar 2021

The Alliance of Digital Technologies and Business: Is There Room for Human Rights?

Yulia Razmetaeva

Abstract In the digital age, technologies are permeating our lives, but control over them is not in our hands. Companies, especially transnational corporations, including those in the legal field, are becoming increasingly influential players. Many digital tools, whose effects are global and unpredictable, belong to businesses and are developed primarily to allow companies to make profit. At the same time, unlike governments with direct human rights obligations, corporations have many more opportunities to act on the edge of law and ethics, or even beyond.

Manipulating our trust and attention, companies influence freedom of expression and diversity of opinions, as well as legitimate democratic processes. Using our data to profile and automate information processing, companies intervene in our privacy. The ever-increasing use of artificial intelligence in the provision of services contributes to algorithmic discrimination. Making consumers dependent on devices, applications, digital platforms and environments companies are widening the 'digital divide', which further distances us from achieving gender, social, political and other kinds of equality.

Digital technologies can potentially improve everyone's lives, promote justice, and help us better respond to global threats. However, in a world where private interests are placed above fundamental rights, the rally for information resources overshadows universal values, and politics has an upper hand over law, these technologies turn out to be dangerous tools. Is there still room for human rights in the fruitful alliance of business and digital technologies?

Y. Razmetaeva (✉)
Department of Human Rights and Legal Methodology, Yaroslav Mudryi National Law University, Kharkiv, Ukraine

Centre for Multidisciplinary Research on Religion and Society, Department of Theology, Uppsala University, Uppsala, Sweden

D. A. Pamplona et al. (eds.), *Business and Human Rights from the Lens of Women*, Interdisciplinary Studies in Human Rights 13,
https://doi.org/10.1007/978-3-032-04036-7_6

1 Introduction

In the digital age, we are in a situation where technology is permeating our lives, but control over it is not in our hands. Companies, especially transnational corporations, are becoming increasingly influential players today. This impact goes well beyond pure business interests and penetrates law-making, as well as decision-making. Moreover, in democracies this impact is even more prominent since democratic processes are slow and multi-staged, allowing businesses to abuse their digital potential even more visibly. Many digital tools, whose effects are global and unpredictable, are in private ownership and are developed primarily for profit. At the same time, unlike governments, most of which recognize direct human rights obligations, corporations have many more opportunities to act on the edge of law and ethics, or even beyond.

Digital technologies can potentially improve everyone's lives, promote justice, and help us better respond to global threats. However, in a world where private interests are placed above fundamental rights, where the rally for information resources overshadows universal values and politics has an upper hand over law, these technologies turn out to be very dangerous tools. Is there still room for human rights in the fruitful alliance of business and digital technologies? This article attempts to answer this question.

The first part of the article looks at companies as the main beneficiaries of digital technologies and their by-products, which are sometimes less obvious. A possibility of a more effective framework for corporate responsibility and business obligations in the field of human rights in the digital age is being considered. It also examines companies' attempts to take on the role of a normative regulator and gain, or even overtake, public trust.

The second part of the article makes assumptions about what conceptual changes are taking place in the sphere of human rights in the digital age, as well as the nature, extent and consequences of a number of threats to the rights associated with the merging of business activities and extensive use of digital technologies. Particular attention is paid to the risks to freedom of expression, privacy and non-discrimination in light of the increasing manipulation of trust, profiling and automated data processing, as well as the implementation and deployment of assisting algorithms and AI-based decision-making.

Part three focuses on the digital divide and how it is related to the deepening injustice. It looks at how companies are widening the digital gap, in particular virtually forcing many to buy new devices and use new applications. This part also contains speculation as to how better human rights protection today depends on digital literacy and uninterrupted Internet access.

Finally, part four seeks to show how businesses in the digital age exploit asymmetries of power. By referring to Kantian ethics, the tendency is shown of companies increasingly viewing technology users as instruments, which, perhaps, strikes at the central idea of human rights—the idea of human dignity.

The methodology of this study includes phenomenological and deontological approaches as a philosophical basis, as well as an analysis of literature focused on business and human rights issues in the digital era. It also includes an analysis of judicial decisions of national and international courts, which (1) reflect the trends of legal thought and prevailing legal doctrines in the digital age, and (2) reflect the reaction to gaps or conflicts in the legal regulation of the digital environment, as well as of activities that have an online component.

2 Companies as the Main Beneficiaries of Digital Technologies

Whether we take advantage of digital technologies or suffer the negative consequences of using them, there are actors who always seem to win. Technologies are developing rapidly and are already shaping the landscape of the modern world quite visibly. As the main creators, owners and promoters of digital technologies, business entities control their development to a significant extent.

It appears that in pursuit of the desired profit, some companies often disrespect both ethical and legal boundaries, attempting to obviate tight legal constraints by seeking more lenient jurisdictions and regimes. This is especially typical of the so-called gig economy, when companies claim that they merely put clients and service providers in touch, not being responsible for the parties' actions. Besides, more often than not, gig economy businesses feel entitled to special conditions as those that promote innovations in society. This is seen, for instance, in cases such as "Asociación Profesional Élite Taxi v. Uber Systems Spain" and "Uber France SAS v. Nabil Bensalem", in which the companies claimed that they should act under special regulation of their services as providing "Information Society services", while in fact providing "services in the field of transport".[1] These cases show how businesses seek to operate in the field of the most favorable legal regulation. This, of course, is not surprising—for centuries, entrepreneurship has been based on exploring "uncharted lands" while at the same time striving to ensure that the benefits outweigh the risks. On the one hand, Uber strives to come across as an innovative company, which should somehow justify a privileged regime for its activities, while on the other hand trying to escape responsibility for multiple violations of both passengers' and drivers' rights. Specifically, it refuses to bear responsibility when drivers abuse or harass passengers, fails to provide any employment protection to the drivers and automatically raises prices for passengers whose phones' batteries are running low. Overall, the picture is rather unsightly.

---

[1] See Asociación Profesional Élite Taxi v. Uber Systems Spain, SL, Case C-434/15, ECLI:EU:C:2017:981; Uber France SAS v. Nabil Bensalem (Criminal proceedings against Uber France), Case C–320/16, ECLI:EU:C:2018:221.

In the digital age, attempts to sell goods or impose services on the basis of the received data become more and more threatening. As was rightly noted, "when information about us is used to influence our decision-making, it does more than diminish our interests – it threatens our autonomy".[2] The sphere of our autonomy is already decreasing today. This is happening, in the first place, due to the fact that we are increasingly forced to rely on the opinions of others (opinion leaders, visible experts, estimates widely covered by the media), as processing the overwhelming amounts of information, fact-checking and assessing the data critically have become an enormous task. Another reason for the shrinking autonomy is that in a world almost devoid of privacy, it is becoming more and more difficult to preserve the space of individual freedom. Finally, autonomy is also threatened because of the targeted influence on us, which seeks to stimulate certain behaviors and is based on the fact that too much about us becomes known to an indefinite circle of people based on the array of the data that is collected and the digital footprints that we leave, voluntarily or involuntarily.

Not only do technologies make it possible for business to influence our choices,—they literally control our actions. Shoshana Zuboff writes about "behavior modification" as a phenomenon central to the functioning of the modern information economy.[3] The worst thing is that since the information economy is built on this modification, the beneficiaries of the digital technologies will strive to hold on to this model.

There is also perhaps a less visible benefit to companies stemming from the ubiquity of digital technology. Business is becoming the holder and driving force of the digital space, so the rules imposed on us go far beyond our Facebook account. In fact, companies create a regulatory framework that receives more social support than the law itself, becoming embodied and reproduced in habitual types of behavior by people themselves. Today, it is claimed, "digital platforms go beyond adding a digital layer to our personal, professional, and political relations: they also add a normative and legal layer, and shape new social contracts".[4]

By operating in the gray areas of law and ethics, and by setting agendas of their own, companies, it seems, get to avoid many restrictions. In particular, when using digital tools, they do not act with the same transparency and accountability as governments or civil society. Businesses also often manage to protect themselves from liability, referring to its belonging to the private sector, when in fact it obviously enters the public space. This is further exacerbated by the unclear distinction between private and public in the digital environment (which, for example, is clearly seen in relation to social networks).

Moreover, businesses seem to be seeking to capitalize on trust and even attention, which has in fact happened to the data, turning it into 'the new gold and oil'. Companies are probably primarily motivated by considerations of profit: it is a good

[2] Susser et al. (2019).

[3] Zuboff (2019).

[4] Shadmy (2019), p. 307.

idea to maintain a social reputation of a high standard in the digital world, where one small and quickly spreading message can seriously strike a giant corporation, and where it becomes more difficult to keep hidden information secret. Companies may not have a long-term plan, but they are taking advantage of the current situation. As a result, we are seeing the attitude to trust as such being transformed.

Marianna Vivitsou and Mohsen Saadatmand see trust as a dynamic process in which there are several participants and whose rules are revised as the established concept of privacy is violated.[5] According to Christopher W. Savage, "ambient trust is not a physical quantity whose extent is determined by objective facts".[6] In the digital age, we are probably (and perhaps unreasonably) giving our trust to companies, at the same time losing trust in governments. As a result, companies actually become actors that gain legitimacy, while governments lose legitimacy. De-legitimating government power can also be associated with undermining public trust in the governments' ability to protect individuals from the consequences of businesses activities. In particular, the weakening of democratic institutions in some countries may be partly due to social media campaigns influencing citizens' participation in electoral processes and their results (as, for example, shown in the Cambridge Analytica case).

Companies' uncontrolled activity and the growing power of business are not the only factors that lead to the violation of the social contract and redistributing legitimacy today. However, they are, perhaps, the most important causes. Such activity also contributes to the shift in the rights and interests of participants in public relations. Business activity in the digital era, besides, exposes the problems that have accumulated (for example, the vulnerability of workers in the gig economy or the deepening of the gender component of the technological divide). Furthermore, it contributes to the formation of such dangers that are mostly not immediately visible, such as the aforementioned narrowing of the scope of privacy, the lasting digital footprint, undermined autonomy, weakening democratic institutions, etc.

In light of the growing influence of business structures and their assuming the role of a public regulator, the thing that does not raise doubts is the need to strengthen the responsibility of companies, in particular by imposing more obligations in the field of human rights.

Over the past decade, a discussion has developed about businesses as human rights addressees, the standards that should be implemented as mandatory, the problems that all stakeholders face.[7] It is also in line with the trends in the discussion of corporate responsibility and business obligations in the digital age. The implementation of obligations based on due diligence,[8] responsibility of companies and incentives for their voluntary observance of human rights in new business conditions,[9] the

[5] Vivitsu and Saadatmand (2016).

[6] Savage (2019), p. 133.

[7] See Aaronson and Higham (2013); Ruggie (2013); Baumann-Pauly and Nolan (2016).

[8] Shackelford (2017).

[9] Ramasastry (2015).

adequacy of current regulatory framework regarding transnational corporations,[10] the provision of a binding business and human rights treaty,[11] the necessity of an international treaty for all business entities, or at least for transnational corporations, as well as other models of business obligations enforcement, are being actively discussed.

Whatever approach is chosen, problems are inevitable. There is no unified model of such obligations framework, both in the sense of a theoretical basis and regulatory support, and it's probably not realistic to expect to have one. It is also difficult to predict the nature and extent of the impact that a business has on human rights, as well as the degree of risk to people and communities. The long-term and indirect negative consequences are also unpredictable. Many companies and officials show resistance to the enforcement of certain human rights obligations.[12] It should be noted that not only is such resistance based on the desire to preserve the space for possible violations and corruption, but also, albeit partially, on the understanding that, given the global, cross-border nature of economic activity in today's world, the developed countries will bear the main burden of obligations. Even in discussions that come to a consensual view of the need for a commitment to business obligations and propose the creation of a relevant international document there are discrepancies as to which business entities should be covered. Two positions have been formed in this regard: imposing binding standards on transnational corporations only or imposing mandatory standards on all types of companies. Here, of course, it is important that thanks to digital technologies the influence of a company in the jurisdiction of one state can extend far beyond the borders of this state. It could be an additional argument in favor of imposing mandatory standards to all types of companies, regardless of their size, as well as of their organizational and legal form.

At the same time, a business can become not only an intruder, but also a human rights protector. Companies can implement innovative technological solutions, quick response protocols, simplified procedures, flexible policies, and productive interaction with consumers. Powerful corporations may demand that their counterparties, as well as public authorities, comply with higher standards, which will positively affect problematic national legal systems. Remarkably, bearing voluntary obligations and providing a high level of human rights protection can be beneficial to businesses, both directly and through competitive and reputational advantages. Modern companies may be interested in maintaining a steady level of user trust, reflected in the positive ratings and "social capital".[13] If a business wants to remain competitive and grow, its long-term interests include using a responsible and ethical approach based on human rights.

---

[10] Santoso (2017).

[11] Bilchitz (2016).

[12] See Grabosch and Scheper (2015), p. 19; Cassell and Ramasastry (2016), pp. 10, 33; Maslow (2019); Favotto and Kollman (2022).

[13] See, e.g., Lins et al. (2019); Del-Castillo-Feito et al. (2022); Rudito et al. (2023).

Brigitte Hamm writes about the struggle for legitimacy that has arisen in the process of shaping modern businesses' human rights obligations and has led to competing projects—voluntary, with broad participation of the parties, and obligatory, with the participation of states at the UN level.[14] Much hope has been tied to the voluntary framework of obligations such as the UN Guiding Principles on Business and Human Rights, Implementing the United Nations "Protect, Respect and Remedy" Framework,[15] but voices are increasingly being heard in support of more binding instruments. In particular, rather stringent obligations and extraterritorial action implies such legislation that returns control over data to users, focused on mechanisms for explicit consent, and obtaining explanations of exactly how companies operate.[16] However, harsher legislation is found in only a few jurisdictions, perhaps those with strongest traditions of respect for individual rights and channels of government accountability.

It is not yet clear what the new global international treaty will look like, and what mechanism—with direct companies' obligations or mediated through governments—will be deployed. At the same time, the changes taking place in the understanding of human rights and the need for their careful balancing and protection against new threats are becoming more evident.

3 What Is Happening to Human Rights Today?

There's an ongoing debate as to the need to expand the concept of human rights to include new rights and increase the scope of established ones,[17] while making a shift towards a more horizontal dimension of rights.[18] While these changes are seen by many as necessary, concerns are also expressed that they may dilute the concept of human rights, lending it false content and ultimately making it ineffective.[19]

As per Tomer Shadmy, "some of the significant legal and moral problems we face today stem from the incompatibility of the modern, state-centric conception of rights to our current transnational, privatized, hyper-connected reality".[20] As Onora O'Neill rightly notes, in recent years, the statist Western notion of rights that has guided, shaped, and justified modern institutions and practices is losing its

[14] Hamm (2022).

[15] Guiding Principles on Business and Human Rights: Implementing the United Nations "Protect, Respect and Remedy". Framework, Annex, U. N. Doc. A/HRC/17/31 (Mar. 21, 2011).

[16] See more Regulation (EU) 2016/679 of the European Parliament and of the Council of 27 April 2016 on the protection of natural persons with regard to the processing of personal data and on the free movement of such data, and repealing Directive 95/46/EC (General Data Protection Regulation) (OJ L 119, 4.5.2016, pp. 1–88).

[17] See Stohl and Stohl (2017); Razmetaeva (2020); Favotto and Kollman (2022).

[18] Knox (2008).

[19] Hannum (2016).

[20] Shadmy (2019), p. 353.

descriptive, normative, and even aspirational power.[21] Attempts to resolve this contradiction and at the same time leave human rights at the basis of the social contract include revising the nature of obligations arising from rights towards a horizontal concept, when not only states, but also individuals, companies, and organizations themselves become their addressees. Such attempts include, in addition, revising approaches to justifying rights.

Particularly, it is proposed to discard the "moral" approach, according to which human rights are considered "as antecedently existing basic moral rights" in favor of the "institutional" approach, which "starts with contemporary human rights practice in which human rights refer to rights enumerated in the Universal Declaration of Human Rights and subsequent international documents, and in which states are the primary duty bearers of human rights".[22] According to this approach, if companies are held accountable for human rights, they should not be placed on a par with states. Although it cannot be argued that companies do not have responsibilities as such, these should be relationships mediated by government institutions, and not direct obligations, in particular, because business lacks mechanisms for responsibility, accountability, power balancing, etc. As can be seen in the case of transnational corporations, if we impose corresponding obligations on them, "we attribute to them a kind of authority that is usually reserved for political and legal institutions".[23]

This approach echoes doubts that companies can bear direct human rights obligations at all, at least without a major reshaping of familiar social structures. That said, certain transformations have already been going on for some time. The restructuring is linked to the threats to human rights in the digital age. While it cannot be said that we have been overlooking threats altogether, we still seem to be underestimating their scale. Above all, under attack are fundamental rights—privacy and freedom of expression—which are the key to securing many other human rights. Serious and poorly tracked threats undermine the right to non-discrimination, or—in the understanding of the Convention for the Protection of Human Rights and Fundamental Freedoms—the prohibition of discrimination, which is the basis for the protection of other individual rights.

There are a number of decisions of the European Court of Human Rights that deal with various violations of fundamental rights related to digital technologies as such, as well as utilizing them in companies' activity. These decisions often contain important positions about the scope of these rights and the legitimate expectations of individuals. For example, in a well known case a company fired an employee as a result of tracking his email messages and accessing his content; however, the employee had not been informed of the nature or extent of the surveillance or the degree of intrusion into his privacy and correspondence[24] or of violation of privacy

[21] O'Neill (2016), p. 6, 164.

[22] Hsieh (2017), p. 297.

[23] Hsieh (2017), p. 307.

[24] See Bărbulescu v România [2017] ECHR 742.

by broadcasting the unblurred applicant's image.[25] There have been a number of precedents that show how the scope of the freedom of expression has changed. For example, the court found that YouTube, as the only platform that provides information of specific interest, particularly on political and social matters, helps to ensure freedom of expression.[26] The importance of hyperlinking for the smooth operation of the Internet was highlighted in Magyar Jeti Zrt v. Hungary.[27] Additionally, the provision by a political party of an app to vote was considered an exercise of its freedom of expression in Magyar Kétfarkú Kutya Párt v. Hungary.[28] A number of decisions relate to those actors, including companies, which allegedly only provide platforms for commenting on the Internet and try to avoid the responsibility inherent in "publishers".[29] This is only a small part of the cases related to the use of new technologies, but they all show the immensity of the task of keeping fundamental rights intact and the difficulty of reaching a common understanding of the rights by different subjects of legal relations in the digital era.

New threats to human rights are emerging from the rise of profiling and automation of data processing, as well as the introduction and deployment of assistive algorithms and AI-based decision-making. In particular, by increasing the share of artificial intelligence in services, companies are not always complying with the due diligence or diversity principles. Moreover, discriminatory practices become increasingly difficult to track down.

For example, the landmark lawsuit "State v. Loomis" on the application of an algorithm to assess risk in sentencing[30] shows that developers are not inclined to reveal all the secrets of what lies at the heart of decisions based on artificial intelligence. In addition, due to deliberate or unconscious underestimation of the possible consequences, business structures often fail to appreciate the genie that is being released (or may be released) out of the bottle.

Importantly, many of the new threats to human rights are hidden, and the negative consequences of many companies' activities can have an effect far delayed in time. This complicates the digital risk assessment. For example, manipulating trust may lead to the prevalence of certain opinions as leading in the digital space. Then spreading and extensive promotion of certain opinions through digital tools affects freedom of expression because at some point it becomes difficult to separate imposed views from one's own opinions or because certain opinions become almost unquestionable. Another example of delayed consequences is people becoming secluded inside their 'filter bubbles'. This, in turn, promotes polarization, as

---

[25] See Bremner v. Turkey [2015] ECHR 877.

[26] See Cengiz and Others v. Turkey 8226/10 (Judgment (Merits and Just Satisfaction): Court (Second Section) French Text, [2015] ECHR 1052.

[27] See Magyar Jeti Zrt v. Hungary 11257/16, [2018] ECHR 990.

[28] See Magyar Kétfarkú Kutya Párt v. Hungary App no 201/17 (ECtHR, 21 January 2020).

[29] See Delfi AS v. Estonia 64569/09 – Grand Chamber Judgment, [2015] ECHR 586; Magyar Tartalomszolgáltatók Egyesülete and Index.hu Zrt v. Hungary 201/17 – 22947/13 (Judgment (Merits and Just Satisfaction): Court (Fourth Section)) [2016] ECHR 135.

[30] See State v. Loomis, 881 N.W.2d 749 (2016).

differing views become more difficult to accept, and certain opinions get excluded from discourse altogether. As a result, the diversity of opinions may be significantly reduced and the legitimacy of democratic processes may be affected.

All these threats are also constantly evolving in unpredictable ways, because the development of digital tools is not happening according to a unified plan. In a sense, they open the door to other dangers and other problems, the consequences of which can be irreparable.

That being said, certain additional complications arise from the need for a complex balancing of rights, as well as a balance of rights and legitimate interests. First of all, we are talking about conflicts of classical fundamental rights, which acquire a new meaning due to changes in the scope of these rights. For example, the balance of freedom of expression and privacy can shift due to the undefined status of statements made in social media (when it is unclear whether the author is a public or private figure, whether the account is official or non-official, etc.). Further complicating the issue is the fact that different privacy plans may be attached to the post ('for the general public' or 'friends only'), as well as a lack of clarity as to whether the author of the statement is a particular public person or an SMM manager. In addition, those rights that are only starting to acquire the status of fundamental in the digital era may come into conflict with the established, 'classical' ones. For example, the clash of the individual's right to be forgotten with the society's right to know (or the public interest in freedom of information) can be hard to resolve because the former is not recognized as a human right in all jurisdictions.

Finally, a dangerous devaluation of the ethical core of human rights as the foundation of our societies can be observed. According to John Tasioulas, who writes about a schism that can be recently observed between the universal human interests or values and the proper judicialization of human rights: "Human rights laws and institutions, after all, are not themselves to be identified with sound human rights morality. They are not the deliverances of perfectly operating reason. To conceive of them in this way is a kind of idolatry, one that confuses man-made institutional means with objective ethical end".[31]

This tendency may lead us to disconnecting the ideal human rights concept from its institutional and practical implementation, the latter being inevitably complicated and even distorted by human imperfection. However, this does not mean that we must accept the possible loss of the central idea of rights. The erosion of the idea of human rights, their inner ethical sense, is something that is possibly happening in the digital age, largely due to businesses being actively promoting reckless digitalization. A significant part of business activity widens the digital divide, contributing to the asymmetry of power and the instrumentalization of users.

[31] Tasioulas (2019), p. 1172.

4 The Digital Divide and Deepening Injustice

The digital divide could be generally defined as inequality in access and use of digital technologies, which deepens general inequality and injustice. Previous research into the digital divide has mainly focused on unequal access to digital technologies, as well as disproportionate opportunities for their use, stemming from a lack of education and skills, as well as learning difficulties prevailing in certain groups of people. A third dimension has been recently added to the discussion, namely—inequality in terms of benefits obtained by those who use digital tools. According to Massimo Ragnedda, the third level of digital divide describes benefits obtained from the previous two and the ability to exploit these benefits in a digital tech-driven market to improve one's life chances.[32] It is businesses that are most often the beneficiaries of the chances, as in many instances they are developers, owners, and active promoters of the technologies. On many occasions, companies are also actors that accumulate the different possibilities of digital technologies, test various options and discover their new facets. Thus, businesses have little if any incentive to try and eliminate the third dimension of the divide.

Besides, a race for the benefits provided by today's digital technologies leads to their unthoughtful development and deployment. Companies may come to market products that are insufficiently researched in terms of their potential delayed and non-obvious harms. As evidenced by the example of large-scale linguistic artificial intelligence models, an explosive mixture can be obtained from seemingly harmless ingredients.

Let's look at the example of big data—a phenomenon characterized by (1) the tremendous amount of data collected, (2) the phenomenal speed at which they are obtained and analyzed.[33] Considering such criteria as timeliness, completeness, and accuracy in connection with big data analytics, it is indicated that the speed of their provision and processing is rocketing, while their origin and structure are changing.[34] All this opacifies the understanding of big data, but their profound impact on privacy issues, including threats that are unpreventable as of today, is undeniable. Undoubtedly, big data can improve private and public life, but at the same time it leads to significant implications for people and groups who are deprived of opportunities to exercise control over big data processing and utilization—the kind of checks and balances that exist in other spheres. In particular, the use of big data leads to a growing reliance on algorithms for their analysis and subsequent decision-taking, and the gradual reduction of human oversight over many automatic processes,[35] actual deanonymization since sensitive user data can be obtained statistically,[36] doubtful consent in case of data reuse, intrusions in privacy, even

[32] Ragnedda (2017), p. 5.

[33] Schaefer (2019).

[34] Wanner and Janiesch (2019).

[35] Mittelstadt (2019).

[36] Vivitsu and Saadatmand (2016).

without the use of personal data, etc. Are companies willing to eventually move away from big data, or at least be more cautious about them? This seems unlikely. On the contrary, the deployment of solutions based on such data has become so ubiquitous (for example, in the fields of transportation or health) that if you pull this beam out of the frame, the entire edifice risks collapsing.

With regard to the digital divide Duncan Campbell wrote:

> Finally, technology transfer is one aspect of the divide which has distinct policy implications. The ubiquity of information is a defining feature of the digital era yet, ironically, technological development in the post-Cold War era has been increasingly dominated by the private sector, rather than by public sector expenditure on research and development. Thus, on the one hand, access to information for application to economic and social ends has never been easier. On the other, the core knowledge permitting technological advance is in the hands – or rather the heads – of major private enterprises.[37]

Twenty years later, these claims still hold true. Moreover, companies are widening the digital divide, urging the use of certain technological solutions in the private and public spheres, as well as virtually forcing consumers to purchase new devices and use new applications. This is only partly due to aggressive marketing as the supply in this case meets the demand. However, once installed, an app will keep calling for multiple updates, restricting the access to your data should you refuse to install those or threatening that the system will malfunction unless updated. Although this is a kind of subtle manipulation rather than gross coercion, it still remains dubious in terms of freedom of choice.

The COVID-19 pandemic is a good example of the difference between forced and voluntary decisions. Many talk about increasing inequality and pressures due to the pandemic, when "the status of digital spaces is switching from an amenity to a necessity".[38] What's more, the leap forward in digital technology has led to persistent behaviors associated with the many transitioning online, and this is not something that is going to disappear anytime soon. As rightly pointed out, "many aspects of life remain significantly altered and will remain heavily reliant on the Internet for some time to come, due to social distancing".[39] In addition, the pandemic has in a sense highlighted the fact that even the first wave (or dimension) of the digital divide has yet to be dealt with. As Najeh Aissaoui writes, "the current crisis has shown that the access divide still requires attention from researchers and policymakers".[40]

Discussing the drastic transition to telehealth-based care, Anita Ramsetty and Cristin Adams write that "those whose access was impeded were the most vulnerable to poor health outcomes related to COVID-19".[41] Similar problems with the vulnerability of individuals and groups were observed in the field of education, which in many countries had moved to the online format. In particular, it is

[37] Campbell (2001), p. 124.

[38] Beaunoyer et al. (2020).

[39] Lai and Widmar (2021), p. 458.

[40] Aissaoui (2021).

[41] Ramsetty and Adams (2020), p. 1147.

emphasized that the burden of educating children, especially those with special educational needs, was "placed on family members".[42] It also highlighted the relationship between socioeconomic status and the digital divide in access to distance learning.[43] Regarding digital health services, digital tracking and tracing systems during the COVID-19 pandemic, Mariarosaria Taddeo wrote: "big parts of the population (20% of the whole population in the UK, 32.1% of the Italian population, and 24% over the Eurozone) are likely to be excluded from these services […] The same percentage of the population is also excluded from digital services that support education, professional opportunities, and social interactions.[44]

The pandemic had definitely deepened the digital divide, already noticeably deepened by business activity. Moreover, effective protection of human rights became in many ways a privilege available to those who have access to digital tools and the skills to use them, as well as stable access to the Internet. Even though the pandemic is over, certain effects of it have lingered, for example the effect of deepening educational inequalities.[45]

One piece of research "showed that what people do online and the skills they have affect outcomes in other domains and that this is independent of the characteristics of the person".[46] Digital skills and access to digital technologies help us advance in other areas, but it is often a privilege that goes unnoticed. Moreover, many important features are already designed by default in such a way that they require a certain level of technological standards (like, for instance, a high-speed broadband connection) as well as digital skills needed (like, registering an account through complex multi-step procedures, dealing with complicated online forms, processing different file formats, etc).

You may have noticed how sometimes, in hindsight, we are surprised at how dramatically the baseline has changed, and at what we have come to take for granted by default. This often concerns improvements in psychological, material, or social well-being. For example, our children often have what we only dreamt of. What used to be a breakthrough verging on a miracle has become a new norm. But at the same time, perhaps unnoticeably, a new level of restrictions are becoming a new norm—restrictions unseen before, caused and enhanced by the ever-advancing technologies.

Being unbothered by a possibility that our digital activity or bits of private communication may end up on other people's screens was the norm before the mass equipping of public spaces with video surveillance cameras and the mass ownership of smartphones. Nowadays, the level of privacy that had existed before the digital era is not expected in many places anymore (and it is now much easier for ordinary people, not only for celebrities hunted by paparazzi's cameras, to become

[42] Petretto et al. (2020), p. 154.

[43] Azubuike et al. (2021).

[44] Taddeo (2020), p. 173.

[45] See Cheshmehzangi et al. (2023); Golden et al. (2023).

[46] Van Deursen and Helsper (2018), p. 2333.

involuntary heroes of memes than thirty years ago). There is probably no denying the sad truth: privacy as we used to know it is lost and there are no more places left where you can feel like an owner of a quiet haven of individual freedom.

The new reality, permeated by digital technologies, can offer opportunities for the protection of human rights that would have been difficult even to imagine a few decades ago. Yet it also creates a level of risk and a depth of inequality that are extremely difficult to overcome.

5 Business, Asymmetry of Power and Instrumentalization

One of the crucial risks is the 'asymmetry of power', which by itself does not always pose danger. However, in the digital era, business can be assumed to be acquiring excessive power, not balanced by any checks and balances. This asymmetry appears to have several manifestations: the asymmetry of knowledge, the asymmetry of control, imbalance of rights and obligations, imbalance of responsibility and, ultimately, the asymmetry of impact.

The power of companies in the digital age is based on knowledge asymmetries. First and foremost, companies often do not disclose either the source code of the algorithms, or the methods they use to process data, or even the details of the settings of the devices and software they sell. The convenience of appealing to trade secrets is pretty obvious here. Secondly, digital technologies are used by many, but few have any understanding of how they work. Thirdly, the skew arises from the accumulation of a huge amount of data in the hands of business structures.

The asymmetry of control is reflected, above all, in the loss of public oversight over companies' compliance with the terms of the social contract. For example, although data, which has become extremely important as a means of influence and an economic resource, is largely produced by people or their activities, people themselves have less and less control over it, while either providing their personal data voluntarily (but still not on the basis of a complete and permanent waiver of the relevant rights), or facing them being collected and processed without explicit consent.

The imbalance of rights and obligations is reflected in the fact that today neither governments, nor individuals united in civil society organizations or the citizens of individual states can exercise full supervision over their observance. Some of the instruments that were concentrated in the hands of institutions and movements of civil society, making it possible to maintain a fair balance, accountability and responsibility, are losing their effectiveness. Moreover, they can be turned against those who use them. In particular, with the example of the Facebook platform, Tomer Shadmy shows how users are regulated and constrained on a daily basis by a system whose decision-making processes are not transparent and not open to any dialogue, argumentation, or interpretation; the execution of decisions in this system is immediate and automatic; rights transform from a product of discourse and the practice of interpretation to a result of the practice of structured coding.[47] Another example would be the use of instant voting on issues of public interest, which is carried out through mobile and stationary devices with visualization and rapid dissemination of results. These results can be presented in a way that helps to sway public opinion in the direction that corporations-owners of digital tools or their customers desire, or even orchestrate public opinion.

The asymmetry in responsibility, already mentioned above, stems from poorly controlled and highly protected from influences and intrusions activities of companies. Being part of the private sector, businesses expect to not be interfered with in the same way as civil society institutions expect to be free from intrusion. Operating in the free market and often lacking rigid regulatory or ethical boundaries, companies gain an unfair advantage over other parties to the social contract. All this gives businesses the opportunity to maximize their benefits for instance, by aggressive use of digital technologies in favor of companies' interests, while minimizing responsibility.

Furthermore, in relation to users, companies are often not equal counterparts. In fact, they create power relationships that are more complex than, for example, boss-subordinate or government-citizen relationships. Companies seem to instrumentalize users.[48] The use of people as instruments, in turn, can strike at the central idea of human rights—the idea of human dignity.

Bearing in mind the universal, non-instrumental principles of interaction, one should turn to the second formulation of the categorical imperative, which reads: "So act that you use humanity, whether in your own person or in the person of any other, always at the same time as an end, never merely as a means".[49] To treat people as a *means*, and not as an *end-in-itself*, means, among other things, to deny people recognition of their value.

Our dependence on digital technology is increasing. Besides, we may be using them to build a significant part of both wealth and expectations, especially in those societies that Luciano Floridi calls "mature information societies".[50] Inevitably, those in possession of the keys to technology gain disproportionate mightiness and may also fail the proverbial test of power, being tempted to abandon non-instrumental principles of interaction.

As it was discussed above, opinions differ as to whether the responsibilities in terms of human rights obligations are to be the same for transnational companies and other businesses, or whether the former should be imposed stricter regulations in order to harness their immense power and disproportionate potential. By the same token, the question arises as to whether the tendency to treat users as tools is pertinent to all types of businesses, or more characteristic of big tech corporations.

---

[47] Shadmy (2019), p. 352.

[48] Hereinafter, I mean "users" in a broad sense, not just those who buy digital technologies from companies. Potentially, the company's efforts are aimed at everyone to whom the business wants to sell any goods and services. Very often today this happens using a variety of digital tools.

[49] Kant (1997 [1785]), p. 38.

[50] Floridi (2016), p. 4.

Even though the difference between large, medium and small companies who possess digital tools is gradually fading away and the dangerous trend of instrumentalization is now seen in many businesses' activity, it seems that tech giants are probably 'setting the tone' for treating users as means. For example, such corporations use users' data they collected "to rank and segment individuals, and then sell those inferences to others or use them to develop new products and service".[51]

Finally, all this is reflected in the asymmetry of impact that is observed in many societies. In the first place, the margin of freedom in the digital space is narrowing as the digital environment is owned or controlled by corporations to an increasing extent. Although we can still see common citizens, without any institutional support, become opinion leaders in social networks, using the opportunities of freedom of expression, gaining popularity through their own web pages or online platforms, which are relatively affordable, making themselves visible to the public is becoming increasingly difficult at least due to the algorithms of digital platforms controlled by corporations. The fact that companies are accumulating technologies, gaining control over information channels, and promoting certain ways of interaction, endows businesses with unprecedented capabilities to maximize their impact. This means that companies that own popular digital tools, software, social media, search engines, and apps have been gaining a range of leverage over individuals, communities and governments.

This correlates with the weakening of state institutions and democratic regimes as such, the rise of populism,[52] and the emergence of radical and polarized opinions[53] coupled with the informational fatigue entailing weakened critical thinking and growing mistrust of public institutions. All this presents even more serious problems for countries that are already characterized by weak democratic institutions, were or have been under the long-term influence of authoritarian and totalitarian regimes.

This trend of the relevant structures weakening and, probably, their failure to ensure the promotion and protection of rights, also makes us consider the possibility of businesses being the party that will actively participate in the process of fulfilling the conditions of the social contract. Discussing human rights protection gaps, Lottie Lane writes that "either the international human rights framework will have to evolve to cover certain non-State actors, or ways of protecting individuals outside of the confines of the legal framework will have to be strengthened".[54]

Potentially, companies can offer their own ways of protecting human rights, which are more effective and efficient than the classical judicial and non-judicial mechanisms, such as instantly banning users spreading hatred in social networks. However, it is in the company's owners' discretion to set criteria for hate speech and

[51] Birch and Cochrane (2021), p. 51.

[52] See, e. g., Van Leeuwen and Halleck-Vega (2021); Rodríguez-Pose et al. (2021); Fortunato and Pecoraro (2022); Mutascu et al. (2025).

[53] See, e.g., Scrivens (2020); Maniou and Bantimaroudis (2021); Bettarelli and Van Haute (2022).

[54] Lane (2018), p. 82.

impose overall censorship schemes, which does not look like promoting the freedom of expression or supporting the social contract as such as the users never willingly entrusted the companies with such regulatory power. Moreover, entrusting certain actors with regulatory power should normally be accompanied by demanding accountability and transparency. In other words, when we entrust human rights standards setting to governments we do this through democratic procedures and with proper checks and balances.

Public trust associated with legitimacy, as discussed above, and individual trust, which appears to be associated with autonomy and, especially, free choice, are gaining importance in the digital age. In terms of individual trust, many of us seem to behave in a rather paradoxical way. On the one hand, we are truly concerned about the power that tech corporations possess and the intrusions that many companies make into our lives on a daily basis. On the other hand, we continue to use software and devices, search engines, smart watches and maps, many of us regarding those as an integral part of our daily routine. In this behavior, however, we perhaps show signs of merely following almost invisible nudges from businesses. Besides, we are not sufficiently protected from the excessive power companies have in the digital age, not least due to governments' apparent neglect of the growing danger.

When during the pandemic Apple and Google agreed to collaborate to create a shared application programming interface, it entailed the growing adherence of governments to the coincident decentralized protocol,—thus, "a decision driven by online service providers will shape the way in which public authorities may design and use their apps and the extent to which these will respect the privacy of their citizens".[55] It seems that companies can already determine not only the future of the digital world, but of the world in general. So there is no exaggeration in seeing a rather bleak picture of what will happen if we do not act now.

6 Conclusions

Is there room for human rights in the ever-expanding realm of threats? We can cautiously assume that there is, as long as we manage to preserve the core ethical underpinning of these rights without neglecting the major changes that the concept of human rights has already undergone. The social contract may need to be revised to include business as a party into the contract. By significantly increasing the responsibility of companies and at the same time strengthening the guarantees for individuals to have control over their lives, a better balance could be achieved. In addition, we may have to come to terms with the fact that no protection system, even the most sophisticated one, will provide sufficient safeguard from all latent threats and their non-obvious consequences in the digital age.

[55] Taddeo (2020), p. 174.

The greatest danger, perhaps, lies in the poorly monitored gradual erosion of the idea of human rights, and in the first place, in the devaluation of human dignity and a failure to perceive everyone as an end-in-itself, and not as a means. The critical changes in public trust and the resulting legitimacy problems open up a wide field for manipulation. A loss of individual trust and a shrinking sphere of autonomy also do not add optimism as to the consequences of businesses' activity.

All these should be the subject of further research, which can be focused on possible ways to overcome the asymmetry of power while preserving the core concept of human rights, and on the consequences of companies' intrusion into the public realm, *de facto* playing the role of normative regulators.

References

Aaronson SA, Higham I (2013) Re-righting business: John Ruggie and the struggle to develop international human rights standards for transnational firms. Hum Rights Q 35(2):333–364

Aissaoui N (2021) The digital divide: a literature review and some directions for future research in light of COVID-19. Global Knowl Mem Commun 71(8/9):686–708. https://doi.org/10.1108/GKMC-06-2020-0075

Azubuike OB, Adegboye O, Quadri H (2021) Who gets to learn in a pandemic? Exploring the digital divide in remote learning during the COVID-19 pandemic in Nigeria. International Journal of Educational Research Open 2: 100022. https://doi.org/10.1016/j.ijedro.2020.100022

Baumann-Pauly D, Nolan J (eds) (2016) Business and human rights. From principles to practice. Routledge

Beaunoyer E, Dupéré S, Guitton MJ (2020) COVID-19 and digital inequalities: reciprocal impacts and mitigation strategies. Comput Hum Behav 111:106424. https://doi.org/10.1016/j.chb.2020.106424

Bettarelli L, Van Haute E (2022) Regional inequalities as drivers of affective polarization. Reg Stud Reg Sci 9(1):549–570. https://doi.org/10.1080/21681376.2022.2117077

Bilchitz D (2016) The necessity for a business and human rights treaty. Bus Hum Rights J 1(2):203–227. https://doi.org/10.1017/bhj.2016.13

Birch K, Cochrane DT (2021) Big Tech: four emerging forms of digital rentiership. Sci Cult 31(1):44–58. https://doi.org/10.1080/09505431.2021.1932794

Campbell D (2001) Can the digital divide be contained? Int Labour Rev 140(2):119–141

Cassell D, Ramasastry A (2016) White Paper: options for a treaty on business and human rights. Notre Dame J Int Comp Law 6(1:4):1–60

Cheshmehzangi A, Zou T, Su Z, Tang T (2023) The growing digital divide in education among primary and secondary children during the COVID-19 pandemic: an overview of social exclusion and education equality issues. J Hum Behav Soc Environ 33(3):434–449. https://doi.org/10.1080/10911359.2022.2062515

Del-Castillo-Feito C, Blanco-González A, Díez-Martín F, Cachón-Rodríguez G (2022) Social capital and organizational legitimacy as competitive advantages in the information and communications technology sector. J High Technol Manag Res 33(2):100441. https://doi.org/10.1016/j.hitech.2022.100441

Favotto A, Kollman K (2022) When rights enter the CSR field: British firms' engagement with human rights and the UN Guiding Principles. Hum Rights Rev 23:21–40. https://doi.org/10.1007/s12142-020-00614-w

Floridi L (2016) Mature information societies—a matter of expectations. Philos Technol 29:1–4. https://doi.org/10.1007/s13347-016-0214-6

Fortunato P, Pecoraro M (2022) Social media, education, and the rise of populist Euroscepticism. Humanit Soc Sci Commun 9:301. https://doi.org/10.1057/s41599-022-01317-y

Golden AR, Srisarajivakul EN, Hasselle AJ, Pfund RA, Knox J (2023) What was a gap is now a chasm: remote schooling, the digital divide, and educational inequities resulting from the COVID-19 pandemic. Curr Opin Psychol 52:101632. https://doi.org/10.1016/j.copsyc.2023.101632

Grabosch R, Scheper C (2015) Corporate obligations with regard to human rights due diligence policy and legal approaches. Friedrich-Ebert-Stiftung. Global Policy and Development Hiroshimastr. Berlin

Hamm B (2022) The struggle for legitimacy in business and human rights regulation—a consideration of the processes leading to the UN Guiding Principles and an international treaty. Hum Rights Rev 23:103–125. https://doi.org/10.1007/s12142-020-00612-y

Hannum H (2016) Reinvigorating human rights for the twenty-first century. Hum Rights Law Rev 16(3):409–451. https://doi.org/10.1093/hrlr/ngw015

Hsieh N (2017) Business responsibilities for human rights: a commentary on Arnold. Bus Hum Rights J 2:297–309. https://doi.org/10.1017/bhj.2017.6

Kant I (1997 [1785]) Groundwork of the Metaphysics of Morals (tr. and ed. by M. Gregor). Cambridge University Press, Cambridge

Knox JH (2008) Horizontal human rights law. Am J Int Law 102(1):1–47

Lai J, Widmar NO (2021) Revisiting the digital divide in the COVID-19 era. Appl Econ Perspect Policy 43(1):458–464. https://doi.org/10.1002/aepp.13104

Lane L (2018) The horizontal effect of international human rights law in practice. A comparative analysis of the general comments and jurisprudence of selected United Nations Human Rights Treaty Monitoring Bodies. Eur J Comp Law Gov 5(1):5–88

Lins KV, Servaes H, Tamayo A (2019) Social capital, trust, and corporate performance: how CSR helped companies during the financial crisis (and why it can keep helping them). J Appl Corp Finance 31(2):59–71. https://doi.org/10.1111/jacf.12347

Maniou TA, Bantimaroudis P (2021) Hybrid salience: examining the role of traditional and digital media in the rise of the Greek radical left. Journalism 22(4):1127–1144. https://doi.org/10.1177/1464884918796587

Maslow SA (2019) Business and ethical challenges: human rights requirements, due diligence, remediation, and brand protection. Business Regulation & Regulated Industries. November 4, 2019. Available at: https://businesslawtoday.org/2019/11/business-ethical-challenges-human-rights-requirements-due-diligence-remediation-brand-protection/. Accessed 10 June 2024

Mittelstadt B (2019) The ethics of biomedical 'big data' analytics. Philos Technol 32:17–21. https://doi.org/10.1007/s13347-019-00344-z

Mutascu M, Strango C, Turcu C (2025) Online social media and populism in Europe. Eur J Polit Econ 86:102619. https://doi.org/10.1016/j.ejpoleco.2024.102619

O'Neill O (2016) Justice across boundaries: whose obligations? Cambridge University Press, Cambridge

Petretto DR, Masala I, Masala C (2020) Special educational needs, distance learning, inclusion and COVID-19. Educ Sci 10(6):154–155. https://doi.org/10.3390/educsci10060154

Ragnedda M (2017) The third digital divide: a Weberian approach to digital inequalities. Routledge, Taylor & Francis Group, London; New York

Ramasastry A (2015) Corporate social responsibility versus business and human rights: bridging the gap between responsibility and accountability. J Hum Rights 14(2):237–259

Ramsetty A, Adams C (2020) Impact of the digital divide in the age of COVID-19. J Am Med Inf Assoc 27(7):1147–1148. https://doi.org/10.1093/jamia/ocaa078

Razmetaeva Y (2020) The right to be forgotten in the European perspective. TalTech J Eur Stud 10(1):58–76. https://doi.org/10.1515/bjes-2020-0004

Rodríguez-Pose A, Lee N, Lipp C (2021) Golfing with Trump. Social capital, decline, inequality, and the rise of populism in the US. Camb J Reg Econ Soc 14(3):457–481. https://doi.org/10.1093/cjres/rsab026

Rudito B, Famiola M, Anggahegari P (2023) Corporate social responsibility and social capital: journey of community engagement toward community empowerment program in developing country. Sustainability 15(1):466. https://doi.org/10.3390/su15010466
Ruggie JG (2013) Just business. Multinational corporations and human rights. Amnesty International Global Ethics Series. W.W. Norton & Company, New York
Santoso B (2017) "Just business" – is the current regulatory framework an adequate solution to human rights abuses by transnational corporations? German Law J 18(3):533–558. https://doi.org/10.1017/S2071832200022057
Savage CW (2019) Managing the ambient trust commons: the economics of online consumer information privacy. Stanford Technol Law Rev 22(1):95–162
Schaefer GO (2019) Ethics in the era of big data. Asian Bioethics Rev 11:169–171. https://doi.org/10.1007/s41649-019-00092-4
Scrivens R (2020) Exploring radical right-wing posting behaviors online. Deviant Behav 42(11):1470–1484. https://doi.org/10.1080/01639625.2020.1756391
Shackelford SJ (2017) Human rights and cybersecurity due diligence: a comparative study. Univ Mich J Law Reform 50(4):859–885
Shadmy T (2019) The new social contract: Facebook's community and our rights. Boston Univ Int Law J 37:307–354
Stohl M, Stohl C (2017) Human rights and corporate social responsibility. In: Brysk A, Stohl M (eds) Expanding human rights. Edward Elgar Publishing, Cheltenham, pp 115–136. https://doi.org/10.4337/9781785368844.00017
Susser D, Roessler B, Nissenbaum H (2019) Technology, autonomy, and manipulation. Internet Policy Rev 8(2). https://doi.org/10.14763/2019.2.1410
Taddeo M (2020) The ethical governance of the digital during and after the COVID-19 pandemic. Minds Mach 30:171–176. https://doi.org/10.1007/s11023-020-09528-5
Tasioulas J (2019) Saving human rights from human rights law. Vanderbilt J Transnatl Law 52:1167–1207
Van Deursen AJAM, Helsper EJ (2018) Collateral benefits of Internet use: explaining the diverse outcomes of engaging with the Internet. New Media Soc 20(7):2333–2351. https://doi.org/10.1177/1461444817715282
Van Leeuwen ES, Halleck-Vega S (2021) Voting and the rise of populism: spatial perspectives and applications across Europe. Reg Sci Policy Pract 13(2):209–220. https://doi.org/10.1111/rsp3.12411
Vivitsu M, Saadatmand M (2016) Privacy in the era of big data and learning analytics: ethical considerations and positions. In: Ethical and Privacy Issues in the Design of Learning Analytics Applications: 2nd Workshop on Ethics & Privacy in Learning Analytics @ LAK1, University of Edinburgh, Edinburgh, UK, April 24, 2016 Learning Analytics Community Exchange LACE
Wanner J, Janiesch C (2019) Big data analytics in sustainability reports: an analysis based on the perceived credibility of corporate published information. Bus Res 12:143–173. https://doi.org/10.1007/s40685-019-0088-4
Zuboff S (2019) The age of surveillance capitalism: the fight for a human future at the new frontier of power. Public Affairs, New York

COVID-19 and Modern Slavery in Brazil: Reflections of the Pandemic in the (Non)Compliance with SDG 8 and Target 8.7

Ana Cláudia Ruy Cardia Atchabahian and Izabela Zonato Villas Boas

Abstract This paper seeks to validate the implications for modern slavery and human trafficking in the post-pandemic scenario in Brazil, especially from sources produced by the main International Organizations operating in this field, such as the United Nations within the United Nations Office for Drugs and Crime (UNODC) and the International Labor Organization, as well as the developments and obstacles presented nationally. As a hypothesis, it is suggested that the consequences of the existing problems in Brazil—and aggravated by the pandemic—may be an obstacle to achieving the Sustainable Development Goal (SDG) 8 and, especially, target 8.7 by 2025. Aiming at reducing vulnerabilities and sustainable development of the economy, society and the environment, the SDGs are integrated, interdependent and indivisible and indicate a list of tasks to be fulfilled by all actors. The paper adopts the inductive method, and the materials used to reach the main conclusions come from primary and secondary sources, such as documents from the United Nations (UN) and its agencies, as well as the International Labor Organization (ILO), and specialized bibliography on modern slavery and human trafficking.

A. C. R. C. Atchabahian (✉)
Mackenzie Presbyterian University (UPM), São Paulo, Brazil

International Law from the Pontifical Catholic University of São Paulo (PUC-SP), São Paulo, Brazil

Pontifical Catholic University of Paraná (PUC-PR), São Paulo, Brazil

I. Z. V. Boas
Mackenzie Presbyterian University (UPM), São Paulo, Brazil

Faculty of Law at Fernandópolis' Educational Foundation, São Paulo, Brazil

International Institute of Legal Sociology, Oñati, Spain

D. A. Pamplona et al. (eds.), *Business and Human Rights from the Lens of Women*, Interdisciplinary Studies in Human Rights 13,
https://doi.org/10.1007/978-3-032-04036-7_7

1 Introduction

The emergence of guidelines for governmental actions at international, national and local levels led the United Nations (UN) to present the Millennium Goals to the international society in 2000. The initiative was the first global policy framework designed for social and global development through eight determinations related to basic rights, namely: hunger eradication, right to education, gender equality, health, environment and development in a broad sense, which were supposed to be implemented by States by 2015.[1]

In 2015, and based on the results obtained with the Millennium Goals, the UN presented the "2030 Agenda", seeking the continuity of that initiative through the introduction of 17 (seventeen) Sustainable Development Goals (SDGs), composed of 169 (one hundred and sixty-nine) targets, which, unlike the previous initiative, must be implemented by States and other entities of international civil society, namely, International Organizations, companies and NGOs, in addition to individuals themselves by the year 2030.[2]

Aiming at reducing vulnerabilities and sustainable development of the economy, society and the environment, the SDGs are integrated, interdependent and indivisible and indicate a list of tasks to be fulfilled by all actors.

Considering that each State is responsible for achieving the SDGs and its targets in accordance with its socioeconomic and cultural criteria, such norms must be equalized domestically. In Brazil, the adaptation of SDGs to the domestic reality has also been under the responsibility of the Institute for Applied Economic Research.

Given that the SDGs are integrated, this research gives greater emphasis to SDG 8, which is intended for Decent Work and Economic Growth, aiming at promoting "sustained, inclusive and sustainable economic growth, full and productive employment and decent work for everyone".[3]

Among SDG 8, the analysis proposed herein focuses especially on target 8.7, which seeks the eradication of forced labor, modern slavery and human trafficking, as well as the elimination, by 2025, of child labor in all its forms.

With the global crisis caused by the SARS-CoV-2 (COVID-19, COVID or pandemic) pandemic, a virus that has circulated the planet since the beginning of 2020 and that resulted in processes of social isolation in all nations (World Health Organization n.d.), emergency actions were adopted by the States to delay the advance of contamination, such as quarantine, isolation and lockdown, which from the beginning had social and economic impacts on a global scale. Consequently, international society in all its spheres needed to seek economic readjustments that would adapt to the impacts of the pandemic.

As a result of the pandemic, the United Nations Office on Drugs and Crime (UNODC) showed that there has been an exponential increase in unemployment

---

[1] Plataforma Agenda 2030 (n.d.).

[2] Plataforma Agenda 2030 (n.d.).

[3] Governo Federal (n.d.-a, n.d.-b, n.d.-c).

and reduction of income, especially concerning informal and low-income workers, which means that people who live in vulnerable conditions find themselves in an even more alarming situation.[4]

In the same sense, the International Labor Organization (ILO) estimated that 114 million people lost their jobs due to the global economic crisis caused by COVID-19.[5] The impacts of combating human trafficking in Brazil should not be forgotten either, especially from that period onwards, which will be the main research problem of the present work.

Vulnerability is a prerequisite for exposing people to the possibility of being victims of crimes that can further aggravate their fragile situation, such as those outlined by SDG 8 and Target 8.7. Given this premise and the increase in the number of unemployed people on the planet (and the consequent worsening of their vulnerability), it is noted that there might be a problem (in Brazil and worldwide) regarding the effective fulfillment of target 8.7 within the deadline determined by the UN.

Thus, as a research problem, this paper seeks to verify the implications for modern slavery and human trafficking in the post-pandemic scenario in Brazil, especially from the materials already produced by the main International Organizations operating in this field, as well as the advances and obstacles presented nationally.

As a hypothesis, it is suggested that the consequences of the existing problems in Brazil—aggravated by the pandemic—may be an obstacle to achieving SDG 8 and, especially, target 8.7 by 2025.

Therefore, the paper will adopt the inductive method, and the materials used to reach the main conclusions come from primary and secondary sources, such as documents from the United Nations (UN) and its agencies, the International Labor Organization (ILO), and a specialized bibliography on modern slavery and human trafficking.

2 COVID-19 and Modern Slavery: Challenges for the Implementation of Target 8.7

SDG 8 is directly aimed at consolidating decent work on the planet. Its fulfillment must necessarily comply with the other SDGs, given its interdependence in ensuring sustainability. Target 8.7, as seen, seeks to eradicate forced labor, modern slavery and human trafficking, as well as the elimination by 2025 of child labor in all its forms.

Concerning human trafficking, the globalizing context currently contributes to the massification of human subjection to the condition of merchandise. In this way, the reduction of the individual to object status, made by other individuals or by

[4] UNODC (2020c).

[5] ILO (2021).

companies, turns out to be a tragic natural consequence of a society that tends to value consumer goods at the expense of human qualities.[6]

As for the trivialization of human exploitation, individuals in this new social model are the first to be subjected to the most inhuman and degrading forms of oppression,[7] such as human trafficking and all forms of exploitation. Due to its high profitability, human trafficking today varies statistically between the second and third illegal modalities with the largest movement of financial resources in the world, together with arms and drug trafficking, in an annual volume of transactions valued at approximately US$150 bi. It is estimated that currently, 21 million people are victims of forced labor, which necessarily presupposes trafficking as a first step in this form of modern slavery[8] with the following exploitation of all human forms.

COVID-19 had global impacts in all sectors, and above all in the world economy. ILO estimates that an increased vulnerability arising from unemployment and the reduction of working hours on the planet tend to worsen the alarming scenario of modern slavery. In the same way that States and other global actors seek ways to prevent the socioeconomic crisis from getting worse from the pandemic, it is possible to infer that human traffickers seek to recruit new individuals to be victims of this crime.

The international reality of trafficking in persons is known especially from the Global Reports on Trafficking in Persons prepared by UNODC, based on its methodology for systematizing data sent by the States.[9] In this sense, the determination of SDG 8 to eliminate such forms of exploitation (which characterize forced labor, human trafficking and modern slavery) and reach a reality of decent work is a measure for a more just and sustainable planetary society.

At the international level, UNODC understands that vulnerable groups and the risks to which they are exposed should not be overlooked in a moment of recovery from the problems exacerbated by the pandemic. In addition, it affirms that the pandemic provides the opportunity to observe deeply rooted inequalities in the global model of economic development that increases marginalization, gender-based violence, exploitation and human trafficking.[10] In other words, it is possible to affirm that COVID did not create new problems but increased the historically proven impacts on latent social inequality worldwide.

To this end, UNODC recommends that to alleviate the economic impact of the pandemic, some actions should be continuously undertaken, such as (i) continuity of monitoring of the pandemic responses; (ii) prevalence of the rule of law culture; (iii) reassurance of access to justice; (iv) surveillance of the applicability of the law through all national and international actors; (v) support from States in combating trafficking in persons; (vi) flexibility of service providers; (vii) systematic

[6] Bauman (1998), p. 34.

[7] Laky (2014), p. 71.

[8] ILO (n.d.).

[9] de Pinto et al. (2018).

[10] UNODC (2020b), p. 26.

collection and data analysis on the impact of COVID-19 on human trafficking, among others.[11]

Concerning the Global Report on Trafficking in Persons 2020, UNODC emphasizes that the consequences of the pandemic will increase unemployment globally, widening social and economic inequalities, impacting the scenario of trafficking in persons around the world—especially considering that people in urgent need of employment are particularly at risk of being trafficked.[12] It also highlights that traffickers and recruiters take advantage of situations of economic need, so that elements related to it, such as poverty, unemployment and low income are highly relevant to explain the social dynamics that govern trafficking.[13] About Brazil, the Report does not provide specific information for the country, but only data that includes South America.

ILO, in turn, emphasizes that the global region most affected by the crisis is the Americas, where a 13.7% loss of working hours was recorded in 2020. In Brazil, however, it is estimated that this loss is higher: 15%.[14]

In Brazil, the scenario does not differ from the global reality. In the third quarter of 2020, the Brazilian Institute of Geography and Statistics recognized that there was a rate of approximately 14.1 million unemployed citizens in the country.[15] Furthermore, the high number of informal workers in Brazil—41.4% of the national population in 2019—often tends to facilitate the precariousness of labor relations, perpetuating the exploratory forms.[16]

With those premises and background, topic two will address the analysis of whether Brazil, with its normative and practical framework, will be able to combat modern slavery to reach the goal of SDG 8 by 2025 and, above all, in a post-pandemic scenario.

3 Projections for a Post-pandemic Scenario in Brazil Regarding the Promotion of Decent Work by 2025

Given that the 2030 Agenda's goals are global and that each State is responsible for its implementation in accordance with its internal reality, it was necessary to adapt that norm to the Brazilian socioeconomic situation, which was done through the work developed by the national Government with the assistance of the Institute of Applied Economic Research.

[11] UNODC (2020b), p. 26.

[12] UNODC (2020a), pp. 23 and 24.

[13] UNODC (2020a), p. 70.

[14] ILO (2021).

[15] IBGE (n.d.).

[16] Antunes (2009), p. 235.

Adapted to Brazil, target 8.7 determines that every work in conditions similar to slavery, human trafficking and child labor, especially in its worst forms, has to be eradicated by 2025. To assist in meeting the target, Brazil created indicator 8.7.1, which aims to analyze the proportion and number of children aged 5-17 years involved in child labor, by sex and age.[17]

The Institute of Applied Economic Research data for SDG 8 demonstrates the existence of sixteen indicators. Concerning target 8.7, its website informs that the data are still under analysis or construction,[18] which, at first, is worrying due to the short period between the crossing of existing data and the establishment of new public policies to achieve the target proposal by the year 2025.

Furthermore, in January 2021, Agência Brasil reported that between 2016 and 2020, the Labor Public Prosecution's Office received more than six thousand complaints related to practices similar to slavery and human trafficking. In addition, only in 2020, more than 900 people were rescued from situations analogous to slavery.[19] In 2021, just in January, approximately 110 people living in this situation were rescued.

As recently pointed out by the deputy national coordinator for the National Department on Combating Slave Labor and Trafficking in Persons (branch of the Labor Public Prosecution's Office), most cases of human trafficking in Brazil happen in rural areas, and there are also several urban rescues in sewing factories and domestic work. He also highlights that victims of this type of crime, in general, live in a situation of great social vulnerability, with poor education and few employment opportunities, which makes them not fully aware of their rights, facilitating the action of criminals in making false promises of great working conditions and remuneration.[20]

Currently, the III National Plan to Combat Trafficking in Persons is in force in Brazil.[21] This public policy,[22] established in 2018 and with a duration of four years, was developed based on thematic axes, with emphasis on accountability, victim assistance and prevention and public awareness, among others (art. 3). However, recent movements contrary to the protection of victims of modern slavery have happened in Brazil—some of them being even stated in governmental policies, namely:

---

[17] IPEA (n.d.).

[18] ODS Brasil (n.d.).

[19] Agência Brasil (2021a).

[20] Agência Brasil (2021b).

[21] Brasil (2018).

[22] The III National Plan to Combat Trafficking in Persons is supported by the National Policy to Combat Trafficking in Persons, established in 2006 in Brazil, two years after the country's adhesion to the Palermo Protocol, the main international norm regarding human trafficking and modern slavery on the planet. BRASIL. This policy and its plans enshrine the recognition that the crime of trafficking in persons must be observed from a multidimensional perspective, that is, public policies to combat trafficking must consider the coordinated action between the actors involved in prevention, repression and accountability of agents involved in human trafficking and assistance to victims of this crime (Brasil 2006; Brasil 2004).

(i) the labor reform in 2017 and the extinction of the Ministry of Labor in 2019; (ii) the attempt to hide from Brazilian society the so-called "dirty list of slave labor"; and (iii) a budget reduction for modern slavery inspections applied by the Federal Government, especially during the pandemic.

In 2017, the labor reform (with amendments to the text of the Brazilian Consolidation of Labor Laws) was the target of disturbing perceptions for the continuity of guaranteeing rights and dignity to workers in the national territory. In addition, there is the issue with the so-called "Register of Employers". Created in 2003, and popularly known as the "dirty list of slave labor", this is a public policy instrument to combat all forms of slavery created by the former Ministry of Labor and has its importance recognized by the Federal Government itself, as it organizes existing national decisions of criminal offenses against slave or forced labor, guarantees its publicity and provides state and social control—especially regarding the possibility of consumers to avoid the consumption of products that do not respect human dignity in their production chains.[23]

Nevertheless, in January 2018, the Brazilian Association of Real Estate Developers, through the Claim of Non-Compliance with a Fundamental Precept (ADPF) No. 509, demanded under the Federal Supreme Court the unconstitutionality of the rule that determined the "dirty list" disclosure, arguing that the publication of that list could only be regulated through a specific law and not by the Executive branch.[24]

In September of the same year, the Federal Supreme Court decided to maintain the disclosure of said list, accepting its compliance with the Brazilian Federal Constitution,[25] especially due to the guarantee of application of constitutionally guaranteed rights to the workers, as well as in connection with the provisions of Law No. 12,527/2011 (also known as the Access to Information Act). Currently, there are approximately 113 companies in this list, ranging from food, textile, among others.[26]

The extinction of the Ministry of Labor was announced through Provisional Measure No. 870, published in 2019, on the first day of President Jair Bolsonaro's government.[27] Among other impacts, the extinction of the Ministry of Labor meant that the inspection of workers became subordinate to the Ministry of Economy, which led to the loss of hierarchy of the Secretary of Labor Inspection, that did not have an independent budget unit to organize actions to combat slavery as well as its management competence for the review of the Regulatory Standards on labor inspection.[28]

[23] Governo Federal (n.d.-a, n.d.-b, n.d.-c).

[24] Conectas Direitos Humanos (2021).

[25] Supremo Tribunal Federal (2020).

[26] Governo Federal (n.d.-a, n.d.-b, n.d.-c).

[27] BRASIL (2019).

[28] Reiner and Baracat (2020).

As for the recent budgetary cut applied by the Federal Government to combat slave and forced labor in Brazil, in 2020 the amount spent for the development of such activities was solely R$1,300,000.00 (one million, three hundred thousand reais).[29] This insignificant amount, considered the lowest in the last ten years, added to the cutback of teams that carry out investigations based on complaints, demonstrate the Government's negligence in the fight against modern slavery in a country of continental dimensions and with substantial socioeconomic inequality, distancing Brazil from meeting the target 8.7 of SDG 8 by 2025.

Among setbacks, however, it is still possible to notice that, even in a pandemic scenario in Brazil and in the world, people in modern slavery were rescued in the country, which can be seen as a positive aspect, but still contrary to the sense of an ideal of eradicating this global problem during this decade. Despite the rescue of people in a situation similar to slavery and forced labor in Brazil in 2020, this number is lower than the statistics of the previous years, raising again the discussion about how Brazil is fighting against modern slavery in its territory and the importance given to that problem.

Those measures also go against international determinations for the Brazilian State, such as the decisions of the Inter-American Court of Human Rights in cases "Trabalhadores da Fazenda Brasil Verde v. Brasil"[30] and "Empregados da Fábrica de Fogos de Santo Antônio de Jesus v. Brasil",[31] both with references to the socioeconomic conditions of the Brazilian population and human trafficking and labor exploitation of men, women, children and adolescents.

With regard to work from digital platforms, the informality resulting from the virtualization of consumer relations in Brazil has generated new problems with workers' exploitation.[32] In a study carried out with application-mediated product delivery companies in 2021, the National Labor Tax Audit concluded that workers registered on the application named "Rappi" should necessarily act according to the rules of the Brazilian Consolidation of Labor Laws, that is, with a formal contract.[33]

Another problem that will have serious consequences for inequality in Brazil and the consequent informality is linked to access to basic education during the pandemic period, especially for children and adolescents enrolled in the public education system. The absence of technological resources on behalf of public schools as well as poor children and families tends to produce disparities in their learning in comparison with children and adolescents enrolled in the private school system.

The lack of access to technology in this case—and which was not resolved by the three Brazilian government spheres until this moment—will bring future impacts that may further compromise the possibility of the vulnerability of children and

[29] G1 (2021).

[30] Inter-American Court of Human Rights (2016).

[31] Inter-American Court of Human Rights (2020).

[32] Cardia and Gamba (2020).

[33] Repórter Brasil (2021).

adolescents who will make up the national workforce in the coming decades.[34] The consequence, therefore, will be once again a setback in labor relations in Brazil, which brings the possibility of new situations of modern slavery in violation of SDG 8 and target 8.7.

Seeking to alleviate the economic impacts of the pandemic, Brazilian Federal Government instituted through Law No. 13,982 of 2020[35] a financial benefit called "Emergency Assistance", aimed at protecting informal workers, individual micro-entrepreneurs, self-employed and unemployed citizens.[36] Law No. 13,982 established the amount of R$ 600.00 (six hundred reais) per month for the Emergency Assistance, a sum close to half of the Brazilian minimum wage (in 2021, of R$ 1,100.00 (one thousand and one hundred reais).[37] This aid was a strong driver of the country's economy at the first moments of the pandemic; however, and as a result of economic inflation, it is still insufficient given the territorial disparities and inequalities existing in the country.[38]

All the situations listed above, added to Brazil's position in the Human Development Index, demonstrate that the country not only is an economy with high socioeconomic inequality, subjecting its citizens to constant conditions of vulnerability but also that, even during the pandemic period, little was done to combat human trafficking and other forms of modern slavery in the country. This scenario is even more noticeable given that, compared to 2018,[39] Brazil lost five positions in 2019 in the world ranking[40] in a scenario that still does not yet have the impacts of the pandemic year.

The problems mentioned above, as seen, are of a past, present and future order and will compromise the Brazilian commitment to complying with SDG 8 by 2025. Past order, as the neglect of the protection of Brazilian workers goes back to the period before the pandemic, dating back its colonial history. Present order, since during the first year of the COVID-19 pandemic little was done to intensify the inspection of situations analogous to slavery, in a movement contrary to expectations, even by budgetary cuts on national operations. Future order, as the present neglect with sectors such as education and informal labor will generate a new mass of informal or even registered workers, with the common characteristic of precariousness at its most varied levels—all vulnerable and susceptible to be victims of modern slavery.

Integrated public policies are needed to put an end to those problems with long-term perspectives and which will hardly result in the complete eradication of slave labor and human trafficking in Brazil by 2025.

---

[34] Gamba and Cardia (2021).

[35] Brasil (2020a).

[36] Caixa Econômica Federal (n.d.).

[37] BRASIL (2020b).

[38] IPEA (2020).

[39] UNDP (2019).

[40] UNDP (2020).

4 Conclusion

This study intended to examine (considering Sustainable Development Goal 8 and its target 8.7, aimed at the eradication of modern slavery, human trafficking and promotion of decent work) the Brazilian situation in a pandemic context, especially regarding the country's ability to achieve that target by the year 2025. From research carried out in primary and secondary sources, it was found that the COVID-19 pandemic brought global impacts of a socioeconomic and environmental nature. Especially on the economic level, the increase in the unemployment around the world has greatly contributed to the expansion of situations of human vulnerability.

As seen in the previous items, vulnerability is one of the main requirements sought by traffickers to recruit individuals who will be exploited in a multiplicity of ways. Trafficking in persons and modern slavery, therefore, go against the ideal of decent work, advocated by SDG 8 and its target 8.7.

It should be remembered, however, that both the COVID-19 pandemic and the violations that already exist on the planet are the result of decades of exploitation of the social, economic and political vulnerabilities of peoples, especially in the world's least developed states. The pandemic, therefore, only enhances existing violations, amplifying its results and bringing serious consequences for a greater number of victims.

In Brazil, although the country has expressly compromised to ensure compliance with the aforementioned target by the year 2025, it has been proven that, despite some efforts to rescue workers in conditions similar to slavery and the implementation of public policies of combating human trafficking, the possibility of eradicating such degrading forms of work by that year is remote. This is because, as seen, there were situations and even public policies that were not consistent with the protection of victims of modern slavery, including (i) the extinction of the Ministry of Labor in 2019 and the labor reform in 2017; (ii) the attempt to hide from Brazilian society the so-called "dirty list of slave labor"; and (iii) the budget reduction for inspections by the Federal Government, especially during the pandemic. Although individuals have been rescued in precarious situations in recent years, it is evident that such numbers are underreported, especially in a country where unemployment has increased, as well as informality, the economic situation remains undefined and even the educational prospects of the national public education have been affected by the global pandemic.

Some possible steps to comply with target 8.7 of SDG 8 would be: (i) the establishment of stricter criteria by the Federal Government for the implementation of SDG 8 and its targets; (ii) the intensification in inspections by the Labor Public Prosecution's Office of situations of modern slavery; (iii) the reinforcement of public policies and the increase in efforts to combat human trafficking in Brazil (both internally and internationally and, mainly, in border regions); (iv) economic incentives for society and for certain essential sectors with a view to rekindle the economy; (v) investments in the public education sector to avoid school dropouts due to inequalities in access to technology in times of remote classes and also after the pandemic.

Such measures must be implemented not only for a short term during the COVID pandemic, but also be part of more permanent policies so Brazil could ensure the attainment of its sustainability through the establishment of strategies of a transversal nature. The target of decent work, therefore, must transcend the pandemic discussion in Brazil, being not only a goal for 2025, but for a more human and decent future for all workers in the country.

References

Agência Brasil (2021a) MPT recebe mais de 6 mil denúncias de escravidão e tráfico de pessoas. Disponível em: https://agenciabrasil.ebc.com.br/direitos-humanos/noticia/2021-01/mpt-recebe-mais-de-6-mil-denuncias-de-escravidao-e-trafico-de-pessoas. Available at: https://agenciabrasil.ebc.com.br/direitos-humanos/noticia/2021-01/mpt-recebe-mais-de-6-mil-denuncias-de-escravidao-e-trafico-de-pessoas. Accessed 17 Feb 2021

Agência Brasil (2021b) Operação resgata cerca de 110 pessoas em situação de escravidão. Available at: https://agenciabrasil.ebc.com.br/direitos-humanos/noticia/2021-01/operacao-resgata-cerca-de-110-pessoas-em-situacao-de-escravidao. Accessed 17 Feb 2021

Antunes R (2009) Século XXI: nova era da precarização estrutural do trabalho? In: Antunes R, Braga R (eds) Infoproletários: Degradação do trabalho virtual. Boitempo, São Paulo, p 235

Bauman Z (1998) O mal-estar da pós-modernidade (M. Gama & C. M. Gama, Trans.). Zahar, Rio de Janeiro

Brasil (2004) Decreto n° 5.017, de 12 de março de 2004. Available at: http://www.planalto.gov.br/ccivil_03/_Ato2004-2006/2004/Decreto/D5017.htm. Accessed 17 Feb 2021

Brasil (2006) Decreto n° 5.948, de 26 de outubro de 2006. Available at: http://www.planalto.gov.br/ccivil_03/_Ato2004-2006/2006/Decreto/D5948.htm. Accessed 17 Feb 2021

Brasil (2018) Decreto n° 9.940, de 03 de julho de 2018. Available at: http://www.planalto.gov.br/ccivil_03/_ato2015-2018/2018/Decreto/D9440.htm. Accessed 17 Feb 2021

Brasil (2019) Medida Provisória n° 870, de 1° de janeiro de 2019. Estabelece a organização básica dos órgãos da Presidência da República e dos Ministérios. Available at: www.planalto.gov.br/ccivil_03/_ato2019-2022/2019/Mpv/mpv870.htm. Accessed 21 Feb 2021

Brasil (2020a) Lei n° 13.982, de 2 de abril de 2020. Altera a Lei n° 8.742, de 7 de dezembro de 1993, para dispor sobre parâmetros adicionais de caracterização da situação de vulnerabilidade social para fins de elegibilidade ao benefício de prestação continuada (BPC), e estabelece medidas excepcionais de proteção social a serem adotadas durante o período de enfrentamento da emergência de saúde pública de importância internacional decorrente do coronavírus (Covid-19) responsável pelo surto de 2019, a que se refere a Lei n° 13.979, de 6 de fevereiro de 2020. Available at: www.planalto.gov.br/ccivil_03/_ato2019-2022/2020/lei/l13982.htm. Accessed 21 Feb 2021

Brasil (2020b) Medida Provisória n° 1021, de 30 de dezembro de 2020. Dispõe sobre o valor do salário mínimo a vigorar a partir de 1° de janeiro de 2021. Available at: www.planalto.gov.br/ccivil_03/_Ato2019-2022/2020/Mpv/mpv1021.htm#:~:text=MEDIDA%20PROVISÓRIA%20N°%201.021%2C%20DE%2030%20DE%20DEZEMBRO%20DE%202020&text=Dispõe%20sobre%20o%20valor%20do,Art. Accessed 21 Feb 2021

Caixa Econômica Federal (n.d.) Auxílio Emergencial. Available at: https://www.caixa.gov.br/auxilio/PAGINAS/DEFAULT2.ASPX. Accessed 19 Feb 2021

Cardia ACR, Gamba JRG (2020) Direitos humanos e tecnologia no contexto pandêmico: a atuação de empresas na violação aos direitos humanos antes e durante a pandemia de COVID-19. In: Abrusio J (ed) Covid-19: impactos jurídicos na tecnologia. D'Plácido, São Paulo, pp 13–32

Conectas Direitos Humanos (2021) STF determina a manutenção da "lista suja" do trabalho escravo. Available at: https://www.conectas.org/noticias/stf-determina-manutencao-da-lista-suja-do-trabalho-escravo. Accessed 19 Feb 2021

de Pinto FCS, Cardia ACR, Placca CA (2018) Estatísticas relacionadas ao tráfico de pessoas: dos relatórios do UNODC à busca de uma metodologia compreensiva sobre o tema. In: Smanio GP, de Pinto FCS, Cardia ACR, Junqueira MA, Andreucci ACPT (eds) Mulheres invisíveis: Panorama internacional e realidade brasileira do tráfico transnacional de mulheres. CRV, Curitiba, pp 57–72

G1 (2021) Em ano de pandemia, verba para combate ao trabalho escravo encolhe mais de 40% e é a menor dos últimos dez anos. Available at: https://g1.globo.com/economia/noticia/2021/02/21/em-ano-de-pandemia-verba-para-combate-ao-trabalho-escravo-encolhe-mais-de-40percent-e-e-a-menor-dos-ultimos-10-anos.ghtml. Accessed 21 Feb 2021

Gamba JRG, Cardia ACR (2021) Escola, pandemia e tecnologia: Impactos iniciais do COVID-19 na educação básica da rede pública de ensino brasileira. In: Andreucci ACPT, Junqueira MA, Dantas TN (eds) Desafios para a proteção de crianças e adolescentes durante a pandemia: construindo estratégias para prevenir o agravamento de desigualdades, vol 1. OAB/ESA Publicações, São Paulo, pp 100–117

Governo Federal (n.d.-a) Cadastro de Empregadores - "Lista Suja". Available at: https://www.gov.br/mdh/pt-br/navegue-por-temas/combate-ao-trabalho-escravo/cadastro-de-empregadores-201clista-suja201d. Accessed 19 Feb 2021

Governo Federal (n.d.-b) Cadastro de Empregadores que tenham submetido trabalhadores a condições análogas à de escravo. Available at: https://sit.trabalho.gov.br/portal/images/CADASTRO_DE_EMPREGADORES/CADASTRO_DE_EMPREGADORES.pdf. Accessed 21 Feb 2020

Governo Federal (n.d.-c) Transformando Nosso Mundo: A Agenda 2030 para o Desenvolvimento Sustentável. Available at: www.itamaraty.gov.br/images/ed_desenvsust/Agenda2030-completo-site.pdf. Accessed 12 Feb 2021

IBGE (n.d.) Desemprego. Available at: https://www.ibge.gov.br/explica/desemprego.php. Accessed 19 Feb 2021

ILO - International Labour Organization (2021) ILO Monitor: COVID-19 and the world of work. Seventh edition 25 January 2021. Available at: https://www.ilo.org/wcmsp5/groups/public/@dgreports/@dcomm/documents/briefingnote/wcms_767028.pdf. Accessed 15 Feb 2021

ILO - International Labour Organization (n.d.) Forced labour, modern slavery and human trafficking. Available at: http://www.ilo.org/global/topics/forced-labour/lang%2D%2Dja/index.htm. Accessed 15 Feb 2021

Inter-American Court of Human Rights (2016) Caso Fazenda Brasil Verde vs. Brasil. Série C, n° 318. Sentença de 20 de outubro de 2016. Available at: http://www.corteidh.or.cr/docs/casos/articulos/seriec_318_esp.pdf. Accessed 12 Jan 2021

Inter-American Court of Human Rights (2020) Caso Empregados da Fábrica de Fogos de Santo Antônio de Jesus vs. Brasil. Série C, n° 407. Sentença de 15 de julho de 2020. Available at: https://www.corteidh.or.cr/docs/casos/articulos/seriec_407_esp.pdf. Accessed 12 Jan 2021

IPEA - Instituto de Pesquisa Econômica Aplicada (2020) Nota Técnica - Proteção Social aos Mais Vulneráveis em Contexto de Pandemia: Algumas Limitações Práticas de Auxílio Emergencial E a Adequação dos Benefícios Eventuais Como Instrumento Complementar de Política Socioassistencial. Abril/2020. Número 67- Diretoria de Estudos e Políticas Sociais. Available at: https://ipea.gov.br/portal/images/stories/PDFs/nota_tecnica/200505_nt_disoc_n67_web.pdf. Accessed 21 Feb 2021

IPEA - Instituto de Pesquisa Econômica Aplicada (n.d.) 8. Trabalho Decente e Crescimento Econômico. Available at: https://www.ipea.gov.br/ods/ods8.html. Accessed 14 Feb 2021

Laky T (2014) Tráfico internacional de mulheres: Nova face de uma velha escravidão (2ª ed.). Editora Prismas, Curitiba

ODS Brasil (n.d.) Objetivo 8 - Emprego Decente e Crescimento Econômico. Available at: https://odsbrasil.gov.br/objetivo/objetivo?n=8. Accessed 14 Feb 2021

Plataforma Agenda 2030 (n.d.) Conheça a Agenda 2030. Available at: www.agenda2030.com.br/sobre/? Accessed 14 Feb 2021

Reiner E, Baracat EM (2020) A extinção do Ministério do Trabalho e seus efeitos na efetividade dos direitos trabalhistas no Brasil. Revista eletrônica do Tribunal Regional do Trabalho da 9ª Região 9(91):121–136. Available at: https://juslaboris.tst.jus.br/bitstream/handle/20.500.12178/180097/2020_reiner_eduardo_extincao_mt.pdf?sequence=1. Accessed 21 Feb 2021

Repórter Brasil (2021) Entregadores são funcionários da Rappi e devem ter carteira assinada, concluem fiscais do trabalho. Available at: https://reporterbrasil.org.br/2021/02/entregadores-sao-funcionarios-da-rappi-e-devem-ter-carteira-assinada-concluem-fiscais-do-trabalho/. Accessed 21 Feb 2021

Supreme Federal Court (2020) Arguição de Descumprimento de Preceito Fundamental 509. Associação Brasileira de Incorporadoras Imobiliárias (ABRAINC) e Ministro de Estado do Trabalho e Previdência Social. Reporter: Ministro Marco Aurélio. Judgment date: 16/09/2020. Available at: redir.stf.jus.br/paginadorpub/paginador.jsp?docTP=TP&docID=754002533. Accessed 19 Feb 2021

UNDP (2019) Human Development Report 2019. Beyond income, beyond averages, beyond today: inequalities in human development in the 21st century. Available at: http://hdr.undp.org/en/content/human-development-report-2019. Accessed 21 Feb 2021

UNDP (2020) Human Development Report 2020. The next frontier: Human development and the Anthropocene. Available at: hdr.undp.org/sites/default/files/hdr2020.pdf. Accessed 21 Feb 2021

UNODC (2020a) Global Report on Trafficking in Persons 2020. United Nations publication, Sales No. E.20.IV.3. Available at: https://www.unodc.org/documents/data-and-analysis/tip/2021/GLOTiP_2020_15jan_web.pdf. Accessed 12 Feb 2021. p 23 e 24

UNODC (2020b) How COVID-19 Restrictions and The Economic Consequences Are Likely To Impact Migrant Smuggling And Cross-Border Trafficking In Persons To Europe And North America. 2020. Available at: https://www.unodc.org/islamicrepublicofiran/en/how-covid-19-restrictions-and-the-economic-consequences-are-likely-to-impact-migrant-smuggling-and-cross-border-trafficking-in-persons-to-europe-and-north-america.html. Accessed Feb 2021, p 26

UNODC (2020c) Impact of the Covid-19 Pandemic on Trafficking in Persons - Preliminary findings and messaging based on rapid stocktaking. Available at: https://www.unodc.org/documents/Advocacy-Section/HTMSS_Thematic_Brief_on_COVID-19.pdf. Accessed 16 Feb 2021, p 01

World Health Organization (n.d.) Coronavirus Disease (COVID-19) Pandemic. Available at: https://www.who.int/emergencies/diseases/novel-coronavirus-2019. Accessed 24 June 2020

Women on Corporate Boards: American, European and Ukrainian Experience to Use Gender Quotas

Tamara Horbachevska-Konstankevych and Olena Uvarova

Abstract In this chapter, we compare the experience of corporate gender quotas implementation American, European and Eastern European traditions. We illustrate the current situation of the women representation in the corporate boards of companies though the example of legislation and judiciary in the USA, EU and Ukraine as countries representing these three traditions. We then underline, what current counter-arguments are used to object corporate gender quotas. We then contribute to the existing discussion by proposing to look at the BHR agenda though the concept of personal autonomy, namely, the principle of 'gendered autonomy'. Such perspective contributes to the debate on the necessity of introducing gender quotas at corporate boards.

1 Introduction

A scientist who writes or speaks on a gender equality issue in the countries of the post-Soviet region is always forced to start with proof that gender inequality[1] exists, in principle, as a phenomenon. Perhaps the exception is when a scientist gets to a conference on women's rights. Gender equality is the subject of political campaigns

[1] While focusing on women\male distinction in gender inequality, we understand gender as not a binary but pluralistic concept including various genders and people who identify themselves as women not depending on their biological or social role characteristic.

T. Horbachevska-Konstankevych (✉)
Law Group, Wageningen University, Wageningen, The Netherlands

Yaroslav Mudryi National Law University, Kharkiv, Ukraine
e-mail: tamara.horbachevska@wur.nl; lena.uvarova@wur.nl

O. Uvarova
UNDP Business and Human Rights ProgrammeYaroslav Mudryi National Law University, Kharkiv, Ukraine
e-mail: o.o.uvarova@nlu.edu.ua

D. A. Pamplona et al. (eds.), *Business and Human Rights from the Lens of Women*, Interdisciplinary Studies in Human Rights 13,
https://doi.org/10.1007/978-3-032-04036-7_8

in the region often. Papers, articles and reports are written on the contradiction of the ideas of gender equality to the values and traditions that are rooted in society. Any public discussion—whether it be a scientific conference or a social media—is accompanied by quite emotional statements about the contrivedness of the problem.

This is the first difference between the Eastern European context, on one side, and the European and American, on the other, where the fact of gender inequality is not put into question. Discussions are ongoing at the next level already—specific measures are being discussed to overcome gender inequality. And one of such discussions is about quotas aimed at ensuring that women are represented in company management.

While Western colleagues are talking about the intensity of discussion of gender quotas, including in the scientific literature,[2] there are very few examples in the Eastern European region and, specifically, in Ukraine. Among the whole variety of literature on the women's representation in company management, we want to note Aaron A. Dhir 'Challenging Boardroom Homogeneity. Corporate Law, Governance, and Diversity'[3] especially because of its strong consonance with our views on this issue in many ways.

We see our contribution to the discussion, first, in referring to the experience of Ukraine as both Eastern European and post-Soviet country and comparing it with American and European experience in the context of such a basic issue as the legitimate aim (important public interest) of using quotas in the management of private companies. Additionally, if Aaron A. Dhir considers the issue of women's representation in company leadership through the lens of the value of diversity (which is the result achieved or the goal to be pursued), we approach this issue from the point of view of the principle of personal autonomy as a normative requirement, which should be addressed to each entity—public or private—that significantly affects the possibility of a person realizing her or his life project.

In our opinion, factors that distinguish all three regions on the approaches to the fulfillment the state's obligation to protect human rights from violations by business (Pillar 1 of the UN Guiding Principles on Business and Human Rights) find their bright manifestation in the of women's representation in company leadership.

In this chapter the following issues will be considered in the context of all three of these regions:

(a) The current situation with the representation of women in the corporate boards of companies in the USA, EU and Ukraine as both Eastern European and post-Soviet state?
(b) What can sufficiently justify introduction of gender quotas at corporate boards?

The chapter proceeds as following. Section 2 analyses legislative framework in the context of gender equality as a state representing both Eastern European and Post-Soviet Region. Section 3 provides an overview of legislative measures introducing corporate gender quotas and their effects on gender equality and women's representation. Section 4 presents a concept of 'gendered autonomy' as a normative

[2] Lépinard and Rubio-Marín (2018), p. 5.

[3] Dhir (2015).

requirement legitimizing introduction of such affirmative actions like obligatory corporate gender quotas. Section 5 concludes.

2 Ukraine as a Country of Both Eastern European and Post-Soviet Region

2.1 General Context

Ukraine is country that represents both Eastern European and Post-Soviet Region that provides an interesting example of a state aiming to integrate into the European context and overcome the rudiments of Post-Soviet legislation.[4] Generally, being transitional economy states, despite having quite different backgrounds, Post-Soviet countries can be characterized as countries with a high level of bureaucracy, a concentration of achieving maximum profit, and weak attention to human rights.[5] The region also suffers from low self-regulation and a weak engagement of non-state actors with BHR and SDGs agendas, as well as a lack of coherent state regulation, leading to so-called 'state controls gaps'.[6] Some facts about USSR which have significant impact to the current situation on the corporate responsibility to respect human rights and gender equality in particularly in this region.

Economic—private business has emerged in the territory of the former USSR only since 1991, with the beginning of privatization. Up to this moment, private entrepreneurship was banned (under the threat of criminal liability), the idea of private property was denied, all enterprises were state-owned. The economy was centralized and administered by command methods as 'the Soviet economy was embedded in the state; the state *was* the economy. Price and employment stability were closely linked to ideological legitimation of regime and system'.[7] The understanding the huge impact of private companies on human rights situation of people is still seen as a new trend in practice. A feature of the general 'prevalence of the state-centric view of human rights' in the field of BHR described by Western European countries scholars[8] is amplified in Ukraine.

All socialist countries, despite their obvious differences, shared the common features of a collectivist ideology, economic centralization, planning, and nationalization. In all such countries, the leadership sought to promote an economic model rooted in ideology but swiftly contradicted by the 'spontaneous' ideologies of various social groups. The outcome was the proliferation of a hidden economy largely

[4] It should be noted that the definition of the post-Soviet region is very conditional. We use this term to refer to countries that were part of the USSR, except for countries that have become EU members (Latvia, Lithuania, Estonia).

[5] UNDP (2023), p. 11.

[6] The UNDP in Ukraine (2022), p. 65.

[7] Hass (2012), p. 5.

[8] Obara (2017) and Bernaz (2016).

based on market transactions but quite at odds with the legal principles of a market economy. In fact, in state socialism, the main problem for those operating in the second (legal or illegal) economy is not market competition but competition to purchase inputs from the official economy. This is why highly corrupt and ritualistic relations with the socialist bureaucracy constitute the central plank in the nonnative order that regulates the unofficial economy.[9]

Legal—the idea of human rights was subordinate to state policy; collective interest prevailed over the individual/private, legal regulation was based on the principle of the supremacy of the state will, but not on the rule of law principle. Ideas of human dignity and personal autonomy were not elements of law understanding.

Ideological—Civil society existed only in shadows of the Party-state. Not ready to burst out with liberalization, civil society instead had to create itself once the Soviet Union and its satellite states were sufficiently weak.[10]

Predictably, while 'the business and human rights field has developed rapidly in the last two decades',[11] the concept of corporate social responsibility of business, which is the ideological foundation of business and human rights concept, emerged in the post-Soviet space in the early 2000s and is still seen as a new trend in practice.

2.2 Gender Equality Issues in the USSR

The ideological basis of the political and legal regime in the USSR was called Marxism-Leninism. Marxism emerged in the nineteenth century as both a critique of capitalism and the main rival of liberalism. This ideology prescribed that women emancipation is possible 'only through the emancipation of the working class by a proletarian revolution that would eliminate private ownership of the means of production, bring women to the production process as the equals of men, and treat childrearing as a social/collective responsibility'.[12]

By decrees adopted in December 1917, the Soviet government granted women the civil rights and freedoms, equating them with men in the face of the law. Simultaneously with the publication of these decrees, all independent women's associations were banned. The Soviet government took over the upholding female interests. Therefore, a completely new phenomenon 'state feminism' arose, within the framework of which 'emancipation' of Soviet citizens was now carried out. The state and the ruling party, within the framework of this policy, patronized the 'women departments', then the 'women councils', formed be the party itself. Soviet women's organizations did not raise questions about gender equality. They

[9] Dallago (1992), p. 9.

[10] Hass (2012), p. 5.

[11] Baumann-Pauly and Nolan (2016), p. 19.

[12] Kabasakal (2015), p. 680.

promoted party decisions that stated the need to 'improve the status of women'.[13] With the establishment of the new Government after the Revolution in 1917 women's rights were proclaimed equal to men's,[14] providing them with a right to work, vote, equal pay and reproductive rights. Economic crisis in the late 20 s, the shift from woman-worker to woman-worker and family caregiver was created within new governmental policies family and work duties of parents and 'steady retreat to conservatism'.[15] Such a shift created a situation when women were working at two works—official workplace and household work[16] and the percent of men's participation in the household was lower[17] despite proclaiming equality between men and women in family duties.[18]

Considering the example of Ukraine, the Constitution of the USSR on March 10, 1919, indirectly guaranteed the right to vote and be elected for all citizens, men and women. Constitution of the USSR, 1929, in Art. 66 stated that.

> Citizens of the Ukrainian Socialist Soviet Republic who have been 18 years old before the election day have the right to vote and to be elected to councils, regardless of sex, religion, race, nationality, etc.

Constitution of the USSR, 1936, in Art. 122 ensured that women in the USSR were granted equal rights with men in all spheres of economic, state, cultural and socio-political life. The exercising these rights by women was ensured by giving women equal rights with men to work, wages, vacations, social security and education, state protection of interests of mother and child.

Soviet legislation was formed aimed to solve 'the women's issue' and ensure equality and freedom of women in a socialist society. The involvement of women in social production was dictated not by the needs of their 'emancipation' as by the needs of modernization of the Soviet economy, its transition from the agrarian to the industrial phase. Beginning in the 1920s, the proportion of women in wage-labor was constantly increasing, though with certain fluctuations. In the 70 s, the share of women in the total number of employees reached 51%, and this figure is maintained until the end of the 80 s. Throughout the 20 years of the 70–80s, 92% of Soviet women of working age worked and studied. Women had two jobs—at their official workplace, doing household work—when the percentage of men's participation in the household was lower[19] despite proclaiming equality between men and women in family duties.[20]

This complex picture shifted again with the collapse of the USSR and the start of the process of economic transformation. Ukraine's rates of wage gap significantly

[13] Chernyakhivska (2016), p. 22.
[14] Tay (1972), pp. 662–692.
[15] Ibid p. 673.
[16] Ibid pp. 674–681.
[17] Ibid p. 690.
[18] Klumbys (2020).
[19] Tay (1972), p. 690.
[20] Klumbys (2020), p. 159.

increased from 1989[21] and a shift back from woman's emancipation towards traditional stereotypic constructs of the female gender was put in place,[22] which is also explained by growing religiosity in some Post-Soviet states such as Central Asia.[23] Fewer gender policies were implemented in newly created states than there were under Soviet gender equality laws, and the effort was made more towards economic stability in gender-neutral norms.

Being progressive and protective in Soviet times, the abovementioned women's rights became discriminative as Gender equality is directly affected by laws and policies that proclaim patriarchal and stereotypic attitudes to women (gender segregation within the labor market on women and men professions, and work responsibilities such as prohibition for sending pregnant women or women with children under 3 years in work business trips even with the will of woman).[24] This is also exacerbated by the practice of differentiation in social, public, and work-life between men and women,[25] and the underestimation of substantive gender equality in the region[26] that make them 'suffer from gender forms of subordination of status and non-recognition'.[27]

In current Ukrainian context, there is a significant problem of informal employment of women at work or decreasing the work hours and creating unpaid leaves[28] because the law and regulations themselves, and court decisions interpreting law provision align with patriarchal approaches towards female workers such as restrictions on women night work, intensified by administrative fines (Uvarova 2017).[29] Legal regulations with the abovementioned Post-Soviet legal norms create a contradiction with a neoliberal economic model now entrenched in Ukraine, thereby maintaining considerable obstacles to the development of corporate responsibility according to international standards (Uvarova 2018).

---

21 Brainerd (2000).

22 Szlek-Miller (1994), pp. 101–114.

23 Ishkanian (2005).

24 See for more Decree (No. 56) of Ministry of Social Policy 'On approval of Methodical recommendations on the inclusion in collective agreements and arrangements of provisions aimed at ensuring equal rights and opportunities for women and men in labor relations' para 3 and UNFPA (2021).

25 Meyersfeld (2013).

26 Vodyannikov (2021).

27 Kharytonova (2020), p. 68.

28 International Labour Organization (2018) and Skoryk (2017).

29 Uvarova (2017).

3 Adopting Women Quotas Experiences

There are different studies presenting both positive and negative impact quotas had on company performance (Atanasov 2016; Ip et al. 2018). Some researchers claim that after such measure was integrated the company performance improved (Kramer et al. 2006)[30] and formed a positive correlation between women on the board and firms' corporate social responsibility ratings or 'social capital' and corporate reputation.[31] Other call introduction of quotas 'an imperfect strategy in an imperfect world'.[32] In contrast, more critical studies question the impact of this measure on deeper structural inequalities and the way businesses operate,[33] or that an ongoing discussion on women at corporate boards relates only to 'privileged white, middle-class, and educated' women, which undermines women of other backgrounds.[34] This section provides an overview of the recent developments in three regions regarding practical impacts of gender quotas.

3.1 *United States*

Until recently, it was believed that it was impossible to imagine the introduction of gender quotas in the United States.[35] Many authors were categorical in their statements that the US Constitution does not allow gender quotas.[36] Moreover, it was argued that.

> in the United States, courts have consistently rejected quotas, as have thinkers across the ideological spectrum. Even supporters of affirmative action have distinguished incremental affirmative action programs from quotas, which have been characterized as malignant, unjustifiable, and inherently wrong.[37]

It was so until the State of California passed the law on mandatory gender quotas for companies' boards. In 2018, California introduced the first state-level obligation for gender-quotas on corporate boards (Senate Bill 826).[38] The study of board composition and stock return data on all firms in the Russell 3000 index from Bloomberg developed by Sunwoo Hwang, Anil Shivdasani, Elena Simintzi in 2018 and summarized the composition of the board of directors of California firms in the sample

[30] Yu and Madison (2021), p. 386; Comi et al. (2020), p. 790 and Atinc et al. (2022).

[31] McCrudden (2012), p. 160.

[32] Seierstad (2016), p. 396.

[33] Barnes and Holman (2020), p. 10.

[34] Terjesen and Sealy (2016), p. 45.

[35] Suk (2012), p. 196.

[36] Magnier and Rosenblum (2014), p. 251.

[37] Ibid p. 252.

[38] See California Senate Bill No. 826 (2018) Chapter 3. 'Directors and Management'.

at the end of their most recent fiscal year.[39] The median board size was eight directors, and the median number of female directors on the board was one. The median percentage of female directors on the board in the sample was 14%. On average, only 4% of firms had a chairwoman on the board, and 7% of firms have a female CEO. More than half of the boards had at least one-woman director, implying that fewer than 50% of firms will be required to add a female director to the board by the end of 2019. To achieve compliance with respect to the law's 2021 requirements, firms needed to add a median of 2 female directors to the board, representing a median increase of 22% in the fraction of female directors. Overall, 27.4% of firms needed to add one female director, 42.5% need to add two female directors, and 16.1% need to add three female directors by 2021 to achieve compliance. The median percentage of female directors on the board of non-California firms is 14%. On average, only 4% of non-California firms had a female chairman of the board, and 4% have a female CEO. If non-California firms were required to comply with California's mandatory board quotas by 2021, they would also have to add a median of 2 female directors to their boards.[40] Generally, the introduced quota requirement had a considerable impact on the corporate landscape for women.[41]

This explains the increased focus on California law. About 12% of all public (traded on stock exchanges) US companies headquartered in California, 602 public firms headquartered in California. By the moment of the statute adaption, 171 (28%) of these firms needed to add a female director by the end of 2019 and 531 (88%) need to add one or more women by 2021.[42] In 2019, women represent, on average, 30% of the board for Russell 3000 firms, but the growth remains at 1%, which makes achieving gender parity in 20 years away.[43]

However, shortly after the adoption of the Senate Bill, a complaint was submitted regarding its unconstitutionality. According to its supporters:

> this "Woman Quota" (SB 826) applies to all businesses across every industry. It applies in perpetuity and irrespective of whether there is any evidence of discrimination in the relevant industry. The law is not only deeply patronizing to women, it is also plainly unconstitutional.[44]

Other lawsuit claimed the Senate Bill is unconstitutional because it 'seeks to force shareholders to perpetuate sex-based discrimination'.[45] Previous case law practice of the U.S. Supreme Court that has rejected quotas, even as it has affirmed the appropriate inclusion of discrete remedies for past discrimination. The seminal case, *Regents of the University of California v. Bakke*, differentiated affirmative

[39] Hwang et al. (2018).

[40] Ibid.

[41] Jain and Mohie Eldin (2024).

[42] Greene et al. (2020).

[43] Gender Diversity Index Report (2024).

[44] See *Creighton Meland v. Alex Padilla, Secretary of State of California* (Case No. 2:19-cv-02288-JAM-AC).

[45] Ibid.

action (which it held was permissible within specific confines) from a quota, which it ruled was impermissible. In considering the legitimacy of a remedy, the U.S. Supreme Court applied strict scrutiny as it had in previous race cases. To survive this highest level of scrutiny, the law in question must involve a compelling governmental interest and be narrowly tailored to achieve that interest. Laws or regulations involving gender are examined under the lower, intermediate scrutiny standard.

Realizing the seriousness of the challenge, the California legislature focused on justifying the measure that was being taken, citing studies pointing to the positive effects of women in companies' board. California law also has a ripple effect as state legislators in New York and New Jersey consider similar mandates. Companies across the country, encouraged by activist investors such as BlackRock, are actively diversifying their boards. However, such legislative regulation requires proper justification of the legitimate aim, and the proportionality of the means used to achieve it in order to have constitutional status. Otherwise, if unconstitutionality would be recognized, the effect may be the opposite. Generally, the introduced quota requirement had a considerable impact in corporate landscape for women.[46] However, the Superior Court of the State of California reversed the Senate Bill 826 in 2022, establishing the violation of the Equal Protection Clause of the California Constitution as lacking legitimation for 'for remedial discrimination'.[47] This judgment also stopped the practice of collecting statistical data regarding women on boards in California.[48]

3.2 *EU Countries*

Regarding EU countries, it worth to consider the legal framework and case-law that exists to address the issue of corporate gender quotas. We do it though the analysis of general *EU legal framework on gender equality, the Directive on Gender Balance in Corporate Boards, and the case-law of CJEU and ECtHR.*

3.2.1 EU Legal Framework and the Directive on Gender Balance in Corporate Boards

Equality between women and men is one of the Union's founding values and core aims under Article 2 and Article 3(3) of the Treaty on European Union (TEU) and Article 8 of the Treaty on the Functioning of the European Union (TFEU),.The principle of positive action and its importance for achieving effective equality between women and men in practice are recognised in Article 157(4) TFEU and in

[46] Jain and Mohie Eldin (2024).

[47] Gibert and Fedorets (2024).

[48] California Secretary of State (2022).

Article 23 of the Charter of Fundamental Rights of the European Union ('the Charter'), which provides that equality between women and men must be ensured in all areas and that the principle of equality shall not prevent the maintenance or adoption of measures providing for specific advantages in favour of the under-represented sex. However, even though the need to establish gender equality is widely recognized in the EU, the legislation applied to achieve this goal often causes quite serious debate. One of the most debatable tools is the use of mandatory 'women quotas'

Frustrated by the slow growth of women's participation in economic decision-making, in 2012, the European Commission proposed a Directive that would establish mandatory quotas for the representation of women in companies' board.[49] Proposed Directive imposed on listed companies which do not have a presence of the under-represented sex of at least 40 per cent of non-executive directors an obligation to make the appointments to those positions on the basis of a comparative analysis of the qualifications of each candidate, by applying pre-established, clear, neutrally formulated and unambiguous criteria, in order to attain the said percentage at the latest by 1 January 2020 (art. 4 (1)). This preference rule provides that, in the presence of equally qualified candidates of both sexes, priority shall be given to the candidate of the under-represented sex unless an objective assessment taking account of all criteria specific to the individual candidates tilts the balance in favour of the candidate of the other sex (art. 4 (3)).

In 2022, the Council of the EU adopted a Directive on Gender Balance in Corporate Boards, requiring companies across the European Union to have 40% of non-executive directors or 33% of all board directors from the underrepresented sex by June 2026.[50] Currently, the average percentage of women at companies' boards in EU is 32.2% and board chairs—8% percent. Cyprus has very low rates (8%), Estonia, Hungary, Bosnia and Herzegovina, Greece—less than 15%.[51] France (46%), Italy (43%), The Netherlands (43%), and United Kingdom (43%) are leaders in this indicator in Europe.[52]

Overall, 8 EU countries have adopted legislation on the application of quotas for the raising representation of women in company boards.[53] However, after the adoption of a new Directive all member states are required to transpose it by 28 December 2024.[54] In 2018, the four countries, which first introduced binding quotas (BE, DE, FR, IT), had 38% women on boards, representing a rise of 28 p.p. since 2010.[55] The models implemented by different countries differ—in some quotas apply only to

[49] Veldman (2023).

[50] See EU Directive 2022/2381 (2022) on Improving The Gender Balance Among Directors Of Listed Companies And Related Measures.

[51] European Women on Boards (2024).

[52] Ibid.

[53] European Institute for Gender Equality (2023), p. 50.

[54] Otto and Müller (2023).

[55] European Women on Boards and Ethics and Boards (2018).

state-owned companies, in some—to all traded on the exchange, in some—only to large ones (Bertrand et al. 2017). Some countries impose tangible sanctions for non-compliance with quotas, some countries impose very conditional sanctions or even dispense with sanctions at first. Belgium, France, Italy, and Norway, penalize firms—with fines, bans on paying existing directors, and even possible dissolution—that fail to comply with the quotas. Germany, the Netherlands, and Spain set quotas but do not sanction companies that do not meet them, while the United Kingdom only sets guidelines for women representation on boards.[56] Still, statistics reveal that initially equal countries in 2010 in gender percentage at corporate boards like Italy (5%) and Greece (6%) became radically different after Italy has introduced obligatory gender quotas in its law—the percentage has changed to 36% in 2019 in comparison to 9% in Greece.[57]

The discussions regarding the Directive are due to a claim that the use of mandatory quotas for women's representation in the board of the companies is a threat to the interests of shareholders and the companies themselves. A similar argument is voiced, as we remember, in the United States by supporters of the unconstitutionality of measures taken in California. According to European law, mandatory quotas must be evaluated in terms of the principle of proportionality. The principle of proportionality states that any policy measure needs to be suitable and necessary to achieve its objectives.

To assess the proportionality of the mandatory quotas is important to determine whether the measure is appropriate and necessary to achieve the aim. In addition, the use of mandatory quotas could potentially lead to adverse effects on the functioning of companies. In this case, the proportionality test will also include weighing competing interests—the freedom of the company to conduct entrepreneurial activities, on the one hand, and achieving gender equality in practice, on the other.[58] The application of the proportionality test is widely used by CJEU and ECtHR.

3.2.2 Case-Law of the European Court of Justice and European Court of Human Rights

In 1995 the European Court of Justice considered the possibility of promoting gender equality by providing a predetermined priority for women in conditions where candidates of both sexes are qualified equally. The *Kalanke* case, the Court had to deal with a more concrete scheme. It examined a law of the German Land of Bremen giving a preference to women in the recruitment for or promotion within the civil service. This preference applied when women and men were equally qualified and when women were under-represented in the relevant sectors (in case of recruitment) or pay brackets (in case of promotion). Under-representation of women was deemed

[56] The Economist (2018).

[57] Latura and Weeks (2023), p. 611.

[58] Leszczynska (2017).

to exist when they did not make up at least 50% of the staff in the sector, or in the individual pay bracket in question.

The Court distinguished equality of results from equal opportunities and ruled that only the latter is acceptable. The judgment in *Kalanke* case created a lot of controversy, perhaps the biggest in the history of the Court's cases on gender equality. Against the usual trend, the Court limited the reach of a protective clause in an equality Directive. Contrary to their usual approach, the national governments reinforced the protection afforded by the Directive by changing the Treaties. After the outcry caused by the *Kalanke* case, in the next round of revision of the treaties in 1997, all national governments agreed to include a new Treaty provision reinforcing the possibility to adopt positive action measures based on gender.[59]

In November 1997, the Court had another judgment in a landmark case *Hellmut Marschall v Land Nordrhein-Westfalen*. It addressed the issue of compliance with the legislation of one of the lands of Germany with EU law. Under the disputed legislation, if in a particular sector women are less than men, then female candidate is given priority in hiring in the case of equal competence and professional skills, unless the male candidate for this job has the specific qualities that will give him the advantage. The Court acknowledged that this provision was not contrary to EU law. The Court considers that when it comes to promotion, there is a tendency to favor men, not women, if they are equally qualified. This situation is caused by deep-rooted prejudiced attitudes and stereotypes about women's roles and opportunities. That is why the equal qualification of women and men candidates does not mean that they have an equal chance. Therefore, provisions such as the provision in German law help prevent actual inequalities by introducing an additional criterion (status of woman), unless the woman is automatically given preference.

The approach that has emerged in the practice of the European Court of Human Rights, requires to prove that quotas are a necessary and proportional means of promoting gender equality. In other words, the State must answer the question: couldn't it be possible to promote it by other, softer tools (training programs, etc.)? The issue of gender quotas has not been widely considered in the practice of the ECtHR yet. However, two cases—*Evnik and Others v. Slovenia*[60] and *Staatkundig Gereformeerde Partij v. the Netherlands*[61]—illustrate the emerging approach of ECtHR regarding obligatory gender quotas. In both cases regarding introducing obligatory gender quota for political parties the ECtHR held that

> <…> the advancement of the equality of the sexes is today a major goal in the member States of the Council of Europe … and that its institutions consider the lack of gender balance in politics to be a threat to the legitimacy of democracy and a violation of the right of gender equality…the interference in question pursued the legitimate aim of strengthening

[59] Barmes (2010), p. 12.

[60] See European Court of Human Rights *Evnik and Others v. Slovenia* no. 54893/18 (12 November 2019).

[61] See European Court of Human Rights *Staatkundig Gereformeerde Partij v. the Netherland* no. 58369/10 (10 July 2012).

> the legitimacy of democracy by ensuring a more balanced participation of women and men in political decision-making.[62]

> <…> nowadays the advancement of the equality of the sexes in the member States of the Council of Europe prevents the State from lending its support to views of the man's role as primordial and the woman's as secondary.[63]

These ECtHR's judgments confirm that 'increasing female participation is a legitimate and favorable aim', to achieve which gender quotas can be an effective measure.[64] Further, it can be assumed how events can develop if the 'gender quotas' case falls into the ECtHR. Imagine a hypothetical case, the subject of which is following: the male applicant believes that his right not to be discriminated against (Article 14 of the European Convention on Human Rights and Fundamental Freedoms) has been violated in the context of the right to privacy (Article 8 of the Convention), since the legislative step to introduce gender quotas has limited his ability to self-realization, minimized its impact on his further professional development. The only grounds for refusal of leadership positions in the company' governance was the use mandatory gender quotas by the company.

First, we can expect that the Court will reiterate that:

> <…> Article 14 affords protection against different treatment, without an objective and reasonable justification, of persons in similar situations. For the purposes of Article 14, a difference of treatment is discriminatory if it "has no objective and reasonable justification", that is, if it does not pursue a "legitimate aim" or if there is not a "reasonable relationship of proportionality between the means employed and the aim sought to be realised".[65]

Recalling *Emel Boyraz v. Turkey* case, it can be assumed that the Court accepts that the situation in the case is covered by Art. 8, 14 of the Convention. If the Court was rephrased a little, it could have noted in this hypothetical case the following:

> <…> The Court considers that the issue to be examined in the present case is not whether the applicant had a right to be recruited to the company's board. His submissions under this head concerned the difference in treatment to which he had been subjected on the ground of his sex.

Next, the Court will ask, *whether the applicant was in an analogous or relevantly similar position*. The Court, as a rule, seeks an answer to this question solely in formal attributes: did the man and woman aspire to the same position. It can be assumed that the answer will be yes. Although it is possible that at this stage the state will be able to prove that women and men applying for a managerial position in the company are not in a similar position due to the existing indirect discrimination. The ECtHR (and CJEU as well) considers statistics an effective means of proving indirect discrimination.

---

[62] See *Evnik and Others v. Slovenia* para 34.

[63] See *Staatkundig Gereformeerde Partij v. the Netherlands* para 73.

[64] Toplak (2019).

[65] See European Court of Human Rights *Bradshaw and Others v. Malta* no. 37121/15 (23 October 2018) para 76.

But let's assume that the Court proceeds to the next question: *Whether the difference in treatment was objectively justified?*

Based on the previous practice of the ECtHR, it can be assumed the answer to this question:

> <…> where a difference of treatment is based on sex, the margin of appreciation afforded to the State is narrow and in such situations the principle of proportionality does not merely require that the measure chosen should in general be suited to the fulfilment of the aim pursued, but it must also be shown that it was necessary in the circumstances.

Approximately the same reasoning algorithm can be expected in a hypothetical case in which the firm itself can act as the applicant and appeal the violation of Article 1 Protocol 1 of the European Convention on human rights and fundamental freedom in connection with a disproportionate interference in the governance of the company. It is not excluded that the Court, for example, will refer to the fact that 'social life is regulated not only by the law but also by different types of social rules. In many fields social self-regulation may yield better results than legal rules',[66] and it will take the position that gender diversity in company governance is a sphere of self-regulation, and the maximum that the state can do in this regard is to conduct information campaigns to create appropriate knowledge and interest in companies. Or it can held that 'positive obligations on the State are inherent in the right to effective respect for private life under Article 8; these obligations may involve the adoption of measures even in the sphere of the relations of individuals between themselves';[67] or that 'a difference in treatment that is aimed at ensuring substantive equality may be justified under Article 14 of the Convention'.[68]

3.3 Ukraine

No country in the Eastern European region has adopted quotas for the representation of women in company boards. The first thing to note is the lack of official statistics or other centralized mechanisms for collecting information on the representation of women in company management, based on which the states of the region could formulate their policies on this issue. This is a common symptom for countries in the region. According to a report from the European Commission on the situation in the region, gender stereotypes and discrimination against women hinder their greater inclusion in the labor market and cause additional barriers to women's entrepreneurship. The document also states that women are employed mostly in services and government institutions with a much lower level of wages than in those

[66] See Dissenting Opinion of Judges Pejchal and Wojtyczek European Court of Human Rights *X. v. The Former Yugoslav Republic of Macedonia* no. 29683/16 (17 January 2019) para 9.

[67] See European Court of Human Rights *Beizaras and Levickas v. Lithuania* no. 41288/15 (14 January 2020) para 110.

[68] See European Court of Human Rights *Ēcis v. Latvia* no. 12879/09 (10 January 2019) para 86.

areas where men dominate. Gender wage gap remains significant and varies from 18.6% In Ukraine[69] to 34% 50%, as in Kazakhstan and Azerbaijan accordingly.[70]

According to the British Council in Ukraine, in the countries of the Eastern Partnership (Armenia, Azerbaijan, Belarus, Georgia, Moldova and Ukraine—all countries of the former USSR), women are underrepresented in economically responsible positions. In 2015, there were 9% of women on the boards of central banks, 15% in the leadership of trade unions, 10% in the leadership of associations of employers, less than 15% in the boards of companies listed on stock exchange quotes.[71] The UN Development Program carried out a special project in Ukraine, an analysis of open information in state registers, which shows the names of managers (but not sex), to determine the percentage of women in company management.[72] While the general percentage of women in leadership positions increased to 40.48% during 2017–2020 and the rise of female entrepreneurship in Ukraine,[73] the rate of women in corporate boards remains the same 30% in 2024.[74] However, there is another significant feature: women are predominantly managing in areas that conform to the stereotypes of traditionally female household and community activities: education and childcare, social assistance (as well as trade union activities), hotels, restaurants, food retailing and clothing, tailoring, beauty salons, tourism, arts and leisure, accounting and auditing. Thus, Ukrainian legislation on women's employment 'is gender-blind rather than gender-sensitive, as it does not address existing imbalances and women's underrepresentation in certain economic areas'.[75]

In Ukraine, there was an attempt to introduce gender quotas (40%) for the representation of women in company board: a draft of the law was submitted to the parliament in 2019 and 2020.[76] However, it provided the quota's application to supervisory boards only (it was not about executive directors) and just to state companies and state banks. To justify the law, the authors of the draft repeated almost completely the arguments contained in the California Law. But the draft of the law was not further considered by parliament. The Law of Ukraine 'On Equal Rights and Opportunities for Women and Men' provides that 'employers can take positive actions to achieve a balanced ratio of women and men in different fields of work, as well as among different categories of workers'.[77]

---

[69] Ministry of Economy of Ukraine (2024).

[70] UNDP (2023), p. 95.

[71] British Council (2018).

[72] UNDP (2017).

[73] Tokar et al. (2023).

[74] Forbes Ukraine (2024).

[75] NIRAS (2023), p. 36.

[76] See Draft Law on Amendments to Certain Legislative Acts on Ensuring Equal Rights and Opportunities for Citizens from Representation in Supervisory Boards and Governing Bodies of State Unitary Enterprises, Economic Societies, and State Bank 3939-IX (3 September 2024).

[77] See The Law of Ukraine 'On Equal Rights and Opportunities for Women and Men' 2866-IV (8 September 2005) Article 17.

The Action Plan for 2019 on the Implementation of the Poverty Reduction Strategy, approved by the Decree of the Cabinet of Ministers of Ukraine in 2019, consisted of a measure of 'introducing gender quotas at state-owned enterprises'.[78] However, it was not implemented. Furthermore, the Strategy of Human Development, which was issued by the President of Ukraine in 2021 and is planned to achieve its objectives by 2025, does not mention the introduction of gender quotas and only refers to the need of 'formation of an effective mechanism for achieving a balanced representation of women and men in the field of politics and public administration, taking into account the categories of civil servants'.[79] Simultaneously, the National Strategy for Closing the Gender Pay Gap until 2030 and approved an Action Plan for 2023–2025 calls for incentives to push employers to introduction of gender quotas in management bodies and in managerial positions.[80] Similarly, the State Strategy for Ensuring Equal Rights and Opportunities of Women and Men for the period up to 2030 and its Operative Plan operationalizes the need for using gender quotas as one of the mechanisms to achieve the balanced representation of women and men in companies decision-making through the implementation of positive actions.[81] However, none of these provisions was implemented in state or corporate level regulations, policies, or practices.

While the main positive point is that the relevant discussions are underway,[82] a key negative tendency is the fact that even supporters of the using of quotas pay little attention to the issue of a legitimate aim, justification for the using quotas. Most often, the need to comply with European practices is called as the main argument, and the justification itself does not go beyond copying arguments presented by colleagues from the United States and EU countries.

Despite a very different history, statistics show that the situation with the representation of women in the leadership of companies in the USA, EU countries and post-Soviet countries is approximately the same. There are various explanations for the low representation of women: social stereotypes, gender stereotypes regarding competence and leadership, as well as the lack of interest on the part of women, and the primary responsibility of women for children and other family members who need of care. Studies show that standards of behavior are heavily dependent on standards of conduct of the previous generation.[83] It explains, among other things, the similarity of the situation in the three regions which are subjects of the attention:

---

[78] See Action Plan for 2019 on the Implementation of the Poverty Reduction Strategy № 86-p (20 February 2019) para. 25.

[79] See The Strategy of Human Development, approved by the Decree of the President of Ukraine № 225/2021 (2 June 2021) the operative aim 5.2.

[80] See Operational Plan Concerning Measures for the Implementation in 2023–2025 of the National Strategy to Overcome the Gender Pay Gap for the Period up to 2030 № 815-p (15 September 2023) the strategic aim 2.

[81] See State Strategy on Ensuring Equal Rights and Opportunities for Women and Men for the Period up to 2030 № 752-p (12 August 2022) the operative aim 1.2.

[82] Sabovchyk (2023).

[83] Farrø and Vella (2013), p. 220.

social norms that determine the vulnerable position of women in certain areas of activity are so ingrained in societies that changing the situation will be possible just by positive measures. The next section elaborates how such measures can normatively ground in the concept of personal autonomy.

4 Discussion

4.1 Legitimate Aim: A Protection of a Personal Autonomy

The equity argument for gender quotas in leadership is based first on achieving higher female representation at the highest positions, which is of symbolic importance, but which only directly affects a small number of women. The argument is also often also based on a notion that female leaders will help other women—either directly, through mentorship or advocacy in their organizations, or indirectly, through inspiration and role model effects.[84] However, the question remains: should the arguments be based on economic effect work in principle? Do they have the opposite, negative, effect? If we make the achievement of gender equality dependent on its positive economic impact on the quality of governance, will then the absence of such a positive effect justify gender inequality? The point is that the legitimate aim should be sufficient to justify the interference of state in the sphere of freedom of entrepreneurship. In this regard, the arguments that are based on respect for human rights themselves as an independent value are much more relevant as gender quotas are needed to: prevent current direct discrimination and address stereotyping; compensate the past discrimination; provide identity and recognition for women; ensure diversity and social cohesion. According to A. A. Dhir.

> state-based intervention is essential to shifting existing norms, but should be based on a combination of factors related to organizational governance and decision making, and the goals of democratizing power and equitably distributing access to opportunities.[85]

However, each of these arguments is based on respect for personal autonomy, which implies the possibility of realizing one's life project. We approach the issue of gender quotas from the point of view of the principle of personal autonomy as a normative requirement, which should be addressed to each entity—public or private—that significantly affects the possibility of a person realizing their life project. The value of autonomy is explained by its origin from the idea of human dignity.[86] Pico Della Mirandola, an Italian thinker of the Renaissance, in the work 'Speech on Human Dignity' (published in 1496) states that 'human dignity is that it itself is the creator of its essence. A person can be who she or he wants to be; she or he makes herself/

---

[84] Miller (2018).

[85] Dhir (2015), p. 5.

[86] Griffin (2009) p. 151.

hisself the one she/he chooses'.[87] This aspect of human dignity is embodied in the idea of personal autonomy, which in its simplest definition is understood as self-regulation (*self-rule, self-legislation*) and *self-government*, when the emphasis is on the possibility of self-direction, free from external forces, or, in the figurative words of J. Raz, *self-authorship*, which has its roots in the Mill's romantic liberalism, who insisted on a variety of 'experiments in life' to find the 'free development of individuality'.[88]

The idea of personal autonomy is made extremely attractive by its obligatory connection with freedom, its understanding as the right not to be interfered with by the state ('to keep it at arm's length')[89] or other actors, except cases when such intervention is justified by a legitimate aim. Personal autonomy is impossible in a situation of paternalistic regulation. But it is also impossible in a situation when a party who is clearly weaker than another party is placed in conditions equal to the last one.

Personal autonomy is closely related to the concepts of agency and capability that all together refer to what a person can freely do in line with their perception of good.[90] In this regard Francesco Laruffa argues that 'at the collective level, social policy should not be assessed in terms of its economic benefits but in terms of its contribution to democracy—the collective dimension of autonomy'.[91] Lorella Terzi argues that autonomy is itself a human capability 'since it is constitutive of agency, and it is situated at the nexus of the freedom to pursue well-being and the freedom to pursue agency goals, while also relating to process freedom'.[92] Personal autonomy as a part of agency views a person as 'an agent broadly capable of considering the various choices available and evaluating their potential outcomes, while bringing about their realization'.[93] Other scholars like Marta Nussbaum present personal autonomy in a political form as by 'creating and protecting spaces in which they can live according to their own views'.[94] Agency as autonomy implies deliberation and realization of 'one's values and goals and the means to achieve them successfully'.[95]

The collective dimension of personal autonomy of women proposes 'gendered autonomy' to address issues of gender equality.[96] Gendered autonomy entails the possibility of an individual women identifying herself as a part of certain gender group in society, to act freely in different social spheres and not being afraid of becoming underprivileged because of belonging to a certain gender group. Corporate gender quota as a positive measure internalizes the possibility to represent different

[87] Pico Della Mirandola (1996).

[88] Taylor (2005), p. 602.

[89] Alldridge and Brants (2001) p. 8.

[90] Laruffa (2020), p. 3; Latkovskis (2021), p. 62.

[91] Laruffa (2020), p. 3.

[92] Terzi (2022), p. 331.

[93] Ibid p. 327.

[94] See Terzi (2022) refferening to Nussbaum at p. 330.

[95] Ibid p. 331.

[96] Sredl (2018).

genders in a decision-making, thus broadly providing the equal space for autonomy to different gender groups, especially to those groups which were previously under-represented at corporate boards. As rightly underscored by Laruffa,

> autonomy at work involves not only the choice of the means to achieve given goals—as often assumed in the sociology of work—but also the possibility to participate at the determination of the ends of production.[97]

Collective dimension of gendered autonomy, where identifying own gender is related to certain gender group in society, is influenced by the 'cultural, economic, social, political and environmental factors on people's desires and visions of the "good life"'.[98] This arguably means that such factors incline what capabilities as a group women get when operating in certain society. As a result, in areas where women are still perceived as a weak sex, 'less agentic, that is, assertive, active, and strong, and more communal, that is, understanding, supportive, and caring, than men… and are, therefore, less likely to emerge as leaders'.[99] This perception illustrates women as is does not intend to hold leadership position, this vision forms adaptive preferences of women as belonging to the group which is not supposed to have leadership positions (Alesina et al. 2013). Adaptive preferences are defined as

> preferences that you hold more because your option set is bad or limited than because of the good-making features of the objects you prefer… you want what you do because it was the best option available to you, and you would have wanted something else instead if you'd had a better or larger set of options.[100]

Being affected by adaptive preferences means that an 'individuals' ability to initiate transformative changes in their environment'[101] does not always constitute independent agency and agency. For instance, the refuse of a women to participate in a decision-making when can be prescribed not by her own will but by circumstances that exist in society.[102] As a result, such adaptive preferences prevent women from realizing their personal autonomy in the decision-making and corporate leadership.

To ensure the flourishing of personal autonomy, an economic system should be reformed as 'a capability-oriented social policy should thus aim at expanding human agency both within and beyond work, enhancing simultaneously the "freedom *from* work" and the "freedom *within* work."'[103] The concept of 'gendered autonomy' provides an insight for women at corporate boards accordingly.

[97] Laruffa (2020), p. 5.

[98] Bonvin and Laruffa (2024), p. 3.

[99] Mölders et al. (2018), pp. 871–872; Comi et al. (2020), p. 773.

[100] Terlazzo (2022), p. 270.

[101] Donald et al. (2020), p. 204.

[102] Ibid.

[103] Laruffa (2020), pp. 6–7.

4.2 *BHR Model of Regulation as Based on Personal Autonomy Approach*

We propose a BHR model of ensuring women's participation in a decision-making at the workplace is based on equality enhanced by the principle of personal autonomy, 'gendered autonomy'.[104] We envision a BHR model that centers the responsibility to recognize and respect human dignity. The BHR model of regulation creates guarantees of personal autonomy because it presumes that a state could not regulate all relations, and some spaces of regulation should be the sphere of the business's responsibility, without any state regulation (protection from paternalism). At the same time, the BHR model considers business as a human rights duty bearer through the prism of responsible business conduct—there is a business duty to respect human rights. In the context of women's rights, Pillar requires that the state applies measures to protect women's rights. Wherever they operate, corporations are part of social fabric, they influence politics, economics, legal, social and cultural rules and practices. Culture can influence gender equality. Having such power, businesses are vested with an obligation to ensure, at the least, that human rights are not harmed, not to engage in direct or indirect discrimination, including on the grounds of sex, etc. It is not enough merely to declare one's commitment to human rights, and it would be odd to deny one's obvious impact on human rights, especially those of vulnerable individuals. Corporate policies and practices 'must fully integrate gender-responsive practices within each area of their business operations'.[105]

Today, corporate observance of human rights requires more than formal compliance with the law. Companies must implement due diligence mechanisms in the field of human rights, prevent risks of human rights violations in their operation, promote human rights values, such as gender equality and non-discrimination. Businesses need to abandon the 'do no harm' approach and to go beyond it. In other words, not only should they, among other things, prevent and mitigate the negative impact of their activities on women's rights, but also actively advance women's rights through gender-transformative measures, i.e., measures that change the underlying power structures and relationships in the form of affirmative actions to promote gender equality and women's rights.

Such affirmative actions can lie in the introduction of corporate gender quotas as to impact adaptive preferences, formed in patriarchal societies for women's role in them. Formed in patriarchal societies the perception of women as not capable to hold leadership position should be reformed with the positive measures such as gender quotas. Therefore, such adaptive preferences should be deconstructed by transformative institutions to ensure different groups can 'develop own aspirations and use their voice to support them and translate them into collective claims and action'.[106]

---

[104] Anderson (2003).

[105] Bourke Martignoni and Umlas (2018), p. 8.

[106] Bonvin and Laruffa (2024), pp. 3–4.

5 Conclusion

In this chapter, we compared the situation in three different regions of the world, which, however, are united by the fact that they all relate to the Western tradition of law, which recognizes the fundamental, priority, universal nature of human rights and personal human autonomy. The legislative requirement to ensure the representation of women on the board of companies is a good example of how law aims to influence existing barriers in practice in providing opportunities for personal autonomy.

The basis of legal regulation in the countries of the Eastern European region still lacks attention to a principle of personal autonomy. Many countries in the region have tried to move away from the state-oriented model of legal regulation, some more, some less successfully. But they still have not come to recognize personal autonomy, particularly, gendered autonomy as a constitutive principle of state regulations and corporate policies. The Eastern-European countries they mainly do not recognize the problem, and therefore in most cases they will not perceive the introduction of quotas to solve it. Keeping in their legal order many manifestations of the paternalistic approach, countries of the region often do not take positive actions to overcome structural discrimination, because they are afraid of being accused of the 'post-Soviet syndrome'. Hence, the perception of measures to ensure gender equality as benefits granted by the state to women is predominant.

EU and US models of legal regulation, on the contrary, are based on the recognition of personal autonomy. Measures to ensure gender equality in these legal systems perform the function of eliminating the barriers that women face in the implementation of their life project and are therefore in a more vulnerable position than men who implement the same life project without such barriers. Because these barriers can exist in both the public and private space, and measures of gender equality ensuring can be implemented in both areas. However, the difference between EU and US experience, in turn, is since the US implements a liberal concept of legal regulation, and in matters of ensuring gender equality, law inevitably encounters another fundamental thesis about the minimal presence of the state, especially when it comes to private entities and their freedoms.

Both the USA and the EU initially did not recognize the possibility of applying gender quotas, especially in private relations. However, over time, the situation has changed, though the government politics and practices on introducing obligatory gender quotas remain complicated. The main challenge facing these states today is the justification of the legitimacy of quotas. Such a challenge is determined by an established model of behavior in society and certain stereotypes of thinking.

In this paper we have argued that the concept of gendered autonomy can be an effective normative ground to reshape such established model of corporate behavior that undermines the role of women in corporate decision-making. As such, gendered autonomy for the decision-making at corporate boards allows to form as 'a capability-oriented' corporate systems that expand human agency both within and beyond work. This concept further allows to change the perception of women as not capable to hold leadership position should be reformed with the positive measures such as gender quotas. The significant improvement of women's representations in corporate boards in countries that introduced obligatory corporate gender quotas proves that such measure is effective in achieving the goal of gender equality, enhanced women agency and expanded gender autonomy. Such experience can also be a platform for developing analogical legislation in countries of Eastern Europe.

References

50/50 Women on Boards (2024) Gender diversity index report. Annual progress report of women corporate directors by race & ethnicity, company size, state, and sector in the U.S. https://5050wob.com/wp-content/uploads/pdf/2024-annual-gender-diversity-index-report.pdf

Alesina A, Giuliano P, Nunn N (2013) The origins of gender roles: women and the plough. Q J Econ 128(2):469–530

Alldridge P, Brants C (2001) Personal autonomy, the private sphere and the criminal law. Hart Publishing, Oxford

Anderson PS (2003) Autonomy, vulnerability and gender. Fem Theory 4(2):149–164

Atanasov A (2016) Are quotas the most suitable tool to ensure equal representation of women in company boards? https://ssrn.com/abstract=2712665

Atinc G, Srivastava S, Taneja S (2022) The impact of gender quotas on corporate boards: a cross-country comparative study. J Manag Gov 26(3):685–706

Barmes L (2010) Navigating multi-layered uncertainty: EU, member state and organizational perspectives on positive action. Queen Mary School of Law, Legal Studies Research Paper. https://ssrn.com/abstract=1538522

Barnes TD, Holman MR (2020) Gender quotas, women's representation, and legislative diversity. J Polit 82(4):1271. https://doi.org/10.1086/708336

Baumann-Pauly D, Nolan J (2016) Business and human rights from principles to practice. Routledge

Bernaz N (2016) Business and human rights: history, law and policy-bridging the accountability gap. Routledge

Bertrand M, Black SE, Jensen S, Lleras-Muney A (2017) Breaking the glass ceiling? The effect of board quotas on female labor market outcomes in Norway. National Bureau of Economic Research, Working Paper Series, Working Paper 20256

Bonvin JM, Laruffa F (2024) Transforming social policies and institutions in a capability perspective: agency, voice and the capability to aspire. J Hum Dev Capab 25(4):575–594

Bourke Martignoni J, Umlas E (2018) Gender responsive due diligence for business actors: human rights-based approaches. Geneva Academy of International Humanitarian Law and Human Rights, Geneva

Brainerd E (2000) Women in transition: changes in gender wage differential in Eastern Europe and the former Soviet Union. Ind Labor Relat Rev 54(1):138–162

British Council (2018) Стан та просування рівних можливостей для жінок та чоловіків у культурних та креативних індустріях в Азербайджані, Вірменії, Грузії та Україні [Stan ta prosuvannya rivnykh mozhlyvostey dlya zhinok ta cholovikiv u kulturnykh ta kreatyvnykh industriyakh v Azerbaydzhani, Virmeniyi, Hruziyi ta Ukrayini, in Ukrainian]. http://www.britishcouncil.org.ua/sites/default/files/gender-equality-and-empowerment-ukr_0.pdf

California Secretary of State (2022) Women on boards. Update. https://www.sos.ca.gov/business-programs/women-boards

Comi S, Grasseni M, Origo F, Pagani L (2020) Where women make difference: gender quotas and firms' performance in three European countries. ILR Rev J Work Policy 73(3):768–793

Dallago B, Ajani G, Grancelli B (1992) Privatization and entrepreneurship in post-socialist countries, Economy, law and society. Macmillan Press LTD

Dhir A (2015) Challenging boardroom homogeneity: corporate law, governance, and diversity. Cambridge University Press

Donald A, Koolwal G, Annan J, Falb K, Goldstein M (2020) Measuring women's agency. Fem Econ 26(3):200–226

EIGE (European Institute for Gender Equality) (2023) Gender Equality Index 2023. Towards a green transition in transport and energy. Publications Office of the European Union

European Women on Boards (EWOB) (2024) Diversity on European Boards. Gender balance is improving – now change must go deeper and wider. https://europeanwomenonboards.eu/wp-content/uploads/2024/03/EWOB-Toolkit-for-change-Gender-diversity-on-European-boards.pdf

European Women on Boards and Ethics & Boards (2018) European Gender Diversity Index (GDI). europeanwomenonboards.eu

Farrø L, Vella F (2013) The intergenerational transmission of gender role attitudes and its implications for female labour force participation. Economica 80(318):219–247

Forbes Ukraine (2024) Дуже мало компаній доросли до корпоративного управління». Як проходить велика корпоратизація українського бізнесу? Дослідження UCGA [Forbes Ukraine (2024) Duzhe malo kompanii dorosly do korporatyvnoho upravlinnia». Yak prokhodyt velyka korporatyzatsiia ukrainskoho biznesu? Doslidzhennia UCGA, in Ukrainian]. https://forbes.ua/money/duzhe-malo-kompaniy-dorosli-do-korporativnogo-upravlinnya-yak-prokhodit-velika-korporatizatsiya-ukrainskogo-biznesu-doslidzhennya-g-radus-10072024-22219

Gibert A, Fedorets A (2024) Lifting women up: gender quotas and the advancement of women on corporate boards. Corp Gov 33:407. https://bpd.cdn.sos.ca.gov/div-on-boards/final-judgment-072022.pdf

Greene D, Intintoli VJ, Kahle KM (2020) Do board gender quotas affect firm value? Evidence from California Senate Bill 826. J Corp Finan 60(1015262):1–21

Griffin J (2009) On human rights. Oxford University Press

Hass J (2012) Rethinking the post-Soviet experience: markets, moral economies, and cultural contradictions of post-socialist Russia. Palgrave Macmillan

Hwang S, Shivdasani A, Simintzi E (2018) Mandating women on boards: evidence from the United States. Kenan Institute of Private Enterprise, Research Paper. https://ssrn.com/abstract=3265783

ILO (International Labour Organization) (2018) Undeclared work in Ukraine: nature, scope and measures to tackle it. https://www.ilo.org/sites/default/files/wcmsp5/groups/public/@ed_dialogue/@lab_admin/documents/projectdocumentation/wcms_630068.pdf

Ip E, Leibbrandt A, Vecci J (2018) How do gender quotas affect hierarchical relationships? Complementary evidence from a representative survey and labor market experiments. CESifo Working Paper Series 6915. https://ssrn.com/abstract=3167115

Ishkanian A (2005) Gendered transitions: the impact of the post-Soviet transition on women in Central Asia and the Caucasus. In: Amineh MP, Houweling H (eds) Central Eurasia in global politics. Brill, pp 161–182

Jain A, Mohie Eldin R (2024) Board diversity and career progression of women: evidence from SB 826. https://ssrn.com/abstract=4787312

Kabasakal Arat ZF (2015) Feminisms, women's rights, and the UN: would achieving gender equality empower women. Am Polit Sci Rev 109(4):674–689

Klumbys V (2020) Equality just over the horizon: Soviet gender equality in law and policy. Lith Hist Stud 24(1):143–181

Kramer VW, Konrad AM, Erkut S (2006) Critical mass on corporate boards: why three or more women enhance governance. Wellesley Centers for Women's Publications Office. https://www.wcwonline.org/vmfiles/CriticalMassExecSummary.pdf

Laruffa F (2020) What is a capability-enhancing social policy? Individual autonomy, democratic citizenship and the insufficiency of the employment-focused paradigm. J Hum Dev Capab 21(1):1–16
Latkovskis I (2021) Capabilities, autonomy, and education: a comprehensive anti-perfectionist capability approach to justice. PhD thesis, University of Glasgow
Latura A, Weeks AC (2023) Corporate board quotas and gender equality policies in the workplace. Am J Polit Sci 67(3):606–622
Lépinard E, Rubio-Marín R (2018) Transforming gender citizenship: the irresistible rise of gender quotas in Europe. Cambridge University Press
Leszczynska M (2017) Mandatory quotas for women on boards of directors in the European Union: harmful to or good for company performance? https://link.springer.com/content/pdf/10.1007/s40804-017-0095-x.pdf
Magnier V, Rosenblum D (2014) Quotas and the transatlantic divergence of corporate governance. Northwest J Int Law Bus 34:249–298
McCrudden C (2012) A comparative taxonomy of 'positive action' and 'affirmative action' policies. Queen's University Belfast Law Research Paper 12-04:157–180
Meyersfeld B (2013) Business, human rights and gender: a legal approach to external and internal considerations. In: Deva S, Bilchitz D (eds) Human rights obligations of business: beyond the corporate responsibility to respect. Cambridge University Press, pp 193–217
Miller AR (2018) Women and leadership. In: Averett S, Argys LM, Hoffman SD (eds) Oxford handbook on women and the economy. Oxford University Press
Ministry of Economy of Ukraine (2024) Reducing the gender pay gap from 18.6% to 13.6% and launching the national campaign 'Sure You Can' - how is Ukraine moving towards women's economic empowerment in times of great war. https://www.kmu.gov.ua/en/news/skorochennia-hendernoho-rozryvu-v-oplati-pratsi-z-186-do-136-ta-start-natsionalnoi-kampanii-zvisno-zmozhesh-iak-ukraina-rukhaietsia-do-ekonomichnoho-upovnovazhennia-zhinok-u-chasy-velykoi-viiny
Mölders S, Brosi P, Bekk M, Spörrle M, Welpe IM (2018) Support for quotas for women in leadership: the influence of gender stereotypes. Hum Resour Manag 57(4):869–882
NIRAS (2023) Country gender profile: Ukraine. https://euneighbourseast.eu/wp-content/uploads/2023/09/eu4genderhelpdesk_ukrainegenderprofile_2023-cgp_v3.pdf
Obara LJ (2017) 'What does this mean?': how UK companies make sense of human rights. Bus Hum Rights J 2(2):249–273
Otto B, Müller R (2023) Gender balance quotas: the key to gender equality? https://www.ibanet.org/gender-balance-quotas-key-gender-equality
Pico Della Mirandola J (1996) On the dignity of man. Gateway Editions
Sabovchyk A (2023) Gender balance in the board of directors. Uzhhorod National University Herald. Series: Law 76(2):257–263
Seierstad C (2016) Beyond the business case: the need for both utility and justice rationales for increasing the share of women on boards. Corp Gov 24(4):390–405
Sredl K (2018) Gendered market subjectivity: autonomy, privilege, and emotional subjectivity in normalizing post-socialist neoliberal ideology. Consum Mark Cult 21(6):532–553
Suk JS (2012) Gender parity and state legitimacy: from public office to corporate boards. Stanford J Law Bus Finance 21(2):194–210
Szlek-Miller S (1994) Gender equality and transition from communism in Eastern Europe. Polish Polit Sci Yearb 24:101–114
Tay A (1972) The status of women in the Soviet Union. Am J Comp Law 20(4):662–692
Taylor RS (2005) Kantian personal autonomy. Political Theory 33(5):602–628
Terjesen S, Sealy R (2016) Board gender quotas: exploring ethical tensions from a multi-theoretical perspective. Bus Ethics Q 26(1):23–65
Terlazzo R (2022) Adaptive preferences as autonomy deficits. In: Colburn B (ed) The Routledge handbook of autonomy. Routledge, pp 270–280

Terzi L (2022) Autonomy and capability. In: Colburn B (ed) The Routledge handbook of autonomy. Routledge, pp 324–334
The Economist (2018) Ten years on from Norway's quota for women on corporate boards. https://www.economist.com/business/2018/02/17/ten-years-on-from-norways-quota-for-women-on-corporate-boards
Tokar V, Vinska O, Novak N, Sierova L (2023) Clustering EU Member-States and Ukraine by female empowerment in business. In: Hamdan H, Buallay A, Arora P, Alsabatin H (eds) From Industry 4.0 to Industry 5.0: mapping the transitions. Springer, Cham, pp 89–99
Toplak (2019) The ECHR and gender quotas in elections. https://www.ejiltalk.org/the-echr-and-gender-quotas-in-elections/
UNDP (United Nations Development Programme) (2017) Жінки та чоловіки на керівних посадах в Україні [Zhinky ta choloviky na kerivnykh posadakh v Ukrayini]. https://platforma-msb.org/wp-content/uploads/2017/11/ZHinky-ta-choloviky-na-kerivnyh-posadah-v-Ukrayini-.pdf
UNDP (United Nations Development Programme) (2022) Business and Human Rights (BHR) in Ukraine. Accelerating sustainable and equitable development through implementation of the UN guiding principles on business and human rights (UNGPs). United Nations Development Programme
UNDP (United Nations Development Programme) (2023) The status of the implementation of the UNGPs on business and human rights in Europe and Central Asia. United Nations Development Programme, Istanbul
UNFPA (United Nations Population Fund) (2021) Чим керуються українці та українки при виборі професії: результати національного дослідження щодо ключових чинників та стереотипів [UNFPA (United Nations Population Fund) (2021) Chym keruiutsia ukraintsi ta ukrainky pry vybori profesii: rezultaty natsionalnoho doslidzhennia shchodo kliuchovykh chynnykiv ta stereotypiv, in Ukrainian]. https://ukraine.unfpa.org/sites/default/files/pub-pdf/prezetation_tramplin_ukr_1.pdf
Veldman A (2023) Gender quota for corporate directors: a task for the European Union? The revival of the directive on gender balanced company boards. Utrecht Law Rev 19(3):44–56
Yu JJ, Madison G (2021) Gender quotas and company financial performance: A systematic review. Econ Aff 41(3):377–390
Водянніков О (2021) Ґендерна рівність. Теорія і практика в порівняльному конституційному праві. OSCE [Vodyannikov O (2021) Genderna rivnist. Teoriia i praktyka v porivnialnomu konstytutsiinomu pravi, OSCE, in Ukrianian]
Скорик М (2017) Гендерна дискримінація у доступі до праці й послуг: оцінка стану впровадження Україною антидискримінаційних Директив Ради ЄС. Аналітичне дослідження. Київ, Бюро соціальних та політичних розробок [Skoryk MM (2017) Henderna dyskryminatsiia u dostupi do pratsi y posluh: otsinka stanu vprovadzhennia Ukrainoiu antydyskryminatsiinykh Dyrektyv Rady YeS. Analitychne doslidzhennia. Kyiv, Biuro sotsialnykh ta politychnykh rozrobok, in Ukrainian]
Уварова О (2017) Принцип недискримінації за ознакою статті в судовій практиці України. Право України 7: 56–66 [Uvarova O (2017) Pryntsyp nedyskryminatsii za oznakoiu statti v sudovii praktytsi Ukrainy. Pravo Ukrainy 7: 56–66, in Ukrianian]
Уварова О (2018) Права жінок та гендерна рівність. Holembovska O. O [Uvarova O (2018) Prava zhinok ta henderna rivnist Navchalnyi posibnyk. Holembovska O, in Ukrainian]
Харитонова О (2020) Людська гідність і гендерна рівність у конституційному просторі. UJCL 4: 61–71 [Kharytonova O (2020) Liudska hidnist i henderna rivnist u konstytutsiinomu prostori. UJCL 4: 61–71, in Ukrianian]
Черняхівська В (2016) Історичний досвід становлення української моделі гендерного паритету. Державне управління: удосконалення та розвиток 10: 21–26 [Chernyakhivska V (2016) Istorychnyy dosvid stanovlennya ukrayinskoi modeli hendernoho parytetu, Derzhavne upravlinnya: udoskonalennya ta rozvytok 10: 21–26, in Ukrainian]

Tarzi I (2022) Autonomy and capability. In: Colburn B (ed) The Routledge handbook of autonomy. Routledge, pp [illegible]
The Economist [illegible] Ten years of [illegible] for women on corporate boards. https://www.economist.com/[illegible]/women-on-corporate-board/
[illegible] V, [illegible] (20[illegible]) Number [illegible] and [illegible] female employees [illegible] Hofmann [illegible] 2017
[illegible] (20[illegible]) [illegible]
[illegible]
UN [illegible] (20[illegible]) [illegible] United Nations Development Programme
UN [illegible]
UNFPA [illegible] United Nations Population Fund (2021) [illegible], in Ukrainian]
Vehkamp A (2023) Gender quota for corporate directors, a task for the European Union. The revival of the directive on gender-balanced company boards. Utrecht Law Rev [illegible]
Yu H, Madison G (2021) Gender quotas and company financial performance: A systematic review. Econ Aff 41(3):377–390
Возвишков О (2021) Гендерна рівність. Теорія і практика в порівняльному конституційному праві. OSCE [Vozvyshkov O (2021) Genderna rivnist. Teoriia i praktyka v porivnialnomu konstytutsiinomu pravi. OSCE, in Ukrainian]
Скорик М (2017) [illegible] [Skoryk M (2017) [illegible], in Ukrainian]
Узарова О (2019) [illegible] Право України 7:56–66 [Uzarova O (2019) [illegible] Pravo Ukrainy 7:56–66, in Ukrainian]
Уварова О (2018) [illegible] [Hofman? [illegible] O (2018) [illegible], in Ukrainian]
Харитонова О (2020) Політика рівності і гендерна рівність у конституційному просторі. ЕПСЦ 4:61–71 [Kharytonova O (2020) [illegible] i genderna rivnist u konstytutsiinomu prostori. EPSC 4:61–71, in Ukrainian]
Черкаська К (2010) Історичний аналіз становлення української моделі гендерної паритету. Державне управління: удосконалення та розвиток 10(21):26 [Cherkaska K (2010) Istorychnyi analiz stanovlennia ukrainskoi modeli gendernoho parytetu. Derzhavne upravlinnia: udoskonalennia ta rozvytok 10(21):26, in Ukrainian]

Voices from the Gobi: Centring Indigenous Women in the Global Standards on Corporate Responsibility for Indigenous Peoples

Otgontuya Davaanyam and Baigalmaa Shurka

Abstract This chapter examines corporate responsibility, Indigenous People's rights, and gender justice through the experiences of Mongolian herder women impacted by mining in the Gobi Desert. Despite international frameworks like the UNGPs and OECD Guidelines, corporate accountability remains largely gender-blind, failing to address Indigenous women's unique vulnerabilities. Using doctrinal analysis and a case study, the paper explores how mining activities disrupts herding practices, displaces communities, and exacerbates gender inequalities. It critiques gaps in Mongolia's legal frameworks, including weak enforcement of Free, Prior, and Informed Consent (FPIC) and Environmental and Social Impact Assessments (ESIAs), which often exclude women's voices. Additionally, it highlights the limitations of Local Cooperation Agreements (LCAs), which reinforce patriarchal decision-making and marginalise herder women in fair benefit-sharing. The study calls for gender-responsive corporate accountability, including stronger FPIC implementation, robust gender impact assessments, and environmental and social safeguards. By centring herder women's experiences, it advocates for corporate and policy reforms that uphold Indigenous sovereignty, environmental sustainability, and gender equity.

1 Introduction

As women scholars and practitioners in business and human rights (BHR), we find it crucial to highlight the often-overlooked challenges faced by indigenous women. Globally, indigenous women endure multiple layers of marginalisation—socio-economic inequalities, environmental injustices, and gender-specific discrimination

O. Davaanyam (✉)
Friedrich-Alexander-Universität Erlangen-Nürnberg, Erlangen, Germany
e-mail: otgontuya.davaanyam@fau.de

B. Shurka
Business and Human Rights Advocate, Ulaanbaatar, Mongolia

D. A. Pamplona et al. (eds.), *Business and Human Rights from the Lens of Women*, Interdisciplinary Studies in Human Rights 13,
https://doi.org/10.1007/978-3-032-04036-7_9

rooted in patriarchal norms.[1] Despite some recognition in international frameworks, their intersectional struggles remain insufficiently addressed.[2] The expansion of extractive industries has resulted in land dispossession, environmental degradation, and cultural erosion for indigenous communities.[3] These impacts, compounded by entrenched gender inequalities, place indigenous women in particularly vulnerable positions.[4]

Companies have key responsibilities towards Indigenous peoples, including obtaining Free, Prior, and Informed Consent (FPIC), ensuring fair benefit-sharing, and conducting environmental and social impact assessment, as outlined in international environmental and BHR frameworks.[5] However, these mechanisms frequently overlook gender-specific needs, which restricts indigenous women's participation in decision-making processes and excludes them from equitable outcomes.[6]

To address this gap, it is essential to adopt gender-responsive and intersectional approaches to these core responsibilities, ensuring that the voices and rights of indigenous women are truly recognised and reflected. This research focuses on Mongolia, a landlocked country in North-East Asia, particularly the experiences of indigenous women (nomadic herders) in the Gobi.[7] Traditionally central to sustaining livelihoods and protecting ecosystems, these herders now face mounting threats from climate change, urbanisation, and mining expansion, leading to economic displacement, cultural loss, and increased negative socio-economic impacts.[8] Although there is substantial research on the impact of mining on Mongolian nomadic herders, most studies emphasise anthropological perspectives rather than legal and human rights frameworks, and lack an explicit focus on gendered impacts.[9] To fill

[1] UN General Assembly (2022) Special Rapportuer on the Rights of Indigenous Peoples: 'Indigenous women and the development, application, preservation and transmission of scientific and technical knowledge' A/HRC/51/28, Geneva, August 2022; UN General Assembly, Violence against Indigenous Women and Girls, Report of the UN Special Rapporteur on the Violence Against Women, its Causes and Consequences, Reem Alsalem' A/HRC/50/26, Geneve, August 2022; Fynn Bruey (2019), p. 500.

[2] Handl et al. (2022), pp. 201–225.

[3] Nissen (2023), pp. 369–402.

[4] Nissen (2023), p. 370.

[5] According to Morgera, international legal materials consistently indicate that environmental impact assessment, FPIC, and fair and equitable benefit-sharing apply to business enterprises in the natural resource sectors, guiding their responsibilities toward Indigenous peoples and local communities. See, Morgera (2020), p. 182.

[6] Handl et al. (2022), p. 209.

[7] Sternberg et al. (2022), p. 1.

[8] Board (2022) 'In the deep, cold Gobi desert, Mongolia's nomadic herders cannot outrun climate change' CNA 2022 https://www.channelnewsasia.com/sustainability/asia-great-climate-frontiers-mongolia-desertification-nomads-herders-gobi-2973316 (last accessed 10 January 2025).

[9] Sternberg et al. (2022), pp. 1–23, Michler et al. (2023), pp. 1–13; Drees et al. (2022), pp. 481–505; Caroline Upton (2010), pp. 865–874, Michler et al. (2024), pp. 1071–1085; Dovchin and Dovchin (2024), pp. 536–559.

this void, this study employs a retrospective ethnographic lens, drawing on the previous work experiences of two female authors—who consulted with Mongolian herder women through public consultations, community governance initiatives, and direct field engagement—alongside existing scholarship on the social and environmental impacts of Mongolia's extractive sector.[10] Our involvement as consultants and advocates provides a critical foundation for analysing the gendered socio-environmental repercussions of mining activities, particularly in the Gobi region. This study is further supported by qualitative studies conducted by international organisations that conducted field visits, surveys and biographic interviews with herders.[11]

This analysis proceeds in three stages, examining corporate human rights and environmental responsibilities and their intersection with Indigenous women's rights, with a focus on herder women. First, the paper critiques global frameworks, using doctrinal analysis, to assess their ability to address the unique, intersectional challenges faced by herder women—particularly those managing livestock and water resources in mining-affected environments. It highlights how these frameworks often overlook Indigenous women's perspectives and needs. Second, a case study from Mongolia illustrates how mining-driven socio-economic changes disproportionately affect nomadic women, providing concrete examples of the broader issues identified in global frameworks and the consequences of inadequate policy design. Finally, the analysis advocates for integrating an intersectional approach into key corporate responsibilities—Free, Prior, and Informed Consent (FPIC), benefit-sharing, and environmental and social impact assessment (ESIA)—at local and international levels. This aims to promote gender-responsive corporate accountability, ensuring Indigenous women's meaningful inclusion in decision-making and equitable access to benefits. By centering herder women's lived experiences, the analysis calls for rethinking BHR regulations and policy paradigms to create more inclusive and just frameworks.

2 Navigating Global Frameworks: Indigenous Women, and Corporate Human Rights Responsibility

This section will outline key global frameworks on corporate responsibility towards Indigenous communities, with a focus on corporate human rights and

[10]The research method described here employs a retrospective ethnographic lens. This approach involves analysing past experiences and data collected in real-world settings to understand cultural, social, or environmental phenomena. For example, see Atkinson and Hammersley (2007), p. 42.

[11]For example, studies such as Daley et al. (2018), Gender, Land and Mining Mongolia (WOLTS Research Report), employed surveys, participatory fieldwork, and biographic interviews specifically targeting female herders to examine the cultural and socio-economic impacts of mining on their lives.

environmental rights responsibilities and the specific obligations of companies to respect and address the rights of Indigenous women in the extractive sector. The analysis will begin by examining how Indigenous women's rights are conceptualised within international frameworks. It will then assess how these rights are incorporated into corporate responsibility standards, highlighting gaps and areas for improvement in the protection of Indigenous women impacted by corporate activities.

2.1 *Invisible Indigenous Women: The Gendered Dimensions of Self-determination in International Law*

The expansion of extractive industries, particularly mining, has long inflicted significant socio-economic disruption on Indigenous and local communities. As scholars have noted, Indigenous peoples' identities and cultures are intrinsically linked to their lands, which serve not only as vital sources of livelihood but also as sites of profound spiritual and cultural significance.[12] In this context, land signifies the essential connection between indigenous peoples and their cultural uniqueness, a relationship that is not easily aligned with the legal concept of individual property.[13] Therefore, the corporate destruction and exploitation of their land can be seen as a "deep assault to the very fabric of the communities".[14] Furthermore, in the context of corporate violations against indigenous peoples, indigenous women experience a compounded form of marginalisation.[15] They not only bear the community-level impacts but also face gender-specific challenges, such as being excluded from critical decision-making processes, losing traditional livelihoods, and facing increased vulnerability to gender-based violence.[16] These intersecting challenges deepen their vulnerability and marginalisation, impeding their ability to protect their rights, lands, and cultural heritage. Additionally, the extractive industries exacerbate existing gender inequalities, as women are disproportionately affected by environmental degradation, forced displacement, and the erosion of socio-economic rights.[17]

---

[12] Cittadino (2019), p. 72; Gottardi (2020), p. 95.

[13] Cittadino (2019), p. 72.

[14] Wettstein (2022), p. 92.

[15] Simons (2017), p. 416; UN General Assembly, Violence against Indigenous Women and Girls, Report of the UN Special Rapporteur on the Violence Against Women, its Causes and Consequences, Reem Alsalem, A/HRC/50/26, Geneva 2022, para 28.

[16] UN General Assembly, Violence against Indigenous Women and Girls, Report of the UN Special Rapporteur on the Violence Against Women, its Causes and Consequences, Reem Alsalem' A/HRC/50/26, Geneva 2022, para 9.

[17] For example, see Amnesty International 'Submission To: UN Committee On The Elimination of All Forms of Discrimination Against Women at Its Eighty-Ninth Session and Tenth Periodic Review of Canada: Resource Extraction and Gender-Based Violence against Indigenous Women

While several international standards have been developed to safeguard Indigenous peoples' rights, including UN Declaration on the Rights of Indigenous Peoples (UNDRIP), International Labour Organisation's Convention No. 169, and Committee on Elimination of Discrimination Against Women (CEDAW) General Recommendation No. 39, as well as corporate responsibility frameworks such as the UN Guiding Principles on Business and Human Rights (UNGPs), the OECD Guidelines for Multinational Enterprises on Responsible Business Conduct, the International Finance Corporation (IFC) Performance Standards, and the Equator Principles, their effectiveness remains limited.[18] Most of these frameworks are non-binding soft law instruments, except for ILO C169, which is only legally enforceable for its limited 22 ratifying states.[19] Despite their recognition and the emphasis on Indigenous peoples' rights, these frameworks inadequately address the specific concerns of Indigenous women. The omission of gender-sensitive and intersectional approaches means that Indigenous women's voices and rights are often marginalised within global standards intended to protect Indigenous peoples as a whole.

At the core of Indigenous People's rights advocacy is the redefinition of self-determination as a collective right, which has been recognised as fundamental by international law.[20] The UNDRIP reflects a consensus that the collective right to self-determination is essential for Indigenous peoples to preserve their distinct identities and exercise their human rights.[21] Self-determination, in this context, is not merely about sovereignty but about ensuring access to political processes that shape the social, economic, and environmental conditions affecting their lives.[22] Recognising this self-determination of the Indigenous people's rights operationalised by the FPIC and ESIAs that cover the adverse impacts on indigenous people, as well as the concept of fair benefit-sharing.[23] However, while this concept has

---

and Girls in Canada, 7-25 October 2024' https://www.amnesty.org/en/documents/amr20/8487/2024/en/ (last accessed 23 January 2025).

[18] UN General Assembly (2007), Resolution 61/295 'United Nations Declaration on the Rights of Indigenous Peoples' (UNDRIP) adopted 13 September 2007; International Labour Organisation 'Indigenous and Tribal Peoples Convention' 1989 (No. 169) adopted 27 June 1989; Committee on the Elimination of Discrimination Against Women (CEDAW) (2022) General Recommendations No. 39 on the rights of Indigenous womens rights CEDAW/C/GC/39 Geneva 2022, UN Human Rights Council (HRC) Guiding Principles on Business and Human Rights: Implementing the United Nations "Protect, Respect and Remedy" Framework Geneva 2011; Organisation for Economic Cooperation and Development (OECD) (2023) Guidelines for Multinational Enterprises on Responsible Business Conduct, Paris 2023, International Finance Corporations (IFC) (2012) 'IFC's Performance Standards on Environmental and Social Sustainability', The Equator Principles (2020) https://equator-principles.com/about-the-equator-principles/ (last accessed 10 January 2025).

[19] International Labour Organisation (ILO) (1989) 'Indigenous and Tribal Peoples Convention' 1989 (No. 169) Adopted on 27 June 1989.

[20] Amaya (1996), p. 80.

[21] UN General Assembly (2007), Resolution 61/295 'United Nations Declaration on the Rights of Indigenous Peoples' (UNDRIP) adopted 13 September 2007, Article 7.2.

[22] Amaya (1996), pp. 80–81.

[23] Morgera (2020), p. 183; Morgera (2016), pp. 123–124.

been instrumental in advancing collective Indigenous people's rights, it largely overlooked the gendered dimensions of self-determination.[24] Indigenous women's unique experiences of marginalisation—arising from the intersection of their individual rights as women and their collective rights as Indigenous peoples—remain insufficiently addressed in these international standards.[25]

Indeed, while both UNDRIP and ILO Convention No. 169 play a critical role in protecting indigenous peoples' rights, emphasising self-determination, land ownership, and the principle of FPIC, which is a cornerstone of UNDRIP that requires states and companies to engage in good-faith consultation and cooperation with Indigenous Peoples, these frameworks fell short in addressing the distinct challenges faced by indigenous women. Although the Special Rapporteur Corpus affirmed that all UNDRIP provisions apply equally to Indigenous women and men, she acknowledged that attention to Indigenous women's unique vulnerabilities remains limited despite widespread abuses.[26] While Articles 21 and 22 emphasise state responsibility towards women and children, they lack clear gender-responsive guidelines.[27] Regarding these articles, the Special Rapporteur recognised UN efforts to urge states to address violence against women.[28] However, the Report of the Special Rapporteur on the situation of human rights defenders, Lawlor recorded at least 331 environmental defenders killed, including 44 women—69% advocating for land, Indigenous, and environmental rights, and 28% defending women's rights.[29] Similarly, ILO Convention No. 169 also promoted consultation but does not mandate gender-responsive engagement, that results in excluding indigenous women and girls from vital decision-making on land and resource issues.[30]

To address this gap, CEDAW General Recommendation No. 39 explicitly recognised the rights of Indigenous women and girls, calling on states to ensure their meaningful participation in land and resource-related decision-making, particularly in the context of their heightened vulnerability in the extractive sector.[31] Paragraph 11 specifically highlighted the gendered dimension of self-determination, affirming Indigenous women's and girls' right to autonomy and the ability to make free,

[24] Kuokkanen (2012), p. 228.

[25] Kuokkanen (2012), p. 228.

[26] UN General Assembly (2015) 'Report of the Special Rapporteur on the rights of indigenous peoples, Victoria Tauli Corpuz' A/HRC/30/41 Geneva 2015, para 7.

[27] UN General Assembly (2007), Resolution 61/295 'United Nations Declaration on the Rights of Indigenous Peoples' (UNDRIP) adopted 13 September 2007, Articles 21 ans 22.

[28] UN General Assembly (2015) 'Report of the Special Rapporteur on the rights of indigenous peoples, Victoria Tauli Corpuz' A/HRC/30/41 Geneva 2015, para 7.

[29] UN ECOSOC (2022) 'Report of the Secretary Gerenal: Achieving gender equality and the empowerment of all women and girls in the context of climate change, environmental and disaster risk reduction policies and programmes, E/CN.6/2022/3 Geneva 2022, para 15.

[30] International Labour Organisation 'Indigenous and Tribal Peoples Convention' 1989 (No. 169) adopted 27 June 1989, Article 6.

[31] Committee on the Elimination of Discrimination Against Women (CEDAW) (2022) General Recommendations No. 39 on the rights of Indigenous womens rights CEDAW/C/GC/39 Geneva 2022.

informed decisions regarding their life plans and health.[32] The recommendation further underscored the existential crises Indigenous women face—stemming from continued land dispossession and the inadequate enforcement of their right to self-determination—which exacerbate their marginalisation and threaten their cultural survival.[33] The Committee emphasised the deep connection between Indigenous women and their lands, which underpins their culture, identity, spirituality, and survival.[34] Despite this, they face insufficient legal recognition of their land rights and significant gaps in law enforcement. The Recommendation calls on states to prevent, address, and sanction all forms of gender-based discrimination and violence against Indigenous women and girls, including violence linked to extractive industries.[35] While the recommendations of CEDAW and the principles outlined in UNDRIP represent important aspirational goals, they remain non-binding and lack effective mechanisms for enforcement, particularly in the realm of corporate and transnational activities. This limitation hinders their practical integration into global operations. Furthermore, there is significant ambiguity concerning the alignment and coherence between these recommendations and existing legal frameworks, raising questions about their compatibility and potential for synergistic implementation.

Moreover, both existing regulations on Indigenous peoples and academic discourse on the subject often overlook the specific concerns of Indigenous women. Scholars, Parisi and Corntassel emphasised that Indigenous women face marginalisation not only within Indigenous rights movements but also within broader women's rights frameworks.[36] This exclusion is perpetuated by the lingering effects of colonial legacies and ongoing imperialist influences, which have prevented the full incorporation of Indigenous women's issues into either discourse.[37] Consequently, Indigenous women continue to experience human rights violations at the intersection of their gender and collective identities.[38] These violations are most evident in cases of environmental degradation, land dispossession, and resource exploitation, which undermine Indigenous sovereignty while disproportionately impacting women, who are left to deal with health crises, forced displacement, and rising levels of violence.[39]

[32] CEDAW (2022) General Recommendations No. 39 on the rights of Indigenous womens rights, CEDAW/C/GC/39 Geneva 2022, para 11.

[33] CEDAW (2022) General Recommendations No. 39 on the rights of Indigenous womens rights CEDAW/C/GC/39 Geneva 2022, para 7.

[34] CEDAW (2022) General Recommendations No. 39 on the rights of Indigenous womens rights CEDAW/C/GC/39 Geneva 2022, para 18.

[35] CEDAW (2022) General Recommendations No. 39 on the rights of Indigenous womens rights CEDAW/C/GC/39 Geneva 2022, para 42(b).

[36] Parisi and Corntassel (2007), pp. 81–98.

[37] Parisi and Corntassel (2007), pp. 86–87.

[38] Kuokkanen (2012), p. 226.

[39] CEDAW (2022) General Recommendations No. 39 on the rights of Indigenous womens rights CEDAW/C/GC/39 Geneva 2022, paras 11–12.

Current international frameworks, though crucial in advancing collective Indigenous peoples' rights, fail to adequately address gender-specific vulnerabilities. This gap underscores the urgent need to rethink self-determination by incorporating Indigenous women's unique experiences and rights. Parisi and Corntassel suggested that the discourse on Indigenous self-determination would be more effective if it recognises individuals as both autonomous and inherently connected to their communities.[40] Strengthening the focus on individual self-determination is essential for making collective self-determination a more practical and inclusive project, particularly for Indigenous women.[41] Since Indigenous peoples' rights are widely understood as both individual and collective, the persistent neglect of Indigenous women's rights cannot be attributed to a conflict between these categories.[42] Rather, it reflects entrenched gender inequalities within both Indigenous and mainstream societies, as evidenced by the continued lack of attention to the high rates of violence against Indigenous women.[43]

Also, cultural differences play a significant role in addressing the rights and concerns of Indigenous women. Indigenous communities vary widely in their lifestyles and connections to the land, which requires nuanced approaches to their protection. The UN Special Rapporteur on the Rights of Indigenous Peoples has highlighted the unique challenges faced by mobile Indigenous groups, such as nomadic tribes, herders, and pastoralists, who voluntarily isolate themselves and depend on sustainable movement across vast territories.[44] While some practice transhumance—the seasonal movement of livestock—others follow irregular or shorter patterns.[45] Their distinct way of life demands context-specific approaches to FPIC, corporate environmental assessments, and consultations. Unfortunately, existing frameworks fail to provide tailored solutions for these communities. For mobile Indigenous peoples, their cultural and physical survival is inextricably linked to their territories.[46] Those living in voluntary isolation avoid external contact, while initial contact groups have only recently interacted with the outside world.[47] Due to a lack of research and data, their existence is often overlooked, enabling economic activities on their lands and further marginalising these vulnerable populations.[48]

---

[40] Parisi and Corntassel (2007), p. 85.

[41] Kuokkanen (2012), p. 230.

[42] Kuokkanen (2012), p. 230.

[43] Seck and Simons (2019), p. 4.

[44] UN (2024) 'Report of the Special Rapporteur on the rights of Indigenous Peoples, José Francisco Calí Tzay - Mobile Indigenous Peoples' UN Doc A/79/160, Geneva 2024.

[45] UN (2024) 'Report of the Special Rapporteur on the rights of Indigenous Peoples, José Francisco Calí Tzay - Mobile Indigenous Peoples' UN Doc A/79/160, Geneva 2024, para 5.

[46] UN (2024) 'Report of the Special Rapporteur on the rights of Indigenous Peoples, José Francisco Calí Tzay - Mobile Indigenous Peoples' UN Doc A/79/160, Geneva 2024, para 5.

[47] UN (2024) 'Report of the Special Rapporteur on the rights of Indigenous Peoples, José Francisco Calí Tzay - Mobile Indigenous Peoples' UN Doc A/79/160, Geneva 2024, paras 5–7.

[48] UN (2024) 'Report of the Special Rapporteur on the rights of Indigenous Peoples, José Francisco Calí Tzay - Mobile Indigenous Peoples' UN Doc A/79/160, Geneva 2024, para 7.

Gender issues further complicate the situation. Mobile Indigenous women, who play a critical role in sustaining pastoral livelihoods and preserving traditional knowledge, face disproportionate threats from displacement, environmental degradation, and social disruption.[49] Despite their essential contributions to their communities, they are often excluded from decision-making processes, deepening their marginalisation.[50] Therefore, it is crucial that frameworks not only account for the mobility and isolation of these communities but also adopt gender-responsive approaches, ensuring that mobile Indigenous women are actively included in all consultations and benefit-sharing processes.

2.2 *Global Standards for Corporate Responsibility to Respect Indigenous People's rights*

While corporate obligations towards indigenous peoples are still not sufficiently developed, specific provisions addressing the rights of indigenous women and girls are notably absent.[51] Additionally, the lack of an intersectional lens within these frameworks limits their ability to effectively address the distinct socio-economic and cultural challenges faced by indigenous women and girls.[52] This section will provide a critical analysis of existing global standards on corporate responsibility towards indigenous people's rights, assess the specific obligations outlined in these frameworks, and evaluate their effectiveness in addressing the unique needs of indigenous women and girls.

Regarding corporate responsibility towards Indigenous peoples, the UNGPs and the OECD Guidelines on serve as overarching frameworks. In the extractive sector, more specific instruments such as the IFC Performance Standards, the Equator Principles and the Principles of the International Councils of Mining and Metals (ICMM) are key instruments. Among these, the UNGPs are the most widely recognised global standard, establishing clear expectations for all businesses to respect internationally recognised human rights. Central to the UNGPs is the concept of corporate due diligence, rooted in the "do no harm" principle, which requires businesses to identify, prevent, and mitigate adverse impacts on both people and the

[49] Swiss Agency for Development and Cooperation SDC (2015) 'Gender Analysis in Pastoral Livestock Herding in Mongolia, Ulaanbaatar 2015, p. 32; Magsar (2024) 'Saalitai Enger: Life of Mongolian herdswoman' Friedrich Ebert Stiftung 13 September 2024 https://asia.fes.de/news/mongolian-herdswoman.html#:~:text=A%20gender%20study%20entitled%20%22The,of%2011.1%20hours%20per%20day (last accessed 12 February 2025).

[50] UN Women (2024) 'Advancing gender-responsive synergies across the Rio Convetions: Gender Equality at the Intersection of Climate Action, Biodiversity Protection and Sustainable Land Management' 2024 https://www.wocan.org/wp-content/uploads/2024/12/brief-advancing-gender-responsive-synergies-across-the-rio-conventions-en.pdf (last accessed 11 January 2025).

[51] See Sect. 2.1 of this paper.

[52] Handl et al. (2022), p. 212.

environment caused by their operations.[53] However, the UNGPs have limitations, particularly in explicitly addressing corporate environmental responsiblities, including those related to the rights of Indigenous Peoples. While there is a brief reference in the commentary on Principle 18, which recommends integrating social and environmental impact assessments, the framework does not provide clear guidance on addressing the rights of Indigenous Peoples.[54]

Additionally, Principles 3 and 12 of the UNGPs call on states and businesses to give special attention to vulnerable groups, including Indigenous peoples.[55] However, the framework fails to specify how such attention should be applied, particularly in the extractive sector, where Indigenous communities face significant risks.[56] Additionally, while the UNGPs acknowledge the need for targeted protections, feminist and intersectional scholars have criticised them for lacking a gender-sensitive approach.[57] The absence of a structural understanding of gender inequality and the failure to incorporate an intersectional framework overlook the distinct challenges faced by Indigenous women, who are particularly vulnerable to marginalisation, violence, and exploitation. Also, scholars argued that both women's rights and Indigenous Peoples' rights are often treated as secondary or 'additional' obligations, rather than integral components of corporate human rights responsibilities.[58] This framing positions these groups as vulnerable populations requiring special protection, rather than as rights-holders whose fundamental rights must be equally prioritised.[59] Consequently, existing frameworks risk reinforcing their marginalisation by failing to recognise their rights as central to broader human rights obligations.

The UN Working Group on Business and Human Rights (WGBHR), tasked with clarifying and advancing the UNGPs framework, sought to address the long-standing gender gap by publishing the Gender Dimensions Report in 2019.[60] This report highlighted the disproportionate and unique impacts that business activities

[53] UN Human Rights Council (HRC) Guiding Principles on Business and Human Rights: Implementing the United Nations "Protect, Respect and Remedy" Framework Geneva 2011, Principle 17; Buhmann et al. (2019), pp. 389–403.

[54] UN Human Rights Council (HRC) Guiding Principles on Business and Human Rights: Implementing the United Nations "Protect, Respect and Remedy" Framework Geneva 2011, Principle 18.

[55] UN Human Rights Council (HRC) Guiding Principles on Business and Human Rights: Implementing the United Nations "Protect, Respect and Remedy" Framework Geneva 2011, Principles 3 and 12.

[56] Simons and Handl (2019), pp. 129–130.

[57] UN Human Rights Council (HRC) Guiding Principles on Business and Human Rights: Implementing the United Nations "Protect, Respect and Remedy" Framework Geneva 2011, Commentaries to the Principles 3 and 12; Handl et al. (2022), p. 212.

[58] Simons and Handl (2019), pp. 134–135.

[59] Handl et al. (2022), p. 213; Simons and Handl (2019), p. 134.

[60] UN WGBHR 'Gender Dimension of the UN Guiding Principles on Business and Human Rights' 2019 https://www.ohchr.org/sites/default/files/Documents/Issues/Business/BookletGenderDimensionsGuidingPrinciples.pdf (last accessed 10 January 2025).

have on women, which are frequently ignored in corporate practices.[61] It underscored the compounded effects of intersecting forms of discrimination and violence, with Indigenous women facing additional challenges due to their layered identities.[62] The report calls on businesses to acknowledge and respond to these intersecting inequalities, which may arise from factors such as age, race, caste, class, ethnicity, religion, language, literacy, socio-economic status, marital status, sexual orientation, gender identity, disability, rural residency, migration status, and Indigenous or minority status.[63]

The gender guidance report also urged businesses to go beyond merely avoiding harm by adopting gender-responsive policies throughout their operations and promoting gender equality in practice. In cases where Indigenous women may be affected, businesses are advised to respect their rights to self-determination and adhere to the principles of FPIC, as outlined in ILO C169 and the UN Declaration on the Rights of Indigenous Peoples (UNDRIP).[64] However, the report's reliance on ILO Convention No. 169 and UNDRIP—both of which are largely gender-blind—remains a significant shortcoming. While these frameworks offer critical protections for Indigenous peoples, as we argued earlier, they failed to adequately integrate a gender-responsive approach or address the specific needs and vulnerabilities of Indigenous women and girls.

The OECD Guidelines recognised that businesses must respect all internationally recognised human rights, with special attention to groups at heightened risk, including Indigenous peoples, and call for compliance with FPIC.[65] While the Guidelines, in contrast to the UNGPs, offer broader coverage of environmental issues, they still lack detailed and specific guidance on corporate responsibilities towards Indigenous peoples.[66] As Morgera highlighted, sector-specific guidance under the OECD Guidelines, such as the OECD-FAO Guidance for Responsible

[61] UN WGBHR 'Gender Dimension of the UN Guiding Principles on Business and Human Rights' 2019 https://www.ohchr.org/sites/default/files/Documents/Issues/Business/BookletGenderDimensionsGuidingPrinciples.pdf (last accessed 10 January 2025), p. 6.

[62] UN WGBHR 'Gender Dimension of the UN Guiding Principles on Business and Human Rights' 2019 https://www.ohchr.org/sites/default/files/Documents/Issues/Business/BookletGenderDimensionsGuidingPrinciples.pdf (last accessed 10 January 2025), Principle 12, Illutsrative actions d.

[63] UN WGBHR 'Gender Dimension of the UN Guiding Principles on Business and Human Rights' 2019 https://www.ohchr.org/sites/default/files/Documents/Issues/Business/BookletGenderDimensionsGuidingPrinciples.pdf (last accessed 10 January 2025), Principles 12, Illutsrative actions d.

[64] UN WGBHR 'Gender Dimension of the UN Guiding Principles on Business and Human Rights' 2019 https://www.ohchr.org/sites/default/files/Documents/Issues/Business/BookletGenderDimensionsGuidingPrinciples.pdf (last accessed 10 January 2025), Principles 12, Illutsrative actions e.

[65] Organisation for Economic Cooperation and Development (OECD) (2023) Guidelines for Multinational Enterprises on Responsible Business Conduct, Paris 2023, Chapter IV: Human Rights, commentary para 45.

[66] Chapter VI: Environment covers broad range of environmental impacts in OECD (2023) Guidelines for Multinational Enterprises on Responsible Business Conduct, Paris 2023.

Agricultural Supply Chains, provides more tailored advice.[67] This guidance emphasised the need for social and environmental impact assessments that consider the adverse impacts on Indigenous peoples, promote FPIC, and encourage benefit-sharing with Indigenous communities in operations involving their lands, resources, and knowledge.[68] Morgera contended that while the OECD-FAO Guidance emphasises benefit-sharing and community development (e.g. job creation, capacity building, infrastructure, and revenue allocation), it fails to prioritise Indigenous peoples' rights or integrate their perspectives meaningfully in corporate decision-making processes.[69] However, compared to frameworks such as UNDRIP and ILO C169, this guidance reflects more on gender impacts in engagement with Indigenous communities. For example, it encourages businesses to consider gender-specific risks in environmental and human rights assessments, ensure equal participation of all stakeholders—including women—and recognise the role of women in agricultural activities, alongside marginalised groups like Indigenous women and migrant workers.[70] Despite these efforts, key concepts such as benefit-sharing and consultation largely overlook women's roles, while intersectional issues remain absent, reflecting a critical gap in ensuring truly inclusive and gender equitable corporate practices.

The IFC Performance Standards provide essential guidelines for private sector actors in extractive industries. Specifically, IFC Performance Standard 7 requires (FPIC) for projects affecting Indigenous peoples.[71] However, it lacks provisions to ensure gender-responsive consultations and meaningful engagement with Indigenous women. The gender dimension is only briefly mentioned, requiring companies to consider women's roles in land and natural resource management during impact assessments.[72] While the IFC Performance Standards play a crucial role in defining corporate responsibilities towards Indigenous communities—particularly in comparison to frameworks like the UNGPs and the OECD Guidelines—by explicitly mandating environmental and social impact assessments, meaningful FPIC, fair benefit-sharing, continuous engagement, remedial actions, and strong recognition of cultural heritage and land relationships, they still leave significant gaps in terms of addressing the needs of the indigenous women. Notably, they fail to address broader gendered impacts, potential unique violations, and the specific

[67] Elisa Morgega (2024), p. 241; OECD and Food and Agriculture Organisation of the United Nations (FAO) (2016) 'OECD-FAO Guidance for Responsible Agriculture Supply Chains' Paris 2016.

[68] OECD and Food and Agriculture Organisation of the United Nations (FAO) (2016) 'OECD-FAO Guidance for Responsible Agriculture Supply Chains' Paris 2016, Annex B. Engagement with Indigenous Peoples, p. 78-84.

[69] Elisa Morgega (2024), pp. 241–242.

[70] OECD and Food and Agriculture Organisation of the United Nations (FAO) (2016) 'OECD-FAO Guidance for Responsible Agriculture Supply Chains' Paris 2016, Annex B. Engagement with Indigenous Peoples, pp. 78–84.

[71] International Finance Corporations (IFC) (2012) 'IFC's Performance Standards on Environmental and Social Sustainability', Standard 7: Indigenous Peoples.

[72] International Finance Corporations (IFC) (2012) 'IFC's Performance Standards on Environmental and Social Sustainability', Standard 7: Indigenous Peoples, para 14.

vulnerabilities faced by Indigenous women. As a result, in practice, according to these frameworks, companies often engage primarily with male community leaders, sidelining women's voices and reinforcing patriarchal structures.[73] This exclusion perpetuates the marginalisation of Indigenous women in resource governance, limiting their ability to influence decisions that directly impact their lives, communities, and environments.

The Equator Principles, which endorse IFC Performance Standard 7, require companies to comply with its guidelines.[74] They further elaborate on the responsibility of companies conducting FPIC, which involves a structured and iterative process of exchanging views and information with affected communities. This process aims to ensure that community perspectives – particularly regarding proposed mitigation measures, benefit-sharing, and implementation – are meaningfully incorporated into corporate decision-making.[75]

However, despite recognising the importance of consultation and FPIC, the Equator Principles provide limited guidance on the specific rights and challenges faced by Indigenous women. While gender and disproportionate gender impacts are briefly mentioned in the potential environmental and social issues to be addressed in the environmental and social assessment documentation, there is no detailed framework for addressing gender-specific concerns or ensuring Indigenous women's active participation in consultations. This omission reinforces the gap in existing frameworks regarding the inclusion of Indigenous women in resource governance and corporate engagement processes.

The International Council on Mining and Metals (ICMM)—a multi-stakeholder initiative representing many of the world's leading mining companies—has adopted 10 principles for responsible mining.[76] Under Principle 3, which focuses on Human Rights, member companies are expected to align with the UNGPs and respect the rights of Indigenous Peoples.[77] However, despite this commitment, the ICMM has been widely criticised for failing to enforce FPIC as a mandatory requirement for its members.[78] Instead of advocating FPIC as a mandatory international obligation, the ICMM merely encourages its adoption, effectively reducing a fundamental

[73] Cahier (2020) 'Securing pathways to environmental justice for Indigenous women Multilateral Development Banks and environmental violence in the Americas' https://voelkerrechtsblog.org/securing-pathways-to-environmental-justice-for-indigenous-women/ 11 May 2020, Volkerrechtblog (last accessed 23 January 2025).

[74] The Equator Principles (2020) Exhibit II: Illustrative List of Potential Environmental and Social Issues to be Addressed in the Environmental and Social Assessment Documentation.

[75] The Equator Principles (2020) Exhibit II: Illustrative List of Potential Environmental and Social Issues to be Addressed in the Environmental and Social Assessment Documentation.

[76] International Council of Mining and Metals (ICMM), Principles – Performance Expectations https://www.icmm.com/en-gb/our-principles (last accessed 10 February 2025).

[77] International Council of Mining and Metals (ICMM), Principles – Performance Expectations, Principle 3.

[78] Owen et al. (2022), p. 3; McInnes et al. (2017), p. 154.

international right to a voluntary, morally driven guideline.[79] This approach contradicts the reality that Indigenous People's rights—including FPIC—are internationally recognised as legally binding obligations, not discretionary principles left to corporate goodwill. By maintaining a non-mandatory stance, the ICMM weakens the enforceability of Indigenous rights, leaving communities vulnerable to exploitation and dispossession.

Although the ICMM recently released a position statement on Indigenous Peoples and mining—a step that might seem as long overdue—it encourages member companies to engage in meaningful consultation and respect Indigenous rights, including seeking consent for any anticipated impacts on their lands and livelihoods.[80] The statement also acknowledges that mining projects can infringe upon these rights and further marginalise vulnerable groups, such as women and girls, elders, Indigenous Peoples in voluntary isolation or initial contact, Mobile Indigenous Peoples, and others facing systemic disadvantages.[81] However, the statement faced strong criticism from SCO advocates for Indigenous Peoples' rights, who argued that the ICMM failed to ensure its members uphold the non-negotiable principle of Free, Prior, and Informed Consent (FPIC) for mining projects.[82] They claimed that FPIC is not just a procedural step but a human rights norm rooted in Indigenous Peoples' rights to self-determination and their lands, as affirmed by UNDRIP and other international laws.[83] Oxfam also criticised the policy for neglecting protections for Indigenous Peoples in voluntary isolation, who face severe health risks from outside contact.[84] Oxfam further argued that while the statement urges companies to "carefully consider" their impact, it stops short of prohibiting mining in areas affecting these communities, contrary to Inter-American Commission on Human Rights guidance on Indigenous Poeples in Voluntary Isolation and Initial

[79] Owen et al. (2022), p. 3.

[80] ICMM (2024) 'Indigenous Peoples: Position Statement' 8 August 2024 https://www.icmm.com/en-gb/our-principles/position-statements/indigenous-peoples (last accessed 12 February 2025).

[81] ICMM (2024) 'Indigenous Peoples: Position Statement' 8 August 2024, Recognition Statement 2, p. 4 https://www.icmm.com/en-gb/our-principles/position-statements/indigenous-peoples (last accessed 12 February 2025).

[82] Right Energy Partnership with Indigenous Peoples (2024) 'Indigenous Peoples' Rights at Risk: ICMM's Position Statement Falls Short on Free, Prior, and Informed Consent' 3 September 2024 https://rightenergypartnership.org/public-statement-on-adoption-of-the-indigenous-peoples-mining-position-statement-of-the-international-council-on-mining-and-metals-icmm/ (last accessed 12 February 2024).

[83] Right Energy Partnership with Indigenous Peoples (2024) 'Indigenous Peoples' Rights at Risk: ICMM's Position Statement Falls Short on Free, Prior, and Informed Consent' 3 September 2024 https://rightenergypartnership.org/public-statement-on-adoption-of-the-indigenous-peoples-mining-position-statement-of-the-international-council-on-mining-and-metals-icmm/ (last accessed 12 February 2024).

[84] Greenspan (2024) 'There's a new standard out. Will mining companies finally get it right with Indigenous Peoples?' Oxfam 2024 https://politicsofpoverty.oxfamamerica.org/new-mining-standard-recognizes-indigenous-peoples-right-to-withhold-consent-for-project-activities-but-will-the-guidance-affect-much-needed-change-in-company-practice/ (last accessed 12 February 2024).

Contact in the Americas.[85] This shows that ICMM lacks actual leverage to ensure its member companies implement FPIC in practice, as it provides no clear framework for evaluating compliance or imposing consequences for non-compliance.

Global corporate responsibility standards—such as the UNGPs, OECD Guidelines, IFC Performance Standards, and Equator Principles—set essential frameworks for Indigenous rights, particularly environmental and social impact assessments (ESIAs), Free, Prior, and Informed Consent (FPIC), and benefit-sharing. However, they remain largely gender-blind, lack intersectional perspectives, and fail to address the cultural and socio-economic marginalisation Indigenous women face. While some frameworks briefly acknowledge gendered impacts, they lack enforceable mechanisms, reinforcing patriarchal structures and excluding women from decision-making.

In contrast, Latin America's regional instruments have made significant strides in addressing the rights of indigneous women. The *American Declaration on the Rights of Indigenous Peoples* (adopted by the Organisation of American States) and the *Escazú Agreement* on environmental rights exemplify a more refined and enforceable approach to Indigenous rights.[86] These frameworks integrate gender considerations, acknowledging the distinct and disproportionate challenges Indigenous women face, including land dispossession, environmental degradation, and gender-based violence. A pivotal actor in this landscape is the Inter-American Commission on Human Rights (IACHR), which has scrutinised state compliance with Indigenous Peoples' rights, issued recommendations, and highlighted systemic abuses.[87] IACHR's report, Indigenous Women and Their Human Rights in the Americas, illustrates how environmental destruction, cultural marginalisation, and poverty intersect to disproportionately impact Indigenous women.[88] By linking environmental protections with Indigenous women's well-being, these regional frameworks set a precedent for more inclusive and accountable corporate responsibility policies.

---

[85] Greenspan (2024) 'There's a new standard out. Will mining companies finally get it right with Indigenous Peoples?' Oxfam 2024 https://politicsofpoverty.oxfamamerica.org/new-mining-standard-recognizes-indigenous-peoples-right-to-withhold-consent-for-project-activities-but-will-the-guidance-affect-much-needed-change-in-company-practice/ (last accessed 12 February 2024); Inter-American Commission on Human Rights (IACHR) (2013) 'Indigenous Peoples in Voluntary Isolation and Initial Contact in the Americas' https://www.oas.org/en/iachr/indigenous/docs/pdf/report-indigenous-peoples-voluntary-isolation.pdf (last accessed 12 February 2024).

[86] The Organisation of American States 'American Declaration on the Rights of Indigenous Peoples' 15 June 2016 https://www.oas.org/en/sare/documents/DecAmIND.pdf#page=9.12 accessed 12 January 2025; The Latin American and Caribbean region (2018) 'Regional Agreement on Access to Information, Public Participation and Justice in Environmental Matters in Latin America and the Caribbean', 2018 https://repositorio.cepal.org/entities/publication/86cae662-f81c-4b45-a04a-058e8d26143c (last accessed 12 January 2025).

[87] International Justice Resource Centre (2017) 'IACHR Report Examines Pervasive Discrimination Against Indigenous Women' 29 November 2017 https://ijrcenter.org/2017/11/29/iachr-report-examines-pervasive-discrimination-against-indigenous-women/ (last accessed 11 February 2025).

[88] Inter-American Commission on Human Rights (IACHR) (2017) 'Indigenous Women' OEA/Ser.L/V/II. 2017 https://www.oas.org/en/iachr/reports/pdfs/indigenouswomen.pdf#page=11.15 (last accessed 28 January 2025).

Beyond corporate-led initiatives, the Convention on Biological Diversity (CBD) offers a more cohesive and binding approach to corporate accountability.[89] Special Rapporteur Morgera has advocated that the CBD establishes a global intergovernmental consensus on corporate obligations, explicitly addressing ESIAs, FPIC, and benefit-sharing.[90] She argued that unlike the IFC and ICMM, which treat Indigenous cultural, land, and water rights as secondary considerations, the CBD centred them into impact assessments, reinforcing corporate accountability.[91] However, without synergy and an integrated approach between the CBD and other international frameworks, corporate responsibility towards Indigenous Peoples will remain fragmented and ineffective, failing to bring about meaningful improvements in safeguarding their rights and livelihoods. In conclusion, corporate responsibility frameworks must move beyond voluntary principles and adopt legally binding commitments. This requires mandating and integrating gender-responsive approaches in the FPIC and ESIAs, enforcing corporate obligations through robust oversight and grievance mechanisms, and prioritising Indigenous Peoples' rights, particularly Indigenous women's cultural and environmental rights in impact assessments.

3 Case Study: Mobile Indigenous Women in the Gobi Confront Mining, Displacement and Land Loss

Mongolia, bordered by China and Russia, is home to vast arid steppes and the Gobi Desert. Traditionally, over a quarter of Mongolia's population has followed a nomadic or semi-nomadic lifestyle. However, this way of life is increasingly under threat from climate change, urbanisation, and the aggressive expansion of the mining industry.[92] In Mongolian culture, the concept of *nutag*—meaning "homeland"—reflects a profound cultural, spiritual, and economic bond with ancestral lands, forming the foundation of herders' way of life.[93] Mongolia's herders, often seen as embodying Indigenous-like traditions, have lived in harmony with nature for centuries, moving with the seasons to sustain their livestock and preserve their ancestral land.[94] Once the backbone of the nation, their nomadic lifestyle now collides with modernization and urban growth, leading to a decline in traditional practices under the pressures of economic development.[95] Yet, women herders have played an

[89] Secretariat of the Convention on Biological Diversity Montreal (2011) 'The Convention on Biological Diversity: Text and Annexes' Montreal 2011.

[90] Morgera (2016), pp, 123–124.

[91] Morgera (2016), pp, 123–124.

[92] UNDP Mongolia (2024) 'Combating Desertification in Mongolia's Gobi: Story of Resilience and Restoration' 28 November 2024 https://www.undp.org/mongolia/stories/combating-desertification-mongolias-gobi-story-resilience-and-restoration (last accessed 9 January 2024).

[93] Dovchin and Dovchin (2024), p. 538.

[94] Dovchin and Dovchin (2024), p. 537.

[95] Harter (2023) 'Dust, hail and bank loans: the Mongolian herders facing life without grass' Guardian 15 November 2023 https://www.theguardian.com/global-development/2023/nov/15/

essential, though often invisible, role in maintaining livelihoods, preserving cultural identity, and ensuring community well-being, even as these challenges intensify.[96]

As other Mongolian scholars asserted, the concept of "*nutag*" represents more than a physical territory; it embodies a holistic, reciprocal relationship between herders, land, and spiritual deities.[97] According to ancestral Mongolian cosmology, the land is not merely a resource or property but a living entity, governed by spiritual forces believed to protect and sustain both human and non-human life.[98] As Dovchin and Dovchin argued, rituals, such as offering the first share of tea to nature spirits, reflect this deeply rooted spiritual connection.[99] However, the rapid growth of mining has disrupted this traditional way of life, severing the spiritual and physical ties nomadic herders have with their nutag and increasing the vulnerability of herder women who bear the brunt of both environmental degradation and social disruption.[100] This section is divided into two parts: the first outlines the general impacts of mining on nomadic herders, specifically herders in the Gobi region, while the second focuses on gender-specific impacts on women nomads.

3.1 *Unearthing Consequences: Mining's Impact on Nomadic Life in the Gobi*

3.1.1 Identity in Limbo: The Struggle for Indigenous Recognition and Cultural Rights

Mongolia's Constitution designates livestock as a "national treasure," yet it fails to recognise the herders who sustain this heritage as essential to the nation's cultural identity.[101] Although Mongolia was once dominated by a herding-based lifestyle, modernisation has reduced the number of active herders to below 30 percent of total

---

dust-hail-and-bank-loans-the-mongolian-herders-facing-life-without-grass#:~:text=Some%2030%25%20of%20Mongolia's%20almost,their%20country's%20association%20with%20pastoralism (last accessed 15 January 2025).

[96] WOLTS (2018) Project Summary: 'Mongolia's female herders, mining and the struggle for land' 2018 https://mokoro.co.uk/wp-content/uploads/2024/11/WOLTS-Mongolia-2-page-research-summary_June2018_English.pdf accessed 9 January 2024.

[97] Dovchin and Dovchin, (2024), pp. 537–538.

[98] Dovchin and Dovchin, (2024), pp. 537–538.

[99] Dovchin and Dovchin, (2024), pp. 551–552.

[100] For example, Mendbayar, Perenlei, and Davaanyam (2022) 'National Baseline Assessment on Business and Human Rights for the National Action Plan on Mongolia' UNDP Mongolia 2022 https://globalnaps.org/wp-content/uploads/2024/02/BHR-NBA-in-Mongolia-report-2022.ENG_.pdf (last accessed 12 January 2025); Institute for Innovative Policies (2018) Human rights impact assessment of mining and transportation from Tavan.

Tolgoi" Human Rights Commission of Mongolia, October 2018, Ulaanbaatar, Mongolia https://www.undp.org/sites/g/files/zskgke326/files/migration/mn/57e653f154778b550b0713b795a0e46c0e784ebbedcb9a5e6742ebcb5b9b0b1a.pdf (last accessed 12 January 2025).

[101] Great Ikh Khural Mongolia (1992) Constitution of Mongolia, 13 January 1992 Ulaanbaatar, Article 5.4.

populations.[102] Although Mongolian herders possess a land-based cultural heritage deeply intertwined with Indigenous practices, they remain excluded from formal recognition as "*uuguul irged*" and receive insufficient legal protections.[103] This omission weakens their cultural rights, land tenure security, and capacity to defend their traditional way of life from industrialization and modern development pressures.[104] Lacking recognition, their claims are marginalised in both national and international legal frameworks. The debate over whether herders should be classified as Indigenous peoples or simply local citizens reveals a troubling ambiguity in how cultural identity is defined. Their profound spiritual and cultural bonds with *nutag*—their homeland—have been nurtured over a millennium, encompassing critical knowledge and heritage that transcend mere property ownership.[105] Consequently, Mongolian herding communities, particularly women and girls, face acute challenges from mining operations—land displacement, cultural erosion, diminished livelihoods, environmental degradation, and exclusion from decision-making—intensified by the absence of formal recognition and inadequate legal safeguards.[106]

In 2024, Mongolia introduced the Law on Herders, aiming to define their legal status and outline their rights and responsibilities.[107] This law marks the first time herders have been comprehensively recognised under domestic legislation. It has several positive aspects, including acknowledging herding as a climate-vulnerable livelihood and incorporating government support measures to help herders adapt to the impacts of climate change.[108]

---

[102] Harter (2023) 'Dust, hail and bank loans: the Mongolian herders facing life without grass' Guardian 15 November 2023 https://www.theguardian.com/global-development/2023/nov/15/dust-hail-and-bank-loans-the-mongolian-herders-facing-life-without-grass#:~:text=Some%2030%25%20of%20Mongolia's%20almost,their%20country's%20association%20with%20pastoralism (last accessed 15 January 2025).

[103] However, already some international organisations working in Mongolia, including Worldwide Fund Mongolia (WWF), Asian Development Bank (ADB) started using this concept in their analysis and report of the adverse impacts on herder communities. For example see, ADB (2020) 'Development plan of the Indigenous communities' April 2020, Ulaanbaatar https://www.adb.org/sites/default/files/project-documents/49430/49430-005-ippf-mn.pdf#page=3.12 accessed 12 January 2025.

[104] Tello (2016) 'I'm not Indigenous!' Identity and Exclusion in Indigenous Development IDB Blog August 2016 https://blogs.iadb.org/sostenibilidad/en/im-not-indigenous-identity-and-exclusion-in-indigenous-development/ (last accessed 12 January 2025).

[105] Dugersuren (2015) "When I was herding I had a plentiful life. Now I am working for another and have lost my independence" Guardian 9 March 2015, https://www.theguardian.com/global-development-professionals-network/2015/mar/09/mongolian-nomads-displacement-mining-impact-development-projects (last accessed 14 January 2025).

[106] In the interview, herders answered that "*They explained that the close relationship between nature and humans played a vital role in deciding the quality of their lives*" in Gardelle and Zhao (2021), p. 13.

[107] Great Ikh Khural Mongolia (2024), The Law on Herder, Ulaanbaatar 2024.

[108] Great Ikh Khural Mongolia (2024), The Law on Herder, Ulaanbaatar 2024, Articles 11 and 12.

However, the law treats herders as a homogeneous group, failing to differentiate them based on their native lands. Some herders reside in the vast steppe, while others are indigenous to the Gobi, where environmental conditions are harsher.[109] Given these differences, their vulnerabilities and needs vary significantly, requiring more tailored policies that address the specific challenges faced by different herding communities. Furthermore, the law frames herders merely as economic actors engaged in livestock husbandry, failing to reflect their deep cultural, spiritual, and ecological ties to their ancestral land *nutag*.[110] By reducing herding to a mere economic activity under domestic law, the legislation disregards the holistic significance of their lifestyle and further erodes their right to self-determination. While the law grants herders access to knowledge and technical support to adapt to climate and market changes, it falls short in guaranteeing fundamental rights.[111] It affirms their contractual right to use pastures and natural resources but lacks critical protections, such as, their right to maintain their traditional nomadic lifestyle, free from forced displacement, their right to actively participate in decision-making processes that affect their lands, livelihoods, and cultural heritage and their right to protect and sustain their spiritual and cultural relationship with their ancestral land.

Furthermore, the law provides for investment and development loans, financial support, and bonuses based on livestock production, reinforcing a market-driven approach.[112] Although these provisions appear to offer significant support, they ultimately fail to address the existential threats herders face from land degradation, resource privatisation, and mining expansion.[113] Without explicit cultural and land rights protections, herders remain vulnerable to economic and political forces that prioritise industrial growth over the survival of their way of life. This recently adopted law shows that Mongolia's development policies may continue to neglect the fundamental reality that herding is more than a livelihood—it is a way of being, a system of ecological knowledge, and a cultural identity deeply woven into the country's heritage. By overlooking these dimensions, the law perpetuates a framework where herders are seen as expendable within Mongolia's modernisation agenda rather than as stewards of a living tradition that deserves legal and institutional protection.

[109] Khaltar (2020) 'Mongolia plans river diversion as mining boom sucks Gobi dry: As herders in the Gobi desert lose livelihoods from pollution and lack of water, the government plans to pipe water across Mongolia Dialogue Earth 14 October 2020 https://dialogue.earth/en/water/mongolia-plans-river-diversion-as-mining-boom-runs-gobi-dry/ (last accessed 14 January 2025).

[110] Great Ikh Khural Mongolia (2011), Employment Support Law, Ulaanbaatar 2011, Article 3.1.9 stated that 'herder is a citizen who conducts animal husbandry to obtain its livelihood'.

[111] Great Ikh Khural Mongolia (2024), The Law on Herder, Ulaanbaatar 2024, Article 5.1.

[112] Great Ikh Khural Mongolia (2024), The Law on Herder, Ulaanbaatar 2024, Article 5.1.3.

[113] UN (2024) 'Report of the Special Rapporteur on the rights of Indigenous Peoples, José Francisco Calí Tzay - Mobile Indigenous Peoples' UN Doc A/79/160, Geneva 2024, para 50.

3.1.2 Land Rights on the Edge: Environmental and Social Crossroads in the Gobi

The Gobi region, home to Mongolia's most expansive mining operations, is also the heartland of many traditional herding communities.[114] Herders in this arid landscape have long adapted to extreme conditions by relying on seasonal mobility, shared pasture resources, and deep cultural ties to their ancestral land.[115] However, the rapid expansion of the extractive industry in the Gobi region has severely disrupted these traditional practices, intensifying land conflicts and threatening the sustainability of pastoralism.[116] Customary land rights are not recognised, as Mongolia's civil code designates all unregistered land as state property, denying Gobi herders formal land tenure despite their long-standing stewardship.[117] This legal framework effectively excludes herders from securing private ownership rights, undermining their traditional livelihoods and connection to their ancestral territories. The recently adopted Law on Herders introduced provisions allowing groups of herders to collectively register pastureland for grazing purposes.[118] While this represents a step toward securing land rights, it remains vague and lack enforcement mechanisms to prevent land grabbing, particularly by mining companies. Without clear legal protections, Gobi herders remain at risk of displacement, as mining operations continue to encroach on traditional grazing territories. According to Dovchin and Dovchin, displacement extends beyond forced eviction to include limiting or banning the vital activities and resources communities rely on for survival as counts as economic displacement.[119] Consequently, the absence of land ownership rights forces herders into an unequal and often involuntary coexistence with mining companies on their ancestral lands. While mining and herding technically share the same space in the Gobi, the reality for herders is one of mounting hardship.[120] Major mining projects like Oyu Tolgoi and Tavan Tolgoi have drastically transformed the landscape,

---

[114] Sternberg et al. (2022).

[115] Sternberg et al. (2022), p. 1.

[116] Sternberg et al. (2022), p. 1-2.

[117] Great Ikh Khural Mongolia (1992) Constitution of Mongolia, 13 January 1992 Ulaanbaatar, Article 6.2.

[118] Great Ikh Khural of Mongolia (2002) The Land Law, Ulaanbaatar 2002, Article 21.4.4.

[119] Dovchin and Dovchin (2024), p. 547.

[120] For example, see For example, Mendbayar et al. (2022) 'National Baseline Assessment on Business and Human Rights for the National Action Plan on Mongolia' UNDP Mongolia 2022 https://globalnaps.org/wp-content/uploads/2024/02/BHR-NBA-in-Mongolia-report-2022.ENG_.pdf (last accessed 12 January 2025); Institute for Innovative Policies (2018) Human rights impact assessment of mining and transportation from TavanTolgoi" National Human Rights Commission of Mongolia, October 2018, Ulaanbaatar, Mongolia https://www.undp.org/sites/g/files/zskgke326/files/migration/mn/57e653f154778b550b0713b795a0e46c0e784ebbedcb9a5e6742ebcb5b9b0b1a.pdf (last accessed 12 January 2025).

fragmenting pastures, depleting vital water resources, and pushing herders into increasingly precarious and unsustainable conditions.[121]

Water is a critical resource in the arid Gobi region, and mining operations require vast quantities for mineral processing. Deep aquifer extraction by mining companies has lowered groundwater levels, reducing the availability of water for herders and their livestock.[122] Many herders have reported that traditional wells have dried up, forcing them to travel longer distances to find water.[123] Additionally, locked wells—controlled by mining companies or local authorities—have further restricted access, intensifying resource competition.[124] Mobility is central to Gobi herding practices, allowing pastoralists to navigate extreme climate variability and prevent overgrazing. However, large-scale mining projects have disrupted these patterns by fencing off grazing areas, constructing roads, and developing industrial infrastructure.[125] This land fragmentation has significantly reduced the availability of quality pasture, forcing herders to overuse smaller grazing areas, accelerating desertification, and threatening livestock health.

The increase in mining-related dust pollution has significantly impacted both livestock and herders. Dust from open-pit mines, transport roads, and heavy machinery coats pastures, reducing the nutritional quality of forage and leading to lower livestock productivity.[126] Cashmere and wool—two of the most valuable products from Gobi herders—are particularly affected, as dust contamination lowers their market value.[127] Additionally, dust inhalation has been linked to respiratory problems in both animals and herders, further deteriorating their quality of life.[128] With shrinking access to pasture and water, many Gobi herders are being pushed out of their traditional livelihoods.

Although the government has established regulations to reduce the environmental and social impacts of mining, enforcement remains weak—largely due to inadequate monitoring. Under the Law on Minerals and the Law on Environmental Impact Assessment (EIA), mining companies are required to conduct thorough assessments to prevent adverse impacts to herder communities, livestock, and ecosystems.[129] However, Social Impact Assessments (SIAs) are only partially covered by the current EIA law, which is now being amended to strengthen social assess-

---

[121] NHRCM (2018) Human rights impact assessment of mining and transportation from TavanTolgoi" Human Rights Commission of Mongolia, October 2018, Ulaanbaatar, Mongolia https://www.undp.org/sites/g/files/zskgke326/files/migration/mn/57e653f154778b550b0713b795a0e46c0e784ebbedcb9a5e6742ebcb5b9b0b1a.pdf (last accessed 12 January 2025).

[122] Dalaibuyan (2022), p. 47.

[123] Sternberg et al. (2022), p. 10.

[124] Sternberg et al. (2022), p. 10.

[125] Sternberg et al. (2022), p. 10.

[126] Mendbayar et al. (2022), p. 61.

[127] Mendbayar et al. (2022), p. 61.

[128] Mendbayar et al. (2022), p. 61.

[129] Great Ikh Khural Mongolia (2006) The Law on Minerals, Ulaanbaatar 2006, Article 39.1.2, The mining license holder must conduct environmental impact assessment. Law on Environmental

ment requirements.[130] The law mandates approved procedures for socioeconomic and health impact assessments and bars financial institutions from supporting activities harmful to society, human health, or the environment.[131] While social assessment is required for high-risk projects, existing regulations primarily focus on natural disaster risk, hazardous chemicals, and OHS, leaving gaps in areas such as social conflict, land acquisition, community impacts, and vulnerable groups.[132] The Ministry of Environment and Tourism is currently revising the EIA law and drafting a new regulation with more explicit social assessment provisions.[133]

The promise of coexistence between mining and herding in the Gobi region has, in reality, translated into a process of displacement and marginalisation for herders. The depletion of water resources, loss of pastureland, environmental pollution, and lack of legal protections have placed immense pressure on pastoralists, eroding their ability to sustain their traditional way of life.

3.1.3 Corporate Responsibility to Indigenous Communities in Domestic Law

Under Article 24.1 of the Law on Minerals, only a business entity holding a valid exploration license may apply for a mining license for the corresponding area.[134] Articles 17.2 and 17.3 assign Aimag and Soum governors the responsibility of gathering proposals from the Soum's Assembly of Citizens' Representatives and communicating their approval or rejection to the Central State Administration for Mining and Geology.[135] In this process, the governor serves as a vital intermediary between mining companies and local herders: they must keep communities informed, address concerns, and seek consent before any exploration begins.

Impact Assessment, Article 7.1. The Impact Assessment consists of general and detailed impact assessment.

[130] World Bank Group (2024) 'Mongolia: Environmental and Social Framework Overview Assessment' June 2024, pp. 55–56 https://documents1.worldbank.org/curated/en/099061924121520889/pdf/P5012251f10a7c0a819e851a2f6bb8ea939.pdf (last accessed 21 January 2025).

[131] The Great Ikh Khural Mongolia (2012) 'The Law on Environmental Impact Assessment' Ulaanbaatar 2012, Article 8.4.

[132] World Bank Group (2024) 'Mongolia: Environmental and Social Framework Overview Assessment' June 2024, pp. 56–57. https://documents1.worldbank.org/curated/en/099061924121520889/pdf/P5012251f10a7c0a819e851a2f6bb8ea939.pdf (last accessed 21 January 2025).

[133] World Bank Group (2024) 'Mongolia: Environmental and Social Framework Overview Assessment' June 2024, p. 30. https://documents1.worldbank.org/curated/en/099061924121520889/pdf/P5012251f10a7c0a819e851a2f6bb8ea939.pdf (last accessed 21 January 2025).

[134] Great Ikh Khural Mongolia (2006) The Law on Minerals, Ulaanbaatar 2006, Article 24.1.

[135] Great Ikh Khural Mongolia (2006) The Law on Minerals, Ulaanbaatar 2006, Articles 17.2 and 17.3.

Additionally, Article 42.2 stipulates that mining companies, in collaboration with local governors, are required to conduct public consultations.[136]

Despite these legal provisions, it remains unclear whether they are consistently enforced. Previous studies and conversations with herders suggest that the requirements often go unmet in practice.[137] While these regulations might appear to somewhat align with the FPIC principles, they lack explicit legal mandates ensuring that consent is truly "free," obtained "prior" to project commencement, and based on full, accessible information. Moreover, for our knowledge and experience, herders have questioned the legitimacy of the Soum's Assembly of Citizens' Representatives, noting the absence of clear rules on how representatives are chosen and how community approval is formally discussed and secured.[138] Other scholars have similarly raised concerns about the ambiguity of decision-making processes that based on the opinion or consent of herders and local communities.[139]

As previously argued, Mongolia's current Environmental Impact Assessment (EIA) law only partially addresses Social Impact Assessments (SIAs). While legislative amendments are in progress to fill these gaps by expanding social assessment requirements, the existing framework still focuses predominantly on natural disasters, hazardous chemicals, and occupational health and safety (OHS).[140] As a result, critical social dimensions—such as land acquisition, community impacts, social conflict, and the needs of vulnerable groups, including women—often go overlooked. A telling example is the recent Environmental and Social Impact Assessment (ESIA) conducted Oyu Tolgoi (OT) (operated by Rio Tinto), Mongolia's largest multinational mining operation.[141] Despite its comprehensive scope, the assessment failed to incorporate a gender-specific analysis and did not meet key international consultation standards, including those outlined in the IFC Performance Standards. This comprehensive assessment failed to address the broader human rights impacts on vulnerable groups, including women and children, overlooking critical issues such as land displacement, social conflicts among herders, gendered workload burdens, access to water, and cultural rights of the nomadic herders.

Beyond securing exploration and mining licenses and conducting feasibility studies, mining projects in Mongolia must also engage in local community consultations through Local Cooperation Agreements (LCAs). In accordance with Article 42.1 of the Law on Minerals, mining companies are required to establish LCAs with local governors, creating a formal mechanism for negotiation and benefit-sharing.[142]

[136] Great Ikh Khural Mongolia (2006) The Law on Minerals, Ulaanbaatar 2006, Article 42.2.

[137] Mendbayar et al. (2022), p. 62; Dovchin and Dovchin (2024), p. 547; Dalaibuyan (2017), p. 5.

[138] Mendbayar et al. (2022), p. 62.

[139] Dalaibuyan (2022), p. 49.

[140] World Bank Group (2024) 'Mongolia: Environmental and Social Framework Overview Assessment' June 2024, p. 30. https://documents1.worldbank.org/curated/en/099061924121520889/pdf/P5012251f10a7c0a819e851a2f6bb8ea939.pdf (last accessed 21 January 2025).

[141] Oyu Tolgoi (2012) 'A Comprehensive Environmental and Social Impact Assessment' 2012 https://www.ot.mn/en/social-responsibility/esia (last accessed 21 January 2025).

[142] Great Ikh Khural Mongolia (2006) The Law on Minerals, Ulaanbaatar 2006, Article 42.1.

These agreements oblige mining license holders to collaborate with local authorities on environmental protection, infrastructure development, and employment initiatives.[143] In 2016, the government introduced a model agreement – the first legislative framework for LCAs—to standardise community engagement and protect the interests of affected communities.[144] Despite this progress, the framework remains vague; it lacks clear procedural guidelines for negotiation, benefit sharing, and robust environmental and social impact assessments.[145]

In practice, LCAs are often short-term (usually one year or less) and focus narrowly on compensatory payments for land and water use rather than fostering enduring, mutually beneficial cooperation.[146] A 2017 LCA between Soum Lun in Tuv Aimag and the state-owned company "Avdarkhairkhan" illustrates these shortcomings: the agreement promises only donation-like benefits—such as improving a parking area near the Soum governor's office and constructing an archery field—while failing to address environmental concerns and community health.[147] Foreign-invested mining ventures—such as Oyu Tolgoi (OT) (operated by Rio Tinto) and Erdene Resource Development (ERD) (a Canadian-based company)—have signed LCAs with local governors in Bayankhongor and Umnugobi, ostensibly to serve the interests of local communities, including nomadic herders.[148] Yet the negotiation processes behind these agreements remain opaque, and there is little publicly available information about how any promised benefits are allocated. This lack of transparency raises serious concerns about whether herders' needs and voices are genuinely accounted for in the final deals.

In 2019, UN Independent Expert Juan Pablo Bohoslavsky visited Mongolia and warned that mining poses serious threats to health, housing, water, and sanitation.[149] He identified a conflict of interest in allowing private consultancy firms—contracted by mining companies—to conduct impact assessments. During a visit to the OT mine, he urged ongoing dialogue with local communities, especially herders, and recommended exploring alternative water sources.[150] He also called for a permanent

[143] Dalaibuyan (2017), p. 6-7; Dalaibuyan (2022), p. 51.

[144] The Government of Mongolia Resolution (2016): Approval of the Model Agreement' between local governor and the mining license holder company, Ulaanbaatar 2016.

[145] Dalaibuyan (2017), p. 9.

[146] Dalaibuyan (2022), pp. 51–52.

[147] Mendbayar et al. (2022), p. 63.

[148] Oyu Tolgoi and UmnuGobi Aimag (2015) Cooperation Agreement April 2015 https://www.iltodgeree.mn/contract/789/view# (last accessed 12 February 2025); Erdene Resource Development (ERD) (2024) Erdene Renews Local Cooperation Agreement and Provides Environmental, Social And Governance Update, 2022 Halifax https://erdene.com/site/assets/files/4351/epr.pdf (last accessed 12 February 2025).

[149] UN (2019) 'Mongolia: UN human rights expert visits to examine financial and economic issues' 29 August 2019 https://www.ohchr.org/en/press-releases/2019/08/mongolia-un-human-rights-expert-visits-examine-financial-and-economic-issues (last accessed 12 February 2025).

[150] UN General Assembly (2020) 'Visit to Mongolia: Report of the Independent Expert on the effects of foreign debt and other related international financial obligations of States on the full

multi-stakeholder platform to address environmental claims, emphasizing that access to water is crucial to herders' livelihoods.[151]

Although Mongolian law requires mining projects to engage local communities and establish (LCAs), these mechanisms often fail to meet international standards such as FPIC and do not align with benefit-sharing principles outlined in the UN Declaration on the Rights of Indigenous Peoples (UNDRIP) and ILO Convention 169. In practice, most LCAs are signed and established without meaningful participation from herders, limiting their ability to influence decisions from the outset.[152] For instance, while ERD and OT's LCAs claim to allocate over one million Canadian dollars for environmental restoration, water and electricity payments, and various community benefits (including health services, employment opportunities, training, and self-employment support), it remains highly questionable whether these provisions genuinely address herders' priorities or effectively preserve their cultural, spiritual, and livelihood needs. In our experience, when herders do participate in the process, they often face severe economic pressures that compel them to focus on short-term compensation rather than long-term rights or more equitable benefit-sharing. Furthermore, many herders lack the legal and technical expertise to fully grasp the implications of these agreements, undermining their ability to engage in meaningful negotiations.[153] As a result, LCAs tend to function more as payment mechanisms for water and land usage rather than meaningful instruments for preventing harm and empowering communities.[154] This undermines the core aim of FPIC—to enable communities to shape decisions about their lands and resources. Strengthening legal protections and ensuring robust enforcement is therefore essential to guarantee that herding communities can genuinely participate in decisions affecting their livelihoods and cultural heritage.

3.2 Women on the Frontlines: Gendered Impacts of Mining in the Gobi

Mongolia's mining boom has received considerable scrutiny for its environmental repercussions and the failure of corporate actors to respect Indigenous Peoples rights. Yet these discussions often overlook the experiences of Mongolian women herders, who bear disproportionate burdens as both economic providers and cultural

---

enjoyment of all human rights, particularly economic, social and cultural rights' 3 January 2020 A/HRC/43/45/Add.2, para 64.

[151] UN General Assembly (2020) 'Visit to Mongolia: Report of the Independent Expert on the effects of foreign debt and other related international financial obligations of States on the full enjoyment of all human rights, particularly economic, social and cultural rights' 3 January 2020 A/HRC/43/45/Add.2, para 102 (n).

[152] Dalaibuyan (2022), pp. 59–60.

[153] Dalaibuyan (2022), p. 59.

[154] Dalaibuyan (2022), pp. 51–52.

stewards.[155] These women carry on centuries-old herding knowledge, manage caregiving responsibilities, and maintain local markets by converting animal byproducts—such as wool, hides, and dairy—into essential goods for their communities.[156] The proverb "every part of the livestock can be used, except its breath" encapsulates their remarkable resourcefulness.[157] Nonetheless, mining-related policies and economic assessments rarely account for women's dual workload or the ways that extractive activities multiply their labour.[158]

The arrival of predominantly male mining workforces into pastoral areas has also introduced new forms of structural violence.[159] Incidents of sexual harassment, assault, and domestic violence have become more common, underscoring how mining operations exacerbate gender-based insecurities.[160] These gendered challenges are compounded by Mongolia's land tenure system, which systematically disadvantages women. While herders can formally register winter and spring shelters, large areas of communal pasture remain state-owned and thus vulnerable to rapid expropriation.[161] Many women do not hold the formal land titles required for compensation when mining operations intrude upon shared grazing lands, further undermining their economic stability.

The economic toll of displacement also falls disproportionately on women. As mining depletes or pollutes water sources and grazing lands, entire families may be forced to relocate to less fertile areas. Women, who typically oversee livestock and finances, find themselves navigating reduced resources and greater financial insecurity.[162] Male outmigration to mining jobs compounds this burden by leaving women

---

[155] For example see reports: Swiss Agency for Development and Cooperation SDC (2015) Gender Analysis in Pastoral Livestock Herding in Mongolia 2015 Ulaanbaatar; Asian Development Bank (2022) 'Women's Resilience in Mongolia: How Laws and Policies Promote Gender Equality in Climate Change and Disaster Risk Management' https://reliefweb.int/report/mongolia/womens-resilience-mongolia-how-laws-and-policies-promote-gender-equality-climate-change-and-disaster-risk-management-june-2022 (last accessed 23 January 2025).

[156] Magsar (2024) 'Saalitai Enger: Life of Mongolian herdswoman' Friedrich Ebert Stiftung 13 September 2024 https://asia.fes.de/news/mongolian-herdswoman.html (last accessed 28 January 2025).

[157] Magsar (2024) 'Saalitai Enger: Life of Mongolian herdswoman' Friedrich Ebert Stiftung 13 September 2024 https://asia.fes.de/news/mongolian-herdswoman.html (last accessed 28 January 2025).

[158] Blades-Barrett (2024) 'Decent Work for Women Herders in Mongolia: What's being done?' 21 November 2024 https://sustainablefibre.org/decent-work-for-women-herders-in-mongolia-whats-being-done/ (last accessed 28 January 2025).

[159] Cane et al. (2014); Cane (2015).

[160] Cane et al. (2014).

[161] Daley, Narangerel, Driscoll et al. (2018) 'Gender, Land and Mining Mongolia' WOLTS Research Report No.1, January 2018, pp. 50–51 https://www.delvedatabase.org/uploads/resources/Gender-Land-and-Mining-in-Mongolia.pdf#page=62.61 (last accessed 25 January 2025).

[162] For example, see National Human Rights Commission of Mongolia 'Report on Human Rights of Women Herders: Enjoyment of rights to be free from sexual and reproductive health' 2019 Ulaanbaatar, pp. 23–27. https://www.uih.mn/upload/sudalgaa/files/220_5565662.pdf#page=28.35 (last accessed 24 January 2025);

to manage split households with minimal support. Beyond these economic pressures, cultural and spiritual ties are frayed.[163] Women herders hold key roles in preserving pastoral traditions and ecological knowledge—much of which is lost or fragmented when ancestral lands (*nutag*) are degraded or seized.[164]

Furthermore, many women herders have stepped forward as active defenders of local ecosystems and endangered species, notably the Gobi bear (Mazaalai) and snow leopards—both of which are native only to Mongolia.[165] However, their activism often draws threats and intimidation from mining firms and local authorities—acts that can be viewed as gendered attacks—highlighting systemic efforts to marginalize women's voices in land governance.[166]

Legal perspective, despite broad acknowledgments of Mongolia's cultural heritage and the importance of its nomadic lifestyle, existing mining governance mechanisms consistently fail to recognise women's indispensable roles in herding communities. The absence of formal land rights leaves women particularly vulnerable to dispossession when communal pastures are allocated for extraction.[167] Despite constitutional commitments to gender equality in Mongolia,[168] rural realities often diverge: women are less visible in local decision-making processes—partly due to childcare and household duties—while men's mobility as herders or miners makes them more prominent in negotiations with companies.[169] Legal frameworks, including the Mongolian Laws on Minerals and Laws on EIAs, contain no explicit or implicit references to the distinct challenges women face. No statutes mandate their involvement in negotiations affecting their social, economic and cultural rights tied to their indigeneous status.

Drawing on our previous work experience, we observed that corporate ESIAs often fail to account for the social and cultural dimensions of women's work. Moreover, the limited community consultations that do take place tend to privilege male perspectives, leaving women's voices marginalised in key decision-making processes.[170] As a result, women face a dual dispossession: they lose both their

---

163 Cane et al. (2014).

164 Sandagdorj (2022), Ulambayar and Fernández-Giménez (2013).

165 For example, see Snow Leopard Trust (2019) 'Women Changing the Face of Comservation' https://snowleopard.org/women-changing-the-face-of-conservation/ (last accessed 24 January 2025).

166 SOMO (2020) 'Case Study: Mongolian environmental defenders sued by Altain Khuder' Mind the Gaps 2020 https://www.mindthegap.ngo/harmful-strategies/undermining-defenders-communities/criminalising-human-rights-defenders/mongolian-environmental-defenders-sued-by-altain-khuder/ (last accessed 24 January 2025).

167 Daley et al. (2018), pp. 99–100 https://www.delvedatabase.org/uploads/resources/Gender-Land-and-Mining-in-Mongolia.pdf#page=62.61 (last accessed 25 January 2025).

168 The Great Ikh Khural of Mongolia (2011) 'The Law on Gender Equality' 2011 Ulaanbaatar. Article 5.1.1.

169 Daley et al. (2018), pp. 39–40 https://www.delvedatabase.org/uploads/resources/Gender-Land-and-Mining-in-Mongolia.pdf#page=62.61 (last accessed 25 January 2025).

170 Daley et al. (2018), pp. 39–40 https://www.delvedatabase.org/uploads/resources/Gender-Land-and-Mining-in-Mongolia.pdf#page=62.61 (last accessed 25 January 2025).

physical land and their role as cultural custodians when mining degrades the ecological systems upon which their livelihoods depend. Where Environmental and Social Impact Assessments (ESIAs) do address environmental and social risks, they consistently fail to incorporate women's knowledge of local ecosystems or acknowledge how environmental degradation intensifies their labour burdens. Essential practices central to cultural and spiritual life—such as wool processing, animal husbandry, and stewardship of ancestral lands—are frequently overlooked, diminishing the role of women as primary guardians of Mongolia's pastoral heritage.[171] This can be also seen from the ESIAs conducted by the OT, which did not really reflect the socio economic rights of woman herders.[172] The ESIA of OT only considered women in employment in mining sector, and very brief mention of women local citizens meeting, however, there is no detailed gender analysis or assessment of how mining-induced environmental and social disruptions specifically impact women's livelihoods, traditional knowledge systems, or cultural practices. Moreover, the assessments neglect to examine how displacement, resource depletion, and economic shifts disproportionately affect women, particularly in terms of access to land, water, and economic opportunities beyond wage labour in mining. Without gender-responsive methodologies and meaningful engagement with local women, these assessments risk reinforcing existing inequalities rather than addressing them.[173] OT is a subsidiary of Rio Tinto, a company regarded as a leader in the responsible mining industry. It ranks 7th overall and 5th in the Extractives sector according to the Corporate Human Rights Benchmark (CHRB).[174] Rio Tinto also holds the 3rd position for governance and policy commitments, remedies and grievance mechanisms, and human rights practices.[175] However, despite these rankings, significant gaps remain in its implementation of human rights standards, particularly concerning Indigenous rights, gender impacts, and meaningful community engagement.

LCAs, which are intended to formalise community engagement and benefit-sharing, further illustrate this exclusion. The LCAs signed by ERD and OT, two major mining operations in Mongolia, lack transparency regarding how women's rights and priorities are incorporated into these agreements.[176] There is little clarity

[171] NHRCM (2019), pp. 23–27.

[172] Oyu Tolgoi (2012) 'A Comprehensive Environmental and Social Impact Assessment' 2012 https://www.ot.mn/en/social-responsibility/esia (last accessed 21 January 2025).

[173] Nidzelskaya and Gorski (2020) 'Addressing Gendered Impacts of Mining through Capacity Building UNEP https://www.environmentalgovernanceprogramme.org/mongolia-addressing-the-gendered-impacts-of-mining-through-capacity-building (last accessed 21 January 2025).

[174] Corporate Human Rights Benchmark (2023) Rio Tinto https://www.worldbenchmarkingalliance.org/publication/chrb/companies/rio-tinto-3/ (last accessed 21 January 2025).

[175] Corporate Human Rights Benchmark (2023) Rio Tinto https://www.worldbenchmarkingalliance.org/publication/chrb/companies/rio-tinto-3/ (last accessed 21 January 2025).

[176] Oyu Tolgoi and UmnuGobi Aimag (2015) Cooperation Agreement April 2015 https://www.iltodgeree.mn/contract/789/view# (last accessed 12 February 2025); Erdene Resource Development (ERD) (2024) Erdene Renews Local Cooperation Agreement and Provides Environmental, Social

on whether women herders have been meaningfully consulted or how their concerns—particularly regarding land access, water security, and economic alternatives—are reflected in these agreements. Instead, the focus tends to remain on broad community benefits, often failing to disaggregate impacts by gender or provide gender-sensitive mitigation measures.

This lack of gender inclusivity in LCAs is not solely the result of corporate negligence but is also tied to the incapacity of local governance structures to enforce inclusive decision-making. However, corporate actors should not use weak local governance as an excuse to exclude women's voices from agreements that directly impact their livelihoods. The failure to ensure gender-responsive consultations and transparent commitments in LCAs underscores a broader issue within Mongolia's mining policies: the disconnect between national legislation, local governance, and international human rights standards. Without actively involving women herders in decision-making processes, safeguarding them against economic and social vulnerabilities, and recognising their ecological expertise, the current system perpetuates gender-based inequalities and threatens the sustainability of traditional herding.

4 Conclusion: Reimagining Corporate Accountability for Indigenous Women—Lessons from the Gobi

Mongolia's experience with large-scale mining on traditional herding lands reflects broader patterns across the Global South, where extractive industries exploit asymmetrical power dynamics at the expense of Indigenous peoples and rural communities. Corporate-led due diligence frameworks such as ESIAs, shaped by Northern-centric models, fail to account for the ancestral, cultural, and spiritual ties Indigenous peoples and nomadic communities have to their lands. By commodifying land and disregarding communal stewardship, these frameworks overlook the full extent of mining's impact—not just on economic survival but on cultural continuity, intergenerational knowledge, and ecological resilience.

For Mongolian herder women, these failures are even more pronounced. Corporate policies rarely acknowledge their multifaceted roles in subsistence production, caregiving, and local economies, nor do they integrate their ecological knowledge into decision-making. Instead, international corporate responsibility frameworks continue to be shaped by industrialised-world assumptions about "development" and "ownership," reinforcing gendered power imbalances that exclude women from governance processes. As a result, companies perpetuate extractive models that prioritise shareholder interests while silencing those most affected by environmental and social harm.

And Governance Update, 2022 Halifax https://erdene.com/site/assets/files/4351/epr.pdf (last accessed 12 February 2025).

One of the key mechanism to address these systemic failures is gender-responsive FPIC. However, in Mongolia, FPIC remains poorly enforced and is often reduced to a box-ticking exercise rather than a genuine right of consent and consultation. To be meaningful, FPIC must explicitly incorporate women's perspectives, ensuring that consultations occur at accessible times, provide childcare support, and include culturally relevant legal guidance. This shift is critical in dismantling patriarchal norms that reduce women to secondary stakeholders and in challenging global governance structures that privilege corporate profit over communal rights.

Similarly, ESIAs must be explicitly gender-sensitive and intersectional, addressing not only economic and environmental risks but also the ways in which mining disrupts food security, water access, and social cohesion. Currently, most ESIAs overlook the gendered impacts on Indigenous women, compounding the broader adverse effects on their communities. They also fail to recognise Indigenous women's roles as environmental stewards and cultural knowledge keepers, as discussed in the previous chapter. From a Global South perspective, this reflects a persistent colonial bias in resource governance, where Indigenous knowledge systems are undervalued or ignored. Integrating women's ecological expertise into impact assessments could support biodiversity conservation, rotational grazing management, and sustainable water use—practices essential to pastoralist survival for generations.

Beyond FPIC and ESIAs, corporate due diligence must move beyond voluntary commitments and weak Corporate Social Responsibility (CSR) programs. The OECD Guidelines and the UNGPs offer general principles, but their lack of enforceability has created significant accountability gaps. Mongolia's reliance on voluntary CSR initiatives mirrors trends across the Global South, where mining companies promote superficial community engagement while sidestepping deeper structural issues such as land dispossession, weak legal protections, and corporate impunity. To ensure corporate accountability, gender impact assessments (GIAs) and binding social and environmental obligations must be made prerequisites for corporate licensing. Without enforceability, local women's voices remain overshadowed by distant shareholders and extractive state policies.

Another overlooked challenge is the failure of global legal frameworks to recognise nomadic and pastoralist communities as Indigenous Peoples. Instruments like ILO C169 and UNDRIP were largely shaped by the experiences of settled Indigenous groups, creating additional hurdles for nomadic populations whose land-use patterns do not fit into rigid legal definitions of territory or ownership. Recognising Mongolian herder women as Indigenous would afford them stronger legal claims to collective tenure, cultural rights, and conservation-based resource management. Without such recognition, they risk continued marginalisation in negotiations with both corporate and government actors.

The struggle of Mongolian herder women also mirrors broader Global South resistance against land dispossession and ecological destruction. From the Amazon to the Sahel, Indigenous women have been at the forefront of defending local ecosystems, often at great personal risk.[177] They often face criminalisation, intimidation, and violence, underscoring the urgent need for stronger legal protections, early-warning systems, and conflict-sensitive approaches in business and human rights governance to address gendered attacks.

Ultimately, Mongolia's mining policies expose the failures of corporate-led governance in addressing structural inequalities. Gender-responsive and intersectional FPIC and ESIAs must become standard practice to ensure that Indigenous women have both a voice and a veto in decisions affecting their lands and livelihoods. For Global South scholars of Business and Human Rights, this is not merely about reforming corporate governance—it is about challenging the global economic order that continues to prioritise capital accumulation over communal survival. By centring the lived experiences of Mongolian herder women and ensuring that international standards are not just adopted but meaningfully enforced, corporate accountability can move beyond performative commitments toward the genuine protection of Indigenous peoples' rights, ecological sustainability, and gender justice.

References

Amaya SJ (1996) Indigenous peoples in international law. OUP

Amazon Frontlines (2024) Indigenous Women Put Their Bodies On the Line to Defend the Amazon. https://amazonfrontlines.org/chronicles/indigenous-women-put-their-bodies-on-the-line-to-defend-the-amazon/. Accessed 12 Feb 2025

Amnesty International (2024) Submission To: UN Committee On The Elimination Of All Forms Of Discrimination Against Women At Its Eighty-Ninth Session and Tenth Periodic Review of Canada: Resource Extraction and Gender-Based Violence against Indigenous Women and Girls in Canada', 7-25 October 2024 https://www.amnesty.org/en/documents/amr20/8487/2024/en/. Accessed 24 Jan 2025

Asian Development Bank (2020) Development plan for Indigenous People. https://www.adb.org/sites/default/files/project-documents/49430/49430-005-ippf-mn.pdf#page=3.12. Accessed 12 Jan 2025

Asian Development Bank (2022) Women's Resilience in Mongolia: How Laws and Policies Promote Gender Equality in Climate Change and Disaster Risk Management. https://reliefweb.int/report/mongolia/womens-resilience-mongolia-how-laws-and-policies-promote-gender-equality-climate-change-and-disaster-risk-management-june-2022. Accessed 23 Jan 2025

Atkinson P, Hammersley M (2007) Ethnogprahy: principles in practice, 3rd edn. Routledge, p 42

Blades-Barrett L (2024) Decent work for women herders in Mongolia: What's being done? 21 November 2024 https://sustainablefibre.org/decent-work-for-women-herders-in-mongolia-whats-being-done/. Accessed 28 Jan 2025

Board J (2022) In the deep, cold Gobi desert, Mongolia's nomadic herders cannot outrun climate change. CNA 2022 https://www.channelnewsasia.com/sustainability/asia-great-climate-frontiers-mongolia-desertification-nomads-herders-gobi-2973316. Accessed 10 Jan 2025

[177] Amazon Frontlines (2024) 'Indigenous Women Put Their Bodies On the Line to Defend the Amazon' https://amazonfrontlines.org/chronicles/indigenous-women-put-their-bodies-on-the-line-to-defend-the-amazon/ (last accessed 12 February 2025).

Buhmann K, Jonsson J, Fisker M (2019) Do no harm and do more good too: connecting the SDGs with business and human rights and political CSR theory. Corp Gov Int J Bus Soc 19(3):389–403

Cahier L (2020) Securing pathways to environmental justice for indigenous women Multilateral Development Banks and environmental violence in the Americas. Volkerrechtsblog https://voelkerrechtsblog.org/securing-pathways-to-environmental-justice-for-indigenous-women/. Accessed 12 Feb 2025

Cane (2015) Social and Gendered Impacts related to Mining, Mongolia. 6 April 2015 https://www.dfat.gov.au/sites/default/files/mongolia-social-gendered-impacts-related-to-mining.pdf#page=11.08. Accessed 24 Jan 2025

Cane, Terbish and Byambasuren (2014) Mapping gender-based Violence and Mining Infrastracture in Mongolian Mining Communities. International Mining for Development Centre. https://internationalwim.org/iwim-reports/mapping-gender-based-violence-and-mining-infrastructure-in-mongolian-mining-communities-2/. Accessed 24 Jan 2025

Chief of Great Ikh Khural Mongolia (2024) The Law on Herder, 2024 Ulaanbaatar, Mongolia

Cittadino F (2019) Incorporating Inidgneous Rights in the international regime on biodiversity protection: access, benefit sharing and conservation in Indigneous land. Brill Nijhoff:72

Committee Against Elimination of Discrimination Against Women (CEDAW) (2022) General Recommendations No. 39 on the rights of Indigenous womens rights 31 October 2022, CEDAW/C/GC/39

Corporate Human Rights Benchmark (2023) Rio Tinto https://www.worldbenchmarkingalliance.org/publication/chrb/companies/rio-tinto-3/. Accessed 21 Jan 2025

Dalaibuyan B (2017) Local level agreements in Mongolia's resource sector: lessons learned and the way forward. Briefing Natural Resource Governance Institute. https://resource4.sodonsolution.org/miningjournal/file/2018/3/93439079559526f7/00d0681cff2c7069.pdf. Accessed 10 Feb 2025

Dalaibuyan B (2022) Negotiating the coexistence of mining and pastoralism in Mongolia. J Contemp East Asian Stud 11:46–63

Daley E, Narangerel Y, Driscoll Z et al (2018) Gender, land and mining Mongolia. WOLTS Research Report No.1, January 2018, pp 39–40. https://www.delvedatabase.org/uploads/resources/Gender-Land-and-Mining-in-Mongolia.pdf#page=62.61. Accessed 25 Jan 2025

Dovchin U, Dovchin S (2024) The discourse of the Anthropocene and posthumanism: Mining-induced loss of traditional land and the Mongolian nomadic herders. Ethnicities 24(4):536–559

Drees L, Liehr S, Batbuyan B, Marg O, Mehring M (2022) In search of a nomadic pastoralism for the 21st century. A transdisciplinary development of future scenarios to foster a social-ecological transformation in Mongolia. Innov Eur J Soc Sci Res 35(3):481–505

Dugersuren S (2015) When I was herding I had a plentiful life. Now I am working for another and have lost my independence. Guardian 9 March 2015, https://www.theguardian.com/global-development-professionals-network/2015/mar/09/mongolian-nomads-displacement-mining-impact-development-projects. Accessed 14 Jan 2025

Erdene Resource Development (ERD) (2024) Erdene Renews Local Cooperation Agreement and Provides Environmental, Social and Governance Update, 2022 Halifax https://erdene.com/site/assets/files/4351/epr.pdf. Accessed 12 Feb 2025

Fynn Bruey V (2019) Indigenous women and international law. In: Rimmer SH, Ogg K (eds) Research handbook on feminist engagement with international law. Edward Elgar Publishing, pp 499–524

Gardelle L, Zhao Z (2021) Being herder in contemporary Mongolia: Nomadic Identity and nationhood building at school. Asian Ethnicity: 1–22

Gottardi F (2020) Modern challenges in international law and Indigenous Rights: The United Nations Declaration on the Rights of Indigenous Peoples, Indigenous Women's Activism, and the Issue of violence against Indigenous Women. Trento Student Law Rev 2(2):93–120

Government of Mongolia (2016) Resolution: 'Approval of the Model Agreement' between local governor and the mining license holder company, 28 March 2016

Great Ikh Khural Mongolia (1992) The Constitution of Mongolia, 1992 Ulaanbaatar, Mongolia
Great Ikh Khural Mongolia (2002) The Land Law, 2002 Ulaanbaatar, Mongolia
Great Ikh Khural Mongolia (2006). The Law on Minerals, 2006 Ulaanbaatar, Mongolia
Great Ikh Khural Mongolia (2011) 'The Employment Support Law' 2011 Ulaanbaatar, Mongolia
Greenspan (2024) There's a new standard out. Will mining companies finally get it right with Indigenous Peoples? Oxfam 2024. https://politicsofpoverty.oxfamamerica.org/new-mining-standard-recognizes-indigenous-peoples-right-to-withhold-consent-for-project-activities-but-will-the-guidance-affect-much-needed-change-in-company-practice/. Accessed 12 Feb 2024
Handl M, Seck SL, Simons P (2022) Gender and intersectionality in business and human rights scholarship. Bus Human Rights J 2:201–225
Harter F (2023) Dust, hail and bank loans: the Mongolian herders facing life without grass. Guardian, 15 November 2023. https://www.theguardian.com/global-development/2023/nov/15/dust-hail-and-bank-loans-the-mongolian-herders-facing-life-without-grass#:~:text=Some%2030%25%20of%20Mongolia's%20almost,their%20country's%20association%20with%20pastoralism. Accessed 15 Jan 2025
ICMM (2024) Indigenous Peoples: Position Statement. 8 August 2024, Recognition Statement 2, p. 4 https://www.icmm.com/en-gb/our-principles/position-statements/indigenous-peoples/ Accessed 12 Feb 2025
Inter-American Commission on Human Rights (IACHR) (2013) Indigenous Peoples in Voluntary Isolation and Initial Contact in the Americas. https://www.oas.org/en/iachr/indigenous/docs/pdf/report-indigenous-peoples-voluntary-isolation.pdf. Accessed 12 Feb 2024
Inter-American Commission on Human Rights (IACHR) (2017) 'Indigenous Women' 2017 https://www.oas.org/en/iachr/reports/pdfs/indigenouswomen.pdf#page=11.15. Accessed 28 Jan 2025
International Council of Mining and Metals (ICMM) (2022) Principles – Performance Expectations. https://www.icmm.com/en-gb/our-principles. Accessed 10 Feb 2025
International Finance Corporations (IFC) (2012) Performance Standards on Environmental and Social Sustainability. https://www.ifc.org/en/insights-reports/2012/ifc-performance-standards. Accessed 10 Jan 2025
International Labour Organisation (ILO) (1989) 'Indigenous and Tribal Peoples Convention' 1989 (No. 169) Adopted on 27 June 1989
Khaltar B (2020) Mongolia plans river diversion as mining boom sucks Gobi dry: As herders in the Gobi desert lose livelihoods from pollution and lack of water, the government plans to pipe water across Mongolia Dialogue Earth 14 October 2020. https://dialogue.earth/en/water/mongolia-plans-river-diversion-as-mining-boom-runs-gobi-dry/. Accessed 14 Jan 2025
Kuokkanen R (2012) Self-determination and Indigenous Women's Rights at the Intersection of International human rights. Human Rights Quart Rev 34(1):225–250
Magsar A (2024) Saalitai Enger: Life of Mongolian herdswoman. Friedrich Ebert Stiftung 13 September 2024 https://asia.fes.de/news/mongolian-herdswoman.html. Accessed 28 Jan 2025
McInnes A, Colchester M, Whiltmore A (2017) Free, prior and informed consent: how to rectify the devastating consequences of harmful mining for Indigenous peoples. Persp Ecol Conserv 15(3):152–160
Mendbayar M, Perenlei M, Davaanyam O (2022) National Baseline Assessment on Business and Human Rights for the National Action Plan on Mongolia
Michler LM, Kaczensky P, Oyunsaikhan G et al (2023) To move or not to move—factors influencing small-scale herder and livestock movements in the Dzungarian Gobi, Mongolia. Reg Environ Change 23:13
Michler LM, Kaczensky P, Batsukh D et al (2024) What will the future bring? – Socio-economic challenges to herder households in the Great Gobi B strictly protected area in Mongolia. Hum Ecol 52:1071–1085
Morgega E (2024) Fair and equitable benefit-sharing in international law. OUP, p 241
Morgera E (2016) Corporate accountability. In: Morgera E, Kulovesi K (eds) Research handbook on international law and natural resources. Edward Elgar, pp 109–135

Morgera E (2020) Corporate environmental accountability in international law, 2nd edn. Oxford University Press, p 182

National Human Rights Commission of Mongolia (NHRCM) (2018) Human Rights Impact Assessment of Coal Mining and Transportation in the Tavan Tolgoi Mining Deposits

National Human Rights Commission of Mongolia NHRCM (2019) Report on Human Rights of Women Herders: Enjoyment of rights to be free from sexual and reproductive health. 2019 Ulaanbaatar

Nidzelskaya E, Gorski A (2020.) Addressing Gendered Impacts of Mining through Capacity Building UNEP https://www.environmentalgovernanceprogramme.org/mongolia-addressing-the-gendered-impacts-of-mining-through-capacity-building. Accessed 21 Jan 2025

Nissen A (2023) Gender-transformative remedies for women human rights defenders. Bus Human Rights J 8:369–402

OECD and Food and Agriculture Organisation of the United Nations (FAO) (2016) OECD-FAO Guidance for Responsible Agriculture Supply Chains. OECD Publishing, Paris. https://mne-guidelines.oecd.org/oecd-fao-guidance.pdf. Accessed 10 Jan 2025

Organisation for Economic Cooperation and Development (OECD) (2023) OECD Guidelines for Multinational Enterprises on Responsible Business Conduct. OECD Publication, Paris

Owen JR, Kemp D, Harris J, Lechner AM, Lèbre É (2022) Fast track to failure? Energy transition minerals and the future of consultation and consent. Energy Res Soc Sci 102665:1–14

Oyu T (2012) A Comprehensive Environmental and Social Impact Assessment. 2012 https://www.ot.mn/en/social-responsibility/esia. Accessed 21 Jan 2025

Oyu T, UmnuGobi A (2015) Cooperation Agreement April 2015 https://www.iltodgeree.mn/contract/789/view#. Accessed 12 Feb 2025

Parisi L, Corntassel J (2007) In pursuit of self-determination: indigenous women's challenges to traditional diplomatic spaces. Can Foreign Policy J 13(3):81–98

Right Energy Partnership with Indigenous Peoples (2024) 'Indigenous Peoples' Rights at Risk: ICMM's Position Statement Falls Short on Free, Prior, and Informed Consent' 3 September 2024 https://rightenergypartnership.org/public-statement-on-adoption-of-the-indigenous-peoples-mining-position-statement-of-the-international-council-on-mining-and-metals-icmm/. Accessed 12 Feb 2024

Sandagdorj (2022) How one woman is fighting to preserve Mongolia's last reindeer herding culture. Global Press Journal https://globalpressjournal.com/asia/mongolia/one-woman-fighting-preserve-mongolias-last-reindeer-herding-culture/ (Accessed 24 January 2025); Ulambayar and Fernández-Giménez (2013).

Seck S, Simons P (2019) Resource extraction and the human rights of women and girls. Can J Women Law 31(1):1–7

Secretariat of the Convention on Biological Diversity Montreal (2011) The convention on biological diversity: text and annexes. Montreal 2011

Simons P (2017) Unsustainable international law: transnational resource extraction and violence against women, Ottawa Faculty of Law Working Paper No. 2019-11: 415–432

Simons P, Handl M (2019) Relations of ruling: feminist critique of the United Nations guiding principles on business and human rights and violence against women in the context of resource extraction. Can J Women Law 31(1):113–150

Snow Leopard Trust (2019) Women Changing the Face of Comservation. https://snowleopard.org/women-changing-the-face-of-conservation/. Accessed 24 Jan 2025

SOMO (2020) Case Study: Mongolian environmental defenders sued by Altain Khuder. Mind the Gaps 2020 https://www.mindthegap.ngo/harmful-strategies/undermining-defenders-communities/criminalising-human-rights-defenders/mongolian-environmental-defenders-sued-by-altain-khuder/. Accessed 24 Jan 2025

Sternberg T, Mayaud JR, Ahearn A (2022) Herd It in the Gobi: deserting pastoralism? Land 11(6):799. https://www.mdpi.com/2073-445X/11/6/799. Accessed 12 Jan 2025

Swiss Agency for Development and Cooperation SDC (2015) Gender analysis in pastoral livestock herding in Mongolia, Ulaanbaatar 2015, p 9

Tello R (2016) I'm not Indigenous!' Identity and Exclusion in Indigenous Development. IDB Blog 1 August 2016. https://blogs.iadb.org/sostenibilidad/en/im-not-indigenous-identity-and-exclusion-in-indigenous-development/. Accessed 12 Jan 2025

The Economic Commission for Latin America (ECLA) (2018) Regional Agreement on Access to Information, Public Participation and Justice in Environmental Matters in Latin America and the Caribbean. 2018 https://repositorio.cepal.org/entities/publication/86cae662-f81c-4b45-a04a-058e8d26143c. Accessed 12 Jan 2025

The Equator Principles (2020). https://equator-principles.com/about-the-equator-principles/. Accessed 10 Jan 2025

The Organisation of American States (OAS) (2016) American Declaration on the Rights of Indigenous Peoples. 15 June 2016 https://www.oas.org/en/sare/documents/DecAmIND.pdf#page=9.12. Accessed 12 Jan 2025

UN (2019) Mongolia: UN human rights expert visits to examine financial and economic issues. 29 August 2019. https://www.ohchr.org/en/press-releases/2019/08/mongolia-un-human-rights-expert-visits-examine-financial-and-economic-issues. Accessed 12 Feb 2025

UN ECOSOC (2022) Report of the Secretary Gerenal: Achieving gender equality and the empowerment of all women and girls in the context of climate change, environmental and disaster risk reduction policies and programmes, E/CN.6/2022/3 Geneva 2022

UN General Assembly (2007) Resolution 61/295 United Nations Declaration on the Rights of Indigneous Peoples (UNDRIP) 13 September 2007, https://www.un.org/development/desa/indigenouspeoples/wp-content/uploads/sites/19/2018/11/UNDRIP_E_web.pdf. Accessed 24 Jan 2025

UN General Assembly (2015) Report of the Special Rapporteur on the rights of indigenous peoples, Victoria Tauli Corpuz'A/HRC/30/41 Geneva 2015

UN General Assembly (2020) Visit to Mongolia: Report of the Independent Expert on the effects of foreign debt and other related international financial obligations of States on the full enjoyment of all human rights, particularly economic, social and cultural rights. 3 January 2020 A/HRC/43/45/Add.2 Geneva 2020

UN General Assembly (2022a) Special Rapportuer on the Rights of Indigenous Peoples: 'Indigenous women and the development, application, preservation and transmission of scientific and technical knowledge' A/HRC/51/28, Geneva 2022

UN General Assembly (2022b) Violence against Indigenous Women and Girls, Report of the UN Special Rapporteur on the Violence Against Women, its Causes and Consequences, Reem Alsalem' A/HRC/50/26, Geneva 2022

UN General Assembly (2024) Report of the Special Rapporteur on the rights of Indigenous Peoples, José Francisco Calí Tzay - Mobile Indigenous Peoples. 16 July 2024, A/79/160.

UN Human Rights Council (HRC) (2011) 'Guiding Principles on Business and Human Rights: Implementing the United Nations "Protect, Respect and Remedy" Framework 2011

UN WGBHR (2019) Gender Dimension of the UN Guiding Principles on Business and Human Rights. https://www.ohchr.org/sites/default/files/Documents/Issues/Business/BookletGenderDimensionsGuidingPrinciples.pdf. Accessed 10 Jan 2025

UN Women (2024) Advancing gender-responsive synergies across the Rio Convetions: Gender Equality at the Intersection of Climate Action, Biodiversity Protection and Sustainable Land Management. https://www.wocan.org/wp-content/uploads/2024/12/brief-advancing-gender-responsive-synergies-across-the-rio-conventions-en.pdf. Accessed 11 Jan 2025

UNDP Mongolia (2024) Combating Desertification in Mongolia's Gobi: Story of Resilience and Restoration. 28 November 2024 https://www.undp.org/mongolia/stories/combating-desertification-mongolias-gobi-story-resilience-and-restoration. Accessed 9 Jan 2024

Upton C (2010) Living off the land: nature and nomadism in Mongolia. Geoforum 41(6):865–874

Wettstein F (2022) Business and human rights: ethical, legal and managerial perspectives. Cambridge University Press, p 92

WOLTS (2018) Project Summary: 'Mongolia's female herders, mining and the struggle for land' 2018 https://mokoro.co.uk/wp-content/uploads/2024/11/WOLTS-Mongolia-2-page-research-summary_June2018_English.pdf. Accessed 9 Jan 2024
World Bank Group (2024) Mongolia: Environmental and Social Framework Overview Assessment. June 2024, p. 56-57. https://documents1.worldbank.org/curated/en/099061924121520889/pdf/P5012251f10a7c0a819e851a2f6bb8ea939.pdf. Accessed 21 Jan 2025
WWF (2024) Promoting Dryland Sustainable Landscapes and Biodiversity Conservation in the Eastern Steppe of Mongolia. https://www.worldwildlife.org/projects/promoting-dryland-sustainable-landscapes-and-biodiversity-conservation-in-the-eastern-steppe-of-mongolia. Accessed 10 Jan 2025

Revisiting Asian Values: A Historical Analysis of Its Correlation with Business and Human Rights Development in Southeast Asia

Loren Bustos and Kania Guzaimi

Abstract The business and human rights (BHR) discourse in Southeast Asia shows a different pattern of responses in the region. While BHR is not entirely a new phenomenon, its rise and integration into mainstream development has been constrained by challenges. Currently, only three countries, out of ten member states of the Association of Southeast Asia Nations (ASEAN), have published the National Action Plan on BHR, which are Thailand, Vietnam, and Indonesia. To analyze the current development of the BHR in the region, this study revisits the notion of *'Asian Values'* (AV), an ideological framework that emerged during the 1980s and 1990s, to justify the distinct cultural, social, political and economic characteristics of the Asian region. Within ASEAN, some of its strongest proponents emerged from the Southeast Asian leadership, such as Lee Kuan Yew of Singapore and Mahathir Mohamad of Malaysia. Although the discussion around Asian Values has been a subject of extensive criticism, the heavy debate serves a *puzzling* question on its correlation and lingering impact to the formation of the Southeast Asian human rights culture. To contribute to the growing discourse on BHR, this paper employs a historical analysis approach that traces the Asian Values' relevance and intersection within the human rights, and BHR discourse. This study will be discussed in two parts; the first part will introduce Asian Values and the long-withstanding Asian Values vs. Human Rights debate. It will analyze two historical developments that witnessed the Asian Values vs. Human Rights tension, first, is being a geopolitical nuance as highlighted in the Bangkok Declaration and Vienna Declaration and, second, is through the impact of the Asian Financial Crisis. The second part of the study is dedicated to an in-depth analysis of finding the underpinnings of Asian Values in shaping human rights. It will examine the emergence of corporate social responsibility, sustainability goals and other BHR-related tools and find correlations

L. Bustos (✉) · K. Guzaimi
Business and Human Rights, Faculty of Political Science, Friedrich-Alexander Universität Erlangen-Nürnberg, Erlangen, Germany
e-mail: loren.bustos@fau.de; kania.guzaimi@fau.de

D. A. Pamplona et al. (eds.), *Business and Human Rights from the Lens of Women*, Interdisciplinary Studies in Human Rights 13,
https://doi.org/10.1007/978-3-032-04036-7_10

as to how the Asian Values principles remain significant in contouring human rights and BHR understanding in these contexts.

1 Introduction

The Business and Human Rights (BHR) discourse has brought about contemporary changes in how human rights connect with businesses, societies, and regional institutions. It has steadily gained momentum, prompting regional initiatives to develop BHR commitments and policies as exemplified in Africa, Europe, and Latin America. In Asia, specifically in Southeast Asia (SEA), BHR is also not an entirely new phenomenon, however, its rise has been constrained by challenges in raising awareness, which has hindered its integration into mainstream development practices. Since the establishment of the UN Guiding Principles on Business and Human Rights (UNGP on BHR) and the promotion of state-level National Action Plans (NAPs) in 2011, only Thailand, Vietnam, and Indonesia have so far been able to actively develop NAPs on UNGP BHR in SEA. The region also suffers from high records of human rights violations in various labor-intensive industries with weak regional human rights protection to oversee these violations. For this reason, it is important to provide a regional context-specific analysis to understand the implementation of BHR in Southeast Asia.

Southeast Asia (SEA) is a region known for its rich blend of cultural, religious, social, and ethnic diversity. Geographically speaking, it is a region that consists of eleven (11) countries namely; Cambodia, Laos, Myanmar, Thailand, and Vietnam in the mainland while Brunei, Indonesia, Timor Leste, Malaysia, Singapore, the Philippines referred to as the island or maritime in Southeast Asia.[1] According to recent report, this region is composed of more than 670 million in population with a productive working-age population (ages 20–59) of 55.8% and a rising middle class.[2] At around the eighteenth and nineteenth centuries, all SEA countries, except for Thailand which remained as an independent Kingdom, experienced subjugation under colonial and imperialist rule.

Following the aftermath of World War II, decolonization movements surged across the Global South, advocating for independence and statehood eventually creating the new independent SEA states. However, although it has been a victorious fight for independence, it was a very challenging transitional period for the former colonized SEA states. The restructuring of the international community and the shifts of new global powers served a complex paradigm. Marked by wounds and traumas stemming from colonial legacies, the path toward statehood was marred by deeply rooted identity crises and social and economic disparities. These challenges

[1] Introduction to Southeast Asia | Asia Society. https://asiasociety.org/education/introduction-southeast-asia. Accessed 15 July 2024.

[2] Putra S (2023) ASEAN Statistical Brief – Vol 3 (December 2023) | ASEANstats Official Web Portal. https://www.aseanstats.org/publication/asb-202312/. Accessed 27 January 2025.

were manifested in their internal conflicts, and political instability throughout their nation-building and political transformations.

According to Narine, "the experience of colonialism deeply affected how the states of Southeast Asia perceived the regional environment."[3] The struggle for independence due to colonialism—to varying degrees—contributed to a worldview that saw the international system as deeply predatory. Besides political transformation, many post-colonial nations also recognized the need to achieve economic and political autonomy and to strive for internal economic growth through industrialization.[4] This realization also manifested in the need to shape a distinct identity-finding pathway, at the national and even regional levels, and epitomized the emergence of the *"we-ness"* aspect in the region. This ideal is not limited to political transformation but also reflects a collective cultural and social identity that emphasizes a sense of community cohesion that aims for regional solidarity, like the Association of the Southeast Asian Nations (ASEAN) that was formed in 1967.

The ASEAN was formed to balance the power rivalry between the West and the East, or between the ideologies of liberalism and communism. In line with its reasons of formation to resist dominant powers, when it comes to human rights, ASEAN also balances between the western human rights narrative as well as the Asian Values (AVs). In light of this, this paper aims to look at the meaning of Asian Values within the SEA context and see how it impacts the human rights 'culture' and normative understanding. First, it is just as crucial to offer an overview that investigates the characteristics of SEA in terms of its identity formation and historical becoming, there is an eminent gap in understanding the underlying values, traditions, and principles that influence the intersections between the human rights norms and practice in respect of the Southeast Asian context in BHR discourse.

In the field of International Relations to Political Sciences disciplines, there is a rich literature that studies ASEAN identity formation that can offer some fundamental references. Within the context of the BHR discourse, this paper aims to contribute to a region-focused discussion and employs a historical analysis approach, to understanding the BHR development in the SEA region, with special attention to revisiting a key ideology called the *Asian Values*, which was at its height at the 1990s across Asia but, still offers and resonates relatively strong explanations of the present 'embodiment' of human rights in the SEA region. In the interest of the study, this will focus mainly on understanding Asian Values within Southeast Asia and may not have further elaborate study on its impact on East and wider Asia. It will also focus on ASEAN with the ten SEA member states, as the organizational body that represents Southeast Asia. We will begin with the discussion on what are Asian Values, followed by the geopolitical tensions between the universality of human rights, and its relevance and reflections to the BHR development in Southeast Asia.

---

[3] Narine (2002), p. 10.

[4] Malcolm (1999), p. 57.

1.1 What Are Asian Values?

When understanding the Asian Values (AV) in the SEA context, it is firstly important to highlight that it is intricately connected with the historical development of the region's identity formation. As Acharya explained, perceived from a constructivist lens, "Identity is socially constructed, combining instrumental logic with habit-forming socialization, norms, and institutions. Moreover, such identity building is not entirely divorced from cultural and historical ties but is reinforced by it."[5] The AV shapes the SEA/ASEAN regional identity by bridging and influencing its 'legal-rational' normative set and the 'sociocultural' normative set. Acharya further argued that the *commonality* of these values can impact state behaviors and create 'collective interests and identities.'[6] Identity building and establishing an internationally recognized society (for this matter the creation of ASEAN and ASEAN Way) were significant endeavors during the post-colonial period.[7] This was also an important point especially at the height of the Cold War when security and conflict issues were a great concern for the newly independent SEA states.

To define and understand AV's claims, it is primarily important to highlight that AV is also not limited to being solely a political ideology, the whole idea behind the AV co-exists with its intricate social, cultural, economic, and even religious justifications as an Asian-wide doctrine. Many scholars, political thinkers, and government elites have utilized AV for different purposes. Major Asian government leaders have long sought a *common* identity that encompasses the uniqueness of Asian characteristics distinct from the Western norms and values. In Mahbuhani's work on *Can Asians Think*[8] he protrudes an important inquiry into whether despite Asia's wide diversity, if it could constitute a 'distinct intellectual framework' that can organizationally guide the Asian communities on its own separate from that of the Western construct. Here, Mahbuhani advocated for the Asian traditions and values especially in the light of the Asian Financial Crisis of 1997.[9]

AV emerged as early as the 1970s but gained much more prominence in the 1980s and early 1990s. As a crucial ideology it aimed to explain the economic and commercial development in Southeast Asia's swift move towards industrial expansion.[10] Baba (2016)[11] categorized that there are two main dimensions for AV; first, is psychological which entails the identity and cultural elements. This prescribes the "self" values and the "we-ness" particularization of the region and its sense of belongingness. While the second-dimension deals with pragmatic aspect, this links

[5] Acharya (2017), p. 26.

[6] Acharya (2001), pp. 27–30.

[7] Haacke (2002), p. 4.

[8] Mahbubani (1998), pp. 123–127.

[9] Sheng (2018), *The Asian Values Debate Returns,* https://www.project-syndicate.org/onpoint/the-asian-values-debate-returns-by-andrew-sheng-2018-03 Accessed 22 January 2025.

[10] Khoo (1999), pp. 177–190.

[11] Baba (2016), p. 101.

to Southeast Asia's strategy to open to transregional economic and trade opportunities as well as facilitating regional allegiances. As associated in the ASEAN Way, the nexus between these two dimensions formulated the distinctive feature of the ASEAN Way's principles, as often described as flexible, inclusive through consensus-building, and non-confrontational through bargaining approach.

Southeast Asia's identity formation embraces a 'pan-Asian unity' that resists the notions of geopolitical power domination, such as the so-called Asian giants Japan and China, or even "American-led globalization and a developing unilateral world system."[12] AV advocates propose shaping its own identity by a combination of socio-economic, intellectual and psychological foundation. Given this dynamic, AV is seen here as a factor that has a potential framework to construct the norms and principles that underpins regional identity. This regional identity is intended to be a collective and shared awareness that can help in constructing regional development, and identity shaping components to foster the Southeast Asian region.[13]

As an identity-shaping element, the AV also sparked controversial debates in the international arena over its purpose and motivations. The debate and criticisms were rhetoric topics by several diplomatic speeches, and high-level meetings with interventions from both advocates and non-advocates of the AV.[14] Some of the leading advocates of the AV were leaders and elites from the SEA communities notably Indonesian Foreign Minister, Ali Alatas, Malaysian prime minister Mahathir Mohamad, and Singaporean prime minister Lee Kuan Yew - just to name a few, were some of the well-known Southeast Asian proponents who rallied for the AV approach in the international setting.[15] As expounded, the Asian nations' assertion of cultural and identity particularization stems from the economic from the Western corporation, as highlighted ASEAN aimed to pursue economic development independently and 'done in their own way.'[16]

Hoon's (2004)[17] identified four key claims of the AV and what sparked the major points of debate in the literature:

(1) human rights are not universal, and neither can they be globalized. They emerge differently according to the context of particular social, economic, cultural, and political conditions;
(2) Asian societies are not centered on the individual but on the family. The nation is like a big family. It supposedly comes naturally for Asians to let the combined interests of the family and the nation go before the interests of each individual;
(3) Asian societies rank social and economic rights over individual political rights and;
(4) Finally, the right of a nation to self-determination includes a government's domestic jurisdiction over human rights. This implies that other nations should not interfere with the internal affairs of a state, including its human rights policy.

[12] Saaler and Szpilman (2011), pp. 1–41.

[13] Baba (2016), p. 105.

[14] Ong (2017), pp. 535–560.

[15] Malcolm (1999), p. 59.

[16] Engle (1999), pp. 314–315.

[17] Hoon (2004), pp. 155–156.

For Lee Kuan Yew and Mahathir Mohamad, they outspokenly argued the traditional and communal aspirations of the AVs, that they seek to create an orderly and harmonious society that respects authorities and at the same time establishes accountability structures for public officials. Additionally, economic development is of the forefront goal of the AV, as resilience, pragmatism, openness to new ideas, and possessing innovative and productive societies. The "Lee hypothesis" also emphasizes the utilization of authoritarian control to achieve these aspirations. Some of the non-advocates of the AV have questioned these claims and aspirations, especially in terms of the 'reach' of which Asian cultures are encompassed. For instance, when most of the advocates argued on using the Confucianism values in AV, as attributed to the shared religious dogma of the many East Asian economic miracles, this is identified as limiting since such belief does not encompass Asian per se, came as problematic to many societies that follow other beliefs such as Muslim, Buddhist, and Christian religious affiliated societies.[18] Amartya Sen (1997) as one of the prominent non-advocates, expressed his concern over the oversimplification of the vast and diversity and heterogeneity of the Asian population, that to be pragmatically clustered under what constitutes AV ideals is doing disservice to the distinct and rich Asian culture.[19]

1.2 *The Asian Values vs. Human Rights Debate*

One of the most pressing debates that the AV advocates oppose is the conceptualization of a universal claim of Human Rights (HR). The debates on *AV vs HR* were magnified upon the 1993 Vienna Conference on Human Rights. For ASEAN states, they raised cautious concerns regarding the establishing of a 'human rights regime.' In their concerns they emphasized that although the region acknowledges and commits to the outlined set of human rights and fundamental freedoms, these stipulations will be addressed in a balanced and modest manner, with specific considerations to ASEAN's distinct cultural, social, economic, and political contexts. Additionally, ASEAN stressed that the promotion and protection of human rights should be free from being politicized by the international community.[20]

The AV vs HR debate can come from many points of perspective, but the predominant arguments are rooted in the tensions, as summarized by Hernandez (1995): (1) universalism vs cultural relativism; (2) the emphasis on duties & obligations over rights-based justifications particularly in relation to the collective rights vs. individual rights debates and; (3) argument prioritizing economic development over civil and political rights.[21] In addition, there is also a looming issue that human

[18] Baba (2016), p. 98.

[19] Sen (1997), pp. 5–32.

[20] Gomez and Ramcharan (2021).

[21] Hernandez (1995), p. 34.

rights is portrayed as a Western concept cloaked to intervene and pressure the international community to adhere to international human rights law and enforcement prescribed by the Western powers.

Many of the Asian governments have criticized how the Western governments and media have attacked human rights violations solely on the grounds of civil and political rights. In the early 1990s this even created serious tensions that would have constrained plans for further cooperation.[22] ASEAN's engagement with human rights appeared to be driven primarily by an emphasis on economic, social, and cultural rights, rather than civil and political rights. This perspective became central to the 'Asian values' debate, where several ASEAN governments favored a culturally relative approach to rights over the concept of universal human rights.[23] In Asian societies, the idea of community-building is very much ingrained in the cultural notion of a harmonious society working and coming together or the so-called "communitarianism."

The creation of *universal human rights* has been viewed by the AV advocates, as rather, individualistic, and not adhering to the ingredient in achieving Asia's economic development. For AV, an archetype societal structure is necessary in achieving societal peace and harmony. This consists of a cohesive community, mutual support and working together, high regard for obedience to social rules, and the presence of a well-respected authority figure who maintains order and asserts leadership. For AV, these elements could foster a more stable society where collective/communitarianism welfare is prioritized over the self-interest of individuals. Advocates of the Asian values position argue that some limitations of human rights are necessary for stability in relatively poor societies striving for economic development, which is itself a precondition for a wide range of political goods.[24]

1.3 Human Rights and Geopolitical Developments

Despite being a strong advocate of the AV that later inspired the ASEAN Way, ASEAN member states displayed a contrasting posture during the Vienna World Conference on Human Rights in 1993. Such conference was a historical moment to strengthen the implementation of human rights globally, through the adoption of the Vienna Declaration and program of actions. Prior to the conference, each regions had regional meetings at Tunis, San Josè, and Bangkok to discuss concerns and contributions within each respective region. The ASEAN member states participated in the regional meeting in Bangkok. In order to understand ASEAN member states' response on human rights, it is crucial to see the geopolitical developments, including the Bangkok Declaration, the Vienna Declaration and development of the ASEAN Free Trade Agreement (AFTA) initiative.

---

[22] See EU-ASEAN Stalemate phase in the 1990s.

[23] Kelsall (2020), p. 120.

[24] Zakaria and Yew (1994), pp. 109–127.

The regional discussion in Bangkok mainly discussed and highlighted the tensions between Asian Values (AV) and the universality of human rights. The Bangkok Declaration emphasized the commitment of Asian governments (including ASEAN member states) toward the United Nations Charter, the International Bill of Rights, and the Universal Declaration of Human Rights, however, it should be based within the principles of national sovereignty and territorial integrity. During the regional meeting, several ASEAN member states and Asian countries questioned the universality of human rights and preferred the cultural relativism perspective of human rights, "It is noteworthy that they did not explicitly reject the validity of human rights but rather contested their universal application."[25] Based on the regional discussion, human rights was perceived as 'Western values' associated with the rule of law, reflects a characteristic of a post-colonial nature of international law.[26]

However, the changes in global economic order and geopolitics had a key impact with the way ASEAN member states shifted strategic response towards Human Rights as exhibited in their responses in international events such as the Bangkok Declaration (1993) and afterward the Vienna World Conference (1993). In the same year, to be more economically resilient, ASEAN was also establishing the first phase of ASEAN Economic Integration through the AFTA (ASEAN Free Trade Agreement) which began to force since 1993–2002.[27] Four new ASEAN Member States, which were Vietnam, Laos, Myanmar, and Cambodia also joined the AFTA. Such economic integration was aimed to prepare ASEAN Member States for global trade liberalization, attract foreign direct investment by multinational corporations, and to position ASEAN's relevance as a major trade and economic bloc. In other words, the AFTA was mainly to attract foreign investment, especially during the 1990s when there was a boom in 'Invest China'. China became the largest recipient of foreign direct investment (FDI) in the developing world since 1993, which reached to US$62 billion by 1997.[28] Such development in China was a concern for the ASEAN member states, leading to the AFTA's establishment.

Upon the rise of China's economic power, ASEAN had to position itself against economic competition in Asia and protect its legitimacy and regional capacity, and one strategy to adapt this is by adhering to internationally acclaimed standards such as Human Rights. For instance, although ASEAN member states have previously debated on the notion of Asian Values during the regional meeting in Bangkok, they neverthless shifted their position by endorsing the universality of human rights during the World Conference on Human Rights in Vienna, despite earlier reservations.[29]

[25] Kinzelbach (2022), p. 186.

[26] Desierto DA (2009) Universalizing Core Human Rights in the 'New' Asean: A Reassessment of Culture and Development Justifications Against the Global Rejection of Impunity.

[27] Ishikawa (2021).

[28] Ma (2000).

[29] Kelsall (2020).

While ASEAN was in the early stages of establishing its human rights mechanism and pursuing economic integration, the region suddenly experienced a major disruption with the onset of the Asian Financial Crisis in 1997–1998. At the height of the Asian Financial Crisis, a lot of reforms emerged from economic and financial to social policies and regulations. The Asian Financial Crisis is a "critical juncture" or a key event that created a major revamping and institutional reconstruction in the business environment. The Asian Financial Crisis impacted the ASEAN member states which forced them to take different measures to face the crisis. For example, some countries had to rely on the International Monetary Fund's support, and some could control their capital. Such measures resulted in ASEAN's disunity and lack of organizational resources and structures.[30]

In light of the Asian Financial Crisis, ASEAN Way, which has influences from the AV ideology, was put into question as an inadequate approach to solving the financial crisis of the region. Thus, ASEAN member states such as Thailand's position, backed by the Philippines, proposed a more "flexible engagement" however, such proposed changes were opposed by other member states. Instead, they agreed to allow 'enhanced interactions' which allowed ASEAN member states to comment on each others' domestic situations if it affected the region.[31] Thus, the ASEAN Way remained in force even after the Asian Financial Crisis, given the principles of non-intervention and non-interference rule in ASEAN member states' domestic affairs.

1.4 Human Rights and Post-Asian Financial Crisis

The Asian Financial Crisis highlighted its catastrophic impact on various social and political concerns. The public dissatisfaction over government regimes combined with poverty, inequality, unemployment crisis, and decreasing quality of life led to a demand to not only fix the ailing economy but also a demand for political transformation. For instance, the economic downturn weakened the Suharto regime when many oppositions challenged and felt distrust towards the long-withstanding authoritarian Suharto governance. The Indonesian community accused the Suharto government of cronyism, graft and corruption, and lack of willingness to deal with the currency crisis effectively.[32]

The Asian Financial Crisis clearly exposed the vulnerability and the failing grasp of authoritarian rhetorics, which eventually contributed to the dwindling down of the AV sentiment, "it was this loss of legitimacy of authoritarian regimes that brought discredit to the Asian Values discourse on human rights"[33] The Asian Financial Crisis rocked the political fundamentals of the AV, which also led to back-

---

[30] Narine (2002).

[31] Ibid.

[32] Eklöf (1999), p. 102; see also Kraft (2001), p. 37.

[33] Kraft (2001), p. 38.

pedaling of some of its strong advocates. The Asian Financial Crisis served as a catalyst to observable shift of how ASEAN approach human rights, "following the Asian financial crisis in 1997 there has been modest progress in terms of the proliferation of discourse on human rights and democracy throughout the region."[34] However, as Kraft shared from an interview conducted with officials from Indonesia and Vietnam, ASEAN still viewed importance of the AV as a 'unifying concept for the multi-ethnic societies of Southeast Asia'.[35]

Out of public's outcry and frustration, the Asian Financial Crisis impact also led to the activation of civil society groups, human rights and social advocates, calling for more transparency and accountability from the governments against corruption. In this argument, supported by the civil societies, there were strong initiatives for developing human rights mechanism throughout Southeast Asia and in ASEAN. For an instance, in Thailand, the Asian Financial Crisis also fast tracked the already progressing movement towards political reform, as included in this movement was the development of the "people's constitution" with inclusion of human rights and a mandated national commission on human rights. This political reform movement is also felt in Malaysia, wherein the public strongly pushed for the establishment of their own human rights commission.[36]

By 2002, the ASEAN member states were able to start recovering from the Asian Financial Crisis. By then the ASEAN Free Trade Area (AFTA) fulfilled its goal – which was to reduce tariffs to 0–5%.[37] Related to the AV's notion of communitarianism, the establishment of the "ASEAN Community" was a significant achievement followed by the ASEAN Concord II (Bali Concord II) in 2003. In this meeting, ASEAN member states formally agreed to build what they call the "ASEAN Community" consisting of three pillars, namely: political and security cooperation, economic cooperation, and socio-cultural cooperation. The ASEAN Community document was the first important development post the Asian Financial Crisis. In the ASEAN Community it emphasized its desire to be 'people-oriented and people-centered,' yet, reference to human rights was not used nor mentioned.[38] ASEAN has instead referred to its commitment to be as *'caring societies'* especially as an integral part of the socio-cultural goals of ASEAN.[39]

By 2004, ASEAN signed the Vientiane Action Programme (VAP) which explicitly used the term 'human rights.' The VAP highlighted the promotion of human rights, placing them under the political and security pillar as opposed to the socio-cultural pillar that they were previously associated with. There are two reasons why a shift towards human rights referencing suddenly became more apparent, firstly, due to Western pressure, which was the mainstream and simplistic understanding.

[34] Mohammad (2002), p. 230.

[35] Kraft (2001), p. 39.

[36] Mohammad (2002), p. 239.

[37] Ishikawa (2021).

[38] Davies (2013).

[39] Ibid.

Secondly, alternative findings by Katsumata stated that ASEAN voluntarily embraced human rights as they wanted to strengthen their legitimacy.[40]

This also reflects, in a way, the way AV is manifested to the hesitation to fully embrace human rights in its identity formation and values-based principles with the ASEAN core characteristics. The VAP covered the ASEAN's program from 2004 until 2010, which eventually led to the formulation of the ASEAN Community, the establishment of the ASEAN Charter in 2007 and also the formation of ASEAN's human rights system. The ASEAN Community consisted of 5 programs of the APSC (ASEAN Political Security Cooperation), 12 programs of the AEC (ASEAN Economic Cooperation), and 4 programs of the ASCC (ASEAN Socio-Cultural Cooperation). Just by looking at the number of programs per pillar, one can see that the AEC was of high priority. Agro-based products, automobiles, electronics, fisheries, rubber-based products, textiles and clothing, wood-based products, air travel, e-ASEAN (ICT), healthcare, and tourism were the sectors that were identified as priorities and were expected to be fully integrated by 2010.[41]

The ASEAN Charter that was ratified in 2008 shows the commitment of the ASEAN Member States to institutionalizing human rights within the region. The first ASEAN human rights body was established in 2007, which was the ASEAN Committee on Migrant Workers. Secondly, in 2009, the ASEAN Intergovernmental Commission on Human Rights (AICHR) was established. Last but not least, the ASEAN Commission on the Promotion and Protection of the Rights of Women and Children (ACWC) was also established in 2010. Although regional human rights bodies were formed, it 'weakened' the ASEAN Charter by reverting ASEAN's commitment to human rights to a more facilitative and consultative role.[42] Given the limitations as imposed by the 'ASEAN way' which derives from the principles of non-interference, the mandate and power of the ASEAN Human Rights Bodies also suffers from lack of strong capacities. For an instance, there are no accountability measures or treaty body monitoring system.

Moreover, the ASEAN Intergovernmental Commission on Human Rights (AICHR), which is the Association of the Southeast Asian Nations (ASEAN) human rights body, is frequently called out for its lack of a robust mechanism for human rights protection and merely being a 'promotional' institution.[43] The AICHR's lack of capacity is often compared to the human rights system of other regional organizations that exist in Africa, Europe and Latin America. This also led grassroots-level CSOs and human rights groups and advocates to urgently call for the need for a Southeast Asia Human Rights body with a much more robust enforcement measure.

The ASEAN Human Rights Bodies are mainly to mainstream and ensure the promotion of human rights within the region, without any enforcement mechanisms. As highlighted below (Table 1):

---

[40] Katsumata (2009).

[41] Ishikawa (2021).

[42] Kelsall (2020).

[43] Wahyuningrum (2021), p. 14.

Table 1 ASEAN Human Rights Bodies

	Members of Commission/ Committee	Mandate	Report to
ACMW	Officials selected by AMS, consists of a mixture of civil society advocates, academics, and government officials from within ASEAN.	–No mandate to monitor AMS' adherence to international human rights conventions. –No established complaints mechanisms –Must report to a different inter-Ministerial body within ASEAN based on the Terms of Reference developed by its commission/committee	The ASEAN Senior Labour Officials Meeting under the ASEAN Socio-Cultural Community Blueprint. But also part of the Political-Security Community blueprint, example: the legally binding instrument for the promotion and protection of the rights of migrant workers.
ACWC			The ASEAN Social Welfare and Development Ministers under the ASEAN Socio-Cultural Community. Its mandate is reduced because doesn't follow under the ASEAN Political-Security agenda
AICHR			The ASEAN Foreign Ministers Meeting (AMM) because it is under the ASEAN Political-Security Community Blueprint

Reference: see (Kelsall 2020)

Over the years, ASEAN has adhered to the stringent principles of non-interference, informality, and high regard for national sovereignty. These principles constitute the "ASEAN Way" which exemplifies the approach ASEAN takes to manage its relations and cooperation.[44] The stringent non-interference principle has played a role in hindering the mandate of the AICHR and the relatively 'hands-off' approach to addressing Human Rights, which is regarded as a matter of state-level concern. The ASEAN principles' approaches are oftentimes associated with and fueled by the fundamental ideologies of the *Asian Values*. This approach warrants thorough exploration to perceive AV's lingering impact on how human rights are valued in the region and the interplay it has with the emerging trends in BHR narratives.

[44] Acharya (2001), p. 6.

2 Reflecting on Asian Values in the ASEAN BHR Discourse: Are There Correlations?

To continue the discussion, this part aim to seek the correlations of the persisting or rather lingering impact of the AV principles that may play an integral role in understanding what shapes the human rights culture in the region. In Southeast Asia, mainstreaming the BHR agenda faces challenges in the region, not only because of the limitation of the human rights institutionalization and mechanism, for instance the limitation of the AICHR, but also because of the lack of proper understanding towards BHR goals. In this section, it will analyze how AV claims, which also fostered the ASEAN Way principles broadly speaking, create an underlying and potential influences on the development of human rights and BHR discourse. To dissect the discussion, it will reflect on the four claims of the AV to the current human rights development and BHR-related tools that may serve assumptions in bridging correlations. As there is no unified BHR approach in ASEAN, several regional governance tools in ASEAN could be used to address BHR issues, which includes the 2002 ASEAN Agreement on Transboundary Haze Pollution (AATHP), the 2017 ASEAN Guideline for CSR on Labour, and the 2023 ASEAN Taxonomy on Sustainable Finance. It will reflect on the design of these tools as influenced by AV claims too (Table 2).

This table analyzes the different arguments of Asian Values and reflects its shared commonality and influences with the ASEAN Way. This also shows the deliberate manifestation of the actual actions and policies taken by ASEAN. In this

Table 2 Reflection on Asian Values, ASEAN Way, and ASEAN Action

Asian Values	ASEAN Way	ASEAN Action
On Human Rights as non-universal	Non-reference of the 'Human Rights' terminology as ASEAN's core values and fundamental principles	Importance of cultural relativism in creating frameworks (i.e., CSR)
On Communitarianism (not centered on individual but on family, communities)	Application in creation the ASEAN 3 Community Pillars (Political-Security, Economic, Socio-Cultural)	Perceived shared cultural principles in CSR models, Transboundary Haze Act given its a shared communitarian problem
On promoting economic growth and resilience	The development of AFTA and AEC among flagship work	Leverage economic objectives (market, investment and financial) Added-value of developing CSR, Sustainability goals
On self-determination	Strict adherence to the principles of non-interference and non-intervention	Adherence to soft laws and policies because of its non-mandatory nature No enforcement, more on voluntary/promotional role

Source: AV claims based on Hoon (2004), ASEAN Website https://asean.org/what-we-do/, and reflection based on own work of the authors

reflection table, it determines how soft law approach and informality, which does not imply interference to the ASEAN intergovernmental system, are still the favorable way to conduct and decide upon human rights initiatives. For an instance, the recognition of CSR models as a voluntary mechanism is much more applicable than having hard law and mandated approaches that entails strict legal requirements in the region. Moreover, as reflected on the importance of collectivism in AV, ASEAN incorporated the sense of community and working together in harmony as constituted in the three community pillars.

First, AV has argued over the non-universality of human rights and the need to consider the distinct social, economic, and cultural characteristics and conditions in relation to human rights agenda-setting. In this aspect, cultural relativism and adaptability of human rights norms to the local environment becomes a key element in embodying its compliance and commitment. Take for an instance the proliferation of the Corporate Social Responsibility (CSR) in ASEAN. One of the conflating issues with less 'familiarity' with BHR could be closely associated with the perceived overlap with CSR. In ASEAN, CSR is especially promoted as part of its sustainability agenda and promotion. ASEAN has pledged commitment to the UN SDGs, integrating global sustainable development principles into their regional framework. The ASEAN Charter of 2015 explicitly underscores the bloc's dedication to achieving "sustainable development for the benefit of the present and future generations," placing the well-being, livelihood, and welfare of its people at the forefront of its community-building efforts.[45] CSR then is a much more well-known strategy in the region embraced by both the private sector and the states.

Over the years, CSR evolved to be a *culturally idiosyncratic* feature within the Asian business models. The coherency and consideration of cultural, social, and traditional nuances in a Southeast Asian business operation has been perceived as an important element to create "transformative" knowledge to gaps between intricate relationships between responsibilities and expected duties of business corporations with the communities. Bindu Sharma further stressed out how the Asian tradition has much to guide the CSR discourse in the own region.[46] At the current stage, it is important to acknowledge that there is more familiarity towards CSR than BHR in the ASEAN region. For instance, ASEAN formally created the ASEAN Guidelines for Corporate Social Responsibility (CSR) on Labour in 2017. In this Guideline they emphasize the purpose of a CSR model that is supposed to be business-friendly and non-imposing, "Continuously and proactively encourage enterprises/establishments to incorporate CSR initiatives, human rights and decent work in their business practices"(ASEAN Guidelines, 2017). Among other international and regional instruments, the ASEAN CSR Guideline made reference to the UN Guiding Principles on Business and Human Rights. In 2011, the UNGP on BHR were adopted around the same time, the ASEAN CSR Network was created. These

[45] PM N (2020) ASEAN's Way to Sustainable Development. In: Disruptive Asia. https://disruptiveasia.asiasociety.org/aseans-way-to-sustainable-development. Accessed 27 January 2025.

[46] Sharma (2013), pp. 19–21.

developments signal, both from a global and regional level, growing debates on the roles of corporations in promoting human rights may it be under the guise of a CSR or BHR narratives. In addition to this, there also contribution from key Southeast Asian leaders in the BHR development, particularly Indonesia's role as the chair of the 61st session of the Commission on Human Rights (2005) which supported the appointment of a special representative of the secretary general (SRSG) on the issue of transnational corporations and human rights.

Moreover, there is no unitary position towards an ASEAN-wide level implementation or declared order to call for BHR initiatives. All the conducted studies are often CSR-focused, as observed from the AICHR's work and agenda, which in one way or another connects with the BHR goals in the region. Even in the AEC (ASEAN Economic Community) Blueprint, there are no references to the role of the Human Rights bodies but only highlight the role of CSR respectively, "The new AEC Blueprint of a commitment to 'working closely with stakeholders towards promoting corporate social responsibility activities' as part of an ongoing process of strengthening the contribution of non-state actors to its integration efforts".[47] The CSR narratives gained attraction when media attention focused on publicizing the abuses done by corporations toward human rights. Another reason is the growing notion of CSR is due to the government's lack of the capacity, policy in place and resources to address business-related human rights violations more effectively which were hard pressed by the complaints by firms and consumers alike and led the MNCs and businesses to take initiative to build CSR-related instruments within their core business models (CSR Baseline Study).

The second refelection, dives into the *communitarianism* or family apparatus referenced in AV argument in connection with CSR. This can be seen in Herrera's work, one of the common thematic that she found that geography, geology, natural resources, history, culture can shape CSR meaningfully. Cultural rootedness highlighted important traditions that encompasses *communitarianism*. For instance, in the Mekong countries, "the concept of collectivism and face play a fundamental role in the development of CSR in the Mekong area." While in Islamic roots, "the concept of "*gotong royong*" (joint/shared responsibility) results in forming impromptu groups to perform tasks for the maintenance and welfare of the village community; and the value of "*tolong menolong*" (mutual help) both in urban and rural areas is embedded in the culture of both countries." This is also present in a Civil Society-Led Philippines, wherein "Culture and tradition influenced the development of CSR in the Philippines. The concept of '*bayanihan*' is the spirit of collectivism that is embedded in the culture of the country. The values of '*pakikipagkapwa*' (a shared sense of humanity), '*pagtutulungan*' (mutual self-help), and '*kawanggawa*' (charity) are also part of Filipino culture" plays a vital role in shaping CSR and

[47] Kelsall (2020).

involvement of civil societies, and businesses in achieving ethical and responsible business practices.[48]

In connection towards building cooperation through collective response, the 2002 ASEAN Agreement on Transboundary Haze Pollution (AATHP) is an agreement among all the AMS to facilitate cooperation and coordination in managing the impact of land and/or forest fires in particular haze pollution arising from such fires (usually caused by corporations). The issue on haze is seen as a transboundary environmental problem shared among the neighboring ASEAN countries. As perceived, a transboundary environmental problem requires communitarian cooperation when inflicted environmental space and natural resources are shared, the agreement needs to promote mutual understanding and exchange knowledge on how to better protect the environment against transboundary haze pollution, this approach creates opportunities for shared and innovative solutions that can fight the common issue.[49] The AATHP may not have a monitoring or enforcement system, but the coordination and collective responsibility aspect that is shared among AMS is crucial in its development. For instance, the creation of the ASEAN Coordinating Centre for Transboundary Haze Pollution Control is placed as a priority to mobilize and mitigate the haze and provide emergency responses if the haze happens.[50]

The third reflection is in connection to AV's argument for social and economic rights over individual and political rights. As depicted in the Human Rights vs AV debate, many of the AV proponents have pushed for economic rights, which focuses on aspects of economic growth and development, as a key priority to fulfill country's stability. This connection could be a point of reflection to potentially leverage BHR. Promoting BHR introduces an added-value aspect that could lead to creating pragmatic strategies for creating responsible yet efficient business model and environment. A model or approach wherein the point for both the economic and human rights agenda can converge. In Blanton and Blanton's study on *What Attracts Foreign Investors?* They argued that good human rights record may encourage FDIs. States with high standards and better governance can serve as advantageous for businesses who are looking to invest in countries with predictability, stable political environment, and reliable and ethical regulatory capacity.[51] Leveraging BHR in this case therefore can be argued as not merely moral and normative imperative but could serve as a pragmatic strategy, which as mentioned aligns with the AV dimension, offering significant cause of economic advantage and sustainable development for ASEAN countries.

With the growing prominence of BHR discourse, ASEAN is gradually realizing the need to align the changing demands of businesses with a more coherent and cohesive regulatory frameworks. For instance, the recent creation of the ASEAN

---

[48] Herrera M, *Corporate Social Responsibility in South East Asia: An Eight Country Analysis*, 16 April 2015, pp. 11–15.

[49] Sunchindah (2015), p. 6.

[50] Mohan (2017).

[51] Blanton and Blanton (2007), p. 153.

Taxanomy for Sustainable Finance V3 (2023) served as an overarching guide and foundational framework to support a just transition while fostering sustainable finance adoption by ASEAN member states. The Taxonomy is tailored to cater to the different ASEAN economies, financial systems, and transition pathways. It provides alignment on underlying principles and serves to inform AMS policy makers and financial sector as well as real economy stakeholders. It contains Essential Criteria, including the 'Social Aspects' and the "Do No Significant Harm" (DNSH) and "Remedial Measures to Transition" (RMT) criteria. Its key priorities include: respect human rights, prevention of forced and child labour, and impact on people living close to investments.[52]The Taxonomy signifies ASEAN's initiative to see the economic aspect and bridge it to the social aspect, as emphasizing the need to respect human rights for an instance.

The fourth connection to AV is with the right of a nation to self-determination which includes a government's jurisdiction over human rights. The development of NAPs on BHR could be associated to this since it is state level, and ASEAN did not have a unified statement about NAPs on BHR. Upon the endorsement of the UNGP on BHR in 2011, notable actions have taken place by various organizations and institutions across the globe. Compared to its other regional counterparts, in Southeast Asia, there is a lack of awareness, understanding, and promulgation of the BHR narrative; UN Guiding Principles on Business and Human Rights (UNGP on BHR) which is reflected in the adoption of National Action Plans (NAPs) and other BHR tools and measures in the region. Even though the UNGPs are instrumental in shaping government policies and corporate behaviors and practices to protect human rights, their implementation encounters many challenges. Many SEA states have different levels of commitment and understanding when it comes to standardizing human rights protection and enforcement. So far, only Thailand, Vietnam, and Indonesia have the NAP on BHR.

On 29 October 2019, after several rounds of consultation, Thailand became the first SEA country and the first in Asia, to adopt a National Action Plan (NAP) on Business and Human Rights (BHR). The adoption of the NAP was initiated by grassroot human rights advocates with the government's groundwork and support from the UNDP's BHR+Asia project. With the creation, it has provided HRDD trainings, different levels of consultations and meetings, (UNDP 2022). The Action Plan aimed to strategies and measures for improving corporate responsibility, enhancing legal and policy frameworks, and strengthening protection mechanisms for affected communities and individuals. However, scholars suggest that the NAP BHR fails to incorporate key elements specific to the Southeast Asian context, such as the informal economy and post conflict situations.[53] Despite critics, Thailand further adopted its second version of NAP on 8 September 2023.

On 14 July 2023, Vietnam published its first "National Action Plan on Solutions to Improve Policy and Legal Framework to Advance Responsible Business Practice

[52] ASEAN Taxonomy 2023.

[53] White (2021), p. 32.

in Viet Nam". The NAP development was led by the Ministry of Justice and issued by the Prime Minister for the period of 2023 - 2027. The NAP in Vietnam do not use the term 'human rights', but rather use the term 'Responsible Business Practice' (RBP). On 26 September 2023, Indonesia released the Presidential Decree Number 60/2023 on the National Strategy on Business and Human Rights for the period of 2023–2025. The strategy provides guidance to Indonesian government agencies and ministries, including regional governments, also to businesses and other stakeholders in Indonesia.

As stated in the above, both countries Vietnam and Indonesia do not use the exact 'NAP on BHR' terms in their policies. In fact, Vietnam do not refer to the term 'human rights' at all, and preferred 'responsible business practice' (RBP). Meanwhile, Indonesia do not use the 'National Action Plan' but rather used the 'National Strategy' on business and human rights. Only Thailand uses the exact NAP on BHR term and are already adopted the second version of the document. Other than these three countries, Malaysia is expected to publish its NAP on BHR in 2024, and the Philippines is also currently developing its version. The rest of ASEAN countries such as Brunei Darussalam, Cambodia, Lao PDR, and Singapore do not clearly indicate their intention to develop NAPBHR.

In conclusion, as discussed above, the integration of Business and Human Rights (BHR) frameworks in Southeast Asia remains a challenge and should consider the existing human rights situation in the context of Southeast Asia which is heavily influenced by the Asian Values (AV), translated into the ASEAN Way. The ASEAN member states could utilize existing regional initiatives, such as the ASEAN Taxonomy for Sustainable Finance, CSR Guidelines on Labour, the Transboundary Haze Act, and work together with the ASEAN Human Rights Bodies, such as AICHR, to further harmonize BHR initiatives in the region. On the other hand, there is opportunity for BHR implementation as Southeast Asia shows a preference towards voluntary, non-interfering mechanisms, in line with the voluntary nature of the UNGPs on BHR.

3 Conclusion

In summary, even though the AV debate receive much clamor in the 1990s, its normative and idealization still influences a degree of characteristics and in shaping the way ASEAN addresses human rights and the limited level of mandate it gives the AICHR. Moving forward, this has a direct impact on addressing specific human rights areas as reflected in the trend of BHR domain in the region. As observed, BHR is slowly becoming a more relevant agenda as it is being referred to, for instance, regional governance tools such as the ASEAN Taxonomy and the ASEAN Guidelines for CSR on Labour, however, it is still widely considered at an exploratory stage.

In the region, there is still a gap on what it can entail to the business environment, thus, BHR requires promotion and raising awareness while at the same time, it is necessary to coherently identify its differences from CSR, which is a much-known approach when it comes to addressing the business, societal and environment-related domains. In SEA, BHR requires more rigorous examination and better understanding. Revisiting the AV, AV's normative assumptions can intersect to the development of BHR understanding in SEA by leveraging cultural, social, and familiar practices that connects and are tangible to the SEA local business environments and governance mechanism (ie., leveraging communitarianism), or for instance, emphasizing the protections of SMEs and Informal Workers which constitutes a large population of the ASEAN economy with a huge labour force.

References

Acharya A (2001) Human security: East versus West. Int J 56:442–460. https://doi.org/10.2307/40203577

Acharya A (2017) 'Theorising the international relations of Asia: necessity or indulgence?' Some reflections. Pac Rev 30:816–828. https://doi.org/10.1080/09512748.2017.1318163

Baba G (2016) Regional commonalities and regional identities: forging a normative understanding of Southeast Asian Identity. J Curr Southeast Asian Aff 35:91–121. https://doi.org/10.1177/186810341603500104

Blanton SL, Blanton RG (2007) What attracts foreign investors? An examination of human rights and foreign direct investment. J Polit 69:143–155. https://doi.org/10.1111/j.1468-2508.2007.00500.x

Davies M (2013) Explaining the Vientiane action programme: ASEAN and the institutionalisation of human rights. Pac Rev 26:385–406. https://doi.org/10.1080/09512748.2013.788066

Eklöf S (1999) Indonesian politics in crisis: the long fall of Suharto, 1996–1998. NIAS Press

Engle K (1999) Culture and human rights: the asian values debate in context millennium issue: shaping the parameters of international law in the new millennium. New York Univ J Int Law Polit 32:291–334

Gomez J, Ramcharan R (2021) Introduction: business and human rights Asia—examining the duty of the state to protect. In: Gomez J, Ramcharan R (eds) Business and human rights in asia. Springer, Singapore, pp 1–18

Haacke J (2002) ASEAN's diplomatic and security culture: origins, development and prospects. Routledge, London

Hernandez CG (1995) ASEAN perspectives on human rights and democracy in international relations. University of the Philippines, Center for Integrative and Development Studies and the U.P. Press

Hoon CY (2004) Revisiting the Asian values argument used by Asian political leaders and its validity

Ishikawa K (2021) The ASEAN economic community and ASEAN economic integration. J Contemp East Asia Stud 10:24–41. https://doi.org/10.1080/24761028.2021.1891702

Katsumata H (2009) ASEAN and human rights: resisting Western pressure or emulating the West? Pac Rev 22:619–637. https://doi.org/10.1080/09512740903329731

Kelsall MS (2020) Horizontal embeddedness, business, and human rights: fostering the corporate responsibility to respect human rights within the ASEAN Community. In: ASEAN law and regional integration. Routledge

Khoo S (1999) Envisioning the Malaysian Nation: ethnic nationalism or corporate capitalism? In: Brehony KJ, Rassool N (eds) Nationalisms old and new. Palgrave Macmillan UK, London, pp 125–153

Kinzelbach K (2022) Asian values versus western values. A false dichotomy. In: Eckel J, Stahl D (eds) Embattled visions: human rights since 1990. Wallstein Verlag, Göttingen, pp 185–206

Kraft HJS (2001) Human rights, ASEAN and constructivism: revisiting the "Asian Values" discourse. Philippine Political Science Journal
Ma J (2000) Introduction and overview. In: Ma J (ed) The Chinese economy in the 1990s. Palgrave Macmillan UK, London, pp 1–14
Mahbubani K (1998) Can Asians think? Natl Interest:27–35
Malcolm ACDK (1999) Human rights and Asian values: developments in Southeast Asia. Lawasia J 1999:57–64
Mohan M (2017) A domestic solution for transboundary harm: Singapore's Haze pollution law. Bus Human Rights J 2:325–333. https://doi.org/10.1017/bhj.2017.10
Narine S (2002) ASEAN in the aftermath: the consequences of the East Asian economic crisis. Glob Gov 8:179–194
Ong DM (2017) The Asian infrastructure investment bank: bringing 'Asian Values' to global economic governance? J Int Econ Law 20:535–560. https://doi.org/10.1093/jiel/jgx025
Saaler S, Szpilman CWA (2011) Pan-Asianism: a documentary history, 1920–present. Rowman & Littlefield Publishers
Sen AK (1997) From income inequality to economic inequality. Southern Econ J 64:384–401. https://doi.org/10.1002/j.2325-8012.1997.tb00063.x
Sharma B (2013) Contextualising CSR in Asia: corporate social responsibility in Asian economies. Lien Centre for Social Innovation: Research
Sunchindah A (2015) Transboundary haze pollution problem in Southeast Asia: reframing ASEAN's response. Working Papers
Wahyuningrum Y (2021) A decade of institutionalizing human rights in ASEAN: progress and challenges. J Human Rights 20:158–175. https://doi.org/10.1080/14754835.2021.1875811
White M (2021) Does the slipper fit? National action plans on business and human rights in South East Asia. In: Gomez J, Ramcharan R (eds) Business and human rights in Asia. Springer, Singapore, pp 21–34
Zakaria F, Yew LK (1994) Culture is destiny: a conversation with Lee Kuan Yew. Foreign Aff 73:109–126. https://doi.org/10.2307/20045923

Framing Private Conduct with the Horizonal Application of Fundamental Rights: Reflections on Brazilian and South African Jurisprudence

Danielle Anne Pamplona

1 Introduction

This paper assesses the different paths traced by the apex courts in Brazil and South Africa in the search for social justice and the concrete implementation of fundamental rights. We have already come a long way in defining what states' human rights obligations are. But the courts will face challenges when attempting to use constitutional and judicial actors to frame corporate conduct. This attempt is a reaction to the growing economic and political power of companies that have historically found themselves outside legal frameworks that impose duties to society and the environment.

Economic activity, frankly in pursuit of profit, often does not respect human beings and nature. Or it only does so if the legal system imposes sanctions for the violations it commits or establishes incentives for them to adopt such conduct. Despite the awareness of the international and local communities, regulating economic activities, especially those which operate transnationally, has been a challenge.

This does not mean that there are no attempts. It is sufficient to remember the initiatives at the UN since the 1970s, which swing like a pendulum between extremes of voluntariness—with self-regulatory models—and regulation—such as the Norms on the Responsibilities of Transnational Corporations and Other Business

D. A. Pamplona (✉)
Pontifical Catholic University of Paranǵ PUCPR, Curitiba, Brazil
e-mail: danielle.pamplona@pucpr.br

D. A. Pamplona et al. (eds.), *Business and Human Rights from the Lens of Women*, Interdisciplinary Studies in Human Rights 13,
https://doi.org/10.1007/978-3-032-04036-7_11

Enterprises with Regard to Human Rights.[1] There are, however, other tools to achieve the same goal and this text sheds light on the role of the Brazilian and South African Constitutional Courts in using one of these tools.

The express insertion in legislative texts of limits on corporations is the recognition, by law, of their power. This recognition, in legal texts, comes in the wake of what the judiciary has been doing at the time of the interpretation of constitutional texts. In the same way that fundamental rights have come to populate constitutional texts as structuring the state and limiting its power, one way to limit corporate power is to recognize that it is obliged to respect the same fundamental rights. This has been proved easier to say than to do.

The paper aims to discuss the use of Constitutional law as a driver to enforce human rights obligations of businesses by evaluating the decisions of the Brazilian and South African Constitutional Courts that seek to impose limits on private parties based on human rights. These courts have decided that fundamental rights, originally inserted in constitutional texts to confront state power, can also be applied in private relations. Recognizing the distinction between the Brazilian and South African regimes, and that only in the latter there is a constitutional clause that unequivocally establishes the possibility of applying human rights to private individuals, the intention of this research is to unveil the reasoning used in both courts, to present a justification for its difference, and to draw parallels between the possible extension of these decisions.

We are aware that the binding nature of private individuals to the Constitution raises a risk that cannot be ignored: that of imposing on people, in the name of constitutional values, behaviour and lifestyles that they themselves reject, to the detriment of their existential freedom.[2] Applying this logic to both natural and juristic persons need some nuances. In this sense, I claim that there must be a difference when facing cases relating to private relations between equals, and cases relating to private relations between individuals in an unbalanced relation of power. Law has also the mission to acknowledge these differences and bring individuals to a balanced relation. This is the promise of the principle of equality: the law recognises that people are not on an equal footing in their relationships, whether for political, economic, age, race or gender reasons, and then promotes their equality.[3] This can occur through legislation, or through interpretation of the law. Legislative examples are many: laws that provide special protection to children, the elderly and consumers are, in fact, recognising the fragility of these people in their relationships. Relationships with corporations also can be many, with customers, suppliers, com-

[1] UN Doc. E/CN.4/Sub.2/2003/12/Rev.2 (2003).

[2] Nino (1989), p. 2.

[3] Bandeira de Mello affirms that "The generic and absolute presumption is that of equality… Once the law is enacted, then the distinctions… formulated by it arise in consideration of the diversity of situations." Mello (1995), p. 47.

munities, employees. It is possible that different legislations regulate these relationships. But given the wide range of cases, it is easier to regulate these relationships through the interpretation of rights. With the strike of a pen, a court can establish the limits of corporate action before the necessary guarantee of the fruition of rights by individuals.

The possibility of extending the protection and respect of fundamental rights to private entities is an encouragement to change the dynamics of the relations of corporations with individuals. The division of state obligations into negative or positive, i.e. into simply avoiding harm or taking active steps to realise a right may pose some challenges. However, the framework of positive/negative duties allows us to identify exactly where we need to evolve. As I attempt to demonstrate in the following sections, if there is horizontal application of fundamental rights, it occurs in terms that guarantee the binding of private entities to negative obligations. We still lack the recognition that private entities also have positive obligations, especially when faced with social, cultural, economic and environmental rights.

The problem faced is basically located in a scenario where the activities of actors with strong economic power are constrained through the recognition of fundamental rights (civil and political, in a first moment, and then, ESC rights). Those who face this challenge are, essentially, countries of the global south. These, lacking in financial resources and development, but abundant in natural resources, find themselves in a situation that has not been easy to solve: the need to respect private law rules concurrently with the need to guarantee citizens' rights. This conundrum's genesis lies in the relationship among state, corporations and individual. My concern guiding this text derives from this relationship. However, in order to demonstrate how the two countries have used a tool for tackling this problem, I ended up observing its use also in relations between private actors that are not companies, in order to understand how the courts have approached the horizontal application of rights. The goal is to evaluate how the horizontal application of fundamental rights has been used by the higher courts in South Africa and Brazil, and to try to assess the extent of this application when the relationship is between individuals and corporations.

2 The Possible Relations Between Fundamental Rights and Private Actors

The formula that fundamental rights arise to limit the State is well known. But this formula proved insufficient to regulate human relations. The application of rights is a courts-task and courts can extend to private entities the application of the limits imposed by fundamental rights on states, what is called by scholarship the horizontal application of fundamental rights. The discussion on the limits of the judicial power to extend to private actors the obligations arising from the granting of fundamental rights are represented by two doctrines. The academic debate in the 50s and

60s in Germany,[4] and the discussion of state action doctrine in the United States,[5] shed light on the possibility of requiring private parties to respect fundamental rights. We aim to evaluate how the South-African and the Brazilian courts face the matter. I will briefly explain each of the theories to the extent that they will be necessary for understanding the arguments made in the analysis of the jurisprudence of the constitutional courts mentioned.

The theory that best captures the separation between fundamental rights and private relations is the so-called 'state action doctrine', forged in the United States. Its main argument is that the incidence of fundamental rights only binds the public power and not private entities, meaning that "the behaviour of private citizens and corporations is not controlled by the Constitution".[6] For those adopting this theory, the constitutional and the private law normative systems cannot be analysed from the point of view of a hierarchy, but should be analysed in the field of competition. Therefore, there can be no prevalence of constitutionalism over private law, at the risk of suppressing private autonomy.[7] Moreover, particularly in the federal model adopted in the United States, it falls to the states and not to the union to legislate on private law. Thus, this theory guarantees total autonomy to the states, preventing federal courts from intervening in private relations.

On the other hand, in Germany, a different doctrine has been developed. When the German Constitutional Court decided on the possibility to apply fundamental rights to private relations, it had to face whether this application would be made directly, extracting from the constitutional text the right to be applied to the concrete case; or if the application would require the mediation of infra-constitutional legislation. The German court concluded that fundamental rights are not suitable to directly resolve a dispute between private entities. Instead, the legislator should guarantee the different positions in private relations through infusing private law with constitutional values. The well-known case Lüth,[8] lays the foundation for a doctrine that has crossed borders to be used in cases where, if fundamental rights cannot bind individuals directly, they can 'legitimise limitations of private autonomy, whether by legislation or by interpretation.'[9] The facts of the case indicate that Erich Lüth, a press director of the city of Hamburg, called for a boycott of the film Immortal Beloved by the filmmaker Veit Harlan, which was to be shown at a film festival in the city. Harlan had been a great filmmaker during the Nazi government and had produced, at the request of Joseph Goebbels, the film Jud Süß, with a clear discriminatory and antisemitic character. Harlan was acquitted in criminal court, and all restrictions on his right to work removed. The lower court therefore ruled that Lüth had no right to promote the boycott, with the clear intention of preventing

[4] Sarmento (2010); Sarlet (2012); Silva (2005).

[5] Peretti (2010), p. 273.

[6] Chemerinsky (1985) pp. 503, 507.

[7] Peretti (2010), p. 273.

[8] Bomhoff (2008). p. 121.

[9] STF, RE 201.819/RJ (11.10.05).

the director's return to the national stage, on the basis of civil legislation that limited the right to free speech when contrary to public policy. His conduct was considered undemocratic and violated Harlan's dignity. Luth appealed to the Constitutional Court on the grounds that his right to freedom of expression was being violated. The Court ruled that the prior judgment violated Luth's freedom of expression, which in turn influenced the way in which the notion of 'contrary to public policy' in the civil law had to be interpreted. The decision inaugurates a new way of applying fundamental rights as it states that 'the constitutional guarantee of individual rights is not simply a guarantee of the classic defensive rights of the citizen against the State. Constitutional rights embody, to quote the Federal Constitutional Court, "at the same time an objective order of values"'.[10] For the Court, "every [private law provision] must be interpreted in the light of fundamental rights".[11] The intake from the decision is that fundamental rights cannot be directly applied in private relations. Law makers and judges must resort to constitutional principles and rights when elaborating or interpreting private rights. The image that reflects this adjustment is a mediation between the legislator, the enforcer of the law and the Constitution.

The main argument for the use of the so called 'drittwirkung' doctrine lies in the fact that the interests of freedom and equality of the individual, which are protected by constitutional provisions, are not only threatened by dangers caused by the state, but also by private individuals with similar power.[12] The emergence of the doctrine, therefore, takes place under the contours of the possibility of applying fundamental rights indirectly, that is, incidentally on infra-constitutional legislation. According to the thesis of the radiating effect, fundamental rights are value-determining foundational norms, which radiate throughout the entire legal system and influence all relationships.[13]

The indirect model of application of fundamental rights in private relations also suggests another possibility, which is the direct application. This will happen if there is no law mediating the application of fundamental rights to private parties. If there is legislation reflecting the legislature's position on the solution of a conflict between the fundamental rights of private individuals, the Court should only apply the statute, or at most, if urged by the right, define whether the legal text infringes the constitutional text. Therefore, once the horizontal application of fundamental rights is contemplated, it can be direct—when a constitutional provision is used directly to settle a case; or indirect—when there is legislation mediating the application of the constitutional provision and the constitutional provision is used to condition the way the legislation applies.

Both South-African and Brazilian apex courts adopt horizontal application. This paper will identify the ways in which they use it and then propose the possible mutual learning from both experiences.

[10] Alexy (2003), pp. 131, 133.

[11] Silva (2004), p. 80.

[12] Borowski (2020), pp. 3, 7.

[13] Borowski (2020), pp. 3, 12.

3 The Brazilian Constitutional Court and the Context of Horizontal Application of Fundamental Rights

3.1 The Brazilian Constitution and Its Application

The Brazilian Constitution has no clause expressly and clearly determining the imposition of fundamental rights on individuals. Article 5, which contains an extensive list of rights, uses a language of granting rights, and not imposing duties. The same article does not exclude rights not expressly provided for by the text and provides for the reception of clauses of human rights treaties with constitutional status.[14] This is the constitutional normative substrate available to the Brazilian Federal Supreme Court to impose respect for fundamental rights.

The relevance of the role of the Courts in establishing, on the one hand, the extent of the limits on power imposed by the Constitution, and on the other, the extent of fundamental rights is part of the development of constitutionalism itself in Latin America. The region saw the end of authoritarian regimes in the late 1980s and early 1990s. Constitutional texts began to present long lists of fundamental rights in a noble position in the text—right at the beginning. In the Brazilian Constitution, more important than the list of rights set out in the 1988 text was the growth in the relevance of constitutional norms, the recognition of their normative force, and the visibility of the judiciary which became the guardian of the civilisational promises of the Constitution, characteristics of what has been called neo-constitutionalism:[15]

> The process of constitutionalisation of legal systems that has taken place in recent times implies that the contemporary jurist should focus on the scope, transformations and meaning of the Constitutions' impacts on contemporary legal and political practice. Neo-constitutionalism thus embraces a series of theoretical reflections that attempt to account for the role of a Constitution that invades the most varied spaces of regulation; spaces that become increasingly refined in the face of a society that evolves in complexity and exponentially multiplies the problems it generates. … [this theory] emphasizes the problems of the indetermination of law and, most importantly, the necessary relations between law, moral and politics…[16]

The author goes further to affirm that the post-war Constitutions are prosperous in fundamental principles and rights that subordinate the legislative will to the content of the justice constitutionally foreseen.

This is a reaction to the old idea that the constitutional text would only serve as a guide for the country's political choices. This then new idea that the content of the Constitution deserved to be applied gained strength. It was something already around Europe in the post-war era, but that could only land in Latin America with

---

[14] Constitutional status is granted in Brazil to a human rights treaty that has been approved by a qualified majority of parliament.

[15] Carbonell (2003).

[16] Rossi (2011), p. 159.

the endings of authoritarian regimes.[17] The constitutional rules came to be understood as containers of meaning that should be reflected in people's lives. And to ensure that this could be achieved, judges—who are competent to make judicial review of laws and administrative acts—were entrusted with the task of inserting the constitutional text into the interpretations and applications of infra-constitutional texts.[18] The content of the constitutional text deserved respect and therefore to be applied in concrete cases and not only to serve as an indication for the best political choices. Ensuring that this was the order of things was left in the hands of the judges, seen even by the population[19] as the ones on whose hands should lay the mandate to define the constitutionality of laws and administrative acts through judicial review. This is the phenomenon of constitutionalisation of the legal order, which has expanded the influence of the Constitution over the entire legal system. There are three dimensions in which this constitutionalisation occurs: the formal dimension, which represents what is expressly written in the Constitution, i.e. the positive constitutional law; the substantial dimension, which stems from the normative, principled dimension of the constitution, whether explicitly (e.g. the social function of property) or implicitly (e.g. the social function of the contract); and the prospective dimension, which is the transformative characteristic of this constitutionalisation, re-signifying legal institutes and institutions, based on the reality of social facts.[20] The consequence of this fresh look at the constitutional text is that norms expressing rights become 'supreme, effectively and directly binding rules which can and must be observed in all operations of interpretation and application of the law'.[21]

It is interesting how Klare's observation about the South African Constitution can also be applied to the Brazilian text, given that '...the drafters cannot have intended dramatically to alter substantive constitutional foundations and assumptions, yet to have left these new rights and duties to be interpreted through the lens of classical legalist methods.'[22]

In this sense, constitutionalisation meant that civil law belongs to the constitutional order; the centrality of the order resides in the constitutional text; and legal institutes—i.e. corporation, property and liability—have been re-signified by a constitutional axiology. This new paradigm valorises principles; adopts more open and flexible methods in legal hermeneutics, with emphasis on balancing; it opens legal argumentation to moral claims; and it recognizes and defends the constitutionalisation of law and the prominent role of the Judiciary in implementing the values of the Constitution.[23] The openness that neo-constitutionalism seems to give to judges has

[17] This ideas will continue to evolve in Latin-America to tackle also coloniality of ideas, including legal ones, breaking away with the claim to epistemic universality enshrined by modernity. Teixeira and Sparemberger (2016), p. 52.

[18] Barroso (2012), pp. 23, 29.

[19] Barroso (2012), p. 27.

[20] Fachin (2015), p. 9.

[21] Sanchis (2007), p. 216.

[22] Klare (1998), pp. 146, 156.

[23] Barroso (2012), p. 80; Barcellos (2005), p. 83.

not gone without criticism: it has been claimed that 'its judicialist bias would be anti-democratic … [and its] preference for principles and weighting over rules and subsumption would be dangerous, especially given the peculiarity of [the Brazilian] legal and political culture'.[24] In fact, Judge Kentridge's comment in the early days of South African jurisprudence would suit Brazil well in the first years of application of neo-constitutionalist ideas:

> While we must always be conscious of the values underlying the Constitution, it is nonetheless our task to interpret a written instrument…… it [is not] easy to avoid the influence of one's personal intellectual and moral preconceptions. But it cannot be too strongly stressed that the Constitution does not mean whatever we might wish it to mean.[25]

The best solution seems to be honest about the inevitability that the interpretation of the Constitution will depend on values outside the Constitution, and to be transparent about the adoption of such factors and their role in the decision-making process. Instead, as pointed below, it seems that the case law in Brazil has turned away from admitting this and has insisted that the Supreme Court magistrates were in fact 'finding' the best possible interpretation of the law. Again, Klare's advice would fit perfectly with the critics of neo-constitutionalism in Brazil when he says 'the legal profession needs to be more candid with itself and with the community at large about the politics of adjudication and to accept more forthrightly our responsibility (however limited and partial) for constructing the social order through adjudicative practices.'[26] Decisions indicating the applicable law without justification led to new regulations in the Civil Procedure Code adopted in 2015.[27] From then on, there is a minimum standard of rationality, in view of the then current practice of rendering decisions that were only formally grounded, with no justification of the position adopted by the courts.

I have no doubt that this then new vision of the Constitution and the constitutional law played a role in the way the horizontal application of rights has been developing in Brazil and the lack of justification when affirming the horizontal application, as I will better explain below. The relevance of the neo-constitutionalism to interpret the Constitutional text as binding private parties has been pointed out by the magistrates themselves, i.e., J Joaquim Barboza, that affirmed that there was no more space for the 'idea that private relations are governed exclusively by civil law' and that the better understanding was that 'they are influenced by public law's principles, emanating predominantly from the decisions issued by the organs of constitutional jurisdiction'.[28]

---

[24] Sarmento (2009), pp. 113, 140.

[25] State v Zuma 1995 (4) BCLR 401 (CC) 17.

[26] Klare (1998), pp. 146,164.

[27] First paragraph of article 489 brings a list of six different situations in which a decision will be considered inadequately reasoned, for example, when the decision invokes reasons that would lend themselves to justify any other decision. CPC Código de Processo Civil (2015).

[28] STF RE 201819/RJ (11.10.05) Concurring Opinion Joaquim Barbosa J, 620.

In Brazil, fundamental rights have always appeared in the constitutional texts and scholarship quickly recognised that their inclusion in a list at the very beginning of the 1988 Constitution indicated the importance that they had come to have. However, it has not been observed that this was a mechanism adopted by the Constituent to increase the power of the judges and diminish the power of Parliament, as Klare tells us that was the case with the South African Constitution of 1996.[29] The strengthening of the judiciary has gradually evolved from justifications in decisions that privileged the constitutional text to the detriment of private law.

3.2 *Brazilian Constitutional Court Jurisprudence*

The Brazilian supreme court, the Federal Supreme Court (STF) has already applied fundamental rights to relations between private parties in some situations. There is no need to seek justification for the application in relations with the public sphere since fundamental rights were created as a limitation on public power. The application in the private sector will happen from the recognition that private persons' freedoms are not absolute, that is, the protection of the freedom of one person may imply the violation of the freedom of another, which will require that the freedom be restricted in a proportional manner.

David Bilchitz affirms that the indirect model of horizontal application of rights 'begins with existing current private law rules and reconsiders them in light of fundamental rights'.[30] In Brazil, with the use of neoconstitutionalist theory, we lend a new meaning to infra-constitutional legislation to adjust them to the constitutional content. There is no doubt, then, that the indirect model is applied.

The first case that would have made it possible to apply a fundamental right to a private relationship, under the 1988 Constitution, was adjudicated by the supreme court in 1995.[31] The discussion was whether an illegal constraint occurs when a factory manager requires the employees of an undergarment industry to comply with a contractual clause, establishing that they should submit to intimate searches, under penalty of dismissal. The first instance recognized the offense to the fundamental right of intimacy of the workers with support from the constitutional text without discussing the horizontal application of fundamental rights, but the appeals court dismissed such offense by submitting the contracting parties to the private contract clause (contractual clauses are law between contracting parties). The STF did not decide on the merits due to the recognition of application of the statute of limitations despite the judge rapporteur's regret for not being able to deal with the relevant fundamental rights issue and the radical contrast of perspectives between the first instance decision on the one hand, and the exaggerated private law approach of the

[29] Klare (1998), pp. 146, 147.

[30] Bilchitz (2022), p. 107.

[31] STF RE 160.222-8 RJ (11.04.95).

court of appeals judgment, on the other. It is impossible to predict what the solution would have been, especially since, years later, when the merit was judged for the first time, the court already had a different composition. The same facts were taken to Court in another identical case,[32] and J Moreira Alves took into consideration the existence of a contract between the parties to give greater importance to private autonomy.

Later, the court was faced with a case in which a cooperative excluded members without respect to the right to a full defense and *audi alteram partem*, fundamental rights expressly provided for in the Constitution.[33] The court decided that the rights of full defense and audi alteram partem should have been assured to the excluded members, ruling for the direct application of the mentioned fundamental rights in the relation between the cooperative and its members; but it did not consider it necessary to justify the application of such rights to relations between private individuals. The fact went not unnoticed by the scholarship: 'The judgment did not dwell on academic considerations about the application of fundamental rights in relations between private individuals.... [the Court] took it as undisputed that there are fundamental rights norms that have a direct effect on relations between private persons,'[34] but there was no discussion on the legal reasoning behind the conclusion.[35] It is worth noticing that not only the court did not explain or justify the use of the specific type of direct application of fundamental rights to private relations but also, it did not discuss the possibility of application of rights to private entities in general.

It was 2005 when a case provoked the STF's explicit consideration of the issue of horizontal application of fundamental rights.[36] The facts of the case reflect an individual who has been expelled from an association for reasons not discussed before the court. He claimed that the expulsion procedure should have observed the constitutional rights of full defense and *audi alteram partem*. The fact that previous decisions took as undisputed that there are fundamental rights norms that directly affect relations between private persons, without discussing the horizontal application of fundamental rights[37] was acknowledged by one of the justices. This decision grants us the most robust reasoning on the subject until now. The case was decided by a majority and four justices rendered their reasons. Gilmar Mendes J observed that to understand fundamental rights as acting only in the relationship between the citizen and the State would end up legitimizing the idea that the individual would enjoy a space free from any state interference. In other words, if fundamental rights only impose obligations on the state as a way of respecting the individual's sphere of action, individuals would have vast areas in which they were unregulated. For

[32] AgRAI 220.459-2/RJ (28.09.99).

[33] STF RE 158.215-4 RS (30.04.96).

[34] Branco (2003).

[35] Sarmento (2005), p. 297, CPC (2015).

[36] STF, RE 201.819/RJ (11.10.05).

[37] Branco (2003).

him, this is untenable, as showed by various conflicts of interest with repercussions in the sphere of fundamental rights that derive from civil law, where the benefit granted to one individual configures the imposition of a restriction on another. Relying on Canaris, he recalled that 'fundamental rights fulfil an important task in the legal order not only as a prohibition of intervention (right of defence), but also as postulates of protection'.[38] The decision recollects in depth the German courts' debate about the immediate or mediate application of fundamental rights over private relations seen above. It also recalls the contention that the direct application of fundamental rights would end up suppressing the principle of private autonomy and would encounter the obstacle in the fact that the subjects of private relations, contrary to what occurs in the State-citizen relationship, deserve, in principle, the same protection. It recalled that German courts concluded that fundamental rights are not suitable to directly resolve a dispute between private entities.[39] Instead, the legislator should guarantee the different positions in private relations by setting different limitations. Citing the decisions of the Bundesvergassungsgericht in the well-known cases of Lüth, Blinkfüer and Wallraff, Gilmar Mendes J concludes that if fundamental rights cannot bind individuals directly, they can 'legitimise limitations of private autonomy, whether by legislation or by interpretation.'[40] This is important because, this Justice found it necessary to justify the fact that he was extending the application of fundamental rights, despite the absence of an express provision to that effect. His opinion mentions Konrad Hesse's doctrine that it is up to the legislator, and if omitted or indifferent, to the judge himself, to interpret private law in the light of fundamental rights, exercising the duty of protection that is imposed on the State. To face the question of the legitimacy of demanding respect for fundamental rights from private individuals, the argument is that private autonomy, which encounters clear limitations of a legal nature, cannot be exercised to the detriment or with disrespect of the rights and guarantees of third parties, especially those that are constitutionally established, because the autonomy of the will does not confer on private individuals, in the domain of its incidence and performance, the power to transgress or ignore the restrictions placed and defined by the Constitution itself.

In other words, the Court established that private autonomy suffers a limitation imposed by fundamental rights: a person can freely act providing that other person's rights are not affected. Of course, the clear shortcoming of this idea is that it admits the clashing of rights without giving further guidance on how to solve the question and reach conclusions. Indeed, by stating the rule that private autonomy is limited by fundamental rights, the Court indicates that individual's fundamental rights might be at odds, but it does not make any attempt to describe how it will decide in favour of any sides. Nevertheless, at this point the Court has framed the idea that fundamental rights' application and normative force are also imposed on private individuals, in their private relations. Here, again, the STF has used the direct

[38] STF, RE 201.819/RJ (11.10.05) 590.

[39] STF, RE 201.819/RJ (11.10.05) 594–603.

[40] STF, RE 201.819/RJ (11.10.05).

application of fundamental rights to impose to the association respect for procedural rights.

J Joaquim Barbosa states that another effect of the almost universal acceptance of the "supremacy of the Constitution and the constitutional jurisdiction as an instrument to ensure it lies in the fact that fundamental rights […], are no longer conceived as limitations imposed solely and exclusively on the State".[41] The truth is that the Court here builds a justification for the application of fundamental rights to private relations grounded on the relevance it gives to fundamental rights. As I will indicate further ahead, this happens due to the *momentum* of constitutional thought and ideas at that point. The grounds supporting this decision refer to the neoconstitutionalist ideals,[42] as the prevalence and valorisation of principles and of the role of the judge. There was a strong reliance on the judiciary to ensure that rights included in the constitutional text would be granted in concrete relations in real life. Assuring realization of fundamental rights was not only expected from the magistrates, but also, they trusted this was their main duty.

Gilmar Mendes J goes on to indicate that the association (the defendant), due to its activity (transfer of fees related to copyrights), performs a predominant function in a certain economic and/or social scope, keeping its members in a relationship of economic and/or social dependency, and therefore, it involves what the judge calls non-state public space. This could have given way to recognize that there is an imbalance of power between the parties, though this issue is not explored in the opinion. It could, in future, be useful to explore it when deciding a case where parties are private persons in an unbalanced relation, as might happen between a natural person and a corporation.[43] The fact that the association provided a public service was decisive for the conclusion reached. The public activity character has, in this case, legitimized the direct application of fundamental rights. In my view, the problem with this argument is that it opens the door for a problematic conclusion: fundamental rights could not and would not be enforced on private entities. This conclusion would not serve the intention to recognize that private entities do need to comply with fundamental rights. But the odd thing is that, despite the STF's reliance on the fact that the public function of the association was paramount to the conclusion that it should be bound by fundamental rights, at the end, it expressly admits the horizontal application of fundamental rights. This point is relevant. The horizontal application theory discusses the possibility of private actor being bound by fundamental rights. If the STF determines that fundamental rights must be respected by

[41] STF, RE 201.819/RJ (11.10.05) Concurring Opinion J Barbosa J 623.

[42] See supra 3.1.

[43] Sarmento created a typology that might help understanding nuances in cases relating to the horizontal application of fundamental rights. He claims, in our view correctly, that fundamental rights can relate to either two different things: to existential choices or to the field of patrimonial and economic life. When fundamental rights relate to existential choices the courts must respect a larger space for individual's decisions; when they relate to patrimonial and economic life (such as a labour contract), courts will have a larger room to interfere and require respect for a specific right (Sarmento 2005, pp. 167, 175).

the association because of the nature of its service (public nature), then there is no need to discuss the horizontal application of fundamental rights since there is no doubt that they are applicable on the public sphere. Even so, the summary of the ruling[44] states that

> Violations of fundamental rights occur not only in relations between the citizen and the State, but also in relations between private individuals and legal entities. Thus, the fundamental rights guaranteed by the Constitution are directly binding not only on the public powers but are also aimed at protecting private individuals against private powers.[45]

One possible way to understand the court ruling would be if the decision merely demonstrates that one of the ways (among others) in which private entities can assume constitutional obligations is through a contract, a concession or if the activity was funded by the state. I strongly believe this reasoning is not sound: on the one hand, fundamental rights bind private persons; on the other hand, the mentioned association must comply with fundamental rights because it provides a public service. The public service provided was the criterion required to enforce respect to fundamental rights. Hence, while the court affirms the application of fundamental rights to private relations, its imposition of the duties seems to turn on the nature of the service provided by the private party. This does not add to clarity since if it is true that one can demand from private parties the respect for fundamental rights, it should be unnecessary to discuss the legal nature of the services provided by them. Evidence for this is the dissenting opinion that concludes the association to be eminently private, and therefore not subject to the constitutional provisions of ample defense and *audi alteram partem.*

In concrete terms, therefore, the relevance of Gilmar Mendes J opinion lies in the account of the historical discussion on the issue of horizontal application of fundamental rights and in the summary of previous decisions from foreign courts, which discussed the *drittwirkung* doctrine. As mentioned, Gilmar Mendes J stated that fundamental rights can legitimise limitations of private autonomy by interpretation. By not facing the reasons why it opted to impose the respect to fundamental rights in this case, if not for the fact of understanding that the association's activity had a public character, I claim it wasted a chance to advance the development of the doctrine. Furthermore, by undoubtedly linking its option to the public characteristic of the activity, it seems to leave further away the possibility of demanding respect for fundamental rights from private parties.

Joaquim Barbosa J, however, reaches the conclusion that private autonomy cannot be exercised to the detriment or with disrespect to the rights and guarantees of third parties, indicating constitutional provisions, namely, the principle of dignity of the person (art.1, III) the principle of solidarity (art.3, I) and the principle of immediate applicability of fundamental rights and guarantees (5, para.1). For this Justice,

---

[44] STF's legal opinions have (often) the following structure: Identification of the appeal; number of the case in the court; the caption; summary of the opinion; the disposition; and then the fact and law of the case.

[45] STF, RE 201819/RJ (11.10.05).

fundamental rights are applicable in the sphere of private relations, and this application must be done sparingly, so as not to overly compress the individual's sphere of private autonomy.[46] He justifies the use of the theory by the 'gradual breaking down of the barriers that separated public and private law by the end of the nineteenth century'. For him, a relevant factor is also the constitutionalisation of private law, i.e., 'the removal of the idea that private relations are governed exclusively by civil law and the understanding that they are influenced by public law's principles, emanating predominantly from the decisions issued by the organs of constitutional jurisdiction'.[47]

When the court once again addressed the topic[48] it was in a judgment that discussed the criteria for refusing the right of association. The appeal could not succeed because the decision would depend on the scrutiny of the factual-probative set, which is not admitted at that level. This would already be enough to decide the appeal, but, even so, Luiz Fux J decided to consider the application of fundamental rights. He stated that the norms that define the fundamental rights and guarantees have immediate application, and the Constitution does not block the radiation of their effects to private relations. Again, there is no justification of the reasons why direct application should be used by Courts, nor discussion about its benefits and harms.

The autonomy of political parties has also been tested against fundamental rights. The STF faced the claim surrounding the unconstitutionality of legislation providing for use by women candidates of a smaller percentage of funds, as it created a limit on their use, placing them in an unequal position.[49] In this case, although the legislation required a minimum number of women candidates, the use of financial resources in equivalent amounts was not assured. The judgment decided that the autonomy of political parties, as legal persons governed by private law, does not absolve them from unconditional respect for fundamental rights and therefore, the legislation was unconstitutional for not respecting the right of equality. In justifying the horizontal application of the fundamental right, Fachin J recalls that 'it is precisely in the artificial segmentation between public and private that the main form of discrimination against women lies.[50] No discussion regarding the option for direct or indirect application of fundamental rights was made. The Court was discussing whether or not the content of a law was constitutional, which is clearly a case of state action: the legislative needs to abide by the fundamental rights, otherwise, the legislation will be void. Although the Court expressly mentions the necessary horizontal application of fundamental rights, by stating that the right of autonomy of political parties must give way, in this case, before the necessary protection of the principle of material equality, I claim a different interpretation of the

46 STF RE 201819/RJ (11.10.05) Concurring Opinion J Barbosa J, 620.

47 STF RE 201819/RJ (11.10.05) Concurring Opinion JBarbosa J, 622.

48 STF ARE 1.008.625 J Luiz Fux (17.03.17).

49 STF ADI 5617 DF.

50 STF ARE 1.008.625 J Luiz Fux (17.03.17), p. 28.

decision. I claim that a judicial review case, as this one, is always a case of applying a fundamental right to the state action, which can be a legislation or an administrative act. But then, why are the justices talking about horizontal application of fundamental rights? The reason is that it was argued that the autonomy of the political parties was threatened and in order to justify why the legislation in case (regulating political parties) was not complying with the Constitution, the justice found it relevant to argue that political parties must abide by the equality principle because of the horizontal application of fundamental rights.

In 2020, the Court faced a dispute over the clause of a supplementary pension fund contract that provided for different applicable rules between men and women regarding the calculation of a supplementary retirement benefit, establishing a lower value for women, considering their smaller contribution time. The complementary social security system in Brazil is private in nature and is financed exclusively by employees and sponsors. The applicability of the right to equality was being discussed because the contracting of a complementary welfare plan occurs by an adhesion contract. The question involves civil law, regarding the regulation of the contract.[51] The Court faced the need to define whether the isonomy principle should also apply to the private contract or should only bind the general pension plans.[52] The Court has expressly recognized the possibility of applying the horizontally fundamental rights in order to protect women's rights. Based on the application of the isonomy principle to private relations as well, the Court established that private parties must submit to the radiating application of fundamental rights, especially that of gender equality.

In another judicial review case,[53] a statute's constitutionality was considered when requiring car rental companies to provide a vehicle adapted for a driver with a disability for every twenty cars in their fleet. As it should be, the case discussed if the legislative product—the statute—was or not complying with the constitutional text. The court framed the dispute around the relationship between the right to free enterprise and the right to equality for people with disabilities. The discussion concerned the constitutionality of an infra-constitutional statute that contained a provision that established an obligation for private parties (the fleet must comprise a minimum number of vehicles for the disabled). Carmen Lúcia J defined that 'the principle of free enterprise, the foundation of the Brazilian economic order, has to be weighed against other constitutional values, such as the social function of

---

[51] The closed private complementary pension plans are ruled by the principle of financial and actuarial balance and, therefore, the contractual provision that defines the percentage of 70% of the difference between the initial earnings and the actual salary for the proportional retirement of women after 25 years of contribution and 80% for the same difference in the complementation of the proportional retirement of men after completing 30 years of contribution does not constitute difference in treatment between the genders, nor does It hurt the equity in the form of participation in the costing, once women collect contributions for a shorter period. Thus, the benefit would be adequate to the technical reserves accumulated during the time of contribution for the payment of the proportional benefit.

[52] STF RE 639138 RS.

[53] STF ADI 5452/DF (2020).

property, consumer protection, protection of the environment and the reduction of social inequalities'.[54] In this case, the proportionality test had to answer if this legislation was a legitimate regulation of the economic order. Carmem Lúcia J mentioned that the principle of proportionality requires that the restriction imposed by the law (requiring a minimum number of adapted cars) on rental companies should not inhibit their economic activity. She analysed the legislation from the perspective of the three elements of proportionality: appropriateness, necessity, and proportionality in the strict sense, and in this case, she held that the law was not effectively inhibiting such activity, so it should be maintained. The decision does not mention the horizontal application of rights, but the Court simply recognises the implications of the law for disabled persons. The relevance of this decision, for the purposes intended here, lies in the grounds for the declaration of constitutionality of the law. The *rationale* might have importance in cases involving private parties in an unbalanced relation. It hints to the interpretation that leads to the conclusion that there is a social function to be played by corporations, and this would be a game changer to provide for respect of fundamental rights in private relations.

It could be claimed that the protection of private autonomy arising from the 1988 Constitution is heterogeneous: stronger, when existential dimensions of human life are at stake; less intense, when it comes to relationships of an exclusively patrimonial nature.[55] In this sense, the objection that imposing obligations on private entities would be an interference in their autonomy would be answered with the consideration that this is not necessarily the logical consequence in any dispute. The fundamental rights in dispute would be more likely to yield to the interest of a legal entity when it comes to property rights on both sides. I understand that the criterion of the nature of the right is not sufficient to establish the cases in which private entities will be bound by the rules of protection and respect for human rights.

I would add that it is also necessary to evaluate the criterion of the imbalance between the parties, which is already fully used. The law re-establishes the balance between parties that, in the world of facts, are in different positions—whether due to their age, sex, economic condition, among others. Thus, there are rules that guarantee greater protection for children and the elderly, for women or for those without economic conditions of subsistence. These rules serve to balance relationships in which these people find themselves by recognizing that, in the world of facts, they are in a condition of vulnerability before others. The law, by looking at and recognizing these vulnerabilities, corrects this imbalance. I argue that these two criteria together can result in decisions that serve the greater purpose of achieving a fairer society with equal access.

The horizontal application of fundamental rights cannot be made in abstract and *a priori*, but rather, different criteria should be analysed in context-sensitive application.[56] In this sense, it is praiseworthy that the STF has identified a criterion to

---

[54] STF ADI 5452/DF (2020), p. 136.

[55] Sarmento (2006), p. 207.

[56] Daniels v Campbell and Others (CCT 40/ 03) [2004] ZACC 14; 2004 (5) SA 331 (CC) 40, 41.

require that private parties respect fundamental rights. Here, it is necessary to discuss whether another element should be added to the equation, that is, vulnerability. Thus, the vulnerability (technical, economic, social) of one individual before another could be the trigger for the horizontal application of fundamental rights. Scholarship already touched on this point when declaring that "the existence of a relative consensus on the possibility of directly transporting the principles relating to the binding application of fundamental rights to the private sphere is noted, since we are undoubtedly dealing with unequal power relations, like those established between private individuals and the public authorities."[57] I would like to build on this idea. It is not an innovation. In this sense, if the court is faced with the request to impose the duty to respect on a corporation—i.e. the right to water, or to health, or to freedom of expression, among others—it would be advisable for the court to depart from the functional criterion and assess the vulnerability of one party before another to then reach its conclusion. That said, a full analysis of the role of vulnerability in the horizontal application of fundamental rights goes beyond the scope of this paper. I introduce it here to support the internal logic of the argument, but my primary aim remains the comparative analysis of how the Brazilian and South African Supreme Courts interpret and apply the principle of horizontal efficacy.

It is argued here that there is a relevant distinction between the two types of relationships between private parties that cannot go unnoticed by the court, and that should produce different consequences for the parties regarding their obligations. This would be a good option to solve cases where there is infra-constitutional legislation whose content and meaning is being disputed by two private actors.[58]

I feel obliged to mention that the discussion on the application of fundamental rights to relations between private individuals, in Brazil, takes on different contours when we are faced with cases decided by specialised labour courts. This is a federal system, organised around a normative framework that is highly protective of workers, dating back to 1943. The 1988 Constitution provides for thirty-four specific rights to workers, in addition to those applicable to all individuals. All are fundamental rights and therefore applicable to labour relations. Thus, it is natural that decisions on labour relations should involve fundamental rights. It stands out that all constitutional labour rights will apply directly to private relations (private employer and his employee). The possibility, the need to discuss the grounds for applying the *drittwirkung* doctrine in relation to corporations emerged in the Air France case[59] before a Labour Court. The court faced the need to define whether applying a contractual clause only to employees originating from the company's head office nation violated the constitutional right to equal treatment. In this case, the company applied different criteria for promotions, more beneficial to French employees, in relation to the Brazilians performing the same tasks. The court ruled that the clause in the

[57] Sarlet (2012), p. 386.

[58] Although this will not solve the disputes where there is no legislation in dispute, as I mention further in the text.

[59] STF RE 161.243-6/DF (29.10.96).

private contract could be tested against the fundamental right to equal treatment, using the direct horizontal application of fundamental rights. This case, however, did not cause a stir among Brazilian academics not only because the STF has not made much out of the application of fundamental rights directly to private relations, but also because, historically, labour law is very protective and is at the forefront of the protection of fundamental rights in the country. Following the language of the Constitution, many of the cases related to the horizontal application of fundamental rights are heard before the specialized labour courts, i.e., the application of the theory justifies the annulment of confidentiality and non-competition clauses for offending the fundamental right to the free exercise of the profession; it also justifies the condemnation for moral damages for late payment of salary or for the employer's intrusion in the employee's private life and intimacy.

The cases we find at the STF involve civil and procedural rights. However, the STF has yet to come across a case in which it is called upon to demand that a corporation respect rights other than equality, procedural and labour rights. When it does, it will need to deepen the reasoning developed in the cases here discussed, providing the legal system with reasons and criteria to use or not the *drittwirkung* doctrine.

As it can be seen, rights in debate when the issue of horizontal application was under scrutiny ranged from the right to equality to procedural protections. It was 2005 when the STF took a closer look at the justification for the application of fundamental rights to private relations. It used a functional basis to determine respect for fundamental rights. On the one hand, this solution avoids the problem of limiting the rights of individuals so that others, who are in principle equal, can exercise their own rights.[60] Thus, seeking in the functional argument the justification for application avoids the conundrum formed when the need arises to apply fundamental rights in relations between two individuals. However, upholding this justification may lead to unsatisfactory results if we are looking at the relationship between two private individuals when one of them is a corporation. Besides that, the utmost critic investigates the fact that if we will agree with the application of fundamental rights to relations where one of the parts functions as state, are we really facing a case of horizontal application?

At first sight we could claim that in a civil law country, the profusion of laws that seek to concretise the constitutional text would prevent discussions about the direct application of fundamental rights. In the existence of an infra-constitutional law regulating the situation of conflicting rights, there is no reason for the court to point to the existence of a case of direct horizontal application. Yet, we have seen cases discussed by the STF were decided with use of the direct application of fundamental rights. I claim that horizontal application should be directly imposed on corporations. Corporations, as private actors, follow the principle of legality that affirms they can act whenever statutes do not prohibit their conduct. It means that, unless there is a statute establishing prohibitions, corporations cannot be charged with

[60] Nino (1989); Forst (2001).

disobedience. We would need legislation proscribing virtually every private conduct that transgress fundamental rights. I believe it is safe to say that this will not happen. Instead, the direct application of constitutional rights can ensure that corporations are prevented from harming rights where statutes are silent in this regard.

A further missed opportunity is the fact that, in the absence of an express constitutional clause enabling such horizontal application, it would have been useful if the Court had used the cases it has faced to define not only whether horizontal application should occur and according to which criteria; but also whether it can be invoked regardless of the type of obligation in dispute, whether positive or negative. In all cases discussed above, the STF was answering the following question: Should this private person respect the fundamental right of an individual, or, in other words, should this private person abide by the fundamental right in case? The STF faced very little problem in defining private persons obligations regarding the cases discussed as a result.

It is difficult to predict, from the decisions evaluated, how the STF will decide cases in which the application of a fundamental right to a corporation is claimed, recognising a positive obligation in relation to an economic, social, environmental or cultural right. Cases that have been decided were proposed against those private parties that are exercising a public function, as private hospitals or schools. I expect, though, that the horizontal application of fundamental rights allowing for imposition of positive duties on corporations will not face hurdles regarding interpretation of the constitutional text. The STF has been flexible in justifying the horizontal application or defining what kind of duties it is imposing to corporations. The difficulty is that it needs to articulate an approach to the horizontal application of rights that will enable it adequately to adjudicate matters that involve positive obligations.

4 The South-African Constitutional Court and the Context Of Horizontal Application of Fundamental Rights

4.1 Transformative Constitutionalism in South-Africa

The moment at which South Africa decided to draft a new constitution, albeit provisional, is of extreme relevance in understanding its content and meaning. It was the first constitutional text after the Apartheid regime. This text contained the anguish and hopes of an entire population oppressed by the regime, and of a population yearning for social justice, reconciliation and a new beginning. The review of the manifestations of those who lived through the moment points to the need for the state powers to justify their decisions. In fact, Mureinik, evaluating the provisional Constitution points to 'a culture of justification—a culture in which every exercise of power is expected to be justified; in which the leadership given by government rests on the cogency of the case offered in defence of its decisions, not the fear inspired by the force of its command. The new order must be a community built on persuasion, not coercion.'[61] This new order seems to fall within the so-called transformative constitutionalism as conceived by Klare:

> By transformative constitutionalism I mean a long-term project of constitutional enactment, interpretation, and enforcement committed (not in isolation, of course, but in a historical context of conducive political developments) to transforming a country's political and social institutions and power relationships in a democratic, participatory, and egalitarian direction. Transformative constitutionalism connotes an enterprise of inducing large-scale social change through nonviolent political processes ground in law. I have in mind a transformation vast enough to be inadequately captured by the phrase 'reform', but something short of or different from 'revolution' in any traditional sense of the word. In the background is an idea of a highly egalitarian, caring, multicultural community, governed through participatory, democratic processes in both the polity and large portions of what we now call the 'private sphere.'[62]

Despite this concept, Moseneke mentions that 'the meaning of transformation in juridical terms is as highly contested as it is difficult to formulate'.[63] Indeed, though there might not exist a univocal concept of transformative constitutionalism, but what can be extracted in common from the different concepts rests in the Interim Constitution,[64] which speaks of a historic bridge between the past of a deeply divided society characterised by strife, conflict, untold suffering and injustice, and a future founded on the recognition of human rights, democracy and peaceful co-existence and development opportunities for all South Africans, irrespective of colour, race, class, belief or sex.[65]

This is not to say that there are no criticism as to the results achieved by the transformative constitutionalism that, for some, despite 'its seemingly radical posturing, has established little more than what can be described as a "discourse of hope" in that whilst pronouncing on structural and redistributive material questions, outside of adjudication its proponents rarely pronounce on these questions.'[66] Still, the relevance of transformative constitutionalism seems to be uncontested, as mentions Sibanda, '[B]oth as a conception of constitutionalism and as a term seeking to define South Africa's constitutional project, transformative constitutionalism has, arguably, assumed a near hallowed status as a descriptor of the current South African project of constitutionalism'.[67] Indeed, the author is emphatic in his criticism and states that transformative constitutionalism is an extension of liberal constitutionalism and not really something different. And this (insertion in liberal constitutionalism) is its weakness, since the search for the best interpretation prevents the realisation of the commitments of the Constitution.[68] This is one of the traps pointed

---

[61] Mureinik (1994), pp. 31, 32.

[62] Klare (1998), pp. 146, 150.

[63] Moseneke (2002), pp. 309, 315.

[64] Langa (2006), pp. 351, 352.

[65] Constitution of the Republic of South Africa, Act 200 of 1993.

[66] Sibanda (2020), pp. 384, 399.

[67] Sibanda (2011), pp. 482, 487.

[68] Sibanda (2011), pp. 482, 494.

by the author. The other would be the belief that a consciousness will or should be generated and shared among the people. If such a shared transformative consciousness exists, we do have transformative constitutionalism; it such consciousness does not exist, the chances for the existence of transformative constitutionalism are much smaller.[69]

In this sense, I claim that the criticism that 'the court-centric discourse of transformative constitutionalism has failed to offer any enduring concrete structural, material or epistemic interventions that gesture towards the disruption of the largely undisturbed patterns of white or Eurocentric economic, social, cultural and epistemic domination'[70] must be met with the warning that the doctrine was design to be applicable at and by the judiciary, as the critic mentions. In fact, the hope seems to be handed to the judicial branch alone, and judges cannot really change realities alone. It takes the joint work of executive and legislative branches, and participation of the society for profound changes to happen.

All this hope is grounded on the letter of the constitution and the desire to build a new structure based on the equality of the parties. It is undoubtedly a reaction to the segregationist regime in place up to then. The transformation promised by the constitutional text involves the creation of new power structures, recognising that power is not exclusively in the hands of the state. On the contrary, South Africa is part of a continent whose history is one of deep exploitation by countries from the northern hemisphere and is aware that violations of rights are not the sole responsibility of the state. This reality might have played a role in the crafting of the 1996 Constitution and its clause 8(2).

It is certain that the neglect of the population's needs was so profound that the 'provision of services to all and the levelling of the economic playing fields that were so drastically skewed by the apartheid system must be absolutely central to any concept of transformative constitutionalism'.[71] Whenever the enjoyment of rights is impaired, the new Constitution and its Bill of Rights will come forward with an answer. There should not make any difference, from the perspective of rights protection, as to who is impairing its enjoyment. This seems to be the right take from the South African Constitution, its Bill of Rights and its provision regarding the horizontal application of fundamental rights. In Brazil, the overture of the constitutional text to rights and the notion that the Constitution should be applicable in any case, led to court conclusions that lack adequate accuracy.

[69] Sibanda (2011), pp. 482, 487–490.

[70] Sibanda (2020), pp. 384, 406.

[71] Langa (2006), pp. 351, 352.

4.2 South African Constitutional Court Jurisprudence

The South Africa constitutional text stems from compromises between opposing parties in a two-stage process of constitution making at the end of the apartheid regime: an interim Constitution in 1993 and the final text in 1996.[72] Promulgated into law by Nelson Mandela, it includes a Bill of Rights that would lead the country into a 'culture of justification'[73] of every exercise of power. As the first democratically drafted constitution, it protects the idea of constitutional supremacy, and leads to the abandonment of parliamentary sovereignty.[74] The text is clear in relation to the application to juridical persons, '[W]here a particular right is deemed to apply to a particular kind of juristic person, the right applies. The issue is thus less one of application than it is of interpretation.'[75]

In the interim Constitution, there was some unclarity as to whether the Bill of Rights applied directly or indirectly. In the Du Plessis case,[76] decided under the interim Constitution which had no provision regarding the binding nature of its Bill of Rights, the majority of the Court insulated the common law from direct application of the substantive provisions of the Bill of Rights.[77] In Du Plessis, the South-African Court made a survey of how foreign courts answered the problem of horizontal application of fundamental rights in the same way the Brazilian Court has done in the considered paradigmatic case decided in 2005. 'The Court reasoned that any provision allowing horizontal application could have, and presumably would have, been made in expressly clear terms'[78] and in the absence of such terms, it found that the private actor involved in the case was not bound to comply with the fundamental rights. In drafting the final Constitution, however, the constitutional assembly included a much clearer indication that the Bill of Rights applies to private persons. Section 8(2) of the South-African Constitution states that a provision of the Bill of Rights binds a natural or a juristic person if, and to the extent that, it is applicable, taking into account the nature of the right and the nature of any duty imposed by the right. The reading seems to lead to the clear and unassailable conclusion that fundamental rights are enforceable against private parties. In any case, the enforcement of the 8(2)) clause of the 1996 Constitution has led to some discussion and robust reasoning.

Ally & Linde differentiate two possibilities: 'direct' application refers to the resolution of a dispute by the application of constitutional rights via section 8 of the

---

[72] To know more see Klug (2010).

[73] 'A culture in which every exercise of power is expected to be justified; in which the leadership given by government rests on the cogency of the case offered in defence of its decidions, not the fear inspired by the force at its command.' Mureinik (1994), pp. 31, 32.

[74] Goldsworthy (2007), p. 267.

[75] Woolman and Bishop (2012), p. 34.

[76] *Du Plessis v De Klerk 1996 (3) SA 850 (CC).*

[77] Woolman and Bishop (2012), p. 5.

[78] Futch (1997), pp. 1009, 1017.

Constitution.[79] Indirect application is used to refer to the application of constitutional values to the common law underlying the dispute via section 39(2) of the Constitution.[80] Meyersfeld, in turn, claims that there are four methods used by the South African Court to apply fundamental rights to private relations. The first is the indirect application when common or customary law is interpreted to impose duties on private parties to promote values of the Bill of Rights; the second method imposes obligations on private parties that derive from statutes that relate to the state's obligation to protect rights where the private party performs a state function; the third occurs when the court grants just and equitable remedies that impose duties on private parties; and finally, the forth relates to the direct application of fundamental rights.[81] I now consider some of the case law in this regard.

In Barkhuizen v Napier,[82] the court considered the application of the Constitution to the law of contract. The matter involved the timeframe an insurance contract allows a person to institute an action and whether it would violate the right of access to courts when too short, on the basis that the term was unreasonable or unfair.[83] The Court trusted the principle of autonomy of contract to decide that the individual had entered the contract fully aware of its terms, and in the absence of reasons why it did not comply with the timeframe, which was not unfair, found in favour of the insurer company. The Court refused to apply fundamental rights directly to evaluate the contract; instead, it proposed that that the principle that a contract cannot be contrary to public policy be used to consider whether any fundamental rights were violated in the context of contract law.[84] So, the Court has used, in this case, the indirect application of fundamental rights using 'the values underlying constitutional rights to fill out "general clauses"—such as public policy—in other areas of the law.'[85] Bilchitz points to the fact that the 'vague reasoning... leads courts to situate non-state actors symmetrically even when there are significant power disparities between them'.[86] The express constitutional clause allowing for the use of horizontal application of fundamental rights might have the effect to make articulation of the Court's reasoning unnecessary, although there is no express indication of this in any of the decisions here mentioned. This leaves more room for the discussion regarding the use of indirect or direct use, but still, it seems that the choice made allows for justices to arrive at any outcome.[87]

---

[79] In my view, 8(1) reflects the state action doctrine since it applies the Bill of Rights to all state organs; 8(2) reflects the direct application of fundamental rights.

[80] Ally and Linde (2021), pp. 275, 290.

[81] Meyersfeld (2020), pp. 439, 440.

[82] Barkhuizen v Napier (CCT72/05) [2007] ZACC 5; 2007 (5) SA 323 (CC).

[83] CC 04 Apr 2007, 48.

[84] Ally and Linde (2021), pp. 275, 288–291.

[85] Bilchitz (2022), p. 128.

[86] Bilchitz (2022), p. 129.

[87] In fact, this is one of the drawbacks of the indirect application model. As explained by Bilchitz (2022), p. 111, this model '... provides no structured reasoning process which determines the manner in which fundamental rights may or may not be limited. The reasoning process in relation to

In line with the Universal Declaration of Human Rights, in the Juma Musjid Case,[88] the South African Court held that even if not subsidized, schools provide the service of basic education, as it is defined by its content (and not by who funds it). The facts of the case relate to a property owned by a private trust who was evicting the public school there established since the government has failed to pay the rent. The trust in this case does not have a positive obligation to provide the right to education, as the State does. The Court held that the constitutional provision that binds private entities to the Bill of Rights does not aim 'to obstruct private autonomy or to impose on a private party the duties of the state in protecting the Bill of Rights. It is rather to require private parties not to interfere with or diminish the enjoyment of a right'.[89] This means, it retains the negative obligation not to infringe the use of the right.[90] Through the direct application model, the Court had to balance the property rights of the trust with the right to education of the children and concluded that the trust had acted reasonably since there were alternative schools where the children could be placed and it had no positive obligation to make its property available for the establishment of a school in perpetuity.[91]

Differently from what we pointed out in the Brazilian case law, where there was no discussion regarding the reasons for applying fundamental rights to private relations or for distinguishing between positive and negative obligations, the South African court, when deciding the Daniels case,[92] defines criteria to assess whether it should impose horizontal obligations on private persons.[93] This case considers the positive obligation of landowners to provide for habitable housing for its workers. It was under discussion if the applicable statute allowed the occupier to make improvements on their minimal housing which was on the premises of the landowner and if she needed authorization for that.[94] The statute provided that, if the occupier left the premises, the landowner has to pay for improvements. The respondents contended that were the Court to recognize the occupier's right to make improvements, the result would be, according to applicable law, the placement of an indirect positive duty on them to pay compensation for said improvements,[95]—in other words, the landowners would pay for the occupier enjoyment of rights. The conclusion of the Court was that the occupier needed to consult the landowner about improvements, although she did not need his authorization. Most importantly for the issue here

---

these 'objective values' appears to be entirely open, offering no clear guidance as to how to address conflicts between important values.'

[88] Governing Body of the Juma Musjid Primary School and others v Essay NO and others 2011 (8) BCLR 761 (CC).

[89] Governing Body of the Juma Musjid Primary School and others v Essay NO and others 2011 (8) BCLR 761 (CC) 58.

[90] Meyersfeld (2020), p. 441.

[91] Bilchitz (2022), p. 345.

[92] Daniels v Scribante and Another (CCT50/16) [2017] ZACC 13; 2017 (4) SA 341 (CC).

[93] Daniels v Scribante and Another (CCT50/16) [2017] ZACC 13; 2017 (4) SA 341 (CC)39–41.

[94] Meyersfeld (2020), p. 468.

[95] Madlanga (2018), pp. 359, 372.

discussed, the Court has established that it should not shy away from imposing a positive obligation on a private person, if after weighing relevant factors that was the conclusion reached. What are those factors? Among others, 'what is the nature of the right; what is the history behind the right; what does the right seek to achieve; how best can that be achieved; what is the potential of invasion of that right by persons other than the state or organs of state; and, would letting private persons off the net not negate the essential content of the right? This is relevant because it secures the possibility of the existence of a positive obligation for the landowner.[96] With that, the Court was indicating that 'the Constitution's project of creating a society that is dignified and equal is not solely the responsibility of the state[97] though the implications on private parties will depend on the specific circumstances of each single case.

Indeed, the ruling regarding the possibility of the existence of positive obligations on private actors and that this possibility will be defined upon scrutiny of specific circumstances of the case was confirmed in Pridwin.[98,99] In this case a private school terminated its contract with parents of two boys, after recurring abusive behaviour from their father against other children, staff and parents. The Court had to determine the content of the school's obligations and to decide if the school's conduct was constitutional, bearing in mind the children's right to education on the one hand, and the private autonomy in a contractual context on the other.[100] It founds that the school had a negative obligation not to impair the children's right to education. In this case, the school had terminated the contract without a hearing which included the children's representation, which impaired their right. Despite assuming the task to provide children with basic education, and therefore assuming the responsibility to fulfil the children's right, the Court does not find a positive obligation on the school arising from there.[101]

The language of the constitutional text in section 8(2) 'clearly points to an interpretative process that goes beyond the strict construction of the text alone ...'[102] opening the venue for expanding the duties of non-state actors to include positive obligations. As has been argued by Liebenberg, when discussing obligations related to socio-economic rights, the SA Constitution does create this possibility when affirms that the Bill of Rights binds a natural or juristic person under certain circumstances and courts are tasked with application or development of common law to the extent that legislation does not provide for the effectiveness of the rights.[103] In other

[96] Madlanga (2018), p. 470.

[97] Madlanga (2018), p. 473.

[98] *AB v Pridwin Preparatory School [2020] ZACC 12.*

[99] Meyersfeld (note 32 above) 475.

[100] Bilchitz (note 34 above) 347.

[101] In fact, as points out Bilchitz, the 'only positive obligation flows from section 29(3) which involves maintaining standards not inferior to public schoos. Ibid. 349.

[102] Cheadle and Davis (1997), pp. 44, 57.

[103] Liebenberg (2013), p. 57.

words, it is in the court's hands to extend or not the application of fundamental rights when it decides it is facing the right circumstances.

5 Final Considerations

While the change in the role of the judiciary in South Africa came from the adoption of the first democratically drafted constitution and constitutional supremacy, with the abandonment of parliamentary sovereignty, in Brazil the change came from the adoption of a constitutional theory that opened up the possibility of dressing the judiciary in new clothes, leaving behind the strict application of the letter of the law, since the possibility of judicial review—used with less intensity until then—already existed.

Among the central characteristics of the new paradigm in Brazil were the relevance of constitutional principles; the opening of legal argumentation to moral dimensions; the recognition and defence of the constitutionalisation of private law and the prominent role of the Judiciary in the agenda for implementing the values of the Constitution.[104] Probably those last two elements were prominent ingredients to allow the judiciary to extend the application of fundamental rights to private relations.

Both countries were facing the clamour of the population, especially the marginalised, for recognition of rights and social justice. This recognition should also occur in relations between private individuals, since the constitutionalisation of rights raises their relevance in the popular imagination.

We may ask whether the Courts already apply horizontal effectiveness. Both do so, as seen above, but then we can ask on what basis they do it and what type of horizontal application they use. South Africa counts on a Federal Constitution that expressly foresees this possibility, Brazil has used neoconstitutionalism. South Africa has admitted indirect application, circumventing the critics toward direct application and the suppression of the role of the legislator in favour of the protagonism of the judge.[105] In Brazil, without further explanation, the STF has been directly applying fundamental rights to private relations. Finally, we may ask whether the application of this doctrine imposes positive or negative obligations to non-state entities.

Negative obligations refer to the duty not to hinder the enjoyment of the right. Positive obligations refer to conduct that guarantees that individuals can enjoy rights. The idea is generally accepted that human rights positive obligations are required of the State. Also, it is generally accepted the extension of negative obligations related to human rights also to non-state entities. Thus, especially in the case

[104] Barcellos (2005).

[105] As noted by Liebenberg (2013), p. 59, in South Africa, laws binding private parties to human rights abound. The relation with the state's duty to protect is clear since under international law states are bound to enact legislation to regulate private actors' conducts.

of civil and political rights, it is simpler to visualize that a private entity should not interfere with their enjoyment. However, the issue is more complex when discussing positive obligations. Not only because they are historically linked to the provision of services by the State and equality rights, but also, and mainly, because the imposition of positive conduct on non-State entities potentially harms private autonomy. Thus, it is relevant to evaluate how the Courts decides cases that discuss positive or negative obligations related to fundamental rights. The analysis of the South-African Court cases led to the conclusion that the court is opening the path for a deeper consideration of positive obligations of private entities. The analysis of the Brazilian Court does not allow any conclusion regarding this issue since there is no systematised reasoning of the nuances surrounding horizontal application of fundamental rights. Both courts can take advantage of what the other has produced, how it has resolved cases involving fundamental rights and private relations.

The positive conclusion is that both courts are on the path to broadening the recognition of obligations on the part of private entities. The analysis leaves no doubt about the relevance of the doctrine of the horizontal application of fundamental rights for the solution of dilemmas created by the transnational action of corporations, by their economic empowerment, and by their freedom of action in weak legal regimes. It is the interpretation and application of the constitutional text that can impose limits on the actions of companies, in favour of the rights of individuals and the construction of social justice.

It is interesting to watch developments in both countries. We see the constitutionalisation of private law invade Brazilian scholarship discussion and influencing the way the STF renders its decision and the criticism points to the lack of justification or to the justification based in values and in the judicial power that could lead to different outcomes. In fact, one of the pillars of the new constitutionalism is the explicit embodiment of values.[106] We also see, in South Africa, transforming constitutionalism revolutionising the language of the constitutional text and demanding an interpretation that promotes social justice. In this sense, it is telling that scholarship sees, in the Daniels case, 'the duties that ownership of land—and property law more generally—comes with in the new constitutional dispensation may differ from the obligations that owners may have had in the pre-constitutional context'.[107]

It is a new reading of the legal system that calls for a real repositioning of the rights protected. At this point, the structural claims behind what happens in both countries are very similar. The striking difference appears on the lack of legal argumentation to address the legal problems before the Brazilian Court (as I claimed, caused by the new constitutionalism) which led to the absence of a clear path and direction regarding the horizontal application of fundamental rights. But we can also find criticism, though different, when we turn our eyes to the South-African Court. The Court might use the language of values which 'reduces the entitlement dimension of rights—and their normative priority—to simply one value to be

[106] Barcellos (2005), p. 102.

[107] Boggenpoel and Slade (2020), p. 398.

considered and weighed amongst many.'[108] Also, despite recognizing, in the Pridwin Case, that private actors are bound by the Bill of Rights, the Court missed the opportunity to go further and constitutionalise contract law.[109]

The concern and commitment in assuring enjoyment of rights has led the STF to directly apply fundamental rights to private relations. This court could profit from the reasoning at the South-African Court and could offer to answer questions that logically relate to the facts and the dispute about the horizontal application of fundamental rights. It is not a matter of requiring one court to reach the same conclusions as another. This is not even the case, given the criticism about the results that the South African Court has delivered. But rather, to draw on experiences that can assist in designing the best *rationale* for applying constitutional rights. In this sense, it may be a good habit to restrict oneself to the core of the demand, and avoid digressions that have no impact on its solution and, on the contrary, may generate doubts about the direction the Court is taking. For its turn, the freedom that the STF has felt to decide the mentioned cases could be exported to countries, as South-Africa, that are discovering the best path to promote social justice, especially before a constitutional text that seems to allow for direct and indirect horizontal application.

Both Courts deal with the question: should a private actor respect my fundamental right? The answers differ as the STF will operate with the direct model and the South African Court will operate with the indirect model. But what if the question specifies the social, economic, cultural or environmental rights?

Note that the courts have already faced cases that discuss economic or social rights in relation to the conduct of a private entity when exercising a function that reflects a state duty. These are the cases seen above related to the rights to education or health. Because service providers, although subject to the private law regime, perform a public service, they will be subject to the norms of protection of fundamental rights. It is a guessing exercise to write about the likely behaviour of both courts when faced with a case that asks whether corporations should respect economic, social, cultural or environmental rights, which demand positive benefits. Especially if their core business is not related to the right that is being claimed. Thus, the ultimate question becomes: should a corporation respect my economic, social, cultural or environmental right?

This piece pointed to the fact that corporations, as other private actors, are bound by the principle of legality and therefore, might act freely as long as legislation does not forbid their conduct. This is relevant because it means that it would be necessary legislation forbidden all and each corporate conduct that violates human rights. It is safe to say that this will not happen, as it is not an option even for the State—for whom rights limitations were created. As I see it, rights provisions serve exactly for imposing limits. If this is the way to impose limits on rights, articulations for the non-applicability of rights to private actors are not sustained. And if the constitutional rights are to be respected, this is a conduct that corporations cannot evade.

---

[108] Bilchitz (2022), p. 111.

[109] Ally and Linde (2021), pp. 275, 291.

The absence of legislation mediating this applicability should also not refrain justices to ask for compliance with the rights enshrined in the Constitution, at least regarding the question related to the respect of rights. We cannot test this at this point since cases taken to both courts, so far, have always rely in either a common law or a statute provision. In this case, i.e., an extractive corporation should respect the rights to health and, when its conducts have negatively impacted it, it should be responsible for it. Of course, the following question would mean a step further, and ask if there are also positive obligations for this corporation, regarding human rights. We have not addressed this in our comments to the case-law since it is the case for a specific study.[110] What can be said from the above is that the negative obligations are inexcusable for corporations with no need for any legislation to enforce it. As mention above, private autonomy encounters clear limitations of a legal nature, and cannot be exercised to the detriment or with disrespect of the rights and guarantees of third parties, especially those that are constitutionally established, because the autonomy of the will does not confer on private individuals, in the domain of its incidence and performance, the power to transgress or ignore the restrictions placed and defined by the Constitution itself.

Fundamental rights are real grounds for holding corporations accountable. Corporations are not in a balanced relationship with individuals and communities. There is a misfit from the beginning of the relationship and the law has the mission, by force of material equality, to re-establish this balance. When re-establishing this balance, whether by means of legislation or adjudication, there is a clash with private autonomy. In the case where one of the parties is a corporation and the imposition of a sanction is sought, it is not a question of disregarding an existing agreement between the parties. It is not about annulling a contractual clause because it offends a fundamental right. The direct application of horizontal effectiveness allows the fundamental right to be the basis of the claim, without the need for infra-constitutional legislation (which in most cases will not exist—the law for the private sector regulates conduct by prohibition). This use of the doctrine will be a huge step for the evolution of private relations, especially for the protection of potential victims of the negative impacts that may occur by the performance of a business activity.

References

Alexy R (2003) Direitos fundamentais, balanceamento e racionalidade. Ratio Juris 16:131–140

[110] The Superior Court of Justice (STJ), the highest court to adjudicate issues arising from the interpretation of federal laws, counts with several decisions in the environmental area, where constitutional provisions are mentioned to support the conviction of private actors. One of these cases arises from the request made by the Public Officer on behalf of some indigenous villages affected by mining activities of a private corporation. The STJ, using the indirect application of fundamental rights to private relations, condemned the company for compensation, among others, for disrespecting the fundamental right to an ecologically balanced environment, essential to a healthy quality of life. Superior Court of Justice STJ RESP 1734459 (2019).

Ally N, Linde D (2021) Pridwin: private school contracts, the bill of rights and a missed opportunity. Const Court Rev 11:275
Barcellos AP (2005) Neoconstitucionalismo, Direitos Fundamentais e Controle das Políticas Públicas. Revista de Direito Administrativo 240:83
Barroso LR (2012) Judicialização, ativismo judicial e legitimidade democrática. (Syn)thesis 5:23–32
Bilchitz D (2022) Fundamental rights and the legal obligations of business. University of Johannesburg
Boggenpoel ZZ, Slade B (2020) Where is property? Some thoughts on the theoretical implications of Daniels v Scribante. Const Court Rev 10:379–399
Bomhoff J (2008) Lüth's 50th anniversary: some comparative observations on the German Foundations of judicial balancing. Germ Law J 2:121–124
Borowski M (2020) La Drittwirkung ante el trasfondo de la transformación de los derechos morales en derechos fundamentals. Revista Derecho del Estado 45:3–27
Branco P (2003) Associações, expulsão de sócios e direitos fundamentais. Direito Público 1:143–157
Carbonell M (2003) Neoconstitucionalismo(s). Trotta, Madrid
Cheadle H, Davis D (1997) The application of the 1996 Constitution in the private sphere. S Afr J Hum Rights 11:44–57
Chemerinsky E (1985) Rethinking state action. Northwest Univ Law Rev 80:503–557
CPC Civil Procedure Code, Law 13.105, March 16th 2015, Brazil. Available at http://www.planalto.gov.br/ccivil_03/_Ato2015-2018/2015/Lei/L13105.htm
Fachin LE (2015) Direito Civil: sentidos, transformações e fim. Renovar
Forst R (2001) Contexts of justice: political philosophy beyond liberalism and communitarianism. University of California Press
Futch D (1997) Du Plessis v. De Klerk: South Africa's bill of rights and the issue of horizontal application. NC J Int Law 22:1009–1037
Goldsworthy JD (2007) Interpreting constitutions: a comparative study. Oxford University Press
Klare K (1998) Legal culture and transformative constitutionalism. S Afr J Hum Rights 14:146–188
Klug H (2010) South Africa: from constitutional promise to social transformation. In: Goldsworthy J (ed) Interpreting constitutions: a comparative study, pp 87–102
Langa P (2006) Transformative constitutionalism. Stellenbosch Law Rev 17:351–364
Liebenberg S (2013) The interpretation of socio-economic rights. In: Woolman S, Bishop M (eds) Constitutional law of South Africa, 2nd edn. OS, pp 1–68
Madlanga M (2018) The Human Rights duties of companies and other private actors in South Africa. Stellenbosch Law Rev 29:359–378
Mello CB (1995) O conteúdo jurídico do princípio da igualdade. Malheiros, São Paulo
Meyersfeld B (2020) The South African constitution and the human-rights obligations of juristic persons. S Afr Law J 137:439–478
Moseneke D (2002) The fourth brain Fischer memorial lecture: transformative adjudication. S Afr J Hum Rights 18:306–315
Mureinik E (1994) A bridge to where? Introducing the interim Bill of Rights. S Afr J Hum Rights 10:31–48
Nino CS (1989) Ética y Derechos Humanos. Astrea, Buenos Aires
Peretti T (2010) Constructing the State Action Doctrine, 1940-1990. Law Soc Inq 35:273–310
Rossi A (2011) Neoconstitucionalismo e a superação da perspectiva positivista do direito. Juruá, Curitiba
Sanchis LP (2007) Justicia constitucional y derechos fundamentals, 3rd edn. Trotta, Madrid
Sarlet I (2012) A eficácia dos direitos fundamentais, 12nd edn. Livraria do Advogado, Porto Alegre
Sarmento D (2005) Os princípios constitucionais da liberdade e da autonomia privada. Boletim Científico Escola Superior Ministério Público da União 14:167–217
Sarmento D (2009) O Neoconstitucionalismo no Brasil: riscos e possibilidades. Revista Brasileira de Estudos Constitucionais 9:95–143

Sarmento D (2010) Direitos fundamentais e relações privadas. Lumen Juris, Porto Alegre
Sibanda S (2011) Not purpose-made! Transformative constitutionalism, post-independence constitutionalism and the struggle to eradicate poverty. Stellenboch Law Rev 3:482–500
Sibanda S (2020) When do you call time on a compromise? South Africa's discourse on transformation and the future of transformative constitutionalism. Law Democr Dev 24:383–410
Silva V (2004) Direitos Fundamentais: conteúdo essencial, restrições e eficácia. Malheiros, São Paulo
Silva V (2005) A constitucionalização do Direito: os direitos fundamentais nas relações entre particulares. Malheiros, São Paulo
Teixeira JP, Sparemberger R (2016) Neoconstitucionalismo europeu e novo constitucionalismo latino-americano: um diálogo possível? Revista Brasileira de Sociologia do Direito 3:52–70
Woolman S, Bishop M (2012) Constitutional law of South Africa. Juta, Cape Town

MIX
Papier aus verantwortungsvollen Quellen
Paper from responsible sources
FSC® C105338

If you have any concerns about our products,
you can contact us on
ProductSafety@springernature.com

In case Publisher is established outside the EU,
the EU authorized representative is:
Springer Nature Customer Service Center GmbH
Europaplatz 3, 69115 Heidelberg, Germany

Printed by Libri Plureos GmbH
in Hamburg, Germany